Rogue	Fighter
Cleric	Sorcerer
Skeleton	Skeleton
Bugbear	Skeleton
Kobold	Kobold
Orc	Orc
Zombie	Zombie
Giant Spider	

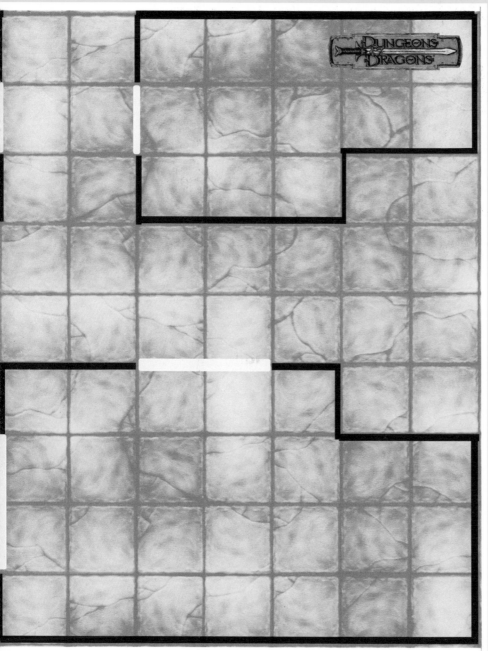

Dungeons & Dragons® FOR DUMMIES®

by Bill Slavicsek and Richard Baker

Foreword by Kim Mohan
Editorial Manager for DUNGEONS & DRAGONS

WILEY

Wiley Publishing, Inc.

Dungeons & Dragons® For Dummies®

Published by
Wiley Publishing, Inc.
111 River Street
Hoboken, NJ 07030-5774
www.wiley.com

WILEY

About the Authors

Bill Slavicsek: Bill Slavicsek began playing the DUNGEONS & DRAGONS roleplaying game with his friends during his formative teenage years in New York City. This was in 1977, the same year that *Star Wars* and Terry Brooks's *The Sword of Shannara* debuted. This trilogy of epic fantasy combined with comic books and horror novels to forever influence Bill's outlook on life and entertainment. In 1986, Bill's hobby became his career when he joined the staff of West End Games. There, as an editor and game designer, Bill worked on a number of board games and roleplaying games, including *Ghostbusters, Paranoia, Star Wars: The Roleplaying Game*, and *Torg: Roleplaying the Possibility Wars*. Later, Bill went on to use his vast knowledge of the *Star Wars* films and associated extensions to write two editions of *A Guide to the Star Wars Universe* for Lucasfilm, Ltd. (published by Del Rey Books).

1n 1993, Bill joined the staff of TSR, Inc., then publishers of the DUNGEONS & DRAGONS game lines, as a game designer and editor. His design credits for the company include the *Alternity Science Fiction Game* (which he co-designed with Richard Baker), the *d20 Modern Roleplaying Game*, the *d20 Star Wars Roleplaying Game*, the *Star Wars Miniatures Game*, *Urban Arcana*, *Council of Wyrms*, and the *Eberron Campaign Setting*.

Since 1997, Bill has been the Director of Roleplaying Games Research and Development for Wizards of the Coast, Inc., the company that now publishes all DUNGEONS & DRAGONS novels and game products. He oversaw the creation of the d20 Roleplaying Game System and the newest edition of the DUNGEONS & DRAGONS game. Bill leads a talented staff of game designers, developers, and editors who produce award-winning game products for DUNGEONS & DRAGONS and other d20 System game lines, including roleplaying game supplements and accessories, adventures and campaign books, and prepainted plastic miniatures. He lives with his wife Michele, two cats, and more comics, toys, and books than he knows what to do with — and that's okay by him.

Richard Baker: Richard Baker is an award-winning game designer and a best-selling author. He's worked on the DUNGEONS & DRAGONS game lines since 1991. Rich traces his D&D experience back to 1979, when he began playing the DUNGEONS & DRAGONS game as a 7th-grader. He spent a significant amount of his high school and college years playing D&D at every opportunity, and after serving as a surface warfare officer in the United States Navy, Rich decided to take a shot at working on the game he grew up playing — and so he joined the staff of TSR, Inc. and became a game designer.

Rich's list of D&D design credits numbers over 50 game products, including the Origins Award-winning *Birthright Campaign Setting*, the *Alternity Science Fiction Roleplaying Game* (which he co-designed with Bill Slavicsek), and the newest edition of the DUNGEONS & DRAGONS game. He has also served as creative director for the Alternity and FORGOTTEN REALMS game lines. As an author, Rich has published seven fantasy and science fiction novels, including *City of Ravens*, *Forsaken House*, and the New York Times bestseller *Condemnation*.

Rich is currently employed as a senior game designer at Wizards of the Coast, Inc. and works every day on new products for the DUNGEONS & DRAGONS game. He married his college sweetheart Kim in 1991; they have two daughters, Alex and Hannah. When he's not writing (a rare occurrence), Rich likes to hike in the Cascades, play wargames, and root for the Philadelphia Phillies — because somebody has to.

Dedication

Bill Slavicsek: To everyone who ever imagined an amazing adventure, I offer this key to D&D. When I first found the game, it helped focus and expand my imagination and creativity. And it was a lot of fun. Today, I still have fun playing the game, and my gaming group meets every Thursday evening to brave whatever new challenges I dream up for them. I hope you'll find the same outlet for imagination and fun as I've enjoyed for almost thirty years.

Richard Baker: To Kim, Alex, and Hannah for being patient with me through nigh-constant work in evenings and on weekends for many months now. I promise that I'm going to take my computer for a drive deep into the woods sometime soon and leave it there so it can't ever find its way home again.

Author's Acknowledgments

Bill Slavicsek: The current edition of the DUNGEONS & DRAGONS game owes its existence to a lot of talented people. The work that Rich and I have done on this *For Dummies* book would not have been possible if not for the original effort of a formidable team of creatives and business people. Peter Adkison, for purchasing TSR, Inc., merging its products and staff with Wizards of the Coast, Inc., and providing the vision for what the new edition of the game would be. My creative team on the massive redesign project, which included Jonathan Tweet, Monte Cook, Skip Williams, Richard Baker, Kim Mohan, Julia

Martin, John Rateliff, Ed Stark, Dawn Murin, Todd Lockwood, and Sam Wood. The business team, past and present, who help bring D&D products to market, which includes Ryan Dancey, Keith Strohm, Cindy Rice, Mary Kirchoff, Anthony Valterra, Chris Toepker, Liz Schuh, Mary Elizabeth Allen, and Charles Ryan.

I have to acknowledge the efforts of my current staff. This amazing collection of designers, developers, and editors work everyday to push the envelope and expand the horizons of our products, and as much as I lead them, they influence the way I think about and approach game design and D&D. Every part of this *For Dummies* book owes at least a little to the ideas and work of Richard Baker, Michele Carter, Andy Collins, Bruce Cordell, Jesse Decker, Michael Donais, Rob Heinsoo, Gwendolyn F.M. Kestrel, Stacy Longstreet, Michelle Lyons, Kim Mohan, David Noonan, Christopher Perkins, John Rateliff, Stephen Schubert, Matthew Sernett, Ed Stark, Chris Thomasson, Rob Watkins, Jennifer Clarke Wilkes, and James Wyatt.

Finally, thanks to everyone at Wiley Publishing who worked with us on this book, including Melody Layne, Christopher Morris, and Jean Rogers, and to everyone at Wizards of the Coast, Inc., who help us make great games on a regular basis.

Richard Baker: Many people of exceptional creativity have worked on the D&D game over the years. Without the work of game designers, editors, and artists such as Gary Gygax, Dave Arneson, Jim Ward, Kim Mohan, Zeb Cook, Jeff Grubb, Steve Winter, Bruce Nesmith, Tim Brown, Troy Denning, Roger Moore, Ed Greenwood, Mike Carr, Harold Johnson, Andrea Hayday, Jon Pickens, Lawrence Schick, Skip Williams, Dave Sutherland, Jeff Easley, Larry Elmore, and countless others, D&D would not have grown into the beloved hobby of millions of fans across the world. Countless other authors, artists, developers, and editors have contributed over the years; we're sorry that we can't thank them all.

A special acknowledgement is in order for Peter Atkinson, Ryan Dancey, and other folks who were instrumental in bringing the D&D game and many of its designers to Wizards of the Coast, Inc. Through their efforts, they reinvented and reinvigorated the game at a difficult and crucial time in its life cycle.

A special thank you to good friends and colleagues who have shared in the authors' own D&D games over the years. Rich would like to thank Ed Stark, John Rateliff, David Eckelberry, Shaun and Miranda Horner, David Wise, Thomas Reid, David Noonan, James Wyatt, Warren Wyman, Duane Maxwell, Andy Weedon, Dale Donovan, Bud Stiles, Thomas Chatburn, Tom Herrington, Doug McNichol, Gary Canter, and Clayton Ball. My games have been the better thanks to your participation.

Publisher's Acknowledgments

We're proud of this book; please send us your comments through our online registration form located at www.dummies.com/register/.

Some of the people who helped bring this book to market include the following:

Acquisitions, Editorial, and Media Development

Project Editor: Christopher Morris

Acquisitions Editor: Melody Layne

Copy Editor: Jean Rogers

Technical Editor: Wizards of the Coast, Inc.

Editorial Manager: Kevin Kirschner

Media Development Supervisor: Richard Graves

Editorial Assistant: Amanda Foxworth

Cartoons: Rich Tennant (www.the5thwave.com)

Composition Services

Project Coordinator: Adrienne Martinez

Layout and Graphics: Joyce Haughey, LeAndra Hosier, Lysney Osborn, Melanee Prendergast, Heather Ryan, Mary Gillot Virgin

Proofreaders: Joe Niesen, Tammy Todd

Indexer: Rebecca R. Plunkett

Art Credits: Des Hanley, Hugh Jamieson, Rob Lazzaretti, Todd Lockwood, Steve Prescott. Wayne Reynolds, Arnie Swekel, Steve Tappin, Lars Grant West, Sam Wood

Publishing and Editorial for Technology Dummies

    Richard Swadley, Vice President and Executive Group Publisher

    Andy Cummings, Vice President and Publisher

    Mary Bednarek, Executive Acquisitions Director

    Mary C. Corder, Editorial Director

Publishing for Consumer Dummies

    Diane Graves Steele, Vice President and Publisher

    Joyce Pepple, Acquisitions Director

Composition Services

    Gerry Fahey, Vice President of Production Services

    Debbie Stailey, Director of Composition Services

Contents at a Glance

Table of Contents

Foreword

*T*wenty-five years ago, I was looking for employment as an editor. What I found, in addition to a great job with *Dragon Magazine*, was this game called DUNGEONS & DRAGONS.

I could tell just by looking through those early rulebooks that the game was in a world all its own. The ideas excited me, and the atmosphere they created was exhilarating. However, those rules didn't do a good job of explaining how to actually *play* the game, and how to get the most out of the experience.

As D&D has evolved over the years, the rules have devoted more and more space to that sort of advice — but DUNGEONS & DRAGONS is, and always will be, a complex, multifaceted game with countless choices and options. Those of us at Wizards of the Coast who create the books that keep the game vibrant and growing will be the first to admit that for a new player, absorbing the *Player's Handbook* can be a daunting task.

That's where *Dungeons & Dragons For Dummies* comes in. With this book, Bill Slavicsek and Richard Baker break down the DUNGEONS & DRAGONS experience into its component parts, making each piece of the whole easy to understand and appreciate.

If their names aren't familiar to you, I'll tell you that Bill and Rich are experts at what they do. As professional writers, they have each created or contributed to dozens of D&D rulebooks and adventures over the last decade and then some. As accomplished Dungeon Masters and players of the game, they bring their love of D&D and their knowledge of the rules to the table every time they get a group together.

D&D is a game about rules. It's also a game about teamwork and social interaction. It's also about many other things, if you want it to be. But at the most fundamental level, it's a game that's meant to be fun to play.

Bill and Rich know how to have fun playing the game and how to make it enjoyable for everyone else. Read on, and let them show you what I mean.

— Kim Mohan

Current Roleplaying Games Editorial Manager at Wizards of the Coast, Inc. Former editor-in-chief of Dragon Magazine *and* Amazing Stories, *managing editor of the three core D&D books:* Player's Handbook, Dungeon Master's Guide, *and* Monster Manual.

Introduction

You crave action and adventure. You revel in the fantastic. You want to play DUNGEONS & DRAGONS. The DUNGEONS & DRAGONS game has been around for more than 30 years, and it stands as the pinnacle of fantasy-adventure games (also known as roleplaying games). The concepts and play patterns of D&D (as it is affectionately called) harken back to the games of make-believe that almost everyone played as a little kid. However, D&D provides form and structure, making game play more satisfying and robust for kids and adults alike.

This book makes the mysterious and often arcane world of fantasy roleplaying, specifically the DUNGEON & DRAGONS game, easier to understand and faster to get into. Get ready to open your imagination, roll some dice, and battle dragons and other magical monsters.

About This Book

We wrote this book to make our favorite hobby game more accessible to every fantasy and gaming fan, from the novice who enjoys fantasy novels such as *The Lord of the Rings* trilogy and has a passing curiosity about DUNGEONS & DRAGONS, to the seasoned D&D player who goes to every convention and has been playing since Gary Gygax and Dave Arneson published the original White Box version of the game. Whether you have yet to play your first game or have been in a regular gaming group for years, our mission is to measurably increase the fun you have playing D&D and your proficiency with the game.

As a new player, this book shows you the basics of the game. You end up with a character to play and enough understanding to confidently take your place at any gaming table. Read this book today, grab a copy of the D&D *Player's Handbook*, and you can play tomorrow without worry or confusion. D&D is a game. Games are fun. We hope to make learning to play fun, too.

For experienced players, we provide hints and tips to elevate your level of play. Character creation, character advancement, combat and encounter strategies, gamemastering — we cover it all. It doesn't matter if you've played once or a hundred times; you can find something in this book to make you a better D&D player or gamemaster (known as a Dungeon Master in D&D lingo).

Why You Need This Book

Novices need *Dungeons & Dragons For Dummies* because it's written by D&D experts to serve as the most comprehensive introduction to the D&D game. You're going to learn things about D&D and fantasy roleplaying that many seasoned gamers still haven't discovered. Do you know the ins and outs of attacks of opportunity? What the best class and race combos are? How to make the most of your character's key abilities? Which monsters can be brought down by what spells and weapons? You can find the answers to all kinds of D&D questions within these pages. And what if you already know a lot about the game? Get ready to learn a good deal more. We've filled this book with inside tips and behind-the-curtain details that you rarely encounter outside the hallowed walls of Wizards of the Coast's fabled RPG R&D department.

We believe that DUNGEONS & DRAGONS speaks to and feeds the human condition. D&D is a game of the imagination, building on the myths and fantasies that have shaped our culture. D&D is a game of endless possibilities, where the only limit on what can happen is what you can imagine. D&D is a social experience, a fun and exciting activity that combines group storytelling and fantasy iconology with strategic challenges and dice rolling. Nothing else — no computer game, no board game, no movie — comes close to delivering the interactive and unlimited adventure of the D&D experience.

From the days of telling stories about trolls and dragons and knights in shining armor around a campfire to the high-tech equivalent that involves computers and high-speed Internet connections, make-believe has advanced along with society. Today, one of the purest expressions of the game is DUNGEONS & DRAGONS. No other outlet for the adventures of armored warriors and powerful wizards is as versatile, creative, or fun as D&D. Get ready to go explore some dungeons and bash some monsters!

How to Use This Book

There's no right or wrong way to use this book. Read it from cover to cover or glance at the table of contents and dive into the chapters or sections that most interest you. If you're a new player, we suggest starting with Part I. You also want to become intimately familiar with the glossary and refer to it often as you explore these pages. If you've played a few games and you're looking to become a better player, check out Part II and Part III. Experienced players will want to look at Part III for insights into the nuances of the game. And those of you who like to be Dungeon Masters (or who aspire to this position) should dive into Part IV. Both longtime players and those new to the world of DUNGEONS & DRAGONS should find something fun and interesting in the Part of Tens.

Much of this book is written with the assumption that you have a D&D *Player's Handbook*. We don't replace the D&D game rules; instead, we try to make them clearer and help you navigate your way through them with inside tips and advice. In addition, you'll need a set of dice (see Chapter 1 for details) to use the practice sessions presented in later chapters, as well as the *battle grid dungeon* and *character and monster markers* included in this book. The battle grid, covered with one-inch squares, when used with the markers, helps show where your character is in relation to other characters and monsters in any particular encounter. We discuss how to use the battle grid in greater depth in Chapter 8.

D&D Terminology

DUNGEONS & DRAGONS has its own lexicon, just like a lot of other intensive activities. Throughout this book, we work to explain things in plain language and to demystify some of the arcane terms and jargon used in the game and rulebooks. Whenever you need some help, flip to the glossary. The glossary is your friend. Still, you should become familiar with the following key terms right off the bat:

- ✔ **DUNGEONS & DRAGONS:** The original roleplaying game of medieval fantasy and adventure. In the game, you take on the role of an imaginary character defined by a series of statistics, cool powers, and magical abilities. The game is played around a table or other comfortable location where books and papers can be spread out and dice can be rolled. D&D (the short form of the name) is a game of your imagination, part group storytelling and part wargame. There are no winners or losers in this game; the point is to build an exciting fantasy story through the actions of your character and the challenges set by the Dungeon Master.

- ✔ **Dungeon Master:** One player is the Dungeon Master (or the DM). While other players control a single character, the DM controls all the monsters and enemies, narrates the action, referees the game, sets up adventures, and develops the campaign. Every D&D game needs a DM.

- ✔ **Player character:** The character controlled by a player is called a player character. A player character might be a powerful fighter, a sneaky rogue, a crafty sorcerer, or a charismatic cleric.

- ✔ **Adventure:** Your character is an adventurer in a fantastic world of magic and monsters. Other characters (controlled by other players) join your adventuring party to explore dungeons and battle amazing creatures such as dragons and trolls. Each quest or story is called an adventure. An adventure might last for a single session of play or stretch over the course of several game sessions.

✔ **Campaign:** The D&D game doesn't end with a single adventure. When the same characters continue from one adventure to another, the overall story is called a campaign.

✔ **Dice:** D&D is a game that uses dice to resolve actions and determine other factors where the outcome isn't certain. The twenty-sided die is the most important, as all major actions in the game are resolved using it. The game also uses a four-sided die, a six-sided die, an eight-sided die, a ten-sided die, and a twelve-sided die. We refer to these dice as d20, d4, d6, d8, d10, and d12. Sometimes, you need to roll multiple dice of a specific shape, such as four six-sided dice. In that case, we use this notation: 4d6. This allows you to generate a result between 4 and 24. Sometimes you need to roll multiple dice and add a modifier, such as two four-sided dice plus two. In that case, we use this notation: 2d4+2. This allows you to generate a result between 4 and 10. (See Chapter 1 for more about D&D dice.)

✔ *Player's Handbook:* One of the three books that make up the rules of the D&D game. This volume contains the basic rules of play and character creation. No D&D player should be caught without one.

✔ *Dungeon Master's Guide:* The second of the three books that make up the rules of the D&D game. This volume contains information that every Dungeon Master needs to run the game, set up adventures, and build campaigns.

✔ *Monster Manual:* The third of the three books that make up the rules of the D&D game. This volume is packed with monsters to challenge even the toughest D&D heroes, and contains information that every player and DM needs to know.

How This Book Is Organized

Dungeons & Dragons For Dummies consists of five parts. The chapters within each part cover specific topics in detail. In each chapter, we start with the basics and build from there. Whenever a point needs further clarification, we cross-reference the appropriate chapter so you can immediately find any additional information you need. In addition, whenever it comes up, we refer you to the appropriate chapter in the D&D *Player's Handbook* or, if necessary, one of the other two books that make up the core rules of the game: the *Dungeon Master's Guide* or the *Monster Manual*.

Part 1: D&D Crash Course

This is your character and these are the dice you roll. We start out with a basic overview of the D&D game, assuming that you're a brand new player who's looking to join an existing gaming group. We give you a little history on how the game began and how it developed, and provide you with ready-to-play characters (called pregenerated characters) so you can join a game right now. We finish off this section with a discussion on starting your own game, just in case you don't currently know anyone who plays.

Part II: Building a D&D Character

Using a pregenerated character is fine, but eventually you'll want to build a character of your very own. In this part, we explain the fine points of character creation and go behind the scenes to discuss character advancement. After all, where your character ends up might be more important than where he or she started. This part of the book is for the player who wants to become more invested in the D&D game. We help you navigate the *Player's Handbook* so that you can make solid, informed decisions about what kind of character you want to build and play.

Part III: Playing Your Best Game

Even expert players should find something new and informative in this part of the book. From effective combat tactics to powerful character combinations, the basics of adventuring party teamwork to advice on good roleplaying, we offer insights into the mechanics of the game and how to be the best D&D player you can be.

Part IV: The Art of Dungeon Mastering

The rest of the book spends a lot of time offering advice and tactics to players. Here's where we provide tips and tricks for that select and important individual who makes every D&D game come alive — the Dungeon Master. It's good to be the DM, and this section of the book starts with the basics of DMing and builds to provide insights that should give even experienced DMs something to think about when running their own games.

Part V: The Part of Tens

No *For Dummies* book is complete without this section of top-ten lists. Helpful and interesting collections of the best spells, monsters, and resources abound throughout these short chapters.

After the last Part of Tens chapter and before the index is the glossary. Perhaps the most often referred to part of this book, the glossary helps you navigate and understand the terms and jargon that pervade the D&D game. Use the glossary often as you use this book and the core D&D rulebooks.

Icons Used in This Book

To guide you along the way and to point out information you really need to know, this book uses the following icons.

This icon points to tips and tricks that make some aspect of the D&D game easier or faster.

Remember these important nuggets, and you'll be a better player or DM.

If you see this icon, read and follow the accompanying directions. This information can prevent you (or your character) from having a very bad day.

Whenever you see this icon, you know we're directing you to more detailed information in one of the D&D core rulebooks — the *Player's Handbook*, *Dungeon Master's Guide*, or *Monster Manual*.

Where Do I Go from Here?

If you're a new player, get a copy of the D&D *Player's Handbook*. If you aspire to be a Dungeon Master, you'll also need the *Dungeon Master's Guide* and the *Monster Manual*. But don't read them yet! The core rulebooks aren't written for novices. Start by digging into the chapters in Part I of this book. We wrote that part specifically to help new players enter the D&D game.

If you've played a time or two (or a hundred!), check out Parts II, III, and IV for D&D gaming advice that anyone interested in the game can use. Part IV is especially relevant if you want to be the Dungeon Master or if you want to improve your already formidable DMing skills.

Our last bit of advice before you move on (and read all of the other nuggets of advice we've packed between these yellow covers) is this: Have fun! D&D is a game. The basics of D&D are straightforward and relatively easy to grasp. Don't let all the details beyond that frighten or confuse you. We're here to help with that, so trust us and let us do our job. For the majority of D&D players around the world, those added details are what make D&D one of the greatest ways they know for spending their leisure time. Explore those details with us, and we think you'll come to the same conclusion.

Part I
D&D Crash Course

The 5th Wave   By Rich Tennant

"I don't want to be Kerwin the Rogue. I want to be Cliff the roofer, who was sent here to check for leaks in the ceiling."

In this part . . .

In this part of the book, we assume that you're a brand-new player. We start out with a bit of background about the Dungeons & Dragons game, and then we dive in and show you how to join an ongoing gaming group. With ready-to-play characters and an overview of the basic rules of play, you can get up to speed quickly and start bashing monsters with the best of them. Near the end of this part, we also offer advice on starting your own gaming group, providing you with every opportunity for getting into the D&D experience!

Chapter 1

Preparing for Adventure

. . . .

In This Chapter

▶ Exploring the origins and objectives of DUNGEONS & DRAGONS

▶ Looking at the components of the game

▶ Explaining role of the Dungeon Master

▶ Examining the things you need to play

▶ Understanding the different expressions of the game

▶ Joining a 1st-level game

. . . .

*E*veryone played make-believe during childhood. Whether you played cops and robbers, cowboys and Indians, superheroes, or firefighters, you opened up your imagination and pretended to be something other than yourself. DUNGEONS & DRAGONS is a game of the imagination, a roleplaying game where players take on the roles of amazing heroes in a medieval fantasy setting. It's just like make-believe, only more sophisticated, grown up, and fun. D&D gives form and structure to your imagination, creating a leisure activity that's more interactive and open-ended than any movie, novel, or computer game.

The backdrop for D&D is a mythological world of fairy tales, epic adventures, and monsters, where heroes gain power and magic to win against all kinds of challenges and villains. This backdrop owes much to fantasy novels, including *The Lord of the Rings* trilogy by J.R.R. Tolkien, but also to a sort of collective consciousness consisting of material from comic books, TV shows, movies, and other fantasy-related influences. Over the course of 30 years, D&D has, in turn, influenced such media and helped set the stage for the computer game industry. This chapter provides an overview of the game and explores some of the topics that we discuss in greater detail throughout the book.

What Is D&D?

The DUNGEONS & DRAGONS roleplaying game is full of fantastic locations, strange creatures, magic items, treasure, and lots of monsters. Imagine an ancient place and time. Imagine a world much like our own, long ago, when armored warriors used swords and bows, castles sat atop wooded hills, and thatched cottages clumped together here and there across the countryside. Imagine that in this ancient time magic really works, and that humans aren't the only intelligent species roaming the land.

D&D lets you explore this imaginary world. With the game, some willing friends, and your imagination, you strike out on epic quests set in this long-ago place that never existed but is as familiar as your own recollections. The D&D game lets you participate in the ultimate interactive story. In this story, you and the other players determine what happens next. How does the adventure end? That's the best part — the ending isn't determined until you and your character get there!

The origin of D&D

It started with wargames, a popular pastime in which participants re-create famous battles on a tabletop using metal figures. In the mid-1960s, Gary Gygax formed a small group of wargamers who met regularly and set out to publish new wargames. This led to the development of the *Chainmail* miniatures rules, and by 1971, Gygax added supplemental rules that expanded the game to include fantastic creatures such as elves, dwarves, and monsters.

In 1972, Dave Arneson came to Gygax with a new take on the traditional wargame. Gone were the massive armies. Each player had a single character, like the "hero" characters in *Chainmail*. A storyteller ran the game, unfolding a narrative in which the players were free to choose their own course of action for their characters. This was a cooperative experience, not a competitive wargame, in which the players joined forces to defeat villains and gain rewards.

This combination of miniatures gaming and player imagination created a totally new experience. Gygax and Arneson collaborated on a set of rules, but they weren't able to find a publisher. So in 1974, Gygax formed a company that eventually was called TSR, Inc. and published DUNGEONS & DRAGONS himself.

In 1977, the rules were totally rewritten and the original DUNGEONS & DRAGONS *Basic Set* was released. Sales rose rapidly and the game became a phenomenon. A year later, a new version of the game, *Advanced DUNGEONS & DRAGONS*, was introduced, published in a series of high-quality hardcover books.

The 1980s continued to see remarkable growth for the game, and new initiatives started during this decade. D&D novels were introduced, a cartoon series debuted on Saturday morning TV, and new fantasy worlds (called *campaign settings*) for D&D such as DRAGONLANCE and FORGOTTEN REALMS appeared. In 1989, the second edition of AD&D hit the shelves, and the 1990s saw the birth of even more campaign settings, including RAVENLOFT, DARK SUN, and PLANESCAPE.

In 1997, TSR changed hands. Wizards of the Coast, makers of the phenomenal trading card game MAGIC: THE GATHERING, purchased the company and moved most of the creative staff to its offices in Washington state. In 2000, the newest edition of the DUNGEONS & DRAGONS game was released, and today the game is more popular than ever. Some 4 million people play D&D every month, using their imaginations and having fun with their friends.

D&D: It's good for you

A few times over the long history of the DUNGEONS & DRAGONS game, some people have tried to knock it as something silly or even harmful. Nothing could be further from the truth. D&D promotes teamwork and socialization. It teaches math and reading skills. It encourages creativity and imaginative problem solving. It's uplifting, inspirational, and thought provoking. And it's fun, too! You sit in the same room with other people, socialize, and create amazingly deep fantasy worlds in which good battles evil on a regular basis — and good usually wins out in the end. What could be better than that?

For a number of reasons, D&D is different from other games you may have played:

- **The play keeps on going:** Like an ongoing television series, your game continues from play session to play session.

- **Your character grows as the game goes on:** You play a character that grows and develops with every adventure he or she participates in.

- **The only limit is your imagination:** The game offers endless possibilities and a multitude of choices because your character can do whatever you can imagine.

- **Everyone wins:** Because the game is really a series of stories told collectively by the players and the Dungeon Master, D&D is a game where everyone wins. If your character survives and wins the day (or dies spectacularly and memorably), and everyone has a good time, then the adventure ends in a win for the group.

Objectives of the D&D Game

D&D is a cooperative game, not a competitive one. In other words, you don't compete against the other players and you don't win by beating them. Instead, there are a lot of different ways to "win" the game. The common denominator in every victory condition is "fun." If you and the other players have fun, everyone wins a game of D&D.

Storytelling

One way to "win" a D&D game is to help the group tell a fun and exciting story. Whether you successfully complete your adventure or fail miserably, if everyone has a good time and you contribute to creating a story that everyone is going to remember, the group wins.

A continuing saga . . .

Unlike other games, each D&D adventure that you play is just one tale in the continuing saga of your player character and the other characters in your group. Of course, you can play a single game session and have a great time, but the real excitement and power of the D&D game comes from watching your character improve and develop from one adventure to the next.

This means that events have consequences. If you find a magic weapon or a potion in one adventure, for example, you can use it in the next. And that evil necromancer that got away? Watch out! He will return in a future adventure to cause you more trouble, just like characters in novels, TV series, and movies.

Adventure goals

Every adventure contains its own set of victory conditions. Sometimes it's as simple as surviving the dungeon and escaping, or defeating the boss villain at the heart of the fortress of evil. Other times, you might have a specific goal to accomplish (take the evil ring and toss it in the volcano) or a specific monster to beat (stop the werewolf before it rampages through the town again). If you achieve the objective of the adventure, the group wins.

Character victories

When you begin playing D&D, your character starts out at 1st level — the lowest experience level. Your character wins each time he or she defeats monsters and gains experience points and treasure. With each new level your character gains, he or she increases in power and reputation. Each increase in wealth, power, and equipment is a win for your character.

Looking at the Components of the Game

You need three distinct components to play a DUNGEONS & DRAGONS game:

- ✔ **Players:** You need players, usually two to six of them, to take on the roles of adventurers in the fantasy world. The adventurers controlled by the players are also called *heroes* or *player characters* (*PCs,* for short).

- ✔ **A Dungeon Master:** The *Dungeon Master (DM)* controls all of the *non-player characters (NPCs)* — the monsters, villains, and other incidental characters that inhabit the fantasy world. The DM sets the pace of the story and referees the action as the adventure unfolds.

✔ **An adventure:** An adventure is the activity that the player characters participate in. An adventure usually consists of a basic plot and a number of encounters. As the players (through their characters) interact with the plot and resolve the encounters, they help the DM tell a story. The cool thing is that every action the player characters perform affects the twists and turns of the plot, so that the outcome of the adventure winds up surprising everyone.

The following sections give more details about all the various parts of the D&D experience.

Players and characters

Like the protagonists of a novel or the heroes of a movie, the action revolves around the characters in a D&D game. Each player creates a character (or selects a ready-to-play character, such as the ones presented in Chapters 3, 4, 5, and 6), a heroic adventurer who is part of a team that regularly delves into dungeons and battles monsters. These characters include mighty fighters, brave clerics, cunning rogues, and powerful sorcerers. You, as a player, play the game while your character takes all the risks.

Playing a D&D character is kind of like acting, except everything happens around the gaming table. You don't have to deliver lines or perform stunts. Just find a comfortable seat, explain what your character is doing, and roll some dice. The scene plays out in your imagination and in the imaginations of the other players.

The Dungeon Master

One player has a special role in a D&D game. This player, the *Dungeon Master* (or *DM*), controls the pace of the story and referees the action along the way. Every D&D game needs a Dungeon Master — you can't play the game without one.

The cool thing about Dungeon Masters is that they allow the game to be totally interactive and open-ended. Players can have their characters attempt anything they can imagine because there's a real, live person sitting in the DM's chair, coordinating the action and determining how every event adds to the story. The game rules and the dice help, but the DM must use his or her imagination to make the world unfold.

The player who decides to take on the role of the Dungeon Master becomes a member of a select group. Not everyone has the dedication and creativity to be a DM, but those that do have a great outlet in the D&D game. The DM defines the game his or her group is going to play, and a good DM results in a great game of D&D.

Some groups use multiple DMs, so that everyone gets to run a player character at some point, and everyone who wants to try their hands at DMing gets the opportunity. Other groups go for years with the same player serving as DM for every game session. It all depends on the desires of the group and the personalities involved.

The adventure

The player characters are the stars of your D&D game, just like the heroes in books or movies. They are adventurers, and adventurers need adventures. A D&D adventure features action, combat, mystery, challenges, and lots and lots of monsters. Adventures come in three forms: full-length adventures published specifically for D&D, adventure hooks in published products that DMs can turn into full-length adventures, and adventures that DMs create for themselves.

Adventures can be as simple as a basic dungeon crawl or as complex as a murder mystery. An adventure can last for a single game session or stretch out over a number of sessions of play. One adventure might take place in a haunted castle, another in a crime-ridden village, a third in the catacombs beneath an ancient graveyard. What makes D&D different from your typical board game is that each adventure is just a single tale in the continuing saga of your player characters. Adventures provide the stage upon which your player characters perform heroic deeds and resolve legendary quests. Anything is possible in a D&D game, and it is through adventures that the possibilities come alive.

Supplies you need

Players and characters, a Dungeon Master, and an adventure — these are the basic components of any DUNGEONS & DRAGONS game. However, you need a few supplies to get the most out of the experience. These things include:

- The D&D game itself
- Special dice
- Character sheets
- Miniatures and battle grids
- Pencils and paper — lots of it

The D&D game

This *For Dummies* book is a great place to start, but eventually you'll need other products and books to get the most from the DUNGEONS & DRAGONS role-playing game. Beginners should pick up the *DUNGEONS & DRAGONS Basic Game*, which includes the basic rules, dice, and many of the other components discussed in this section, all in one convenient box.

If you want to progress beyond the basics, you'll need the three core books, all published by Wizards of the Coast, that comprise the full D&D game:

- ✔ **Player's Handbook:** Presents the rules of the game from the player's point of view and provides details on creating characters, outfitting adventurers, and playing the game.

- ✔ **Dungeon Master's Guide:** Presents the rules of the game from the Dungeon Master's point of view and provides detailed advice on running games, creating adventures, sustaining campaigns, and awarding experience to player characters. It also contains a selection of magic items and a fold-out battle grid to enhance play.

- ✔ **Monster Manual:** Presents hundreds of creatures to use in any D&D game. From low-level to high-level, friendly to hostile, each creature has an illustration, game tactics, and statistics for ease of use.

The DM needs all three books, but players can usually get by with just a copy of the *Player's Handbook*.

Dice

Dice are used to determine the outcome of actions in the game. If you want your character to try something — such as attack the ogre, disarm the trap, or search for clues — the dice are used whenever the result isn't a sure thing. The D&D game uses dice of different shapes. Each player should have his or her own set of dice with which to play the game. Players get possessive and protective of their dice, and having your own set means you can customize it (dice come in all kinds of styles and colors). Game play also proceeds more smoothly when you don't have to pass the dice around when sharing among players.

A set of dice for the D&D game includes at least the following (see Figure 1-1):

- ✔ One four-sided die (referred to as a d4)
- ✔ Four six-sided dice (d6)

✔ One eight-sided die (d8)

✔ Two ten-sided dice (d10)

   When these two dice are rolled together, they can produce any digit
   between 01 and 100. For this reason, these two dice are often called
   percentile dice (d%). Some dice sets include a d90 (a die that has sides
   expressed in tens — 10, 20, 30, and so on) to make rolling percentile
   dice easier.

✔ One twelve-sided die (d12)

✔ One twenty-sided die (d20)

Figure 1-1: The basic dice for D&D.

The d20 determines character success at any given action, while the other
dice determine what happens if an action succeeds.

Character sheets

Your D&D character is defined by a series of key statistics, as well as by the
background story you create for the character. These statistics and other key
information are contained on a character sheet. As your character participates
in adventures, these statistics change.

This book contains a series of basic character sheets that provide ready-to-
play characters. These can be found in Chapters 3, 4, 5, and 6.

Miniatures and a battle grid

While most of the action of D&D occurs in the imaginations of the participants, it is often very helpful to display certain information where everyone
can see it. Combat situations, for example, work better when the players and
DM know where all the participants are (characters and monsters) in relation
to one another. D&D uses a one-inch grid, called the battle grid, to represent
where the action takes place. To represent the characters and monsters, the
players and DM place miniatures or other markers on the battle grid.

This book contains a sample battle grid and markers to use in your first few
D&D experiences. We discuss the use of these items in Chapter 8.

Other play surfaces can be found in the *Dungeon Master's Guide* and the *D&D Basic Game*. Official prepainted plastic D&D miniatures can be found in the *D&D Basic Game*, as well as in *D&D Miniatures* booster packs, available wherever fine hobby games are sold.

Pencils, paper, and graph paper

You'll want a means for keeping notes and recording important information during game play, so have a lot of pencils, scrap paper, and graph paper available. Use the scrap paper for notes about the adventure (write down the names of NPCs and places, any treasure your character acquires, and any other details that you might forget or think may be important later). One player might take the role of note keeper, or each player may want to take his or her own notes. Use the graph paper to sketch a map of the area the PCs are exploring — players want to map the dungeon as they explore it, while the DM uses graph paper to design the whole dungeon before the adventurers enter it.

One Game Rule to Rule Them All

The DUNGEONS & DRAGONS game is built around a core mechanic. This core mechanic is used to resolve all actions in the game, keeping play fast and intuitive.

The Core Game Mechanic: Whenever your character attempts an action that has a chance of failure associated with it, roll a twenty-sided die (d20). The higher the roll, the better the character's chances of succeeding in that action.

Character actions boil down to three basic types:

- ✔ **Attack rolls:** A roll to determine if your character succeeds at attacking a monster or other opponent. Using a longsword against a monster, for example, requires an attack roll.
- ✔ **Skill checks:** A roll to determine if your character uses a skill successfully. Using the Climb skill to scale a wall, for example, requires a skill check.
- ✔ **Ability checks:** A roll to determine if your character succeeds at attempting to do something to which no specific skill really applies. Attempting to bash open a dungeon door, for example, requires a Strength ability check.

To determine if any of these actions are successful, follow these steps:

1. **Roll a d20.**
2. **Add any relevant modifiers.**
3. **Compare the result to a target number.**

Expressions of D&D

The primary expression of Dungeons & Dragons takes the form of the D&D roleplaying game (RPG). This is where the whole thing started, and the RPG is still going strong after 30 years. This expression is presented in the three core rule-books (*Player's Handbook, Dungeon Master's Guide,* and *Monster Manual*) and a plethora of supplements and accessories that expand the world of D&D. This *For Dummies* book focuses on the RPG experience and tries to make it clearer and easier to get into. But other expressions of D&D exist. Here are a few that you might want to check out:

✔ **Dungeons & Dragons miniatures:** Official D&D prepainted plastic miniatures are available for use with the RPG. From hero characters to monsters such as bugbears, mind flayers, beholders, and more, a wide selection of the most popular and iconic D&D creatures can be found in randomly assorted booster packs. These miniature figures can also be used for a more competitive experience, a head-to-head skirmish game where players create warbands of D&D characters and creatures to throw against each other. If this concept (which goes back to D&D's roots) interests you, look for the *D&D Miniatures Starter Set* and *Booster Packs.*

✔ **Dungeons & Dragons novels:** Wizards of the Coast publishes fantasy novels set in the worlds of Dungeons & Dragons. Some of the most popular series include novels set in the Forgotten Realms and Dragonlance campaigns, and the young adult Knights of the Silver Dragon series for younger readers.

✔ ***Dragon Magazine* and *Dungeon Magazine:*** Paizo Publishing, in cooperation with Wizards of the Coast, publishes two monthly magazines dedicated to the Dungeons & Dragons game. *Dragon Magazine* provides a player's perspective on the hobby, offering loads of new options to add to your game. Consider it to be a monthly supplement full of new feats, spells, and magic items, as well as new player character races and prestige classes, and tons of roleplaying and tactical advice to make any player better at the game. The companion periodical, *Dungeon Magazine,* is the definitive monthly resource for D&D Dungeon Masters. It features DM advice, dungeon lairs, and ready-to-play adventures that can be dropped into any D&D campaign. Together, these magazines are a must-have for serious D&D players and DMs everywhere. You can learn more about these magazines and find subscription information on the Web at www.paizo.com.

✔ **Computer and console games:** You might be more familiar with Dungeons & Dragons through the computer and video games that have been released over the years. The computer game industry grew out of the paper RPGs created by D&D, and today Atari continues to publish licensed games set in the worlds of Dungeons & Dragons. Popular titles include *Baldur's Gate, Neverwinter Nights,* and *Temple of Elemental Evil,* and more games for both console platforms and computers are on the way.

If the result equals or exceeds the target number, the action succeeds. A result less than the target number indicates that the action fails. Target numbers, also called the Difficulty Class (or DC) for a particular task or action, come from a variety of places. Some are set by the action itself and are defined in the rules, while other times, the target numbers are determined by the Dungeon Master. For more details, see Chapter 7.

Joining a D&D Game

The best way to learn how to play DUNGEONS & DRAGONS is to jump right in. If you know other players who have a regular game, this book provides you with everything you need to join an existing game. The ready-to-play characters in Chapters 3, 4, 5, and 6 are 1st-level characters, completely built and outfitted for their first adventure. If you want to join a higher-level game, Chapter 9 presents one of these characters at greater levels of experience — specifically, at 4th level and at 8th level — giving you a little more latitude in where to start.

If you don't have an existing game group to join, you'll have to start your own. Chapter 9 discusses organizing your own game group.

Whether you join an existing group or start your own, we urge you to get moving. Every day you wait means one less day of getting in on the fun and excitement of D&D.

The best place to start

Other than this nifty *For Dummies* book, where's the best place to start learning the DUNGEONS & DRAGONS game? Well, we wrote this book to be a great starting point as well as a perfect companion to the full D&D game. Don't be afraid to just start out using the material in this book.

At some point, however, you need to get one of the D&D games. If you're brand new to the concept of roleplaying games, we urge you to buy the DUNGEONS & DRAGONS *Basic Game*. This jam-packed box includes dice, versatile battle grid tiles, miniatures, and ready-to-play characters. This *For Dummies* book makes a great companion for learning to play with the *Basic Game*.

If you have some knowledge and experience with D&D or games like it, you might be ready to leap right into the core rulebooks. This trinity of knowledge comes in the form of the *Player's Handbook*,

Dungeon Master's Guide, and *Monster Manual*. These volumes are available at fine hobby game stores and bookstores, and with this *For Dummies* book at your side, you should have no trouble navigating your way through them. If you go this route, you'll need to buy a set of dice too, because the books don't come with them.

If you'd rather approach the D&D experience through a more competitive expression, check out the DUNGEONS & DRAGONS *Miniatures Starter Set*. It includes dice and rules for building warbands full of D&D creatures and heroes, and presents a straight-forward version of D&D's core game mechanic. The great thing about D&D is that if you understand the basics, you can play either a competitive skirmish game or a cooperative roleplaying adventure.

Chapter 2

Your First Character

*Y*our interface with the fantastic adventures of DUNGEONS & DRAGONS is your *player character* (also called a *PC*). Like the hero of a novel, the star of a movie, or the character in a computer game, your player character (along with the other player characters in your adventuring party, run by other players) is at the center of all the action. Unlike the heroes of novels, movies, or even computer games, however, a D&D player character has no script to follow. *You* determine the course of every adventure through the actions you have your character take — and the only limit is your own imagination.

In this chapter, we examine the basics of what makes a D&D player character tick. From game statistics to race and class abilities, this chapter provides an overview so that you can get a handle on the character you're going to play. This is all in preparation for selecting one of the ready-to-play characters presented in Chapters 3 through 6. In those chapters, we've done all the work of creating characters so that you can spend time getting familiar with all of the game concepts. Later in the book, we walk you through the process of character creation so that you can use this book and the core D&D rulebooks to make your very own player character from scratch.

Defining Your Character

A DUNGEONS & DRAGONS player character lives in an ancient time, in a world much like ours was in medieval times, when knights and castles filled the land. Imagine this place, where magic really works and dragons roam in the dark beyond the firelight. Your character might be a strong fighter or a nimble rogue, a wise cleric or a charismatic sorcerer. Every day, your character explores the unknown places of the world, seeking monsters to slay and treasure to win. Every adventure that your character survives makes him or her a little more powerful, a little more famous, and a little richer.

D&D is a game, and so you need some way to express and describe your character in the context of the game world. Your fighter, for example, might be "extremely strong but not too bright," and those characteristics need to be translated into game terms. The following sections provide an overview of the things you'll find on your *character sheet,* a record of your character's game statistics.

Name

Every great character has a great name. You may have a name all picked out from the moment you conceive your character, or you may figure it out after you've determined all of your character's game statistics. Great names are evocative. They fit the mood of the story and world in which the character adventures. John Savage is a great name for a character in a spy thriller set in the modern world, but it doesn't work so well for a character in a D&D fantasy world.

The characters presented for your use in Chapters 3, 4, 5, and 6 have names already assigned to them. Chapter 2 of the *Player's Handbook* also lists sample names based on race. Those are good places to start when you decide to create your own character from scratch (which we discuss in Part II).

Race

In the fantasy world of Dungeons & Dragons, humans aren't the only intelligent race walking around. Other intelligent races share their adventures, and your character can belong to any of these. To start, we present only a few of the possible races you could choose from. The D&D *Player's Handbook* has additional races that make great player characters.

These races are drawn from myth and legend, and they are similar to the imaginary races that populate many popular fantasy worlds. For D&D, the races we begin with are *humans, dwarves, elves,* and *halflings.* More detailed information on the character races can be found in Chapter 13. Here's a quick rundown on the benefits of each:

- **Humans:** These are people just like you and us. They are adaptable, flexible, and extremely ambitious. Compared to the other races, humans are relatively short-lived. In game terms, humans get an extra feat and four extra skill points to reflect their natural tendencies.

- **Dwarves:** The members of this race are hearty and steadfast, standing about 4½ feet tall but powerfully built and extremely broad. They have a strong connection to mountains and rocky places. They can live to be more than 400 years old. In game terms, dwarves receive a +2 to Constitution and a –2 to Charisma (see the "Ability scores" section, later in this chapter). They also receive bonuses against poison, spells, and magical effects. Dwarves also have darkvision, the ability to see up to 60 feet in the dark.

✔ **Elves:** Elves have a strong connection to the natural world, especially woodlands. They can live to be more than 700 years old. Known for being artists of both song and magic, elves have an affinity for spellcasting and lore. They stand about 5½ feet tall, appearing graceful and frail. Elves receive a +2 to Dexterity and a –2 to Constitution (see the "Ability scores" section). They are immune to sleep effects and receive a bonus against enchantment spells. Elves have low-light vision and a racial bonus on Listen, Search, and Spot checks (see the "Skills" section, later in this chapter).

✔ **Halflings:** The members of this race are clever and capable — much more so than their small size might indicate. Standing about 3 feet tall, with slim, muscular builds, halflings are athletic and outgoing. Curious to a fault and usually with a daring to match, halflings love to explore. They tend to live well past 100. Halflings receive a +2 Dexterity and a –2 Strength to reflect their small statures. They also receive bonuses to Climb, Jump, Listen, and Move Silently checks (see the "Skills" section), as well as a bonus to all saving throws due to their fearlessness and ability to avoid damage.

Class

In addition to your character's name (Regdar, perhaps) and race (human, for example), your character is most easily identified by his or her class. A *class* is kind of like a profession or vocation. It determines what role the character plays in the adventuring party. In this book, we present four of the most popular D&D classes for your use. More can be found in the D&D *Player's Handbook*.

The four basic classes are *fighter, rogue, sorcerer,* and *cleric*. More detailed information on the character classes can be found in Chapter 11. Here's a quick overview of each class:

✔ **Fighters:** These characters are warriors with exceptional combat capabilities and weapon skills. Nobody kills monsters and stands at the front of an adventuring party as well as the fighter.

✔ **Rogues:** Members of this class rely on tricks, cunning, and stealth to get through a dungeon and save the day. Rogues are great at getting past locked doors, scouting, spying, and attacking from the shadows.

✔ **Sorcerers:** These are spellcasters, calling on powerful magic spells to fight monsters and protect their teammates. Sorcerers need to stay out of direct combat, but the power they bring to the adventure makes them worthy members of any party.

✔ **Clerics:** These characters focus the might of divine magic to cast healing and protective spells. A good second-line warrior as well, a cleric might be one of the most versatile members of an adventuring party.

So, your character might be Regdar the human fighter, for example.

Level and XP

Level is a description of your character's relative degree of power. A 10th-level character, for example, is more powerful and able to take on tougher challenges than a 5th-level character. With each new level your character attains, he or she becomes more powerful and capable. Your character begins play at 1st level.

Experience points (XP) are the numerical measure of your character's personal achievements. Your character earns experience points by defeating opponents and overcoming challenges. When your character's XP total reaches various milestones, he or she gains new levels. At 0 XP, for example, your character is 1st level. At 1,000 XP, your character attains 2nd level. More information on XP and levels can be found in Chapter 18.

Ability scores

The primary expression of your character in game terms starts with his or her ability scores. Every D&D character is defined by six abilities — Strength, Dexterity, Constitution, Intelligence, Wisdom, and Charisma. (See Chapter 12 for more information about ability scores.) Each ability gets a score, a number that determines how good your character will be at different tasks in the game.

The average score for everyday people in a D&D world is 10 or 11. Player characters are heroes, and so they are better than everyday folk. The average ability score for a player character is 12 or 13.

During character creation, you can generate numbers between 3 (a terrible score) and 18 (an excellent score). The characters presented for your use in Chapters 3 through 6 already have their ability scores and other statistics figured out, so you can start playing immediately.

Special abilities

If it hasn't been made clear yet, your player character is special. He or she stands above the normal people and becomes a hero in the world. As such, your character has special abilities. These might be based on your character's class or race, or tied to certain feats you have selected.

For example, Regdar the fighter has taken the Power Attack feat. This provides him with the special ability to reduce the effectiveness of his attack roll in order to increase the damage he deals on a successful hit. Another example of a special ability is Wellyn the sorcerer's ability to cast arcane spells.

Key statistics

Your character has a number of key statistics that you'll refer to over and over through the course of play. These appear right at the top of the ready-to-play character sheets presented in Chapters 3 through 6. More details on how to use these statistics can be found in Chapter 7. Here's a quick rundown on these statistics:

- ✔ **Initiative modifier:** This modifier is used to determine who goes first in a combat round.

- ✔ **Speed:** This value shows how far your character can move (measured in feet) in a round.

- ✔ **Attack and damage modifiers:** These numbers are associated with your character's weapons of choice, show what you must roll to attack opponents, and how much damage your character does if the attack succeeds.

- ✔ **Armor Class (or AC):** This value is what opponents need to roll to hit your character during combat.

- ✔ **Hit points (or hp):** This number defines how much damage your character can withstand before being defeated in combat. When your character runs out of hit points, he or she is defeated.

Feats

Feats provide special bonuses or capabilities for your character. Sometimes a feat provides a totally new power for your character. Other feats improve powers your character already has. The ready-to-play characters in Chapters 3 through 6 have already had feats selected for them. For more information about selecting your own feats, see Chapter 14.

Skills

Skills represent the training and education your character has beyond the combat and spellcasting inherent to his or her class. Depending on your character's class, your character will have a greater or lesser amount of skills to call upon. Rogues, for example, receive a large number of points with which to buy and improve skills. Fighters, on the other hand, just don't go in much for studying, and therefore receive a much smaller number of skill points to use.

Skills have already been selected for the ready-to-play characters presented in Chapters 3 through 6. Additional information on skills can be found in Chapter 15.

Gear

Every D&D player character must be well prepared for adventuring life. This is reflected not only in the class, skills, and feats the character has, but in the gear the character carries. From weapons and armor to rations, sleeping rolls and rope, torches, flint and steel, and the backpack to carry it all in, no adventurer goes naked into a dungeon.

Equipment has already been selected for the ready-to-play characters presented in Chapters 3 through 6. Additional information on adventuring gear can be found in Chapter 16.

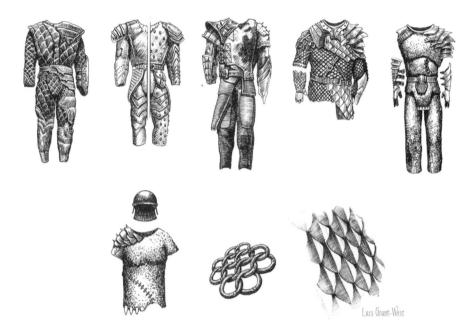

Lars Grant-West

Spells

Characters with a spellcasting class possess spells. In this book, the spellcasting classes we cover are the sorcerer (an arcane spellcaster) and the cleric (a divine spellcaster). The D&D *Player's Handbook* presents other spellcasting class options.

A spell is a one-time magical effect. Some spells deal damage to either a single opponent or a group of opponents. Other spells heal adventuring companions who have been injured in combat. There are all kinds of spells with all kinds of different magical effects.

The sorcerer (one of the spellcasting character classes presented in this book) casts arcane spells. Arcane spells tend to be offensive in nature. The cleric (another spellcasting character class in this book) casts divine spells. Divine spells tend to be helpful and defensive in nature, providing healing or effects that improve or otherwise benefit the party.

Spells have already been selected for the ready-to-play spellcasters presented in Chapters 5 and 6. Additional information on spells can be found in Chapter 17.

Playing Your Character

As stated earlier in this chapter, the way you interface with the D&D world is through your player character. Your character is your eyes and ears in the fantasy world, as well as your hands and feet. You can interact with the world your Dungeon Master presents in any way you want through your character. The only limit is your imagination — and sometimes how well you roll the dice. The following sections tell you how to get the most out of your player characters.

Taking turns

When you're caught up in a game, it's easy to care only about whose turn it is during combat and other dramatic situations (such as when dealing with a trap or obstacle). Try not to forget that there are other people playing the game with you. When you really get into your character and the fantasy, you might have a tendency to hog all of the DM's attention. Resist that urge! Let every player have a turn talking to the DM, asking questions, or describing what his or her character wants to do. It's only fair, and it makes the game work much better. Besides, much of the fun is in seeing what the other players are thinking and how they're reacting to their characters' actions.

During combat situations, everyone makes an initiative roll to determine the order of play. We cover initiative and game play in greater detail in Chapter 7.

Roleplaying

D&D is a roleplaying game. That means that your character is much more than just a collection of game statistics (though those have their place). Take those game statistics and build a personality for your character. Remember that your character is a hero and is part of a team, but otherwise let your imagination be your guide. What sets your character apart are the quirks and mannerisms you bring to the role.

Players are not characters

Always keep in mind that you and your character are two different people. You have knowledge as a player that your character doesn't have. Your character shouldn't know what die rolls have been made or other things that don't make up his or her "character knowledge." Characters never talk about Armor Class or hit points or ability scores. They can discuss the quality of their armor, their general health, and their comparative strengths and weaknesses, but never the game mechanics behind those things.

Be sure to let the DM and the other players know when you're speaking as your character or as yourself, if there is any confusion. When

you remember the difference between you the player and your character, everyone can have more fun roleplaying.

A good Dungeon Master may say during the game "You don't know that" or "You wouldn't think of that," meaning that you're confusing player knowledge with character knowledge. Good players learn to avoid this type of problem by keeping the two separate.

Players don't swing swords, cast spells, disarm traps, or die fighting monsters. Characters, on the other hand, do all this and more over the course of a typical adventure.

D&D is a game. Have fun with it. You don't have to use funny voices or accents or anything like that. Just determine how your character would act in any given situation and remain true to the character as the adventure unfolds. Soon, your character will develop a personality all of his or her own, and the game, in turn, will take on a fantastic life that makes each session fun to play.

Your imagination is the limit

In addition to attacking, casting spells, and using skills, characters can do all sorts of things. The only limit to what a character can do is the player's imagination and the rulings of the Dungeon Master. Depending on the situation, your character might bash apart a cabinet to find a secret compartment, make a rope out of bed sheets, or try to build a trap out of spare parts in an evil wizard's workshop. The DM decides if an idea works or not, sometimes calling for die rolls to help determine the outcome.

Choosing Your Character

The earlier sections in this chapter cover the basics. After you have a handle on the basic stuff, select your own character from those presented over the next four chapters. There's no right or wrong way to choose a character. You might like the picture of the character and decide to play that character because he or she looks cool and heroic. You might really want to play a specific class and/or race. Of course, you should read through all the material, but in the end, go with your gut and choose the character that most appeals to you. Here are some recommendations:

- **Fighters:** You want to play a fighter if being in the thick of combat appeals to you. Fighters always have something to do, no matter what challenge appears before them. Fighters are also among the easiest characters to play because they do one thing and they do it well — they fight. If you want to play a fighter, turn to Chapter 3 and select one of the ready-to-play fighters presented therein.

- **Rogues:** You want to play a rogue if being sneaky and cunning appeals to you. Rogues have plenty of skills to call upon, and they excel at making sneak attacks on their enemies. Rogues have a few more options than fighters, making them slightly more complex to play, but they're still a good choice for those new to the game and the concepts of D&D. If you want to play a rogue, turn to Chapter 4 and select one of the ready-to-play rogues presented therein.

- **Sorcerers:** You want to play a sorcerer if casting flashy spells appeals to you. Sorcerers cast arcane spells that deal damage or protect the party. Sorcerers are harder to play than fighters or rogues due to the slight complexity of spellcasting, but the rewards for playing a sorcerer well can be very satisfying. If you want to play a sorcerer, turn to Chapter 5 and select one of the ready-to-play sorcerers presented therein.

- **Clerics:** You want to play a cleric if spellcasting, up close combat, and helping others appeals to you. Clerics cast defensive and helpful divine spells that give the entire party a boost. In addition, they have the ability to fight alongside fighters when the monsters charge in fast and furiously. If you want to play a cleric, turn to Chapter 6 and select one of the ready-to-play clerics presented therein.

Creating your own character

We recommend starting out by using one of the ready-to-play characters. This allows you to get right into the game and get a feel for it without a lot of upfront preparation. However, one of the great joys of the D&D game is creating your own character and watching him or her develop and grow over the course of a long and exciting campaign. When you're ready to create your own character from scratch, the information in Part II guides you through the process of using the D&D *Player's Handbook* to build exactly the character you want to play.

Chapter 3

Starting Out as a Fighter

*T*he fighter is the quintessential DUNGEONS & DRAGONS player character. As the name of the class implies, the fighter has the best all-around fighting capabilities. A fighter usually has a good Strength score to better use melee weapons, such as swords and axes. A good Dexterity score helps bolster a fighter's use of ranged weapons, such as bows, as well as his or her Armor Class.

Fighters can use any kind of armor, shield, or most weapons without penalty. They are trained in all types of combat.

Your character can take any approach to the fighter class. He might be a questing knight, a king's champion, or an elite foot soldier. She might be a mercenary, a raider, or a thug. Some fighters use their expertise for the greater good, while others are only interested in personal gain.

Some fighters take up the sword to escape life on the farm. Whether a fighter receives formal training in an army or local militia, or is self-taught but battle tested, he or she stands at the front of any adventuring party. A fighter provides combat prowess, high hit points, and good defense to the party. In return, the fighter seeks magical support, healing, and scouting skills from comrades. As part of a team, the fighter protects the other party members and wades in to defeat the tough opponents. In other words, the fighter's job is to fight.

In this chapter, we provide a bit of advice on who might want to play a fighter character and how to play a fighter character if that's the route you decide to go. The rest of the chapter features four ready-to-play fighter characters that you can use to kick-start your adventuring career.

Who Should Play a Fighter?

The fighter is among the easiest, most straightforward characters to play. Anyone brand new to the concept of D&D and roleplaying might want to start out with a fighter character. If you think that being in the center of most combat encounters will appeal to you, or if you like the idea of playing a physically powerful character, then the fighter is the class for you.

Every adventuring party needs at least one fighter. In a party of four, a solid fighter is essential to success. In a party of five or six, two fighters really provide a lot of offense and make adventuring that much easier.

How to Play a Fighter

The fighter does one thing and he or she does it well. Combat is the fighter's bread and butter, so if you play a fighter, you have to be ready to wade into battle whenever monsters or other opponents appear. A melee-oriented fighter (a fighter who uses close-quarter weapons such as swords) wants to get up close and personal with the enemy, and usually wants to take on the toughest opponent personally. A ranged fighter (a fighter who uses ranged weapons such as bows) wants to attack opponents from a distance, at least for the first few rounds of battle. The ranged fighter should always have at least some skill with a melee weapon, however, because very few opponents stand around at a distance to get shot at for very long. And when they rush in, it's a good idea to have a secondary weapon (say, a longsword) for defense.

Fighters should be brave and stalwart, gutsy and heroic. Later, you can play with the baselines and portray any kind of fighter you want, but to start out, go with the tried-and-true basics. Fighters live for the thrill of combat and the excitement of adventure. And woe to any evil that happens to cross their path!

Have fun with the idea of being a physical powerhouse, a combat expert, and a master of weapons. That's the fighter's portfolio, and you should play it for all it's worth. That doesn't mean you shouldn't play smart, however. If your fighter blindly rushes into combat and gets killed, then the rest of your team will be in real trouble. Be cautious, but not too cautious. Above all, be a hero.

Selecting a Fighter

The rest of this chapter features four ready-to-play fighter characters:

- ✔ Regdar is a human male who excels at close combat with his powerful greatsword.
- ✔ Brenna is a human female who also wields a greatsword.
- ✔ Tordek is a dwarf male who uses a dwarven waraxe.
- ✔ Quarion is an elf male who prefers ranged combat with his longbow, though he carries a longsword for those times when he has to fight in close quarters.

Any of these characters make a great fighter and a worthy member of any adventuring party. Pick the one that most appeals to you, and then turn to Chapter 7 for a quick overview of game play.

Regdar, Human Fighter

Regdar is a champion of good, pledging his mighty sword to the cause of justice. He adventures to put down evil and to gain skill and experience that he can use in his crusade. Of all the weapons he has trained to use, Regdar prefers his greatsword, even though it requires two hands to use and thus prevents him from using a shield to protect himself. Regdar's job on an adventuring team is to kill the monsters and protect his teammates.

Initiative	**+1**

When combat starts, the character with the highest initiative check goes first.

Speed	**4**

You can move 4 squares per turn.

Armor Class	**15**

Opponents need to roll this number or better to hit you.

Hit Points	**12**

If you run out of hit points, you are defeated.

Greatsword	**d20+4**
Damage	**2d6+3**

Special Abilities

Cleave: Once per round, if you kill an opponent with your greatsword, you can immediately make a greatsword attack against another opponent if there's one next to you.

Power Attack: If you wish, before you attack, you can take a −1 penalty on the attack roll. If you hit, you deal +2 damage.

Shortbow	**d20+2**
Damage	**d6**

When you attack, decide which weapon you're going to use. Then roll the twenty-sided die and add the bonus. If the result is equal to or higher than the opponent's Armor Class, you hit. Roll other dice as listed for damage. Damage reduces the opponent's hit points.

Skills

When you use a skill, roll the twenty-sided die and add or subtract, as the skill says. If you roll high enough, you succeed.

The Dungeon Master knows how high you need to roll.

Diplomacy   d20+1
    Use this skill to convince and persuade others.

Hide   d20–3
    Use this skill to conceal yourself so that others can't see you.

Listen   d20+1
    Use this skill to hear opponents on the other side of a dungeon door.

Move Silently   d20–3
    Use this skill to sneak around quietly.

Search   d20
    Use this skill to locate secret doors and hidden treasure.

Spot   d20+1
    Use this skill to notice opponents lurking in the shadows.

Saving Throws

When you make a saving throw, roll the twenty-sided die and add or subtract as shown.

Fortitude   d20+4
    To resist poison, stunning, and similar effects.

Reflex   d20+1
    To avoid traps, dragon breath, and similar hazards.

Will   d20–1
    To resist mental attacks.

Armor

Regdar wears scale mail armor.

Weapons and Gear

Regdar carries a greatsword, a shortbow, 20 arrows, a backpack, 10 torches, and flint and steel.

Regdar

Race: Human
Class: Fighter
Level: 1st
Alignment: Good

Ability Scores

           Score   Bonus*

STRENGTH   **15**   **+2**
Bonus applies to sword attack and damage, kicking down doors.

DEXTERITY   **12**   **+1**
Bonus applies to Armor Class, bow attack, Reflex saving throws, Hide and Move Silently skills.

CONSTITUTION   **14**   **+2**
Bonus applies to hit points, Fortitude saving throws.

INTELLIGENCE   **10**   **+0**
Bonus applies to Search skill.

WISDOM   **8**   **–1**
Penalty applies to Will saving throws, Listen and Spot skills.

CHARISMA   **13**   **+1**
Bonus applies to Diplomacy skill.

* Bonuses and penalties have already been calculated into your statistics.

Feats

Cleave, Power Attack: See Special Abilities.

Weapon Focus (Greatsword): +1 to attack, already calculated into statistics.

Gold Pieces (gp)   Experience Points (XP)

—————————   —————————

Brenna, Human Fighter

Brenna fights for the joy of battle and the thrill of defeating evil monsters. She craves excitement and challenges that test her skills and courage. Brenna wields a powerful greatsword, and she keeps a number of daggers on hand to throw when she needs a ranged weapon. Brenna's job on an adventuring team is to kill the monsters and protect her teammates.

Initiative **+1**
When combat starts, the character with the highest initiative check goes first.

Speed **6**
You can move 6 squares per turn.

Armor Class **15**
Opponents need to roll this number or better to hit you.

Hit Points **11**
If you run out of hit points, you are defeated.

Special Abilities

Cleave: Once per round, if you kill an opponent with your greatsword, you can immediately make a greatsword attack against another opponent if there's one next to you.

Power Attack: If you wish, before you attack, you can take a –1 penalty on the attack roll. If you hit, you deal +2 damage.

Greatsword **d20+4**
Damage **2d6+3**

Dagger **d20+2**
Damage **d4**
When you attack, decide which weapon you're going to use. Then roll the twenty-sided die and add the bonus. If the result is equal to or higher than the opponent's Armor Class, you hit. Roll other dice as listed for damage. Damage reduces the opponent's hit points.

Skills

When you use a skill, roll the twenty-sided die and add or subtract, as the skill says. If you roll high enough, you succeed.

The Dungeon Master knows how high you need to roll.

Diplomacy   d20+4
  Use this skill to convince and persuade others.

Jump   d20+4
  Use this skill to leap over pits or fences.

Listen   d20–1
  Use this skill to hear opponents on the other side of a dungeon door.

Move Silently   d20–1
  Use this skill to sneak around quietly.

Search   d20
  Use this skill to locate secret doors and hidden treasure.

Spot   d20–1
  Use this skill to notice opponents lurking in the shadows.

Saving Throws

When you make a saving throw, roll the twenty-sided die and add or subtract as shown.

Fortitude   d20+3
  To resist poison, stunning, and similar effects.

Reflex   d20+1
  To avoid traps, dragon breath, and similar hazards.

Will   d20–1
  To resist mental attacks.

Armor

Brenna wears chain shirt armor.

Weapons and Gear

Brenna carries a greatsword, 3 daggers to throw, a backpack, 10 torches, and flint and steel.

Brenna

Race: Human
Class: Fighter
Level: 1st
Alignment: Neutral

Ability Scores

	Score	Bonus*

STRENGTH   **15**   **+2**
Bonus applies to sword attack and damage, kicking down doors, Jump skill.

DEXTERITY   **12**   **+1**
Bonus applies to Armor Class, ranged attack, Reflex saving throws, Move Silently skill.

CONSTITUTION   **13**   **+1**
Bonus applies to hit points, Fortitude saving throws.

INTELLIGENCE   **10**   **+0**
Bonus applies to Search skill.

WISDOM   **8**   **–1**
Penalty applies to Will saving throws, Listen and Spot skills.

CHARISMA   **14**   **+2**
Bonus applies to Diplomacy skill.

* Bonuses and penalties have already been calculated into your statistics.

Feats

Cleave, Power Attack: See Special Abilities.

Weapon Focus (Greatsword): +1 to attack, already calculated into statistics.

<u>Gold Pieces (gp)</u>   <u>Experience Points (XP)</u>

_____   _____

Tordek, Dwarf Fighter

Tordek quests to prove himself to his warclan. He refuses to return to his dwarven homeland until he has made a name for himself that his clan can be proud of. He believes the best way to accomplish this is through battle and adventuring. Tordek uses a waraxe in combat. Tordek's job on an adventuring team is to kill the monsters and protect his teammates.

Initiative   **+1**

When combat starts, the character with the highest initiative check goes first.

Speed   **4**

You can move 4 squares per turn.

Armor Class   **17**
   (against giants)   **21**

Opponents need to roll this number or better to hit you.

Hit Points   **13**

If you run out of hit points, you are defeated.

Special Abilities

Power Attack: If you wish, before you attack, you can take a –1 penalty on the attack roll. If you hit, you deal +2 damage.

Dwarven Waraxe   **d20+4**
   Damage   **d10+2**

Shortbow   **d20+2**
   Damage   **d6**

When you attack, decide which weapon you're going to use. Then roll the twenty-sided die and add the bonus. If the result is equal to or higher than the opponent's Armor Class, you hit. Roll other dice as listed for damage. Damage reduces the opponent's hit points.

Skills

When you use a skill, roll the twenty-sided die and add or subtract, as the skill says. If you roll high enough, you succeed.

The Dungeon Master knows how high you need to roll.

Intimidate   d20+2
  Use this skill to threaten an opponent into backing down.

Jump   d20
  Use this skill to leap over pits or fences.

Listen   d20+1
  Use this skill to hear opponents on the other side of a dungeon door.

Search   d20
  Use this skill to locate secret doors and hidden treasure.

Spot   d20+1
  Use this skill to notice opponents lurking in the shadows.

Saving Throws

When you make a saving throw, roll the twenty-sided die and add or subtract as shown.

Fortitude   d20+5
  To resist poison, stunning, and similar effects.

Reflex   d20+1
  To avoid traps, dragon breath, and similar hazards.

Will   d20+1
  To resist mental attacks.

Armor

Tordek wears scale mail armor and carries a heavy wooden shield.

Weapons and Gear

Tordek carries a dwarven waraxe, a shortbow, 20 arrows, a backpack, a sack, and flint and steel.

Tordek

Race: Dwarf
Class: Fighter
Level: 1st
Alignment: Neutral

Ability Scores

	Score	Bonus*
STRENGTH	15	+2

Bonus applies to waraxe attack and damage, kicking down doors, and Jump skill.

DEXTERITY	13	+1

Bonus applies to Armor Class, bow attack, and Reflex saving throws.

CONSTITUTION	16	+3

Bonus applies to hit points, Fortitude saving throws.

INTELLIGENCE	10	+0

Bonus applies to Search skill.

WISDOM	12	+1

Bonus applies to Will saving throws, Listen and Spot skills.

CHARISMA	6	–2

Penalty applies to Intimidate skill.

* Bonuses and penalties have already been calculated into your statistics.

Feats

Power Attack: See Special Abilities.

Weapon Focus (Dwarven Waraxe): +1 to attack, already calculated into statistics.

<u>Gold Pieces (gp)</u>   <u>Experience Points (XP)</u>

_____   _____

Quarion, Elf Fighter

Quarion has taken to the life of adventuring to satisfy his wanderlust. He believes in setting his own pace and wandering freely from dungeon to dungeon in search of adventure and glory. Quarion never goes into a battle without his trusty elven longbow and longsword at his side. Quarion's job on an adventuring team is to kill the monsters and protect his teammates.

Initiative	+3

When combat starts, the character with the highest initiative check goes first.

Speed	4

You can move 4 squares per turn.

Armor Class	17

Opponents need to roll this number or better to hit you.

Hit Points	11

If you run out of hit points, you are defeated.

Special Abilities

Point Blank Shot: If you make a ranged attack on an opponent within 6 squares (30 feet) of you, you get a +1 bonus on attack and damage rolls. So, your longbow attack becomes d20+6 with d8+1 damage when attacking an opponent at ranges of up to 6 squares.

Longbow	d20+5
Damage	d8

Longsword	d20+1
Damage	d8+1

When you attack, decide which weapon you're going to use. Then roll the twenty-sided die and add the bonus. If the result is equal to or higher than the opponent's Armor Class, you hit. Roll other dice as listed for damage. Damage reduces the opponent's hit points.

Skills

When you use a skill, roll the twenty-sided die and add or subtract, as the skill says. If you roll high enough, you succeed.

The Dungeon Master knows how high you need to roll.

Climb   d20+1
    Use this skill to scale a cliff or climb out of a pit.

Intimidate   d20–1
    Use this skill to threaten an opponent into backing down.

Listen   d20+3
    Use this skill to hear opponents on the other side of a dungeon door.

Search   d20+2
    Use this skill to locate secret doors and hidden treasure.

Spot   d20+5
    Use this skill to notice opponents lurking in the shadows.

Saving Throws

When you make a saving throw, roll the twenty-sided die and add or subtract as shown.

Fortitude   d20+3
    To resist poison, stunning, and similar effects.

Reflex   d20+3
    To avoid traps, dragon breath, and similar hazards.

Will   d20+1
    To resist mental attacks.

Armor

Quarion wears elven scale mail armor.

Weapons and Gear

Quarion carries a longbow, a longsword, 20 arrows, and a backpack.

Quarion

Race: Elf
Class: Fighter
Level: 1st
Alignment: Good

Ability Scores

	Score	Bonus*
STRENGTH	13	+1

Bonus applies to sword attack and damage, kicking down doors, and Climb skill.

DEXTERITY	17	+3

Bonus applies to Armor Class, bow attack, and Reflex saving throws.

CONSTITUTION	12	+1

Bonus applies to hit points, Fortitude saving throws.

INTELLIGENCE	10	+0

Bonus applies to Search skill.

WISDOM	12	+1

Bonus applies to Will saving throws, Listen and Spot skills.

CHARISMA	8	–1

Penalty applies to Intimidate skill.

* Bonuses and penalties have already been calculated into your statistics.

Feats

Point Blank Shot: See Special Abilities.

Weapon Focus (Longbow): +1 to attack, already calculated into statistics.

Gold Pieces (gp)   Experience Points (XP)

_____ _____

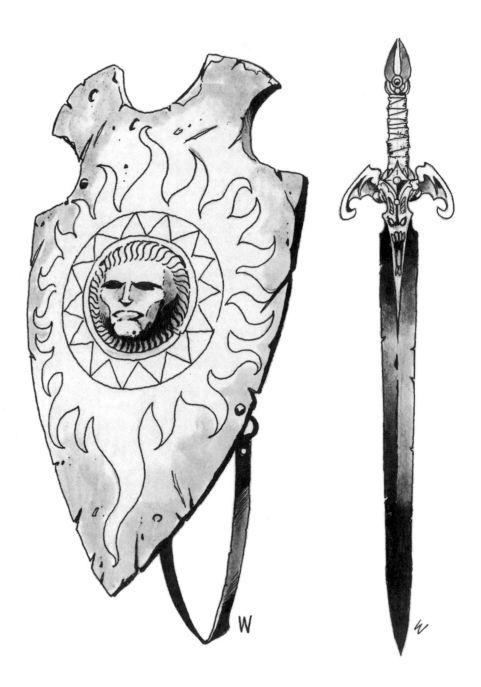

Chapter 4

Starting Out as a Rogue

. . . .

In This Chapter

▶ Understanding the rogue class

▶ Exploring who should play a rogue

▶ Discovering how to play a rogue

▶ Meeting three ready-to-play rogues

. . . .

The rogue has been part of the DUNGEONS & DRAGONS experience from the beginning. In the early days, this class was called the thief, but as player characters, rogues can and should be so much more than that title implies. A rogue is an expert in the use of all kinds of skills, excelling at sneaking around, scouting, and disarming traps. A rogue usually has a good Dexterity score to improve his or her success with many of the class's primary skills, as well as to bolster his or her Armor Class and ranged attacks.

Rogues can use only light armor, simple weapons, rapiers, and shortbows. Using heavier armor, shields, or martial weapons provides a penalty to a rogue's attacks and skill checks. (Certain skills, such as Open Lock and Disable Device, require the use of thieves' tools, which is a kit that contains tools such as metal picks, clamps, a small saw, a small hammer, and skeleton keys.)

Your character can take any approach to the rogue class. He might be a stealthy thief, a silver-tongued trickster, or an elite scout. She might be a spy, a thug, or a diplomat. All rogues are versatile, adaptable, and resourceful.

Rogues adventure to get something they want. Some want information and experience, others loot. Some rogues seek fame, others infamy. Many also see every adventure as a challenge — figuring out how best to avoid a guard, circumvent a trap, or avoid setting off an alarm. A rogue's role in an adventuring party depends on the skills the character has learned. As part of a team, the rogue looks for opportunities to make ranged attacks or to strike from hiding, while using stealth and evasion to serve as party scout.

In this chapter, we provide a bit of advice on who might want to play a rogue character and how to play a rogue character if that's the route you decide to go. The rest of the chapter features three ready-to-play rogue characters that you can use to kick-start your adventuring career.

Who Should Play a Rogue?

The rogue isn't as dedicated to a single mode of play as the fighter, but this class makes a good starting point for new players who aren't afraid of making a few decisions during the game. If you like to solve puzzles, or if you want to play a character that is equal parts skillful, cunning, and stealthy, then the rogue is the class for you.

Every adventuring party needs one rogue. In a party of four, a skillful rogue is essential to success. In a larger party, a single rogue still provides the abilities to avoid or overcome traps and hazardous obstacles. More than one rogue might be overkill, and you could be sacrificing other skill sets that the party might desperately need.

How to Play a Rogue

The rogue has a number of skills and abilities that make him or her an essential part of any adventuring team. Stealth and skills are the rogue's tools of trade, so if you play a rogue, you have to be ready for anything. Battle isn't the rogue's primary function. Instead, the rogue scouts for the party, uses skills to deal with traps and locked doors, and usually has enough other skills to be a jack-of-all-trades. Though a rogue's low hit points and attack bonus (compared to a fighter) make close-quarters battle even more dangerous for a character of this class, a rogue does have a special sneak attack that can deliver an amazing amount of damage on a successful hit. A rogue's skill with a ranged weapon usually allows him or her to help the party by attacking opponents from a distance.

Rogues should be curious and daring. Later, you can play with the baselines and portray any kind of rogue you want, but to start out, go with the tried-and-true basics. You live for the thrill of adventure. You seek challenges to overcome, and you just have to open that locked door to see what's waiting on the other side. And if you can pick up some gold along the way, so much the better!

Have fun with the idea of being a skilled expert who's dexterous and stealthy. Use your skills and abilities often and the rewards will come to you. While all rogues have a little bit of thief in them (or in some cases, a lot), the code of the adventuring party urges you not to steal from your teammates. After all, everyone in the team needs to be able to trust each other to work best, and the rogue should work extra hard not to be the cause of strife and unrest in the party. Be curious and a little reckless, but not too reckless. Above all, be a hero.

Selecting a Rogue

The rest of this chapter features three ready-to-play rogue characters:

- ✔ Kerwyn is a human male who excels at getting into locked places and swings a rapier with wild abandon.
- ✔ Shadow is a human female who uses stealth as a weapon and has a good mix of useful skills.
- ✔ Lidda is a halfling female who is quick on her feet and deadly when striking from the shadows.

Any of these characters make a great rogue and a worthy member of any adventuring party. Pick the one that most appeals to you, and then turn to Chapter 7 for a quick overview of game play.

Kerwyn, Human Rogue

Kerwyn is a good-hearted rogue with a thirst for adventure. He sees every quest as a challenge to do his best and help his companions — and if he earns some gold along the way, even better. Kerwyn's weapon of choice is the rapier, and the blade sings in his skilled hands. Kerwyn's job on an adventuring team is to handle tricky challenges such as locked doors and traps.

Initiative   **+6**
When combat starts, the character with the highest initiative check goes first.

Speed   **6**
You can move 6 squares per turn.

Armor Class   **14**
Opponents need to roll this number or better to hit you.

Hit Points   **8**
If you run out of hit points, you are defeated.

Rapier	d20+1
Damage	d6+1

Special Abilities

Sneak Attack: On the first round of combat, if you attack an opponent before it acts, you deal +d6 damage. Or if you flank an opponent (so that you and an ally are on opposite sides of it), you deal +d6 damage with your rapier. Sneak attacks don't work against undead creatures. Ranged sneak attacks don't work past 6 squares (30 feet).

Shortbow	d20+2
Damage	d6

When you attack, decide which weapon you're going to use. Then roll the twenty-sided die and add the bonus. If the result is equal to or higher than the opponent's Armor Class, you hit. Roll other dice as listed for damage. Damage reduces the opponent's hit points.

Skills

When you use a skill, roll the twenty-sided die and add or subtract, as the skill says. If you roll high enough, you succeed.

The DM knows how high you need to roll.

Disable Device   d20+6
     Use this skill to jam or disarm traps.

Heal   d20+2
     Use this skill to stabilize a dying companion.

Hide   d20+6
     Use this skill to conceal yourself so that others can't see you.

Listen   d20+5
     Use this skill to hear opponents on the other side of a dungeon door.

Move Silently   d20+6
     Use this skill to sneak around quietly.

Open Lock   d20+8
     Use this skill to pick a lock.

Search   d20+4
     Use this skill to locate secret doors and hidden treasure.

Spot   d20+5
     Use this skill to notice opponents lurking in the shadows.

Saving Throws

When you make a saving throw, roll the twenty-sided die and add or subtract as shown.

Fortitude   d20+2
     To resist poison, stunning, and similar effects.

Reflex   d20+4
     To avoid traps, dragon breath, and similar hazards.

Will   d20+1
     To resist mental attacks.

Armor, Weapons, and Gear

Kerwyn wears leather armor and carries a rapier, a shortbow, 20 arrows, a backpack, 10 torches, flint and steel, and thieves' tools.

Kerwyn

Race: Human
Class: Rogue
Level: 1st
Alignment: Good

Ability Scores

	Score	Bonus*
STRENGTH	**12**	**+1**

Bonus applies to rapier attack and damage, kicking down doors.

DEXTERITY	**15**	**+2**

Bonus applies to Armor Class, bow attack, Reflex saving throws, Hide, Move Silently, and Open Lock skills.

CONSTITUTION	**14**	**+2**

Bonus applies to hit points, Fortitude saves.

INTELLIGENCE	**10**	**+0**

Bonus applies to Disable Device and Search skills.

WISDOM	**13**	**+1**

Bonus applies to Will saving throws, Listen and Spot skills.

CHARISMA	**8**	**–1**

Penalty applies to Diplomacy skill.

* Bonuses and penalties have already been calculated into your statistics.

Feats

Improved Initiative: You have a +4 bonus on your initiative checks.

Nimble Fingers: You have a +2 bonus on Disable Device and Open Locks checks.

Gold Pieces (gp)   Experience Points (XP)

_____   _____

Shadow, Human Rogue

Shadow slips through every adventure with quiet determination and impressive skill. She has a powerful desire to overcome every challenge and a fondness for expensive treasure. She also has a charismatic way with people, and she uses this to the benefit of herself and her team. Shadow's job on an adventuring team is to handle tricky challenges such as locked doors and traps.

Special Abilities

Dodge: Select an opponent on your turn. You receive a +1 dodge bonus to Armor Class against that foe until the beginning of your next turn.

Sneak Attack: On the first round of combat, if you attack an opponent before it acts, you deal +d6 damage. Or if you flank an opponent (so that you and an ally are on opposite sides of it), you deal +d6 damage with your rapier. Sneak attacks don't work against undead creatures. Ranged sneak attacks don't work past 6 squares (30 feet).

Initiative   **+6**
When combat starts, the character with the highest initiative check goes first.

Speed   **6**
You can move 6 squares per turn.

Armor Class   **14**
Opponents need to roll this number or better to hit you.

Hit Points   **7**
If you run out of hit points, you are defeated.

Rapier   **d20+2**
    Damage   **d6+2**

Hand Crossbow   **d20–2**
    Damage   **d4**
When you attack, decide which weapon you're going to use. Then roll the twenty-sided die and add the bonus. If the result is equal to or higher than the opponent's Armor Class, you hit. Roll other dice as listed for damage. Damage reduces the opponent's hit points.

Skills

When you use a skill, roll the twenty-sided die and add or subtract, as the skill says. If you roll high enough, you succeed.

The DM knows how high you need to roll.

Diplomacy   d20+5
Use this skill to convince and persuade others.

Disable Device   d20+6
Use this skill to jam or disarm traps.

Hide   d20+6
Use this skill to conceal yourself so that others can't see you.

Listen   d20+3
Use this skill to hear opponents on the other side of a dungeon door.

Move Silently   d20+6
Use this skill to sneak around quietly.

Open Lock   d20+6
Use this skill to pick a lock.

Search   d20+4
Use this skill to locate secret doors.

Spot   d20+3
Use this skill to notice opponents lurking in the shadows.

Saving Throws

When you make a saving throw, roll the twenty-sided die and add or subtract as shown.

Fortitude   d20+1
To resist poison, stunning, and similar effects.

Reflex   d20+4
To avoid traps, dragon breath, and similar hazards.

Will   d20–1
To resist mental attacks.

Armor, Weapons, and Gear

Shadow wears leather armor and carries a rapier, a hand crossbow, 20 bolts, a backpack, 10 torches, flint and steel, and thieves' tools.

Shadow

Race: Human
Class: Rogue
Level: 1st
Alignment: Neutral

Ability Scores

	Score	Bonus*

STRENGTH   **14**   **+2**
Bonus applies to rapier attack and damage, kicking down doors, Jump skill.

DEXTERITY   **15**   **+2**
Bonus applies to Armor Class, ranged attack, Reflex saving throws, Move Silently skill.

CONSTITUTION   **12**   **+1**
Bonus applies to hit points, Fortitude saving throws.

INTELLIGENCE   **10**   **+0**
Bonus applies to Search skill.

WISDOM   **8**   **–1**
Penalty applies to Will saving throws, Listen and Spot skills.

CHARISMA   **13**   **+1**
Bonus applies to Diplomacy skill.

* Bonuses and penalties have already been calculated into your statistics.

Feats

Dodge: See Special Abilities.

Improved Initiative: You have a +4 bonus on your initiative checks.

Gold Pieces (gp)   Experience Points (XP)

_____   _____

Lidda, Halfling Rogue

Lidda, like all halflings, stands about half as tall as a human. She's sneaky, curious, and extremely fond of shiny objects. Her career as a rogue began when she left her home to wander in search of adventure. Lidda's job on an adventuring team is to handle tricky challenges, such as locked doors and traps.

Initiative   **+7**
When combat starts, the character with the highest initiative check goes first.

Speed   **4**
You can move 4 squares per turn.

Armor Class   **16**
Opponents need to roll this number or better to hit you.

Hit Points   **7**
If you run out of hit points, you are defeated.

Special Abilities

Sneak Attack: On the first round of combat, if you attack an opponent before it acts, you deal +d6 damage. Or if you flank an opponent (so that you and an ally are on opposite sides of it), you deal +d6 damage with your rapier. Sneak attacks don't work against undead creatures. Ranged sneak attacks don't work past 6 squares (30 feet).

Rapier   **d20+1**
    Damage   **d4**

Shortbow   **d20+4**
    Damage   **d4**
When you attack, decide which weapon you're going to use. Then roll the twenty-sided die and add the bonus. If the result is equal to or higher than the opponent's Armor Class, you hit. Roll other dice as listed for damage. Damage reduces the opponent's hit points.

Skills

When you use a skill, roll the twenty-sided die and add or subtract, as the skill says. If you roll high enough, you succeed.

The DM knows how high you need to roll.

Climb   d20+4
Use this skill to scale a cliff or exit a pit.

Decipher Script   d20+6
Use this skill to interpret ancient runes.

Diplomacy   d20+3
Use this skill to convince and persuade others.

Disable Device   d20+6
Use this skill to jam or disarm traps.

Hide   d20+7
Use this skill to conceal yourself from view.

Listen   d20+4
Use this skill to hear opponents on the other side of a dungeon door.

Move Silently   d20+7
Use this skill to sneak around quietly.

Open Lock   d20+7
Use this skill to pick a lock.

Search   d20+6
Use this skill to locate secret doors.

Spot   d20+4
Use this skill to notice hidden opponents.

Saving Throws

When you make a saving throw, roll the twenty-sided die and add or subtract as shown.

Fortitude   d20+1
To resist poison, stunning, and similar effects.

Reflex   d20+5
To avoid traps, dragon breath, and similar hazards.

Will   d20+0
To resist mental attacks.

Armor, Weapons, and Gear

Lidda wears leather armor and carries a rapier, shortbow, 20 arrows, a backpack, 10 torches, flint and steel, and thieves' tools.

Lidda

Race: Halfling
Class: Rogue
Level: 1st
Alignment: Neutral

Ability Scores

           Score   Bonus*

STRENGTH   **10**   **+0**
Bonus applies to rapier attack and damage, kicking down doors, Climb skill.

DEXTERITY   **17**   **+3**
Bonus applies to Armor Class, ranged attack, Reflex saving throws, Hide, Open Lock, Move Silently skills.

CONSTITUTION   **13**   **+1**
Bonus applies to hit points, Fortitude saving throws.

INTELLIGENCE   **14**   **+2**
Bonus applies to Decipher Script, Disable Device, Search skills.

WISDOM   **10**   **+0**
Bonus applies to Will saving throws, Listen and Spot skills.

CHARISMA   **8**   **−1**
Penalty applies to Diplomacy skill.

* Bonuses and penalties have already been calculated into your statistics.

Feats

Improved Initiative: You have a +4 bonus on your initiative checks.

Gold Pieces (gp)   Experience Points (XP)

_____   _____

Chapter 5

Starting Out as a Sorcerer

. . . .

In This Chapter

▶ Understanding the sorcerer class

▶ Exploring who should play a sorcerer

▶ Discovering how to play a sorcerer

▶ Meeting three ready-to-play sorcerers

. . . .

*T*he sorcerer is an arcane spellcaster who uses magic for attack, defense, and a myriad of other uses. A sorcerer approaches magic as an art, using raw power, directed at will, to cast spells. A sorcerer requires a good Charisma score, as this ability determines how powerful the sorcerer can ultimately become. Good Dexterity and Constitution scores also help keep the sorcerer alive when trouble appears.

Sorcerers are only proficient with simple weapons. Armor interferes with spellcasting, so sorcerers usually avoid it.

Your character can take any approach to the sorcerer class. Most sorcerers believe that their power comes from within themselves, and many believe that the source of that power comes from dragon ancestors whose blood courses through them. Whatever the truth, sorcerers tend to be proud, confident, and introspective.

Sorcerers adventure to improve their abilities. Their spellcasting ability comes from within themselves, and it can only be honed and developed through use. A sorcerer's role in an adventuring party depends on the spells the character has learned. As part of a team, the sorcerer uses his or her powerful presence (thanks to a high Charisma score) to negotiate and bargain on behalf of the party, all the while watching for the best opportunity to cast a spell.

Who Should Play a Sorcerer?

Spellcasting can be tricky, but every party needs a spellcaster, and the rewards for playing one can be high. If you want to play a character with a bit of an exotic nature and a selection of powerful spells at the ready, then the sorcerer is the class for you.

Every adventuring party should have a sorcerer for the magical might the class provides. An arcane spellcaster has access to magical spells that can complement or enhance the natural abilities of nonspellcasters such as fighters and rogues. In a party of four, the sorcerer's offensive magic can be every bit as important as the fighter's greatsword. To get the most out of a sorcerer in a party of five or six, it makes sense to team up with another spellcaster, either another sorcerer (with a different selection of spells) or a cleric.

How to Play a Sorcerer

The sorcerer is not a melee combatant. When a battle breaks out, the sorcerer wants to be at a distance, casting spells or using a ranged weapon. A sorcerer can't stand up to a lot of physical damage, and so must rely on other team members to provide defense. What the sorcerer has is a selection of spells that he or she can cast multiple times. A sorcerer with damage-dealing spells can become a primary source of a party's offensive punch. A sorcerer with charms and illusions, on the other hand, plays a subtler role in a party's success.

Sorcerers should be confident and a little mysterious. They have good interpersonal skills and often possess a presence that demands attention. As a sorcerer, you adventure to test the limits of your power — and by testing them, to surpass them.

Have fun playing a good-looking, exotic, mysterious spellcaster with a touch of dragon in your blood. Cast spells at opportune times to help your party, and then stand back and provide ranged attacks to supplement the offensive melee capabilities of the fighter and cleric. Test yourself and your team often, for in the test is perfection. Above all, be a hero.

Selecting a Sorcerer

The rest of this chapter features three ready-to-play sorcerer characters:

- ✔ Wellyn is a human male who spends a lot of time thinking but has offensive spells at the ready.

- ✔ Eronni is a human female who prefers to tantalize and confuse her enemies, but she can deal damage when she has to.

- ✔ Valanthe is an elf female who mixes offense with defense to best serve her team.

Any of these characters make a great sorcerer and a worthy member of any adventuring party. Pick the one that most appeals to you, and then turn to Chapter 7 for a quick overview of game play.

Wellyn, Human Sorcerer

Wellyn adventures to seek the true source of his arcane abilities. He believes that the blood of dragons runs through his veins, but a part of him needs proof that this is so. Wellyn's job on an adventuring team is to cast spells against the most deadly opponents, or when they will be most helpful.

Initiative   **+2**
When combat starts, the character with the highest initiative check goes first.

Speed   **6**
You can move 6 squares per turn.

Armor Class   **12**
Opponents need to roll this number or better to hit you.

Hit Points   **8**
If you run out of hit points, you are defeated.

Special Abilities

Spells: You can cast a total of five 0-level spells and four 1st-level spells per day.

0-Level Spell Choices

Acid Splash: Deals d3 acid damage to target.

Daze: Humanoid creature loses next turn; resists on a Will save of 13+.

Flare: Dazzles one creature (–1 on attack rolls) for 1 minute (10 rounds).

Light: Object shines like a torch.

1st-Level Spell Choices

Burning Hands: Blast of flame deals d4 fire damage to all targets within 3 squares.

Magic Missile: Deals d4+1 damage to target.

| **Quarterstaff** | **d20–1** |
| **Damage** | **d6–1** |

| **Light Crossbow** | **d20+2** |
| **Damage** | **d8** |

When you attack, decide which weapon you're going to use. Then roll the twenty-sided die and add the bonus. If the result is equal to or higher than the opponent's Armor Class, you hit. Roll other dice as listed for damage. Damage reduces the opponent's hit points.

Skills

When you use a skill, roll the twenty-sided die and add or subtract, as the skill says. If you roll high enough, you succeed.

The Dungeon Master knows how high you need to roll.

Bluff   d20+4
  Use this skill to trick others.

Concentration   d20+3
  Use this skill to cast a spell while being attacked.

Diplomacy   d20+6
  Use this skill to convince and persuade others.

Listen   d20+1
  Use this skill to hear opponents on the other side of a dungeon door.

Search   d20
  Use this skill to locate secret doors and hidden treasure.

Spot   d20+1
  Use this skill to notice opponents lurking in the shadows.

Saving Throws

When you make a saving throw, roll the twenty-sided die and add or subtract as shown.

Fortitude   d20+1
  To resist poison, stunning, and similar effects.

Reflex   d20+2
  To avoid traps, dragon breath, and similar hazards.

Will   d20+3
  To resist mental attacks.

Armor, Weapons, and Gear

Wellyn wears no armor. He carries a quarterstaff, a light crossbow, 20 bolts, a backpack, 2 torches, flint and steel, and a pouch of spell components.

Wellyn

Race: Human
Class: Sorcerer
Level: 1st
Alignment: Neutral

Ability Scores

	Score	Bonus*

STRENGTH   **8**   **−1**
Penalty applies to quarterstaff attack and damage, kicking down doors.

DEXTERITY   **15**   **+2**
Bonus applies to Armor Class, crossbow attack, Reflex saving throws.

CONSTITUTION   **13**   **+1**
Bonus applies to hit points, Concentration skill, Fortitude saves.

INTELLIGENCE   **10**   **+0**
Bonus applies to Search skill.

WISDOM   **12**   **+1**
Bonus applies to Will saving throws, Listen and Spot skills.

CHARISMA   **14**   **+2**
Bonus applies to Bluff and Diplomacy skills, and spells per day.

* Bonuses and penalties have already been calculated into your statistics.

Feats

Combat Casting: You have a +4 bonus on Concentration checks for defensive casting.

Toughness: You have +3 hit points.

Gold Pieces (gp)   Experience Points (XP)

_____   _____

Eronni, Human Sorcerer

Eronni adventures to test and improve her arcane abilities. She believes that the blood of dragons runs through her veins, and she wants to use her gift to defeat evil. Eronni's job on an adventuring team is to cast spells against the most deadly opponents, or when they will be most helpful.

Initiative   **+2**
When combat starts, the character with the highest initiative check goes first.

Speed   **6**
You can move 6 squares per turn.

Armor Class   **12**
Opponents need to roll this number or better to hit you.

Hit Points   **8**
If you run out of hit points, you are defeated.

Special Abilities

Spells: You can cast a total of five 0-level spells and four 1st-level spells per day.

0-Level Spell Choices

Detect Magic: Detect spells and magic items within 12 squares (60 feet).
Flare: Dazzles one creature (–1 on attack rolls) for 1 minute (10 rounds).
Ray of Frost: Deal d3 cold damage to target.
Read Magic: Read scrolls and arcane writing.

1st-Level Spell Choices

Mage Armor: You get a +4 armor bonus that lasts for one hour of game time (usually one encounter).
Magic Missile: Deals d4+1 damage to target.

| **Dagger** | **d20+1** |
| **Damage** | **d4+1** |

| **Light Crossbow** | **d20+2** |
| **Damage** | **d8** |

When you attack, decide which weapon you're going to use. Then roll the twenty-sided die and add the bonus. If the result is equal to or higher than the opponent's Armor Class, you hit. Roll other dice as listed for damage. Damage reduces the opponent's hit points.

Skills

When you use a skill, roll the twenty-sided die and add or subtract, as the skill says. If you roll high enough, you succeed.

The Dungeon Master knows how high you need to roll.

Bluff   d20+2
    Use this skill to trick others.

Concentration   d20+3
    Use this skill to cast a spell while being attacked.

Diplomacy   d20+3
    Use this skill to convince and persuade others.

Listen   d20
    Use this skill to hear opponents on the other side of a dungeon door.

Search   d20−1
    Use this skill to locate secret doors and hidden treasure.

Spot   d20
    Use this skill to notice opponents lurking in the shadows.

Saving Throws

When you make a saving throw, roll the twenty-sided die and add or subtract as shown.

Fortitude   d20+1
    To resist poison, stunning, and similar effects.

Reflex   d20+2
    To avoid traps, dragon breath, and similar hazards.

Will   d20+2
    To resist mental attacks.

Armor, Weapons, and Gear

Eronni wears no armor. She carries a dagger, a light crossbow, 20 bolts, a backpack, 2 torches, flint and steel, and a pouch of spell components.

Eronni

Race: Human
Class: Sorcerer
Level: 1st
Alignment: Good

Ability Scores

	Score	Bonus*
STRENGTH	**12**	**+1**

Bonus applies to dagger attack and damage, kicking down doors.

	Score	Bonus*
DEXTERITY	**15**	**+2**

Bonus applies to Armor Class, ranged attack, Reflex saving throws.

CONSTITUTION	**13**	**+1**

Bonus applies to hit points, Fortitude saving throws, Concentration skill.

INTELLIGENCE	**8**	**−1**

Penalty applies to Search skill.

WISDOM	**10**	**+0**

Bonus applies to Will saving throws, Listen and Spot skills.

CHARISMA	**14**	**+2**

Bonus applies to Bluff and Diplomacy skills, spells per day.

* Bonuses and penalties have already been calculated into your statistics.

Feats

Improved Initiative: You have a +4 bonus on initiative checks.

Toughness: You have +3 hit points.

Gold Pieces (gp)   Experience Points (XP)

_____   _____

Valanthe, Elf Sorcerer

Valanthe travels the land, seeking to improve her magical abilities and determine whether her elf heritage or dragon blood will mark her destiny. Valanthe's job on an adventuring team is to cast spells against the most deadly opponents, or when they will be most helpful.

Initiative   **+3**
When combat starts, the character with the highest initiative check goes first.

Speed   **6**
You can move 6 squares per turn.

Armor Class   **13**
Opponents need to roll this number or better to hit you.

Hit Points   **8**
If you run out of hit points, you are defeated.

Special Abilities

Spells: You can cast a total of five 0-level spells and four 1st-level spells per day.

0-Level Spell Choices
Detect Magic: Detect spells and magic items within 12 squares (60 feet).
Flare: Dazzles one creature (–1 on attack rolls) for 1 minute (10 rounds).
Read Magic: Read scrolls and arcane writing.
Resistance: Target gains +1 on saving throws for 1 minute (10 rounds).
1st-Level Spell Choices
Magic Missile: Deals d4+1 damage to target.
Magic Weapon: Gives a weapon a +1 enhancement bonus on attack and damage rolls that lasts for one minute (10 rounds).

| **Spear** | **d20–1** |
| **Damage** | **d8–1** |

| **Light Crossbow** | **d20+3** |
| **Damage** | **d8** |

When you attack, decide which weapon you're going to use. Then roll the twenty-sided die and add the bonus. If the result is equal to or higher than the opponent's Armor Class, you hit. Roll other dice as listed for damage. Damage reduces the opponent's hit points.

Skills

When you use a skill, roll the twenty-sided die and add or subtract, as the skill says. If you roll high enough, you succeed.

The Dungeon Master knows how high you need to roll.

Concentration   d20+3
 Use this skill to cast a spell while being attacked.

Diplomacy   d20+2
 Use this skill to convince and persuade others.

Heal   d20+2
 Use this skill to stabilize a dying companion.

Listen   d20+3
 Use this skill to hear opponents on the other side of a dungeon door.

Search   d20+2
 Use this skill to locate secret doors and hidden treasure.

Spot   d20+4
 Use this skill to notice opponents lurking in the shadows.

Saving Throws

When you make a saving throw, roll the twenty-sided die and add or subtract as shown.

Fortitude   d20+1
 To resist poison, stunning, and similar effects.

Reflex   d20+3
 To avoid traps, dragon breath, and similar hazards.

Will   d20+3
 To resist mental attacks.

Armor, Weapons, and Gear

Valanthe wears no armor. She carries a spear, a light crossbow, 20 bolts, a backpack, 2 torches, flint and steel, and a pouch of spell components.

Valanthe

Race: Elf
Class: Sorcerer
Level: 1st
Alignment: Good

Ability Scores

	Score	Bonus*

STRENGTH   **8**   **−1**
Penalty applies to spear attack and damage, kicking down doors.

DEXTERITY   **16**   **+3**
Bonus applies to Armor Class, ranged attack, Reflex saving throws.

CONSTITUTION   **13**   **+1**
Bonus applies to hit points, Fortitude saving throws, Concentration skill.

INTELLIGENCE   **10**   **+0**
Bonus applies to Search skill.

WISDOM   **12**   **+1**
Bonus applies to Will saving throws, Heal, Listen, and Spot skills.

CHARISMA   **13**   **+1**
Bonus applies to Diplomacy skill, spells per day.

* Bonuses and penalties have already been calculated into your statistics.

Feats

Toughness: You have +3 hit points.

Gold Pieces (gp)   Experience Points (XP)

_____   _____

Chapter 6

Starting Out as a Cleric

· ·

In This Chapter

▶ Understanding the cleric class

▶ Exploring who should play a cleric

▶ Discovering how to play a cleric

▶ Meeting three ready-to-play clerics

· ·

*N*o fantasy world is complete without a pantheon of mythical gods to add flavor, color, and background to the setting. And no DUNGEONS & DRAGONS adventuring party is complete without a servant of the gods — the cleric. A cleric uses divine magic and decent combat abilities to aid a party. A cleric needs a good Wisdom score to bolster his or her divine spells. A good Constitution score improves a cleric's hit points so he or she can wade into battle when called upon, and a good Charisma score improves the class's ability to *turn undead* (the ability to repel or destroy undead creatures such as skeletons and zombies).

Clerics can use any kind of armor and shield, and they can use all simple weapons without penalty. To use weapons that fall into other categories without penalty, such as martial weapons (which include longswords and warhammers), a cleric needs to select the appropriate feat.

Clerics adventure to support the causes of their gods, to help those in need, and to work to improve the reputation of their deities and temples. In addition to following their faith, clerics might have any common motivation for adventuring as well. Clerics can seek fame, treasure, and power, just like any other class.

An adventuring cleric devotes his or her life to a god's service from a young age. A cleric uses divine magic to aid the party, using healing spells and boosting spells to best advantage. Having the second-best combat skills of the four core classes, the cleric provides melee support and often wades in to stand beside the fighter in battle. The cleric's job is to defend and heal with spells, and to fight when battle rages.

Who Should Play a Cleric?

The cleric can be somewhat complex to play due to the class's proficiency in both combat and divine magic. However, this combination makes the cleric not only necessary for any adventuring team, but a lot of fun to play, too. If you think that playing a supporting role, helping your teammates, and occasionally mixing it up in battle sounds like the kind of character you want to play, then the cleric is the class for you.

Every adventuring party needs at least one cleric. In a party of four, a cleric is essential to success. In a party of five or six, two clerics can provide a lot of healing and defense, making adventuring that much easier.

How to Play a Cleric

In an adventuring party, the cleric is everybody's friend. Through the use of divine magic, a cleric can make a fighter stronger or a rogue quicker for a short period of time, for example, and everyone can benefit from a timely healing spell in the middle of a grueling battle. Some clerics serve a cause or an ideal instead of a god, but all clerics work to promote the source of their divine power.

Clerics should be brave and helpful, faithful and heroic. Later, you can play with the baselines and portray any kind of cleric you want, but to start out, go with the tried-and-true basics. You live to help others and serve your god. You hate evil in all its forms, and you have a special loathing for the undead.

Have fun with the idea of being the one that the rest of the party counts on for healing and defense. Don't be afraid to pick up your mace and mix it up with the monsters, but that should take second place to providing divine support for the team. Be devoted to your cause and your teammates. Above all, be a hero.

Selecting a Cleric

The rest of this chapter features three ready-to-play cleric characters, all of which combine healing and defensive magic with good combat skills:

- ✔ Jerek is a human male in service to Ehlonna, the goddess of the forests.
- ✔ Tiann is a human female who follows the path of Heironeous, the god of valor.
- ✔ Eberk is a dwarf male who is devoted to Moradin, the god of dwarves.

Any of these characters make a great cleric and a worthy member of any adventuring party. Pick the one that most appeals to you, and then turn to Chapter 7 for a quick overview of game play.

Jerek, Human Cleric

Jerek follows Ehlonna, the goddess of woodlands. His training has included healing magic and melee combat. He loves nature and the creatures of the forests. Jerek's job on an adventuring team is to protect his teammates with spells, but he can hold his own in a fight, too.

Initiative   **+5**
When combat starts, the character with the highest initiative check goes first.

Speed   **4**
You can move 4 squares per turn.

Armor Class   **16**
Opponents need to roll this number or better to hit you.

Hit Points   **12**
If you run out of hit points, you are defeated.

Special Abilities

Spells: Cast each spell once per day. You can cast *cure light wounds* (heal d8+1 damage) in place of any 1st-level spell.

<u>0-Level Spells</u>
Cure Minor Wounds: Heal 1 point of damage.
Light: Object shines like a torch.
Virtue: Target gains 1 temporary hit point.
<u>1st-Level Spells</u>
Bless: Team gains a +1 bonus on attack rolls that lasts for one minute (10 rounds).
Magic Weapon: Weapon gains a +1 bonus on attack and damage rolls that lasts for one minute (10 rounds).
Protection from Evil: +2 Armor Class and +2 saves against evil creatures that lasts for one minute (10 rounds).

Heavy Mace   **d20+2**
    Damage   **d8+2**

Light Crossbow   **d20+1**
    Damage   **d8**
When you attack, decide which weapon you're going to use. Then roll the twenty-sided die and add the bonus. If the result is equal to or higher than the opponent's Armor Class, you hit. Roll other dice as listed for damage. Damage reduces the opponent's hit points.

Skills

When you use a skill, roll the twenty-sided die and add or subtract, as the skill says. If you roll high enough, you succeed.

The Dungeon Master knows how high you need to roll.

Diplomacy   d20+3
> Use this skill to convince and persuade others.

Heal   d20+2
> Use this skill to stabilize a dying companion.

Listen   d20+2
> Use this skill to hear opponents on the other side of a dungeon door.

Search   d20+2
> Use this skill to locate secret doors and hidden treasure.

Spot   d20+2
> Use this skill to notice opponents lurking in the shadows.

Saving Throws

When you make a saving throw, roll the twenty-sided die and add or subtract as shown.

Fortitude   d20+3
> To resist poison, stunning, and similar effects.

Reflex   d20+1
> To avoid traps, dragon breath, and similar hazards.

Will   d20+4
> To resist mental attacks.

Armor

Jerek wears scale mail armor and carries a light wooden shield.

Weapons and Gear

Jerek carries a heavy mace, a light crossbow, 20 bolts, a backpack, 10 torches, flint and steel, holy symbol, and a potion of *cure light wounds* (heal d8+1 points of damage, one use).

Jerek

Race: Human
Class: Cleric
Level: 1st
Alignment: Good

Ability Scores

	Score	Bonus*

STRENGTH   **14**   **+2**
Bonus applies to mace attack and damage, kicking down doors.

DEXTERITY   **12**   **+1**
Bonus applies to Armor Class, crossbow attack, Reflex saving throws.

CONSTITUTION   **13**   **+1**
Bonus applies to hit points, Fortitude saving throws.

INTELLIGENCE   **10**   **+0**
Bonus applies to Search skill.

WISDOM   **15**   **+2**
Bonus applies to Will saving throws, Heal, Listen, and Spot skills, spells per day.

CHARISMA   **8**   **–1**
Penalty applies to Diplomacy skill and turn undead checks.

* Bonuses and penalties have already been calculated into your statistics.

Feats

Improved Initiative: You have a +4 bonus on your initiative checks.

Toughness: You have +3 hit points.

<u>Gold Pieces (gp)</u>   <u>Experience Points (XP)</u>

_____   _____

Tiann, Human Cleric

Tiann follows Heironeous, the god of valor. Her training has included both healing magic and combat skills. As part of her faith, Tiann promotes justice and honor. Tiann's job on an adventuring team is to protect her teammates with spells, but she can hold her own in a fight, too.

Special Abilities

Spells: Cast each spell once per day. You can cast *cure light wounds* (heal d8+1 damage) in place of any 1st-level spell.

0-Level Spells
Cure Minor Wounds: Heal 1 point of damage.

Detect Magic: Detect spells and magic items within 12 squares (60 feet).

Resistance: Target gains +1 on saving throws that lasts for one minute (10 rounds).

1st-Level Spells
Bless: Team gains a +1 bonus on attack rolls that lasts for one minute (10 rounds).

Divine Favor: You gain +1 bonus on attacks and damage rolls that lasts for one minute (10 rounds).

Protection from Evil: +2 Armor Class and +2 saves against evil creatures that lasts for one minute (10 rounds).

Initiative   **+1**

When combat starts, the character with the highest initiative check goes first.

Speed   **4**

You can move 4 squares per turn.

Armor Class   **16**

Opponents need to roll this number or better to hit you.

Hit Points   **13**

If you run out of hit points, you are defeated.

Heavy Mace   **d20+2**
Damage   **d8+1**

Light Crossbow   **d20+1**
Damage   **d8**

When you attack, decide which weapon you're going to use. Then roll the twenty-sided die and add the bonus. If the result is equal to or higher than the opponent's Armor Class, you hit. Roll other dice as listed for damage. Damage reduces the opponent's hit points.

Skills

When you use a skill, roll the twenty-sided die and add or subtract, as the skill says. If you roll high enough, you succeed.

The Dungeon Master knows how high you need to roll.

Diplomacy   d20+4
  Use this skill to convince and persuade others.

Heal   d20+2
  Use this skill to stabilize a dying companion.

Search   d20
  Use this skill to locate secret doors and hidden treasure.

Spot   d20+2
  Use this skill to notice opponents lurking in the shadows.

Saving Throws

When you make a saving throw, roll the twenty-sided die and add or subtract as shown.

Fortitude   d20+4
  To resist poison, stunning, and similar effects.

Reflex   d20+1
  To avoid traps, dragon breath, and similar hazards.

Will   d20+4
  To resist mental attacks.

Armor

Tiann wears scale mail armor and carries a light wooden shield.

Weapons and Gear

Tiann carries a heavy mace, light crossbow, 20 bolts, holy symbol, a backpack, 10 torches, flint and steel, a potion of *cure light wounds* (heals d8+1 points of damage, one use), and a 50-foot coil of rope.

Tiann

Race: Human
Class: Cleric
Level: 1st
Alignment: Good

Ability Scores

	Score	Bonus*

STRENGTH **12** **+1**
Bonus applies to mace attack and damage, kicking down doors.

DEXTERITY **13** **+1**
Bonus applies to Armor Class, ranged attack, Reflex saving throws.

CONSTITUTION **14** **+2**
Bonus applies to hit points, Fortitude saving throws.

INTELLIGENCE **8** **−1**
Penalty applies to Search skill.

WISDOM **15** **+2**
Bonus applies to Will saving throws, Heal and Spot skills, and spells per day.

CHARISMA **10** **+0**
Bonus applies to Diplomacy skill and turn undead checks.

* Bonuses and penalties have already been calculated into your statistics.

Feats

Toughness: You have +3 hit points.

Weapon Focus (Heavy Mace): +1 to attack, already calculated into statistics.

Gold Pieces (gp)   Experience Points (XP)

_____   _____

Eberk, Dwarf Cleric

Eberk follows Moradin, the god of dwarves. His training has included both healing magic and the warhammer. Thanks to his faith, dungeons hold no fear for Eberk. Eberk's job on an adventuring team is to protect his teammates with spells, but he can hold his own in a fight, too.

Special Abilities

Spells: Cast each spell once per day. You can cast *cure light wounds* (heal d8+1 damage) in place of any 1st-level spell.

0-Level Spells

Cure Minor Wounds: Heal 1 point of damage.

Detect Magic: Detect spells and magic items within 12 squares (60 feet).

Read Magic: Read scrolls and magic writing.

1st-Level Spells

Bless: Team gains a +1 bonus on attack rolls that lasts for one minute (10 rounds).

Divine Favor: You gain +1 bonus on attacks and damage rolls that lasts for one minute (10 rounds).

Protection from Evil: +2 Armor Class and +2 saves against evil creatures that lasts for one minute (10 rounds).

Initiative   **−1**
When combat starts, the character with the highest initiative check goes first.

Speed   **4**
You can move 4 squares per turn.

Armor Class   **15**
   (against giants)   **19**
Opponents need to roll this number or better to hit you.

Hit Points   **11**
If you run out of hit points, you are defeated.

Warhammer   **d20+1**
   Damage   **d8+1**
When you attack, decide which weapon you're going to use. Then roll the twenty-sided die and add the bonus. If the result is equal to or higher than the opponent's Armor Class, you hit. Roll other dice as listed for damage. Damage reduces the opponent's hit points.

Skills

When you use a skill, roll the twenty-sided die and add or subtract, as the skill says. If you roll high enough, you succeed.

The Dungeon Master knows how high you need to roll.

Diplomacy   d20+4
> Use this skill to convince and persuade others.

Listen   d20+3
> Use this skill to hear opponents on the other side of a dungeon door.

Search   d20
> Use this skill to locate secret doors and hidden treasure.

Spot   d20+3
> Use this skill to notice opponents lurking in the shadows.

Saving Throws

When you make a saving throw, roll the twenty-sided die and add or subtract as shown.

Fortitude   d20+5
> To resist poison, stunning, and similar effects.

Reflex   d20–1
> To avoid traps, dragon breath, and similar hazards.

Will   d20+4
> To resist mental attacks.

Armor

Eberk wears scale mail armor and carries a heavy wooden shield.

Weapons and Gear

Eberk carries a warhammer, holy symbol, a backpack, and a potion of *cure light wounds* (heals d8+1 points of damage, one use).

Eberk

Race: Dwarf
Class: Cleric
Level: 1st
Alignment: Good

Ability Scores

	Score	Bonus*
STRENGTH	**12**	**+1**

Bonus applies to warhammer attack and damage, kicking down doors.

DEXTERITY	**8**	**–1**

Penalty applies to Armor Class and Reflex saving throws.

CONSTITUTION	**16**	**+3**

Bonus applies to hit points, Fortitude saving throws.

INTELLIGENCE	**10**	**+0**

Bonus applies to Search skill.

WISDOM	**15**	**+2**

Bonus applies to Will saving throws, Listen and Spot skills, spells per day.

CHARISMA	**11**	**+0**

Bonus applies to Diplomacy skill and to turn undead checks.

* Bonuses and penalties have already been calculated into your statistics.

Feats

Martial Weapon Proficiency (warhammer): Eberk can use a warhammer, even though clerics can't usually use one.

<u>Gold Pieces (gp)</u>   <u>Experience Points (XP)</u>

_____   _____

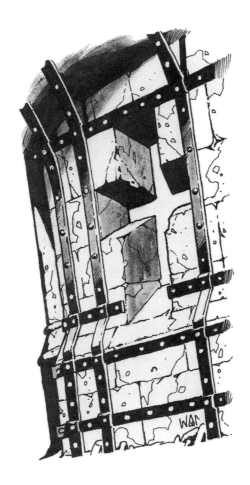

Chapter 7

Playing the Game

Although the heart of the DUNGEONS & DRAGONS game is imagination and adventure, and your character can attempt to do anything you can think of, the best way to learn how to apply the game mechanics is by examining D&D combat. So in this chapter, we show you how to play the game from the perspective of beating up the monsters — that's something that happens in almost every D&D adventure.

Refer to one of the ready-to-play character sheets from Chapters 3 through 6 when reading this chapter.

Understanding the D&D Game

Every DUNGEONS & DRAGONS game is an adventure. From an epic quest to a humble dungeon crawl, an adventure breaks down into three basic types of encounters:

> ✔ **Roleplaying encounters:** These encounters present players with situations in which they can roleplay their characters and interact with each other and with those characters controlled by the Dungeon Master (known as *nonplayer characters,* or *NPCs*). Trading, negotiating, or simply talking to locals are among the types of roleplaying encounters you may participate in. Skills like Bluff, Diplomacy, and Intimidate are sometimes employed during these encounters, but many times, no dice rolls are necessary at all. Roleplaying encounters can lead to challenge or combat encounters, or they can be self-contained discussions between characters.

  ✔ **Challenge encounters:** Encounters of this type revolve around characters struggling against natural or man-made hazards, such as trying to cross a lake of fire or dealing with a poison-needle trap on a locked chest. These encounters require skill checks, ability checks, or saving throws to navigate.

  ✔ **Combat encounters:** These make up the heart of many D&D adventures. When no other option presents itself for dealing with monsters or other opponents (such as brigands, thugs, raiders, or pirates), the D&D character hefts sword, staff, or axe and wades into battle. Combat encounters are the most rigidly structured times in the game, where most of the core rules come into play. When most people talk about playing D&D, this is the part of the game they envision. We show you how to play the game using the combat encounter structure throughout the rest of this chapter.

Rolling Dice

To provide tension, suspense, and an element of luck, the DUNGEONS & DRAGONS game uses dice to determine the outcome of actions where failure has a consequence. Fighting a monster, picking a lock, disarming a trap, leaping over a pit of molten lava — the game provides a method for determining success or failure based on a character's skills and abilities and adding a touch of luck for drama and excitement. Rolling dice is fun, and D&D allows for plenty of dice-rolling action in every adventure.

Remember the Core Game Mechanic: Whenever your character attempts an action that has a chance of failure associated with it, roll a twenty-sided die (d20). The higher the roll, the better the chance of success.

These character actions boil down to attack rolls, skill checks, and ability checks. To determine if any of these actions are successful, you follow these steps:

  1. **Roll a d20.**

  2. **Add any relevant modifiers.**

  3. **Compare the result to a target number.**

     If the result equals or exceeds the target number, the action succeeds. A result of less than the target number indicates that the action fails. For any task or action, target numbers, also called the *Difficulty Class* (or *DC*), come from a variety of places. Some are set by the action itself and are defined in the rules, and others are determined by the Dungeon Master. An opponent's Armor Class, for example, is the target number needed to make a successful attack.

For example, if Regdar the fighter wants to attack the fearsome bugbear with his greatsword, his player rolls a twenty-sided die and adds 4 (his attack roll modifier). If the result is 17 or better, his attack hits (17 is the bugbear's Armor Class). The player then rolls dice to determine how much damage the attack deals to the bugbear. To find out how much damage Regdar deals with his greatsword, Regdar's player rolls 2d6+3 (two six-sided dice and adds 3, for a result between 5 and 15).

Combat Basics

As characters adventure into mysterious forests or dark dungeons, they often encounter monsters of all shapes and sizes. In the inevitable battles that ensue, you use dice and your character's statistics to determine the course of combat. Players roll dice for their characters. The Dungeon Master rolls dice for the monsters (or whatever opponents the player characters are facing).

In a combat encounter, you put miniature figures for each character and monster on a battle grid. Players take turns in order, one after the other, moving their figures on the battle grid to show where their characters are moving in the battle, placing the figures next to or within sight of the monsters that their characters are attacking. (See Chapter 8 for more about using the battle grid.) You roll a die to see if an attack hits. If it hits, you roll dice to determine how much damage the attack deals.

Determining who goes first

Every character and monster has an *initiative modifier*. This is a bonus or penalty added to a d20 roll called an *initiative check*. Everyone makes an initiative check at the start of a combat encounter. This sets the order of play for the entire encounter, as follows:

1. **Players make initiative checks for their characters by making a d20 roll and adding initiative modifiers.**

2. **The Dungeon Master makes an initiative check for the monsters, one roll for all opponents. If an encounter features different types of monsters with different initiative modifiers, use the highest modifier when making the check.**

3. **The Dungeon Master jots down all the results on scrap paper to establish an initiative order, from highest result to lowest result.**

4. **The character or creature with the highest initiative result goes first and takes a turn, followed by the next highest result, and so on.**

5. **When everyone has had a turn, the round ends.**

   The second round uses the same order, starting with the character with the highest initiative result. Continue until the battle ends.

The DM's initiative log for a combat encounter might look like this:

Lidda	25
Wellyn	17
Regdar	10
Monsters	7
Eberk	4

This indicates the order in which each character will act in each round of the encounter. Notice that the DM makes a single roll for all of the monsters in the encounter, and all the monsters act after Regdar but before Eberk. (Eberk's player rolled a poor initiative result.)

On your turn in combat, your character can do any one of the following actions:

- ✔ Move and attack.
- ✔ Attack and move.
- ✔ Just move.
- ✔ Just attack.

Moving in combat

D&D is a game of imagination, but sometimes it gets really hard to visualize exactly what is going on in combat situations. When your character, other player characters, and several monsters are all attacking and moving around, it helps to have a clear visual representation so everyone knows exactly where each character and monster is during the battle. This is where miniature figures and the battle grid come into play. Each character and monster has its own miniature (or some other marker to represent it). At the beginning of a combat encounter, the players and the DM arrange the figures or markers on the battle grid to show the positions of all of the characters and monsters. Chapter 8 covers using the battle grid in detail.

Your character's speed is listed on the character sheet (see Chapters 3 through 6). For simplicity, the speed is expressed in squares, showing how many squares the character (represented by a miniature or some other marker) can move on the battle grid. Each square on the battle grid represents an area that is 5 feet wide, so a character with a speed of 6 can move up to 30 feet in a single round. Here are some guidelines to remember when gauging movement:

- ✔ **Speed:** Your character can move up to his or her speed in squares in a single round. Of course, your character can move less if you prefer.

- ✔ **Diagonals:** When your character moves diagonally on the battle grid, the first diagonal square you move into counts as 1 square, the second diagonal counts as 2 squares, the third as 1 square, the fourth as 2 squares, and so on. You can think of each diagonal square as 1.5 squares for the purposes of moving and determining distances.

- ✔ **Friends:** Your character can move through a square occupied by one of his or her teammates, but your character can't stop in that square.

- ✔ **Monsters:** Your character can't move through squares occupied by monsters or other opponents. If your character moves next to a monster or other opponent, your character must stop or the monster gets a free attack against him or her right away. This free attack is called an *attack of opportunity.* If you start your turn with your character next to a monster (or other opponent), your character can only move one square. If your character moves farther, the monster gets an attack of opportunity against him or her.

- ✔ **Just moving:** If all you want to do on your turn is move, your character can move up to twice his or her speed. So, if Regdar decides to just move on his turn, he can move up to 8 squares (or 40 feet).

Attacking with a weapon

In the D&D game, the two basic ways to attack with weapons are as follows:

- ✔ **Melee attacks:** These attacks require the use of a melee weapon (such as a sword or mace), and your character must be next to an enemy to make a melee attack.

- ✔ **Ranged attacks:** Attacks of this sort require the use of a ranged weapon (such as a shortbow or crossbow), and there must be at least 1 square between your character and an enemy on the battle grid in order for your character to make a ranged attack. You must be able to draw an imaginary line between your character and the enemy target. If walls, monsters, or another character completely blocks the path between your character's square and the target's square, you can't make a ranged attack because your character doesn't have a clear line of sight.

The attack and damage rolling process is as follows:

1. **Decide which weapon your character is using to make the attack.**

2. **Roll a d20 and add the bonus or penalty listed for that weapon.**

3. **If the result of the roll and modifier is equal to or higher than the monster's Armor Class, your attack hits.**

4. **If the attack hits, roll the type of die indicated for the weapon's damage and add the listed modifier (if any).**

5. **Damage reduces the monster's hit points; if the monster's hit points drop to 0, it's defeated.**

At higher levels, your character can make more than one attack per turn. To do so, however, you can only attack. You can't move and make multiple attacks on a turn.

Damage and dying

When characters and monsters attack and hit (that is, when they achieve a result that equals or exceeds the target's Armor Class), they deal *damage* to their target. Damage reduces hit points, but has no other effect on a target. A character or monster with 1 hit point is as strong and healthy as one with 25 hit points — except that the character or monster is closer to 0 hit points. And 0 hit points is bad.

When a monster's hit points are reduced to 0, it is dead and defeated.

When a character's hit points are reduced to 0, he can take only a single move on his turn. If he tries to do anything else, he falls to -1 hit points immediately thereafter.

When a player character's hit points are reduced to 1 or lower, the character falls to the ground, unconscious but not yet dead — the character is dying. Each round thereafter, the character loses 1 hit point. When the character's hit points drop to –10, he or she dies.

Healing a dying character

Each round, a dying character has a 10 percent chance of becoming *stable,* meaning that the character is no longer losing hit points, but he or she is still unconscious. To roll a percentage, you roll two ten-sided dice, indicating before hand which is the first digit (the ten's place) and which is the second digit (the one's place). (Some ten-sided dice have two numbers on each side, from 00 to 90, to indicate that die is to be used for the ten's place when rolling a percentage.) For example, a result of 0 (or 00) on the first die and 8 on the second die generates 08 percent, indicating that the character stabilizes.

A character with the Heal skill can stop a dying character's loss of hit points with a skill check result of 15 or better. This action takes the place of an attack.

Any amount of magical healing also stops a dying character's loss of hit points. If magical healing raises a character's hit points to 1 or more, the character can resume acting as normal.

What Else Can You Do During Combat?

Besides moving and attacking, a character can take these actions during a combat round:

- ✔ Move and cast a spell, or cast a spell and move.
- ✔ Switch weapons (but not move).
- ✔ Move and reload a crossbow (but not attack).
- ✔ Reload a crossbow and attack (but not move).
- ✔ Perform another action (for example, kick open a door or pick up an object).

Casting spells

In most cases, a cleric or sorcerer can cast a spell before or after moving. This counts as the character's attack for the round. At higher levels, your character will learn spells that require the whole turn to cast, but all of the spells provided on the ready-to-play character sheets take only part of the turn. Here are some guidelines about casting spells during combat:

- **Divine spells:** Clerics cast divine spells. The ready-to-play clerics (see Chapter 6) can cast each of their listed spells once per day. After a period of prayer and preparation, the spells are once again available for use. This prayer period consists of meditating for one hour in a relatively peaceful environment at a specific time each day, usually dawn, dusk, noon, or midnight. (See Chapter 17 for more about using and preparing spells.) Clerics can also replace a prepared spell with a *cure* spell. For example, Eberk can cast *cure light wounds* instead of his *bless* spell, should he so desire. In such a case, Eberk is deciding to forego the benefits of a *bless* spell for the day in favor of providing healing magic for himself or a teammate.

- **Arcane spells:** Sorcerers cast arcane spells. A sorcerer can cast a certain number of spells per day, but the spell cast must come from the character's selection of known spells (see Chapter 5 for the known spells of the ready-to-play sorcerers). For example, Wellyn can cast four 1st-level spells every day. He knows two 1st-level spells: *burning hands* and *magic missile*. So, during a day of adventuring, Wellyn might cast two *burning hands* spells and two *magic missile* spells, or four *magic missile* spells, or any other combination that adds up to four. After a night of rest (at least 8 hours), the sorcerer's spell slots are once again available to use. The sorcerer concentrates for 15 minutes and readies his mind to cast his daily allotment of spells. (See Chapter 17 for more about using and preparing spells.)

- **Monsters and opponents:** If a monster or other opponent is adjacent to a spellcaster, casting a spell provokes an immediate attack from the monster (an attack of opportunity). Should the attack succeed, the spellcaster must make a successful Concentration skill check (DC equals 10 plus the damage the monster deals) to cast the spell. If the skill check fails, the spell can't be cast this turn.

- **Rolling:** You don't have to roll a die for your character to succeed at casting a spell. As long as your character has a spell available, just say that he or she is casting it. You might have to roll a die to see how much damage a spell deals, or how many hit points it cures, or whatever. Sometimes, a monster gets a saving throw to avoid some or all of a spell's effects.

Saving throws

Every character and monster has modifiers for the three types of saving throws in the game (Fortitude, Reflex, and Will saves). A *saving throw* is a die roll you make to protect your character from certain types of danger. When you need to make a saving throw, the Dungeon Master will tell you. You don't choose which type of save to make; that's determined by the nature of the danger.

To make a saving throw, roll a twenty-sided die and add the modifier for the particular type of save you are trying to make. The DM will tell you what a successful roll (or a failure) indicates. Chapter 10 discusses saving throws in more detail.

Switching weapons

At the start of a combat, your character either has a specific weapon in hand or draws a weapon. You can have your character switch weapons during combat (sheathing a longsword and drawing a longbow, for example), but doing so takes the entire turn.

Reloading a crossbow

Crossbows take time to reload. On a turn after your character shoots a crossbow, he or she can reload the weapon and shoot, or your character can move and reload. Your character can't do all three things — reload, shoot, and move — in the same turn.

Longbows and shortbows don't require extra time to reload.

Special Combat Rules

The following sections describe a couple of special rules that may come into play during a combat encounter.

Shooting into a fight

Some player characters have ranged weapons. They can fire these at monsters as they see fit. When the monster they want to shoot is mixing it up with another player character in close-quarters (melee) combat, it becomes harder to accurately use a ranged weapon. To make a ranged attack against a monster that is next to a teammate, your character gets a –4 penalty to the attack roll because it's hard to shoot the monster when the monster is so close to his or her friend.

For example, Lidda wants to make an attack with her shortbow (a ranged weapon) against the orc engaged in melee combat with Regdar. Lidda's player normally makes a d20+4 roll to try to attack the orc with her shortbow. Because the monster is in melee with Regdar (her teammate), she makes the attack with a –4 penalty. The attack roll is now d20.

Flanking

You can employ a combat tactic called *flanking* to get an advantage against an opponent. If your character and a teammate's are on opposite sides of a monster, you each get a +2 bonus on attack rolls against that monster.

For example, Lidda draws her rapier and moves to the opposite side of the orc. Now Lidda and Regdar are flanking the monster. This provides them both with a +2 bonus. Now Lidda's rapier attack is d20+3 and Regdar's greatsword attack increases to d20+6.

Exploring the Dungeon

Outside of combat, D&D play can be very casual. The Dungeon Master tells the players what their characters see (and hear, and smell, and so on) and asks them what they do. Players don't have to act in any particular order, though the DM may impose some structure just so everyone gets to do what they want to do. If you use the battle grid during these casual periods, it's probably just to see where the characters are in relation to each other. Here's an example of dungeon exploration:

> **Dungeon Master:** "The 10-foot-wide corridor you've been following ends in a locked wooden door. What do you want to do?"
>
> **Lidda's player:** "I try to unlock the door."
>
> **Dungeon Master:** "Okay. Make an Open Lock check."
>
> **Lidda's player:** *Rolls a d20 and adds 7 (her Open Lock modifier) to the result.* "I got a 16."
>
> **Dungeon Master:** "The lock clicks open."
>
> **Regdar's player:** "Now that the door is unlocked, I step past Lidda and open the door."
>
> **Dungeon Master:** "The doors swings open with a slight creak. Inside, you see a small gold statue sitting atop a waist-high pedestal in the center of the room."
>
> **Lidda's player:** "I walk up and take a look."
>
> **Valanthe's player:** "So do I."
>
> **Eberk's player:** "I'll stand in the doorway in case something goes wrong."
>
> **Regdar's player:** "Lidda's always getting into trouble. I'll step into the room but stand back, ready to move if Lidda and Valanthe set off a trap."
>
> **Dungeon Master:** "Okay. Valanthe and Lidda look at the statue. It appears to be made of gold. It seems heavy, even if it isn't more than a foot and a half tall. It's carved in the shape of a dragon, and there is some kind of writing near the base that you can't read."
>
> **Valanthe's player:** "I cast *detect magic*."
>
> **Dungeon Master:** "The statue glows with an aura of magic. Everyone make a Spot check."
>
> **All players:** *All of the players roll d20s and add their Spot skill modifiers. Regdar's player lucks out and gets the highest result, an 18.*
>
> **Dungeon Master:** "While the rest of you stare at the golden statue, Regdar notices that a panel in the far wall has swung aside. Beyond, Regdar sees

a dark opening. Something has begun to emerge from that opening, but only Regdar sees it. What are you going to do?"

What happens next? That depends on the Dungeon Master and the actions of the players!

What can you do while exploring?

While exploring a dungeon or other adventure location, characters can do any of the following actions:

- ✔ Search the walls for secret doors.
- ✔ Listen at doors.
- ✔ Check doors to see if they are locked.
- ✔ Force open or unlock a door.
- ✔ Search rooms for treasure.
- ✔ Manipulate levers or push statues.
- ✔ Use the Intimidate skill to frighten a kobold, for example, into telling the party what waits around the bend.
- ✔ Do anything else you can think of!

Characters can do all sorts of things as they explore an adventure location. They might break apart a cabinet to locate a secret compartment, gather sand into a pouch, try to build a makeshift bridge out of a table, or do whatever else the players can think of.

The Dungeon Master decides whether or not something the characters try actually works. Some things are easy and characters can succeed automatically. It doesn't take any special skill or luck to fill a pouch with sand, for example.

Other actions are impossible. No character can smash through a 12-inch thick, solid stone wall by hitting it with his or her fist.

When there's a possibility of either success or failure, and the task doesn't relate to any particular skill, the DM calls for an ability check.

Ability checks

To make an ability check, a player rolls a d20 and adds his or her character's bonus associated with the ability that best fits the action. If the DM decides that the result is high enough, using the sample DCs provided in the D&D

rulebooks as a guide, the character succeeds. Here are some examples of ability checks and the DCs required to succeed:

- ✔ Trying to break down a strong wooden door requires a DC 18 Strength check.
- ✔ Attempting to thread a needle requires a DC 5 Dexterity check.
- ✔ Holding your breath for a long time requires a DC 10 Constitution check.
- ✔ Navigating a challenging maze requires a DC 20 Intelligence check.
- ✔ Recognizing the NPC rogue who was following your character at the market requires a DC 10 Wisdom check.
- ✔ Making sure your character gets noticed in a crowd requires a DC 15 Charisma check.

Chapter 8

Practice Session

. . . .

In This Chapter

▶ Using the battle grid and character markers

▶ Testing player characters against each other

▶ Testing player characters against monsters

▶ Adding story elements to make an adventure

. . . .

*I*n the preceding chapters, we present an overview of the basics of the DUNGEONS & DRAGONS game, we introduce a group of ready-to-play characters, and we show you how to make attack and damage rolls, skill checks, and saving throws. After going over the basics, you can actually roll some dice and see how it all comes together at the gaming table.

This chapter takes you on a tour of a sample play session of DUNGEONS & DRAGONS. Note that you need a set of D&D dice to participate in this practice session. You can get a set of D&D dice at your local game store or bookstore, or you can buy a set from any online game seller. When you get your dice, continue with this practice session.

The Battle Grid and Markers

The DUNGEONS & DRAGONS game uses three-dimensional components to help players visualize scenes and work through tactics and strategy in combat. Miniatures and a battle grid provide the best way to visualize the action. A fold-out battle grid is included with this book. One side has an open grid that can be used to replicate any dungeon scene. The other side is set up as a portion of a dungeon and can be used with the sample adventure presented in Chapter 24.

A battle grid consists of a grid of 1-inch squares. You can count distances in squares, or you can convert to the game world dimensions of 1 square equals 5 feet. For example, Regdar has a speed of 4, meaning that he can move 4 squares (20 feet) in a turn and make an attack.

You use the battle grid and miniatures or other markers (see the following section, "Markers") to show the marching order of your group of adventurers or the relative location of characters and monsters in any given encounter.

The best use for the battle grid is for when the characters stumble or charge into combat. When you can see how far away or how close the monster is, as well as where other player characters are in relation to it and your character, you can plan better moves and make full use of the environment during combat encounters.

A larger version of the battle grid can be found in the D&D *Dungeon Master's Guide*. More durable grids made of vinyl can be purchased at game and hobby stores or from online game sellers.

Markers

The battle grid only works if you use something to represent player characters and monsters. The battle grid in this book features cut-out markers that include a mix of characters and monsters. Carefully cut apart the markers and set them aside for later use. If you're ambitious, you can gather a bunch of DUNGEONS & DRAGONS miniatures to use instead of the markers.

Most characters and many monsters are considered to be Medium in size. A Medium character occupies a single square on the battle grid. Large creatures occupy a 2 x 2 area, or 4 squares. Only one character or creature can occupy a square. Characters can move through squares occupied by friendly characters, but they can't move through squares occupied by enemies. Characters can't stop moving in an occupied square (whether the occupier is a friend or enemy doesn't matter). (For the purposes of the battle grid, Small characters — such as Lidda — occupy a single square.)

Moving on the battle grid

In a turn, your character can move up to a number of squares equal to his or her speed and make an attack. If you just want to move your character (making no attack), your character can move up to twice his or her speed. For example, Regdar has a speed of 4. In a turn, he can move up to 4 squares and make an attack, or he can move up to 8 squares if he doesn't make an attack. (See Figure 8-1.)

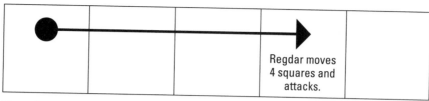

Figure 8-1: Non-diagonal movement.

When measuring diagonal distances, the first diagonal counts as 1 square, the second diagonal counts as 2 squares, the third diagonal counts as 1 square, the fourth diagonal counts as 2 squares, and so on. Think of each diagonal as 1.5 squares. So, Regdar can move 3 squares (1+2+1 = 4) along a diagonal path and make an attack against a monster on his turn. (See Figure 8-2.)

The extra cost for diagonal movement applies only to movement and determining distance for ranged attacks and spells. A character using a melee weapon can always attack a monster in any adjacent square — diagonal or non-diagonal from his or her position.

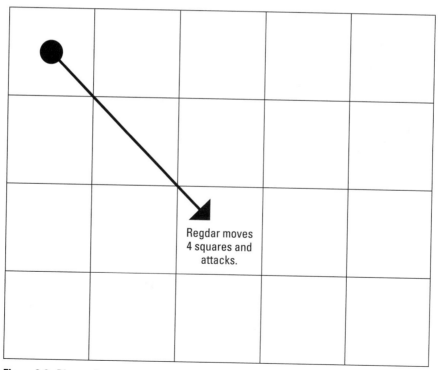

Figure 8-2: Diagonal movement.

Practice: A Sparring Match

The first way to test the game and run your character through the paces is to have a practice fight against another character. Pick the character you want to play from the ready-to-play characters presented in Chapters 3 through 6. Have a friend pick a different character. We suggest that each of you select a fighter from Chapter 3 for your first practice session. Fighters are the easiest and most straightforward characters to play.

Understand that this practice session's purpose is to give you and a friend a feel for the game mechanics. A full-scale D&D game requires a Dungeon Master to run the adventure. To give you a sense of moving and fighting D&D style, we focus on the basics with a scenario that would almost never happen in the game — you and your friend would instead be playing characters on the same adventuring team, and so your characters wouldn't be fighting each other. Another way to think of this practice session is that your characters are sparring or practicing, not fighting to the death.

Next, carefully cut out two of the player character markers, one for each player.

Placing characters on the battle grid

Before you get started with combat, you need to set up a few things. Here's how:

1. **Set the battle grid included with this book on the table between you and your friend.**

2. **Place your character marker in one of the grid's corners.**

   Your opponent places his or her marker in the opposite corner diagonally across the grid.

3. **Each of you rolls initiative. Roll the d20 and add your initiative modifier. The character with the highest result acts first, and then you take turns for the rest of this combat.**

   For example, Redgar's player rolls a 10 and adds +1 for a result of 11. Tordek's player rolls a 14 and adds +1 for a result of 15. Tordek goes first, then Regdar, then Tordek, and so on until one of the characters wins the practice battle.

What to do on a turn

Each turn, a character can move and attack, attack and move, or just move (which allows the character to move up to twice his or her speed). Because fighters really love to get up close and personal in a battle, the first couple of turns, they will either make a ranged attack and move or just move to close the distance between them and the enemy.

Remember that to make an attack, you roll a d20 and add the modifier for the weapon your character is using. If an attack hits (you get a result that's equal to or higher than your opponent's Armor Class), roll the die or dice listed for the weapon's damage. Damage reduces a character's hit points.

When one character is reduced to 0 or fewer hit points, he or she is defeated. The other character wins the practice session!

Example of a sparring match

To help you get a better idea of the intricacies of game combat, we've added a blow-by-blow example of combat between the fighter Tordek and the fighter Regdar. Here's how it would happen:

Turn 1 — Tordek: Tordek got a higher initiative result, so he goes first. He starts off by making a ranged attack with his shortbow. He rolls a 7 on the d20 and adds +2 (the modifier for his shortbow attack) for a result of 9. Regdar has an Armor Class of 15, so Tordek's attack misses. Then Tordek moves 4 squares closer to Regdar. Tordek has attacked and moved. His turn ends.

Turn 1 — Regdar: Regdar goes next. He decides to do the same thing. He rolls a 17 and adds +2 for a result of 19 with his shortbow attack. That's higher than Tordek's Armor Class of 17, so the attack hits. Regdar rolls damage next. He rolls a 2 on a d6 (the damage die for his shortbow). Tordek reduces his hit points by 2. He now has 11 hit points remaining. Regdar then moves 4 squares closer to Tordek, and his turn ends.

Turn 2 — Tordek: Tordek is still far enough away that he decides to make another ranged attack against Regdar. He rolls an 11 and adds +2. The result of 13 is not high enough to equal or beat Regdar's Armor Class. He moves 4 squares closer to Regdar and his turn ends.

Turn 2 — Regdar: Regdar decides to spend this turn switching weapons. He puts away his shortbow and draws his greatsword, in anticipation of the melee battle to come.

Turn 3 — Tordek: Tordek moves closer and makes another ranged attack. This time he rolls a 15 and adds +2 for a result of 17. He hits Regdar! He rolls a 4 on a d6 and deals 4 points of damage. Regdar now has 8 hit points remaining.

Turn 3 — Regdar: Regdar moves next to Tordek on this turn and makes an attack with his greatsword. He rolls a 15 and adds +4 (the modifier for his greatsword) for 19. That's a hit! Regdar rolls two six-sided dice and adds +3 to deal damage. He rolls a 2 and a 5 on the dice, for a total of 10 (2+5+3). Tordek has 1 hit point left!

Turn 4 — Tordek: Tordek spends the turn switching weapons. He now wields a dwarven waraxe.

Turn 4 — Regdar: Regdar attacks again. He rolls a 2, and the result of 6 isn't enough to hit Tordek.

Turn 5 — Tordek: Now Tordek gets a chance to make a melee attack. His modifier for the waraxe is +4. He rolls a 12, and the result of 16 (12+4) is a hit. The waraxe deals d10+2 damage, and Tordek's result is 6. Regdar has 2 hit points remaining.

How does this tense practice session end? Grab the character sheets and dice and find out for yourself!

Player Characters versus Monsters

The next practice session involves player characters and monsters. This is closer to a real combat encounter that you would have in any D&D adventure. You need players; say there are four of you, one to play a character of each class. You need a Dungeon Master to run the monsters. Have each player select a character to play. The DM should carefully cut out the two orc markers; these are the monsters that the four player characters will face in this practice session. Note that both orcs have the same statistics and the same amount of hit points.

Placing characters on the battle grid

Set the battle grid included with this book on the table and make sure the players and DM can comfortably sit around the play area with room for character sheets and dice rolling. The four player characters start on one end of the battle grid. The DM places the two orc markers anywhere in the middle of the battle grid.

Next, everyone rolls initiative. Roll the d20 and add your character's initiative modifier. The DM makes a single roll that covers both orcs. (The orc statistics can be found in the "Orc" sidebar on the next page.) The DM jots down each character's result, in order, from highest to lowest. That sets the order of play for this combat encounter.

For example, Redgar rolls a 10 and adds +1 for a result of 11. Shadow rolls a 14 and adds +6 for a result of 20. Wellyn rolls a 16 and adds +2 for a result of 18. Eberk rolls a 3 and adds –1 for a result of 2. The DM rolls a 5 and adds +0 for a result of 5 for the orcs. So, the initiative order for this combat looks like this:

Shadow	20
Wellyn	18
Regdar	11
Orcs	5
Eberk	2

What to do on a turn

Each turn, a character can move and attack, attack and move, or just move (which allows the character to move up to twice his or her speed). The orcs have the same options.

Remember that to make an attack, you roll a d20 and add the modifier for the weapon your character is using. If an attack hits (you get a result that's equal to or higher than your opponent's Armor Class), roll the die or dice listed for the weapon's damage. Damage reduces a character's (or monster's) hit points.

If the characters reduce both orcs to 0 hit points, the characters win the combat. If the orcs reduce all of the characters to 0 hit points, the orcs win the combat.

The Dungeon Master

The presence of a Dungeon Master turns D&D from a board game into a role-playing game where anything can happen. You can run this practice session with the DM simply controlling the actions of the monsters, or you can let the DM practice his or her DMing skills. A Dungeon Master isn't competing against the players (even though he or she controls their opponents in an adventure). The DM sets the scene, describes the action, and calls for skill checks and other rolls when necessary.

Orc

Orcs are aggressive humanoids with gray skin, coarse hair, and boarlike faces. They hate adventurers and seek to destroy them on sight.

Initiative	+0	**Armor Class**	13
Speed	6	**Hit Points**	5
Falchion	d20+4	**Falchion Damage**	2d4+4
Throwing Javelin	d20+1	**Throwing Javelin Damage**	d6+3
Skill: Listen	d20+1	**Skill: Spot**	d20+1

Example of player versus monster combat

Here's how the first round of this combat encounter might play out:

Turn 1 — Shadow: Shadow goes first (she had the highest initiative result). She draws her hand crossbow and fires at the orc on the right. She rolls a 4 on the d20 and adds her modifier of –2 for a result of 2. That's not enough to hit the orc's Armor Class of 13, and the hand crossbow bolt whizzes past the orc's head.

Turn 1 — Wellyn: Wellyn acts next. He decides to use a spell against the orc on the right. He declares that he is casting a *magic missile* spell. No attack roll is necessary for this particular spell; the magic missile leaps from Wellyn's finger and automatically hits the orc. Wellyn's player rolls damage and deals 4 points of damage to the orc on the right. The DM makes a note that the orc has 1 hit point remaining.

Turn 1 — Regdar: Regdar acts next. He isn't close enough to move and attack an orc, but he can just move (effectively moving twice) to cover 8 squares and wind up next to the orc on the left.

Turn 1 — Orcs: The orcs get to act now. The orc on the left swings his *falchion* (a big, curved sword) at Regdar. The DM rolls a d20 and adds the orc's modifier of +4 for a result of 16. That's a hit! The orc deals 10 points of damage to Regdar, leaving the fighter with 2 hit points.

Turn 1 — Eberk: Eberk has a turn now. He moves up behind Regdar so that he can cast a *cure light wounds* spell on his next turn and heal some of the damage to the fighter.

The first round of the combat has ended. Will the adventurers beat the orcs and win the day? Roll some dice and find out by playing through this scenario yourself!

Adding Story Elements

The DUNGEONS & DRAGONS game provides a platform for players to tell exciting stories in a medieval fantasy world. It's easy for the Dungeon Master to add story elements to an encounter and for the players to imagine what kinds of things their characters will do. In this section, we take the orc battle example and add some story elements to it.

Use the dungeon side of the battle grid. Pick any room and place the markers for the two orcs anywhere within it. Let the player characters start outside the room, somewhere down the corridor. The DM decides that the orcs have recently raided a human village, and now they're inside this dungeon room dividing their spoils. Maybe the orcs have a sack of ten silver pieces, a rusty sword, a scrawny dog tied to a table leg, and a scroll they stole from an empty farmhouse. The orcs are laughing and congratulating themselves in their course language when the player characters reach the corridor beyond.

Now the DM calls for Listen skill checks. The DM decides that it isn't too hard to hear the orcs and sets a target of 10 (called the Difficulty Class or DC) for the check. If any of the characters get a result of 10 or better on their check, they hear the noise coming from the room.

If the characters all fail to hear the noise, then the DM can see if the orcs hear the approaching characters. Because the orcs are laughing and talking, the DM decides that they'd have a harder time hearing the player characters and sets the DC at 15.

Now, maybe the characters know that something is in the room, maybe they don't. Maybe the orcs know the characters are coming, maybe they don't. The DM can use this information to build tension and drama as the characters move closer to the room.

When the characters finally reach the room and look in, they see the two orcs, a table, and the spoils from the village. Can the adventurers defeat the orcs? Will the orcs try to fight or beg for their lives? What about the spoils? Is the rusty sword enchanted with magic power? Did the scroll belong to a wizard or does it have some important message scrawled upon its surface? Maybe it's a map to another dungeon and some fantastic treasure.

Story isn't hard, and the elements it brings to the game are fun! Give it a try after you've had some combat practice.

Chapter 9

Finding a D&D Game to Join

UNGEONS & DRAGONS is a cooperative game; you need at least one other person to play with, and preferably as many as five or six people altogether. One person is the Dungeon Master, the player who runs the monsters, presents the dungeon or adventure, and generally keeps the game moving. Everybody else is a player character — a player who runs a single character in the DM's adventure.

In this chapter, we take a look at finding a game to play in, organizing your own game if you can't (or don't want to) find another game to play in, and joining a high-level game. We also provide you with a ready-to-play character at 4th level and at 8th level — Regdar, the human fighter.

A Typical Game Session

You might wonder what a D&D game session looks like. What do people wear, what do they bring, how long do they play, and where do they play? The best comparison for a D&D game is a regular Friday night poker game. People dress casual, they usually meet at somebody's house, they bring some snacks or drinks and what they need to play, and the game usually runs three or four hours — sometimes longer, sometimes shorter.

When you get invited to join a D&D game, it's a good idea to ask or check about the following:

- ✔ **When is the game?** Make sure you're punctual!

- ✔ **Where is the game?** Make sure you get good directions to the host's house or the hobby store, library, community center, or such place where the game is taking place. Get a street address and use MapQuest (www.mapquest.com) if you need to, or arrange to ride to the game with a friend.

- ✔ **Who's the Dungeon Master?** As a new player, the DM is your best friend. Get in touch with the DM a day or two before the game and find out what he or she expects of you.

- ✔ **Ask what game materials you can bring.** Most players show up for a game with the *Player's Handbook,* a set of D&D dice, something to write with and on, and their character sheet. Bring this *For Dummies* book if you expect to play one of the ready-made characters presented in Chapters 3 through 6.

- ✔ **Ask if you can bring food and beverages.** Bring some cash so you can pitch in for a pizza or something.

- ✔ **Don't assume it's okay to bring children.** Older children may very well want to play in the game with you, and that's something you need to clear with the people you will be playing with. Younger children demand your time and attention, and they will probably make things difficult for you and for everybody else. D&D night is probably a good time to get a babysitter.

The first few times you play, it's a good idea to do a lot of listening and watching and not so much talking. As you're learning your character's abilities and figuring out how the game works, pay attention to how the other players conduct themselves at the table. You can take your cues from them.

Finding Someone to Play With

So, say that you bought the *Player's Handbook*, flipped through the book you're holding in your hands, and have generally decided you'd like to play some D&D. How do you go about finding a game to play in? You've got two basic choices: Find someone else's game to join or organize your own game.

Joining someone else's game

This is probably the easiest way to go if you're a novice at D&D. Find an existing group of players who are willing to make some room for you at the table and begin playing with those folks. Every week, hundreds of thousands of people gather for regular D&D games with friends or strangers, just like people fall into regular poker games, bowling leagues, or bingo nights. All you have to do is identify an existing group somewhere near you and let them know you're interested.

So where do you find a D&D group meeting in your town? Try the following:

- **Friends and family:** Ask people you know to find out if somebody is in a game or if that person knows somebody who's in a game.

- **Gaming clubs:** Many high schools and colleges have active gaming clubs. If you're a student, see if your school has a club or organization that sponsors regular games.

- **The friendly local gaming store:** People looking for players to join their game, or people looking for games to join, often post messages in local hobby stores. You won't find this sort of "player corkboard" at a big bookstore that carries D&D books — you'll need to find local hobby stores for this kind of search. The best hobby stores often sponsor games right on-site, which is a great way to meet people you might want to game with.

- **The Internet:** Some popular Web sites or message boards frequented by D&D fans include "players seeking players" posts. A good site for this sort of thing is www.wizards.com/community. If you're under 18, please check with your parents before you start trying to meet strangers online.

- **The RPGA:** This stands for Roleplaying Gamers Association, a worldwide network of D&D fans. Contact the RPGA at www.wizards.com/rpga and ask them if there are any RPGA chapters in your hometown.

Now, here's the hard part: Most gamers understand that it can be difficult to find a game to play in, but you need to show some courtesy when you ask to join a gaming group of strangers. Try something like, "I understand you run a regular D&D game. I'm interested in trying it out. Are you looking for new players?" Don't take it too personally if the answer is no; it's not unusual for Dungeon Masters to decline to add new players if they're already running a game with a lot of players in it.

Organizing your own game

If you can't locate an existing game to join, you'll need to organize your own game. Most players expect a D&D game to be an ongoing, regularly scheduled event — just like that weekly poker night we were talking about.

Your first order of business is finding a Dungeon Master (DM). Chances are good that you know someone — or know someone who knows someone — who's played D&D before and can serve as the gamemaster. If at all possible, you want an experienced player to be your group's DM. Failing that, you'll need to choose a DM for your new game. Because you're trying to organize the thing, you might as well take a stab at it.

After you've determined who's going to be the DM, you need to round up a group of reliable and interested players. Ideally, you'd like to start with three to five players and one Dungeon Master. To find players, ask friends first. Family members are okay, but we suggest siblings or cousins — if you bring a parent or child to a game where most other people are about your age, you may create an awkward social dynamic for everybody else (of course, if *everybody* at the table is in your immediate family, that's not a problem).

If you can't find enough players by asking people you know, you can try fishing for fellow gamers in your town. Post notices at your local hobby store or look for school gaming clubs (if you're a student, that is).

After you've gathered enough people to play, choose a place and a time to meet. In the long run, you'd like to find a good game night that could be regularly scheduled for everybody in your game, but when you're just starting it, there's no reason you can't schedule your games one at a time. Find a place where you can put half-a-dozen people around a good-sized table and not bother other folks by making a lot of noise. If you play at a house where there will be small children around, make sure that somebody (preferably, someone who's not trying to play D&D with you) will be able to pay attention to the kids and keep them entertained.

The *D&D Basic Game*

If you're a novice, and everyone you're playing with is a novice too, we highly recommend that you get your hands on the *D&D Basic Game* and start there. The *D&D Basic Game* includes dice, miniatures, ready-to-play characters, a battle grid, and ready-to-run dungeon scenarios. It's the best starting place for people who have never played the game before, and you'll have a much easier time learning the ropes with the *Basic Game* than you will with the *Player's Handbook* and *Dungeon Master's Guide*.

Starting Off with a High-Level Character

When you join a gaming group that's been playing together for a while, there's an excellent chance that their characters are well past 1st level. For example, you might be told something like, "Great, glad you can join the game — bring a 4th-level character on Saturday!"

Most Dungeon Masters have some ground rules for how new characters can join the game, so you should ask ahead of time who's going to be the Dungeon Master and find out from that person how you should build a character to suit. Don't be afraid to ask for help getting ready. But sometimes you might be joining a game blind, without any knowledge of who's DMing, what sort of game they're running, or how to get a character ready to play fast. For those circumstances, we provide you with a 4th-level and 8th-level version of Regdar, the fighter (see Chapter 3 for Regdar at 1st level). As a new player, you'll find that the easiest character class to play at higher levels is the fighter. When you get to your new game, tell the Dungeon Master that you're ready to play a 4th-level fighter or an 8th-level fighter out of this book, if it's okay by him or her.

If you want to play a fighter with Regdar's stats but don't like the name, change it to something you like. If you prefer a female character, you need only change the name or use the character sheet for Brenna. Brenna has similar game statistics to Redgar, so your character's gender is simply a matter of preference.

Regdar, 4th-Level Human Fighter

As a 4th-level character, Regdar has learned a number of new feats and skills since he was 1st level. He uses better equipment and fights much more effectively than he did at 1st level.

Initiative   **+5**

When combat starts, the character with the highest initiative check goes first.

Speed   **4**

You can move 4 squares per turn.

Armor Class   **20**

Opponents need to roll this number or better to hit you.

Hit Points   **34**

If you run out of hit points, see rules for damage and dying in Chapter 7.

| Greatsword | d20+9 |
| Damage | 2d6+7 |

| Longbow | d20+6 |
| Damage | 1d8+3 |

Special Abilities

Cleave: Once per round, if you kill an opponent with your greatsword, you can immediately make a greatsword attack against another opponent if there's one next to you.

Power Attack: If you wish, before you attack, you can take a –4 penalty on the attack roll. If you hit, you deal +8 damage.

Skills

When you use a skill, roll the twenty-sided die and add or subtract, as the skill says. If you roll high enough, you succeed. The Dungeon Master knows how high you need to roll.

Climb   d20
   Use this skill to climb cliffs or rough walls.

Diplomacy   d20+2
   Use this skill to convince and persuade others.

Hide   d20–3
   Use this skill to conceal yourself.

Listen   d20+1
   Use this skill to hear opponents on the other side of a dungeon door.

Move Silently   d20–3
   Use this skill to sneak around quietly.

Search   d20
   Use this skill to locate secret doors and hidden treasure.

Spot   d20+1
   Use this skill to notice hidden opponents.

Saving Throws

When you make a saving throw, roll the twenty-sided die and add or subtract as shown.

Fortitude   d20+6
    To resist poison, stunning, and similar effects.

Reflex   d20+2
    To avoid traps, dragon breath, and similar hazards.

Will   d20+2
    To resist mental attacks.

Armor

Regdar wears magical *+1 full plate armor*. This means that the armor gives a +1 bonus to his AC, as compared to non-magical full plate armor. (The bonus is already included in Regdar's AC entry.)

Weapons and Gear

Regdar carries a magical *+1 greatsword,* a masterwork composite longbow, 20 arrows, a backpack, 6 sunrods, flint, steel, 50 feet of rope, and a grappling hook. Regdar's greatsword gives him a +1 bonus on attack and damage rolls (already included in his attack entry.)

Ability Scores

STRENGTH   **16**   **+3**
Bonus applies to sword attack and damage, Climb skill, and kicking down doors.

DEXTERITY   **12**   **+1**
Bonus applies to Armor Class, bow attack, Reflex saving throws, Hide and Move Silently skills.

CONSTITUTION   **14**   **+2**
Bonus applies to hit points, Fortitude saving throws.

INTELLIGENCE   **10**   **+0**
Bonus applies to Search skill.

WISDOM   **8**   **–1**
Penalty applies to Will saving throws, Listen and Spot skills.

CHARISMA   **13**   **+1**
Bonus applies to Diplomacy skill.

* Bonuses and penalties have already been calculated into your statistics.

Feats

Cleave, Power Attack: See Special Abilities.

Weapon Focus (Greatsword): +1 to attack, already calculated into statistics.

Weapon Specialization (Greatsword): +2 to damage, already calculated into statistics.

Iron Will: +2 to Will saves, already calculated into statistics.

Improved Initiative: +4 to initiative checks, already calculated into statistics.

Regdar, 8th-Level Human Fighter

As D&D characters gain levels, they generally find better and better magic items in treasure hoards. By 8th level, Regdar carries a number of magic items that help him fight better.

Initiative   +5

When combat starts, the character with the highest initiative check goes first.

Speed   4

You can move 4 squares per turn.

Armor Class   22

Opponents need to roll this number or better to hit you.

Hit Points   72

If you run out of hit points, see rules for damage and dying in Chapter 7.

Greatsword   d20+16/+11

If you move and attack, you make a single attack at +16. If you don't move, you can make two attacks: one at +16 and one at +11.

Damage   2d6+10

Longbow   d20+10/+5

If you move and attack, you make a single attack at +10. If you don't move, you can make two attacks: one at +10 and one at +5.

Damage   1d8+5

Special Abilities

Great Cleave: If you kill an opponent with your greatsword, you can immediately make a greatsword attack against another opponent if there's one next to you. There is no limit to the number of times per round you can do this.

Improved Bull Rush: You can try to shove an opponent out of your way instead of taking an attack. You roll d20+8; your opponent rolls d20 + his Strength bonus. If you win, you shove your opponent back 1 square.

Power Attack: If you wish, before you attack, you can take a –6 penalty on the attack roll. If you hit, you deal +12 damage.

Skills

When you use a skill, roll the twenty-sided die and add or subtract, as the skill says. If you roll high enough, you succeed. The Dungeon Master knows how high you need to roll.

Climb   d20+3
  Use this skill to climb cliffs or rough walls.

Diplomacy   d20+3
  Use this skill to convince and persuade others.

Hide   d20–2
  Use this skill to conceal yourself.

Listen   d20+2
  Use this skill to hear opponents on the other side of a dungeon door.

Move Silently   d20–2
  Use this skill to sneak around quietly.

Search   d20

Use this skill to locate secret doors and hidden treasure.

Spot   d20+2

Use this skill to notice hidden opponents.

Saving Throws

When you make a saving throw, roll the twenty-sided die and add or subtract as shown.

Fortitude   d20+10

To resist poison, stunning, and similar effects.

Reflex   d20+4

To avoid traps, dragon breath, and similar hazards.

Will   d20+4

To resist mental attacks.

Armor

Regdar wears magical *+2 full plate armor* and has a magical *+1 ring of protection.* The ring adds a +1 bonus to Regdar's AC (already included in AC entry).

Weapons and Gear

Regdar carries a magical *+2 greatsword,* a magical *+1 composite longbow,* magic *+2 gauntlets of ogre power,* a magical *+2 amulet of health,* a magical *+1 cloak of resistance,* 20 arrows, a backpack, 6 sun-rods, flint, steel, 50 feet of rope, and a grappling hook. The gauntlets add a +2 bonus to Regdar's Strength score; the amulet adds a +2 bonus to Regdar's Constitution score; and the cloak adds a +1 bonus to Regdar's saving throws (already included).

Ability Scores

STRENGTH   **18**   **+4**

Bonus applies to sword attack and damage, Climb skill, and kicking down doors.

DEXTERITY   **13**   **+1**

Bonus applies to Armor Class, bow attack, Reflex saving throws, Hide and Move Silently skills.

CONSTITUTION   **16**   **+3**

Bonus applies to hit points, Fortitude saving throws.

INTELLIGENCE   **10**   **+0**

Bonus applies to Search skill.

WISDOM   **8**   **–1**

Penalty applies to Will saving throws, Listen and Spot skills.

CHARISMA   **13**   **+1**

Bonus applies to Diplomacy skill.

* Bonuses and penalties have already been calculated into your statistics.

Feats

Improved Bull Rush, Great Cleave, Power Attack: See Special Abilities.

Greater Weapon Focus (Greatsword): +2 to attack, already calculated into statistics.

Weapon Specialization (Greatsword): +2 to damage, already calculated into statistics.

Iron Will: +2 to Will saves, already calculated into statistics.

Improved Initiative: +4 to initiative checks, already calculated into statistics

Part II
Building a D&D Character

The 5th Wave   By Rich Tennant

"Someone should tell your sister the name of the game is 'Dungeons & Dragons', not 'Basements & Dingbats'!"

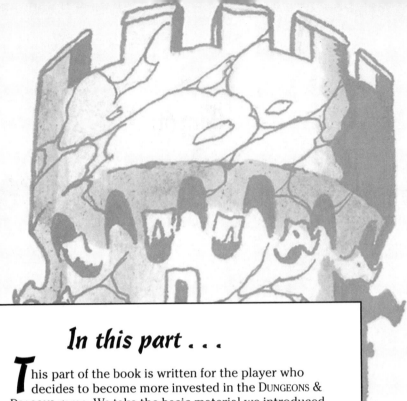

In this part . . .

This part of the book is written for the player who decides to become more invested in the DUNGEONS & DRAGONS game. We take the basic material we introduced earlier in the book and expand upon it. In this part, we help you navigate the D&D *Player's Handbook* and show you how to make solid, informed choices about the kind of character you want to build and how to best play that character at the gaming table. From fully defining the D&D character to examining classes, races, and feat and skill choices, we walk you through the character creation process and tell you what to look for as you gain experience and "level up" your character.

Chapter 10

Defining Your Character

. . . .

In This Chapter

▶ Understanding the D&D character sheet

▶ Creating your own characters

▶ Defining D&D game statistics

▶ Making the most informed choices during character creation

. . . .

This is the part of the book where you move on from basic game concepts and dive head-first into the full DUNGEONS & DRAGONS rules experience. Don't worry, we help you through it. And when you're done, you'll see that even the advanced rules aren't that tough or scary. Just keep the basics from Part I in mind, and we'll handle the rest.

At this point, we figure that you've used one of the ready-to-play characters from Part I to play a game or two of D&D. Now you're ready to create your own character from the ground up. After all, creativity is one of the most compelling aspects of roleplaying, and it all starts with your player character.

In this chapter, you take a more detailed look at the D&D character. We go over all the basic statistics again, but this time delving into all of the possible things you can do with them. This chapter helps you navigate the rest of Part II, explaining the parts of a full D&D character sheet and then pointing you to the information you need to fill out each section as you create your own character.

Your Character Sheet

A D&D character record sheet contains all the pertinent information and game statistics for your player character. A character sheet can be as simple as a blank piece of paper upon which you've written down all of your character's statistics. Or you could use the two-page character sheet that you can photo-copy in the back of the D&D *Player's Handbook* (see Figures 10-1 and 10-2). For really invested players, you can buy the official D&D *Deluxe Player Character Sheets* package that provides four-page character sheet folios for every class. Use whichever version of the character sheet that you feel most comfortable with. The information that follows pertains to all versions of D&D character sheets.

Figure 10-1: The character sheet from the *Player's Handbook* (front side).

There are numerous ways to approach the creation of a D&D character. Some people start out knowing exactly the kind of character they want to play, from race and class to specific roleplaying quirks and background information. Others let the dice fall where they may and then build their characters around the ability scores they rolled. Then there are those who know one aspect of the character they want to play (either the race or class, for example) and then decide on the rest after they see how the dice come out. These are all acceptable ways to approach character creation. Throughout the chapters in this part, we provide details to help you make informed decisions, no matter which approach you take.

Figure 10-2: The character sheet from the *Player's Handbook* (back side).

Filling Out the Character Sheet

You can fill out your character sheet in any order that makes sense to you. We discuss the various sections of the character sheet in the order they appear, however, so you can more easily reference the material.

Names

There's a place on the front of the character sheet for your name and your character's name. A cool, evocative name helps set the personality of your character and contributes to the tone of the campaign, so choose your character's name wisely. A campaign with characters named Elfy, Sugarplum, Bennie, and Toejam has a very different feel than one that features Regdar, Lidda, Wellyn, and Jerek. Talk with your Dungeon Master and the other players to decide what kind of names (and what kind of campaign) you all want to play, and then name your character accordingly. A good, solid name is important, and even though it appears at the top of your character sheet, this is the piece of information you'll probably record last, after you see how the rest of your character's statistics turn out and you've had a chance to think about it.

The D&D *Player's Handbook* provides lists of sample names by character race in Chapter 2. Feel free to use one of these names or to draw inspiration from them as you craft your own name for your character.

Class and level

Class, perhaps more than any other characteristic, has the most profound effect on your character's adventuring career. Class helps determine a character's role in the adventuring party and provides a character with special qualities that set him or her apart from the rest of the team. You can select a class and then apply your ability scores appropriately, or you can roll ability scores and select a class that takes best advantage of your results.

Character level is usually easy when you're creating a starting character: All characters start at 1st level unless the Dungeon Master gives you different instructions. (Sometimes a DM has characters start at a level more suitable for the campaign he or she plans to run, such as 3rd level if the DM wants the characters to have a little experience prior to the start of the campaign.)

Chapter 11 provides detailed information on choosing a class. Chapter 18 discusses levels and character advancement for when you're ready to improve your character.

Race

Another key defining aspect of a D&D character is the fantasy race the character belongs to. In addition to humans, the fantasy worlds of D&D are inhabited by all kinds of amazing, intelligent beings. Want to play an enigmatic elf? How about a dour dwarf? Maybe a dangerously curious halfling? Race provides more than a colorful hook for roleplaying. Each race has ability adjustments, a favored class, and special abilities to help set it apart from the others. After you've decided on a race for your character, record it on the character sheet.

Chapter 13 discusses the core D&D races in more detail and provides the information you need to choose among them.

Alignment and deity

Where does your character fit into the ongoing struggle between good and evil? It's a big question, but the answer to it (or at least the trip to discover the answer) pervades every fantasy epic from *The Lord of the Rings* to the *Tales of King Arthur and the Knights of the Round Table*. The same is true of any DUNGEONS & DRAGONS campaign. In the D&D game, your character's general moral and personal attitudes are represented by the character's alignment. Whether you choose to be lawful good or chaotic evil, alignment is a tool for developing your character's identity in the game. Alignment isn't designed to be restrictive, and characters can always behave inconsistently from time to time. It is used to provide a broad range of touchstones upon which you can develop your character.

The thing to remember with alignment is that players should talk about their choices before setting anything in stone. For example, your Dungeon Master may have a particular type of campaign in mind, one that works best if the characters all have complimentary alignments. Sometimes the tension generated by having a chaotic evil character in with a group of lawful good ones can be fun, but often such deviations lead to troublesome play and hard feelings. Better to all move in compatible directions than in competitive ones when playing D&D.

Another thing to consider when choosing your character's alignment is that D&D is really about heroes. The game works best when player characters choose alignments that are either good or neutral in outlook. Antiheroes and villains have their place in fantasy stories, but the most memorable, long-lasting D&D campaigns focus on the good guys.

Along with alignment, a character's choice of deity can help create a background and personality that makes the roleplaying stronger. A character's deity is a personal choice, though the game provides guidelines by providing two helpful tables, "Deities by Race" and "Deities by Class," on page 106 of the *Player's Handbook*. Now, every campaign is different and may have a different selection of deities. Your Dungeon Master will tell you if you should select a deity from the list in the *Player's Handbook* or from some other source (such as the *Forgotten Realms Campaign Setting*).

In the end, character alignment and deity choice are mostly for flavor and to help you roleplay your character better. Your choice of deity is more important if you're playing a cleric; see Chapter 11 and Chapter 17 for more information.

Character description

The next section of the character sheet provides a place to record information that helps describe your character but has little effect on game play. Of these, only the Size and Age entries have game mechanics associated with them. Most player characters are either Small or Medium in size, and most starting characters are barely into the adult age category when they begin adventuring.

Most of the character races, including dwarves, elves, and humans, are Medium in size. That's the standard, and there are no special bonuses or penalties associated with characters of this size. Medium characters occupy a single square on the battle grid. Small characters, such as halflings, also take up a single square.

Halflings are Small in size. Small characters gain a +1 size bonus to Armor Class, a +1 size bonus on attack rolls, and a +4 bonus on Hide checks. On the other hand, they have to use smaller weapons that deal less damage, they generally move about ⅔ as fast as Medium characters, and their lifting and carrying limits are ¾ of those of Medium characters. For more details about Small characters, see the halfling entry in Chapter 13.

Age, height, and weight for your character are determined by personal choice (and DM approval) or by random generation. See "Vital Statistics" in Chapter 6 of the D&D *Player's Handbook* for details and associated tables.

What you put in the Gender, Eyes, Hair, and Skin entries are all personal choices that have almost no effect in the game. Male and female characters are totally equal, and few in the fantasy worlds of D&D care if a character's skin is brown, pink, or metallic gold. Chapter 2 in the *Player's Handbook* talks about the general appearance of each of the races, and you can use the descriptions there as a starting point.

Ability scores

In addition to class, race, and level, a character's ability scores provide the base upon which your character grows and develops. Consider ability scores the frame upon which the rest of your statistics are hung. Every character has six ability scores: Strength, Dexterity, Constitution, Intelligence, Wisdom, and Charisma. These scores provide modifiers that effect everything from attacks and damage rolls to skill checks and saving throws.

Chapter 12 provides more information about ability scores and how they are used.

Hit points

When combat begins, your character's hit points (hp) are literally all that stands between a character and certain death. Class and level determine your character's hit point total, adjusted by your character's Constitution modifier. Lose a few hit points in battle? No problem! Your character continues to function without any ill effects as long as he or she has at least 1 hit point remaining. That's heroic and fantastic, and that's pure D&D.

When your character takes damage in battle or through some other method (such as a trap or a natural hazard), that damage reduces your character's hit point total. When your character's hit point total reaches 0, he or she is disabled. When it reaches –1, he or she is dying. When it drops to –10, your character is dead. (See Chapter 7 for rules on dying characters.)

Healing, whether natural or magical in nature, can restore lost hit points back up to your original total, but even getting healed back up to 1 hit point means that your character is ready to get back into the action.

Each character class has an associated Hit Die. Fighters, for example, have a d10 Hit Die, while sorcerers have a d4 Hit Die. At 1st level, all characters receive the maximum hit points based on their class's Hit Die — so a 1st-level fighter gets 10 hit points! But you're not done yet. You also get to apply your character's Constitution modifier to the hit point total. For example, Regdar the fighter has a +2 Constitution modifier, so his hit point total at 1st level is 12. When a character reaches 2nd level (and for every level he or she gains thereafter), you roll the appropriate die (the Hit Die), adding the character's Constitution modifier, and then add the result to your character's hit point total. Regdar, for example, adds d10+2 to his hit point total each time he goes up a level.

Armor Class

Armor Class (AC) represents how hard it is for opponents to hit your character in combat. It's the attack roll result — the target number — that an opponent needs to achieve to hit you. Every character and creature in the game starts with a base AC of 10. Various factors combine to improve or reduce that number. Your character's AC is determined as follows:

AC = 10 + armor bonus + shield bonus + Dexterity modifier + size modifier

Not every character will have all of these components. Some characters use armor, some don't. Some carry shields, some don't. Some have Dexterity or size modifiers, some don't. Add up all the modifiers you have that apply to determine your character's Armor Class.

For example, Regdar's AC is 15 because he wears scale mail armor (+4) and has a Dexterity modifier of +1 (10+4+1 = 15). Lidda, on the other hand, has an AC of 16 because she wears leather armor (+2), has a Dexterity modifier of +3, and a size modifier of +1 due to her Small size (10+2+3+1 = 16).

Every character also has target numbers to hit based on situations where the full Armor Class isn't applicable. These situations are as follows:

> ✔ **Touch AC:** Touch attacks, such as attacks with certain spells (the *chill touch* spell, for example), disregard armor and shield bonuses. Your touch AC doesn't include any bonuses for armor or shield, but all other modifiers

apply, such as Dexterity and size modifiers. In the previous examples, Regdar's touch AC is 11, while Lidda's touch AC is 14. You'll never have to guess if an attack is a touch attack: Touch attacks or spells are defined as such in the descriptions of the monsters or spells in the official rulebooks.

✔ **Flat-footed AC:** Characters are considered to be flat-footed at the start of a battle, before they have had a chance to act (before their first turn in the initiative order). A character can't use his or her Dexterity modifier when flat-footed. Bonuses for size, armor, and shield still apply. In the previous examples, Regdar's flat-footed AC is 14. Lidda's flat-footed AC is 13.

Record your character's touch AC and flat-footed AC in the appropriate places on your character sheet.

Speed

A character's speed shows how far the character can move in a round and still do something else, such as make an attack or cast a spell. Speed can be displayed as a number of feet or squares the character can move and do something else. Your character's speed is determined by his or her race and by the type of armor that he or she is wearing. If you decide to just move in a round, your character can move up to twice his or her speed.

Dwarves and halflings have a speed of 20 feet (4 squares). A dwarf always has a speed of 20 feet, but a halfling's speed is reduced to 15 feet (3 squares) if he or she is wearing medium or heavy armor. Humans and elves have a speed of 30 feet (6 squares). This is reduced to 20 feet (4 squares) if they wear medium or heavy armor.

Initiative

Initiative is a Dexterity check. Your character's initiative modifier is the same value as his or her Dexterity modifier. However, you can improve your character's initiative by selecting the Improved Initiative feat (see Chapter 5 of the *Player's Handbook* for this and other feat descriptions).

Saving throws

There are more dangers in D&D worlds than simply being attacked by sword, bow, or claw. Environmental hazards, magical attacks, poisons, and mental attacks are among the numerous other dangers adventurers face on a daily basis. Saving throws can help characters reduce or even avoid the effects of these dangers.

To determine your saving throw modifier in each case, add the base save bonus (determined by your character's class — see Chapter 11) and the appropriate ability modifier. The three types of saving throws are

- ✔ **Fortitude saves:** This type of save measures your character's ability to withstand attacks against his or her health and vitality, such as poison, disease, and energy drain. Apply your character's Constitution modifier to the base save to determine the Fortitude save.

- ✔ **Reflex saves:** This save tests your character's ability to react quickly enough to avoid area attacks such as breath weapons and *fireball* spells, or effects such as pit traps and falling boulders. Apply your character's Dexterity modifier to the base save to determine the Reflex save.

- ✔ **Will saves:** This type of save reflects your character's resistance to mental influence and mental-attacking magical effects, such as psionic attacks and illusion spells. Apply your character's Wisdom modifier to the base save to determine the Will save.

The target number (or Difficulty Class) for a saving throw is determined by the attack or hazard itself. Your Dungeon Master probably won't reveal the DC but will instead simply ask you to roll the appropriate saving throw (roll a d20 and add the modifier for the saving throw) and tell him or her the resulting number. The DM will then let you know if your character failed or succeeded at the save. In extreme cases, or when the DM really wants to keep the players in suspense, he or she may make the rolls for the characters in secret.

Base attack bonus

Every class provides a base attack bonus. This bonus improves as a character gains levels in a particular class. The combat-oriented classes (including the fighter) have a better base attack bonus than more cerebral classes (such as the sorcerer). Find your character's base attack bonus on the appropriate class table in Chapter 3 of the D&D *Player's Handbook* and record it in this section of your character sheet.

Attacks

Your character sheet provides space to record a number of different attack options for your character. This allows you to list a few different melee weapons and ranged weapons, depending on what your character is carrying and what he or she has trained to use. Record the attack bonus for each type of attack you might make. Remember that, when attacking, you make an attack roll with a d20 and add your attack bonus to try to get a result that's equal to or greater than your target's AC.

Your character's attack bonus with a melee weapon is determined as follows:

Attack bonus (melee weapon) = base attack bonus + Strength modifier + size modifier + weapon bonus

Note that not every character will have a weapon bonus. Any bonus provided by the weapon is due to using a magical weapon or because of a feat.

For example, Regdar's attack bonus with his greatsword is +4 — base attack bonus +1, Strength modifier +2, and +1 for taking the Weapon Focus (greatsword) feat.

Your character's attack bonus with a ranged weapon is calculated as follows:

Attack bonus (ranged weapon) = base attack bonus + Dexterity modifier + size modifier + weapon bonus – range penalty

Again, note that any bonus provided by the weapon is due to using a magical weapon or because of a feat. The *range penalty* exists only when your character is far away from the target. At great distances, the target is harder to hit, thus the range penalty. (Check the "Range Increment" description on page 114 of the *Player's Handbook* for more information; also see the weapons tables on pages 116–117 to find the range increment for each weapon.)

For example, Lidda's attack bonus with her shortbow is +4 — base attack +0, Dexterity modifier +3, and size modifier +1. The shortbow has a range increment of 60 feet. Each full range increment (every 60 feet between Lidda and her target, in this case) imposes a cumulative –2 penalty on the attack roll. So, if Lidda fires her shortbow at an orc that's 70 feet away, she takes –2 to her attack roll (lowering her attack bonus to +2) because the orc is farther than one range increment away.

Every weapon brings its own statistics to the table, and these should be recorded on your character sheet as well. A weapon has a damage rating that tells you what to roll to deal damage after a successful attack. A weapon also has a critical attack range, a number or series of numbers you roll on the d20 to determine if your attack is a critical attack (or a crit). You can find these details on the weapons tables in Chapter 7 of the *Player's Handbook*. When you attack with a melee weapon, you deal extra damage equal to your Strength bonus (or 1.5 times your Strength bonus if it's a weapon you wield with two hands, such as a greatsword).

Skills

Every character has skills that represent a variety of training and experience in different areas. Your character receives a number of skill points at each level based on class and Intelligence modifier. See Chapter 11 for more details on skill points per class per level.

Skills are divided into two categories: class skills and cross-class skills. *Class skills* are skills that members of your character's class might learn in the course of their training. Spend 1 skill point on a class skill and you get 1 rank in the skill. *Cross-class skills* are skills that are not class skills for your character class, and so they are harder to learn. Spend 1 skill point on a cross-class skill and you get ½ rank in the skill. (In other words, it takes 2 skill points to buy 1 rank in a cross-class skill.)

Every skill has a key ability. For example, the key ability for the Climb skill is Strength. You apply the modifier for a skill's key ability to determine your skill modifier. You also apply your ranks in the skill and any other modifiers that may by applicable, such as modifiers provided by feats. On your character sheet, record all these numbers in the appropriate sections and total them to get each skill modifier.

For example, take a look at Lidda the rogue's Move Silently skill. Her Dexterity modifier, the key ability for the skill, is +3. She buys 2 ranks in the skill, spending 2 skill points (Move Silently is a class skill for rogues). She also has a miscellaneous modifier, in this case a +2 racial bonus that all halflings receive for this skill. That gives her a Move Silently skill modifier of +7 (3+2+2 = 7).

To use a skill, you make a skill check. A *skill check* is a d20 roll to which you add your skill modifier. So, when Lidda makes a Move Silently check to quietly cross the chamber full of sleeping kobolds, she rolls d20+7.

For more information on skills, see Chapter 15.

Feats

Feats provide characters with new capabilities or improve existing abilities in meaningful ways. A character either has a feat or not; you don't buy them with points and you don't improve them with ranks. A character gains a feat at 1st level and at other levels as he or she advances. Human characters gain a bonus feat at 1st level, so they get to select two feats during character creation. In addition, certain classes gain bonus feats at different levels. A fighter, for example, gains a bonus feat at 1st level. So, Regdar the human fighter starts play with three feats — one that every character gets, one bonus feat for being human, and one bonus feat for being a fighter.

Jot down the name of the feat or feats you select on the back of your character sheet, as well as a brief description of the benefit it provides or the page number of the *Player's Handbook* where you can look up the details when you need to.

For more details about feats, see Chapter 14.

Special abilities

Your character's race and class provide certain special abilites. Record these in the section on the back of the character sheet.

For more information on race abilities, see Chapter 13. For more information about class abilities, see Chapter 11.

Spells

Characters who have spellcasting classes choose a selection of spells. For example, clerics and sorcerers are spellcasters and have spells. If you're playing a sorcerer, record your character's known spells in the spaces on the back of the character sheet. If you're playing a cleric, you may want to write down your character's prepared spells for that day on a piece of scrap paper, especially if you expect to prepare different spells during the course of the adventure.

For more information on spells, see Chapter 17.

Gear

Characters need equipment, and all kinds of adventuring gear is available to get your character through the toughest dungeons. List the equipment your character hauls around in the spaces provided on the character sheet.

For more information about adventuring gear, see Chapter 16.

Making Informed Choices

The rest of Part II walks you through the various components of your character and gives you the information and advice you need to make decisions about character creation. Which class is right for you? How should you distribute ability scores? What feats and skills should you select? What kind of gear should your character carry around? These questions and more are examined in Chapters 11 through 18. Take each chapter one at a time, and by the end, you'll be ready to make informed choices throughout the character-creation process.

Chapter 11

Choosing a Class

In This Chapter

▶ Discovering class and level benefits

▶ Exploring the fighter class

▶ Examining the rogue class

▶ Understanding the sorcerer class

▶ Understanding the cleric class

▶ Finding out about other classes in the game

UNGEONS & DRAGONS characters all share a thirst for excitement and a need to adventure. They just have to explore the dark places of the world and find increasingly difficult challenges with which to test themselves. Where characters differ is in the way they approach each adventure and what knowledge and abilities they bring to the table. A character's class and level, in large part, determines this approach. This chapter discusses both of these characteristics.

Your character's class is his or her profession or vocation. The class you select determines much of what your character can do in the game. Your character's combat prowess, magical aptitude, skills, and other qualities are defined and given boundaries by his or her class.

Your character's level shows how much experience and training he or she has acquired. A 1st-level character, for example, appears extremely green next to a 10th-level character.

When you're creating a character, the class you want to play suggests where you should assign ability scores and even hints at which races are most appropriate to play. In all cases, however, these are only suggestions. D&D is a game about choices and options, not restrictions. You can always play against type if that better fits the concept you have for the character you want to play.

Chapter 3 of the *Player's Handbook* goes into greater depth on character classes and level benefits. Check it out after you read through this chapter.

Class and Level Benefits

Three factors determine success or failure when characters perform actions in the game:

- ✔ A random factor (the d20 die roll)
- ✔ Innate ability (provided by your character's ability score modifiers)
- ✔ Experience and training (represented by your character's class and level)

Base attack bonus

In Chapter 7, we explore the basics of making attack rolls. This section looks deeper into where the base component of an attack roll comes from.

It starts with your character's base attack bonus. Your character's class provides a base attack bonus that increases as your character gains levels. How quickly this bonus increases is dependent upon one of three base attack bonus progressions: good, average, and poor. Classes with a martial bend, such as the fighter class, use the good base attack bonus progression. Classes that take a more cerebral approach to adventuring, such as the sorcerer class, use the poor base attack bonus progression to simulate a lack of combat training. Classes that combine combat training with other focuses, such as the cleric and rogue classes, use the average base attack bonus progression.

Table 3-1 in the *Player's Handbook* shows the three base attack bonus progressions. In addition, each class table in Chapter 3 of the *Player's Handbook* repeats this information as it applies to a particular class.

The difference between a good progression and a poor progression is how fast it improves as your character goes up in level. A good progression, for example, improves every level. A poor progression improves at about half that rate. So, by the time a character with a good progression reaches 4th level, his or her base attack bonus is +4. A character with a poor progression, in contrast, has a +2 base attack bonus at 4th level.

At 1st level, a character's base attack bonus is either +1 (if his or her class uses the good progression) or +0 (if his or her class uses the average or poor progressions). At higher levels, multiple bonuses are shown. Each bonus represents an additional attack the character can make in a round. To use these additional attacks, the character can't move in the round. Making multiple attacks, if you have them, is called using a full-round action.

For example, Regdar's base attack bonus at 8th level looks like this:

+8/+3

This means that if Regdar uses a full-round action (in other words, if he just attacks in the round), his base attack bonus for his first attack is +8 and his base attack bonus for his second attack is +3.

What does this mean when deciding on a class?

If you want your character to be good at making attacks, select a class that uses the good base attack bonus progression. If you want to temper attack power with other skills, select a class that uses the average base attack bonus progression. If you want to be an arcane spellcaster, you have to go with the poor base attack bonus progression — but these classes make up for low attack power with powerful spells.

Classes and base attack bonuses

We focus on four classes throughout this *For Dummies* book: fighters, rogues, sorcerers, and clerics. These are the easiest, most straightforward character classes to play. There are other classes available in the D&D *Player's Handbook*, however. Table 11-1 shows, at a glance, which base attack bonus progression each class uses.

Table 11-1	Class Base Attack Bonus Progressions
Class	*Base Attack Bonus Progression*
Barbarian	Good
Bard	Average
Cleric	Average
Druid	Average
Fighter	Good
Monk	Average
Paladin	Good
Ranger	Good
Rogue	Average
Sorcerer	Poor
Wizard	Poor

Base save bonus

Just as with base attack bonuses, character class provides different progressions for base save bonuses. As the name implies, these form the basis for your character's saving throws throughout the game. There are good base save bonuses and poor base save bonuses. Every class assigns either a good or poor progression to the three types of saves: Fortitude, Reflex, and Will.

Table 3-1 in the *Player's Handbook* shows the two base save bonus progressions. In addition, each class table in Chapter 3 of the *Player's Handbook* repeats this information as it applies to a particular class.

This information is good to have when making a decision about the class you want to play, but you probably won't select a class because it has a good or poor base bonus in your favorite type of save.

Table 11-2 shows, at a glance, which base save bonus progression each class uses for the three types of saves.

Table 11-2	Class Base Save Bonus Progression		
Class	*Fortitude Save*	*Reflex Save*	*Will Save*
Barbarian	Good	Poor	Poor
Bard	Poor	Good	Good
Cleric	Good	Poor	Good
Druid	Good	Poor	Good
Fighter	Good	Poor	Poor
Monk	Good	Good	Good
Paladin	Good	Poor	Poor
Ranger	Good	Good	Poor
Rogue	Poor	Good	Poor
Sorcerer	Poor	Poor	Good
Wizard	Poor	Poor	Good

Level benefits

As characters advance in level, their base attack bonuses and base save bonuses get better. The rate at which these bonuses improve depends on the type of progression each bonus uses. For example, the fighter's good base attack bonus progresses at a faster rate than either the rogue's average progression or the sorcerer's poor progression.

Level for characters of all classes is based on the number of experience points (XP) a character has earned in the course of his or her adventures. (Your DM will tell you how many experience points your character earned for the adventure at the end of each game session. For more on gaining XP, see Chapter 18.) Table 3-2 in the *Player's Handbook* shows how many experience points a character needs to attain a particular level.

For example, all characters start out with 0 XP at 1st level. A character earns experience for defeating monsters and completing adventures. When a 1st-level character accumulates a total of 1,000 XP, he or she advances to 2nd level. To reach 3rd level, a character needs to accumulate 3,000 XP, and so on, as shown on Table 3-2 in the *Player's Handbook.*

A character's level provides other benefits and essential information, as described in the next few sections.

Class skill maximum ranks

Your character selects skills from a list that's specifically geared toward a particular class. Any skills you select from your character's class list are called class skills. The number of ranks you can spend skill points on for any given class skill is determined by your level, as shown on Table 3-2 in the *Player's Handbook.* The rule is easy to remember, though. The maximum number of ranks you can have in a class skill is equal to your character's level +3.

For example, at 1st level, Regdar can buy a maximum of 4 ranks in any of his class skills. (For more on skills and skill ranks, see Chapter 15.)

Cross-class skill maximum ranks

Any skill not featured on your character's class skills list is considered to be a cross-class skill. Cross-class skills cost twice as many skill points to buy as class skills. The number of ranks you can spend skill points on for any given cross-class skill is determined by your character's level, as shown on Table 3-2 in the *Player's Handbook.* The maximum number of ranks you can buy in a cross-class skill is equal to one-half your maximum for class skills.

For example, at 1st level, Regdar can buy a maximum of 2 ranks in any cross-class skill. These 2 ranks would cost the same as buying 4 ranks in a class skill. (For more on cross-class skills, see Chapter 15.)

Feats

Characters gain feats according to level. All characters start with one feat at 1st level. Each character can select a new feat every time he or she attains a level divisible by three. That means that Regdar selects new feats at 3rd, 6th, 9th, 12th, 15th, and 18th level, for example, as shown on Table 3-2 in the *Player's Handbook*.

These feats are given to every character, regardless of class. However, class features may provide additional feats at different levels; these are called bonus feats. (For more on feats, see Chapter 14.)

Ability score increases

Characters increase their ability scores as they advance in level. A character can increase any single ability score by 1 point every time he or she attains a level divisible by four. That means that Lidda increases one of her ability scores by 1 point at 4th, 8th, 12th, 16th, and 20th level, for example, as shown on Table 3-2 in the *Player's Handbook*. So, upon achieving 4th level, Lidda could increase her Dexterity score from 17 to 18. (For more on ability scores, see Chapter 12.)

Class Descriptions

Each class description in the *Player's Handbook* provides key information about the class. Where should you put your best ability scores? What alignment can your character select as a member of this class? What Hit Die do members of this class use to determine their hit points? What base attack and base save progressions does the class use? What skills are considered to be class skills for characters that select this class? What weapons and armor can characters with this class use without penalty? What spells, if any, are available to this class? What other unique capabilities do members of this class possess?

All these questions are covered in the class descriptions. In the rest of this chapter, we explore some of the answers as they relate to four of the classes — fighter, rogue, sorcerer, and cleric — so that you can decide which one you want to play.

The fighter is the best class

Characters of the fighter class have the best all-around fighting capabilities. Deciding to play a fighter means that your character is going to have a lot of hit points for his or her level, good attack scores, good damage capabilities, and a direct approach to game play. That makes the fighter class particularly attractive to new players and players that don't want to deal with the intricacies of spellcasting and skill use.

The fighter's job in any adventuring group is to be a frontline combatant. Good armor and high hit points make a fighter a tank, able to absorb punishment that other characters have little hope of withstanding for very long. Good attacks and high damage potential make a fighter the character best suited to take the battle right to the monsters.

Fighters can select any alignment. All races have fighters, so a fighter character can be created using any of the D&D races. Of the races described in this book, humans and dwarves make the strongest melee-oriented fighters. Elves and halflings can be powerful ranged fighters, due to their Dexterity adjustments. (See Chapter 13 for more on races.)

Fighters get a lot of bonus feats to choose from, as well as bonus feat slots at different levels to take advantage of that. Fighters are proficient in all simple and martial weapons, as well as in all armor types, which makes them very versatile as far as adventuring gear goes.

Fighters start out with 6d4 × 10 gold pieces. Buy the best armor and weapons you can afford to take full advantage of the fighter's built-in benefits.

The *Player's Handbook* offers additional player character races. Of the additional races, the half-orc really takes to the fighter class thanks to his or her Strength adjustment. If you want to play a powerful melee-oriented fighter, you might want to consider playing a half-orc.

Abilities

If you decide to play a fighter, you should consider putting your highest ability score in Strength. Strength modifies both melee attacks and damage, and that's usually where fighters want to excel. Other important abilities for fighters include Constitution, which modifies the fighter's hit point total, and Dexterity, which modifies the fighter's ranged attacks and Armor Class.

Hit Die

The fighter uses a d10 Hit Die. This means that at 1st level, a fighter has 10 hit points (modified by his or her Constitution score). Every level thereafter, the fighter rolls d10 and adds his or her Constitution modifier to determine a new hit point total.

If you like to play a character with a lot of hit points, you can't do much better than the fighter class.

Skills

You won't be playing a scholar when you play a fighter. Fighters have a small selection of class skills and a small amount of skill points to use every level. A fighter begins play with (2 + Intelligence modifier) × 4 skill points. At 2nd level and every level thereafter, a fighter gains 2 + Intelligence modifier skill points to spend to improve existing skills or to buy new ones.

Because the fighter has such a limited number of skill points to spend, you don't want to try to dabble in a lot of different skills. Select a couple of key skills that you think you want your character to be good at, and spend your skill points on just those skills at every opportunity.

The class skills most important to a fighter are Climb, Jump, and Intimidate. The cross-class skill you might want to consider putting ranks in is Spot, because it helps you notice clues and avoid surprises. In the dangerous worlds of D&D, that's always a good thing.

See Chapter 15 for more information on skills.

Fighter class features

As befits the easiest class to play, the fighter has very few special class features. What the fighter does have is a good base attack bonus that increases by 1 point every level, good Fortitude saves, the ability to use any armor and any simple and martial weapons without penalty (and without spending a precious feat), and a ton of bonus feats that help to enhance the class's natural combat capabilities.

The rogue is the best class

Selecting the rogue class is the smartest thing you can do if you want to play a character that relies on skills, stealth, and sneak attacks to get to the center of a dungeon and back again. Rogues come in all kinds of varieties, from the smuggler with a heart of gold to the expert spy who uses craftiness and a silver tongue to accomplish the nearly impossible. If you pick this class, you will be able to hold your own in combat, especially if you can attack from a distance or out of the shadows. The rogue has a few special abilities that make the class slightly more complex than the fighter, but without the added complications of spellcasting.

The rogue's job in any adventuring group is to be versatile and resourceful. A rogue usually has a trick up his or her sleeve to get the team out of any jam. Need a lock opened? Need a trap disarmed? Need to sneak past the sleeping dragon? The rogue is the character for the job. When it comes to combat, a rogue prefers to make opportunistic strikes from the shadows or to use a ranged weapon that keeps his or her body out of harm's way. And, while not capable of casting spells from memory like a sorcerer, a rogue can use the Use Magic Device skill to cast spells from scrolls or use just about any kind of magic item if the party needs that kind of assistance.

Rogues can select any alignment, though they tend to avoid lawful outlooks on life. All races have rogues, so a rogue character can be created using any of the D&D races. Of the races described in this book, halflings and elves make the best rogues due to their Dexterity adjustments. Humans also make decent rogues, especially because of the extra skill points that human characters receive every level. (See Chapter 13 for more on races.)

Rogues are proficient in all simple weapons and light armor, as well as with hand crossbows, rapiers, shortbows, and short swords. Rogues don't do well with heavier armor and shields, and they are penalized for using such items in the course of an adventure.

Rogues start out with 5d4 × 10 gold pieces. Buy some leather armor, a short sword, a light crossbow, and thieves' tools as soon as you are able.

The _Player's Handbook_ offers additional player character races. Of the additional races, the half-elf can make a very good rogue due to the racial bonuses he or she receives to the Diplomacy, Gather Information, Listen, Search, and Spot skills.

Abilities

If you decide to play a rogue, you should consider putting your highest ability score in Dexterity. Dexterity modifies many of the rogue's signature skills, as well as Armor Class and ranged attacks. Other important abilities for rogues include Intelligence, which modifies the rogue's skill point total, and Wisdom, which modifies many of the skills the rogue wants to use on a regular basis.

Hit Die

The rogue uses a d6 Hit Die. This means that at 1st level, a rogue has 6 hit points (modified by his or her Constitution score). Every level thereafter, the rogue rolls d6 and adds his or her Constitution modifier to determine a new hit point total.

Skills

The rogue has the most class skills of all the player character races presented in the _Player's Handbook_. To take advantage of all those skill options, the rogue also has the most skill points. A rogue begins play with (8 + Intelligence modifier) × 4 skill points. At 2nd level and every level thereafter, a rogue gains 8 + Intelligence modifier skill points to spend to improve existing skills or buy new ones.

Because the rogue has such a large number of skill points to spend, you can keep strong scores in a relatively large number of skills. Even so, your character will never have enough points to be good at _everything_. Decide what kind of rogue you want to play, and concentrate on the skills that will enhance that character. It's always better to put as many ranks into key skills as possible — more ranks means a better chance to succeed, and the rogue never wants to be caught short using a skill that could mean life or death for the party.

The class skills most important to a rogue depend on what kind of rogue you want to play. Want to be a thief? Concentrate on improving Hide, Move Silently, Open Lock, and Search. Want to deal with the hazards of the dungeon? Spend your skill points on Balance, Climb, Disable Device, Listen, Open Lock, and Spot. Want your rogue to be the silver-tongued diplomat in the group? Then focus on Bluff, Diplomacy, Disguise, Gather Information, Intimidate, and Sense Motive.

Two additional skills to consider as you build your rogue are Tumble and Use Magic Device. Tumble provides a rogue with the ability to take less damage from a fall and to roll through enemy-occupied squares or threatened squares where the character would otherwise be subject to an attack of opportunity. You still have to make a successful skill check, but the character has options not available to anyone else in the party. Use Magic Device provides a rogue with the chance of activating magic devices, such as scrolls and wands, which a character with a non-spellcasting class usually doesn't have. Buy ranks in this skill if you want your rogue to back up the sorcerer in the party. You never know when the rogue might be the last character standing and his or her ability to activate a scroll might be all that stands between the adventurers and certain defeat.

As far as cross-class skills go, you might want to consider spending some of the rogue's wealth of skill points on Knowledge skills. A lot of useful information can be gained by making successful Knowledge checks at the appropriate moments, and you might want your rogue to know a thing or two about arcane lore or dungeoneering.

If you like to play a character with a lot of skill points and a lot of class skills to spend them on, you can't do better than the rogue class.

See Chapter 15 for more information on skills.

Rogue class features

In addition to being highly skilled, a rogue has a sixth sense for avoiding danger. As a rogue advances in level, the class provides a number of danger-avoiding abilities that give the rogue a definite edge when it comes to adventuring. These include *trapfinding* (the ability to search for mundane and magical traps), *evasion* (which improves the benefit of successful Reflex saves), *trap sense* (an intuitive alarm that provides a bonus to Reflex saves and Armor Class when used to avoid traps), and *uncanny dodge* (an ability that allows a rogue to retain his or her Dexterity bonus to Armor Class even when surprised or caught flat-footed). These features are gained automatically at specific rogue levels, and many of them improve at even higher levels.

The rogue is naturally a master of *sneak attacks* (attacks made from hiding or when the rogue's opponent has his or her attention focused elsewhere). At 1st level, a successful sneak attack increases the amount of damage the rogue's weapon deals by 1d6 points. In addition to rolling a weapon's normal damage, you roll a six-sided die. This extra damage increases as the rogue gains levels. At 3rd level, for example, a rogue's sneak attack added damage is +2d6. It continues to improve, every other level, until it hits +10d6 at 19th level!

The sorcerer is the best class

You want to select the sorcerer class for your character if you want to play an arcane spellcaster. If calling forth magical energy, shaping it into powerful spells, and unleashing those spells upon monsters and other opponents appeals to your sense of play, then the sorcerer class is the one for you. A sorcerer's spell selection helps define his or her role in the party, and the class has few special features beyond the ability to cast arcane spells. That ability, however, provides the class with a huge advantage that allows characters who go this route to shine.

The sorcerer's job in any adventuring group is to cast arcane spells. Want to be an offensive powerhouse? Select spells that deal damage. Want to be subtle in your spellcasting? Choose spells such as charms and illusions. In addition, because the sorcerer usually has a high Charisma score, a character with this class often serves as the spokesperson for the adventuring party. Using spells to complement their natural talents allows sorcerers to gain information and influence others better than almost anyone.

Sorcerers can select any alignment, though they tend to favor chaos over law due to the way in which they approach spellcasting. All races have sorcerers, so a sorcerer character can be created using any of the D&D races. Of the races described in this book, elves make the best sorcerers due to their natural inclination toward magic. Humans also make good sorcerers. (See Chapter 13 for more on races.)

Sorcerers are proficient with all simple weapons. They aren't proficient with any armor types or shields, and armor actually interferes with their ability to cast spells.

Sorcerers start out with 3d4 × 10 gold pieces. Pick up the best simple weapons you can afford, both a melee weapon (for up-close combat) and a ranged weapon. Because you don't need to purchase armor, you might want to consider buying some of the adventuring gear the party as a whole would benefit from, such as rope and a lantern. You should also consider paying the cost to summon a familiar at the first opportunity (see the later section, "Sorcerer class features"). And don't forget to buy a pouch to carry your spell components in.

The *Player's Handbook* offers a second arcane spellcasting class: the wizard. Where the sorcerer approaches spellcasting more as an art than a science, working through intuition rather than careful training and study, the wizard is all about research. For this reason, the wizard has a wider selection of spells to call upon, whereas the sorcerer tends to be a specialist. As such, the sorcerer is slightly easier to play. That's why we discuss the sorcerer class in this book instead of the wizard.

Abilities

If you decide to play a sorcerer, you should consider putting your highest ability score in Charisma. Charisma determines the level of power of the spells you cast, how many spells you can cast per day, and how difficult those spells are to resist. See Chapter 17 for more about spells and spellcasting.

Other important abilities for sorcerers include Dexterity, which modifies the sorcerer's Armor Class and ranged weapon attacks, and Constitution, which modifies the number of hit points the sorcerer gains each level and helps improve important Concentration skill checks.

Hit Die

The sorcerer uses a d4 Hit Die. This means that at 1st level, a sorcerer has 4 hit points (modified by his or her Constitution score). Every level thereafter, the sorcerer rolls a d4 and adds his or her Constitution modifier to determine a new hit point total.

The sorcerer, compared to the other classes, doesn't have a lot of hit points. A character with this class doesn't want to get into a prolonged melee battle with any monster. The best way to play a sorcerer during a battle is to stand back, use spells to attack or otherwise aid the party, and then switch to a ranged weapon and attack from a distance. The sorcerer is just too fragile, due to low hit points and Armor Class, to stand toe-to-toe with monsters the way the fighter or cleric does.

If you're playing a sorcerer character, you might want to consider selecting the Toughness feat. Every time you take this feat (and it can be taken as many times as you like, each time you can select a new feat), you add 3 hit points to your hit point total. Check out the ready-to-play version of Wellyn in Chapter 5. He has a total of 8 hit points thanks to his Hit Die (d4), his Constitution modifier (+1), and the Toughness feat (+3). That makes him twice as hard to defeat as he would have been if he had settled for just the hit points provided by his Hit Die.

Skills

The sorcerer has a very small selection of class skills and skill points. Training and education just aren't the sorcerer's approach to the world. A sorcerer begins play with (2 + Intelligence modifier) × 4 skill points. At 2nd level and every level thereafter, a sorcerer gains 2 + Intelligence modifier skill points to spend to improve existing skills or buy new ones.

Because the sorcerer has such a limited number of skill points to spend, you don't want to try to dabble in a lot of different skills. Select a couple of key skills that you think you want your character to be good at, and spend your skill points on just those skills at every opportunity.

The class skills most important to a sorcerer are Concentration, Knowledge (arcana), and Spellcraft. Concentration helps a sorcerer complete the casting of a spell even if he or she is interrupted by an attack. Knowledge (arcana) helps a sorcerer understand arcane spells and other magical knowledge. Spellcraft, a special skill only available to classes that cast spells, allows a character to identify spells and magical effects as they are cast. The cross-class skills you might want to consider putting ranks in are any of the Charisma-based skills, so you can take advantage of that ability's modifier.

See Chapter 15 for more information on skills.

Sorcerer class features

Sorcerers cast arcane spells. What gives sorcerers the edge is that they can cast any spell they know without the need for preparation. This is different from the way the cleric or wizard casts spells, and it gives the sorcerer a lot of flexibility when it comes to casting spells. Sorcerers get more spells to cast per day than a wizard, but conversely have a smaller pool of known spells to draw from. For this reason, you need to very carefully select the spells that your character knows. Look to collect spells that complement each other or play to other strengths the character has. It helps if you determine what kind of sorcerer you want to play. The offense-oriented sorcerer looks for spells that pack a lot of damage, while the sorcerer who decides to play to his or her Charisma-based skills looks to add illusions and charms to his or her repertoire of spells.

The sorcerer also has the ability to summon a familiar at any time, starting as early as 1st level. A *familiar* is a magical beast that resembles a small, mundane animal, but is unusually tough and intelligent. In addition to the animal's normal abilities, it becomes magically linked to its summoner and grants special abilities, such as bonuses to skill checks or saves, or extra hit points. The two relevant costs associated with summoning a familiar are time (24 hours) and magical materials (worth 100 gold pieces).

Page 52 of the *Player's Handbook* provides a list of familiars and the benefits they provide. Choose the animal you want, spend the time and money, and then take advantage of the benefits that a familiar provides.

The cleric is the best class

The cleric is the class for you if you want to play a character that has a profound connection to a higher power. With divine spells, decent combat prowess, and the ability to repel undead monsters, the cleric combines elements of spellcasting and martial skills to bolster any adventuring group. The cleric's spells revolve around healing damage and enhancing the abilities of other party members. These enhancements, commonly called *buffs,* allow the cleric to make everybody around him or her better.

The cleric's job in any adventuring group is to cast divine spells that provide healing, defense, and secret knowledge from on high. By casting spells on his or her teammates, a cleric can make a fighter more powerful, a rogue more effective, and a sorcerer more charismatic. Thanks to solid armor and weapons options, the cleric makes a good secondary combat character, able to provide support for the frontline fighter.

A cleric can select any alignment, as long as that alignment coincides with that of the deity the character serves. All races have clerics, so a cleric character can be created using any of the D&D races. Of the races described in this book, humans and dwarves make the best clerics. (See Chapter 13 for more on races.)

Clerics are trained to use all simple weapons, all types of armor, and most types of shields. Divine magic isn't adversely affected by armor the same way that arcane magic is, so the cleric can benefit from the protection of the best armor he or she can afford.

Clerics start out with 5d4 × 10 gold pieces. Pick up the best simple weapons you can afford, both a melee weapon (for up-close combat) and a ranged weapon. Because clerics can use any kind of armor, buy the best armor your character can afford and wear it proudly. You also need to purchase a holy symbol for your character to channel the power of his or her faith for the purposes of turning (or repelling) undead creatures.

The *Player's Handbook* features a selection of sample deities that can be used in any D&D campaign world. You can find these starting on page 106. Pick a deity for your cleric that corresponds with your character's alignment and race. Remember that, as a cleric, your character gains domain spells and favored weapons based on your choice of a deity.

Abilities

If you decide to play a cleric, you should consider putting your highest ability score in Wisdom. Wisdom determines the level of power of the spells you cast, how many spells you can cast per day, and how difficult those spells are to resist. See Chapter 17 for more about spells and spellcasting.

Other important abilities for clerics include Constitution, which modifies the number of hit points clerics gain at each level, and Charisma, which improves their ability to turn undead creatures.

Hit Die

The cleric uses a d8 Hit Die. This means that at 1st level, a cleric has 8 hit points (modified by his or her Constitution score). Every level thereafter, the cleric rolls a d8 and adds his or her Constitution modifier to determine a new hit point total.

Skills

The cleric has a small selection of class skills and a very small amount of skill points. A cleric begins play with (2 + Intelligence modifier) × 4 skill points. At 2nd level and every level thereafter, a cleric gains 2 + Intelligence modifier skill points to spend to improve existing skills or buy new ones.

Because the cleric has such a limited number of skill points to spend, you don't want to try to dabble in a lot of different skills. Select a couple of key skills that you think you want your character to be good at, and spend your skill points on just those skills at every opportunity.

The class skills most important to a cleric are Concentration, Diplomacy, and Heal. Concentration helps a cleric complete the casting of a spell even if he or she is interrupted by an attack. Diplomacy takes advantage of a cleric's good Charisma modifier to negotiate effectively and influence others. Heal supplements clerics' magical healing powers with mundane medical skill, allowing clerics to help hurt allies even if they have expended their daily allotment of spells. Clerics also gain additional class skills based on the domains associated with their deities. A cleric that chooses the Travel domain adds the Survival skill to his or her class skill list, for example.

See Chapter 15 for more information on skills.

Cleric class features

Clerics cast divine spells. Divine spells come from a higher power, a deity that your cleric has chosen to follow. When you select the cleric class, you must pick a deity. This fantasy god has a selection of associated domains. Choose two of the deity's associated domains. These domains provide bonus spells and granted powers that come to the cleric from on high. You'll find details on deities and domains in Chapter 6 of the *Player's Handbook*.

Clerics must prepare their spells in advance. This means that you must choose the spells you want to have available for your character to cast at the beginning of a day, before the cleric goes adventuring. In game terms, clerics spend one hour in daily meditation, filling themselves with divine energy that can be expelled at will as a prepared spell. As a player, you record one spell for each open spell slot you have on your character sheet or scrap paper. When your character casts a spell (and uses up a spell slot), cross off that spell in your list of preselected spells.

A cleric with a good or neutral alignment can use stored spell energy to cast a healing spell in place of a previously prepared spell. This means that a cleric never has to prepare healing spells; he or she can spontaneously cast a healing spell of the same level (or lower) as any prepared spell on his or her list. To do so, the cleric loses the prepared spell for the day and instead casts a healing spell of the same level (or lower). Jerek, for example, can decide to lose his prepared *magic weapon* spell and instead cast a *cure light wounds* on an injured companion.

Bring what your friends need

If you don't have a clear idea about the type of character you want to play, or if it doesn't really matter too much to you, then take a look at what types of characters the other players are creating and work to fill the holes. Does your party need a frontline combat specialist? Consider creating a fighter. Is the party lacking in spellcasting? Think about playing either a sorcerer or cleric.

No one else going for the rogue? Get in there and make a rogue to be proud of. An adventuring party is a team, and a team needs a variety of skills and abilities. When nothing else suggests itself, look for a way to shore up your team's chances by creating a character that fills a gap or provides a desperately needed ability.

A cleric can't cast a spontaneous healing spell in place of a domain spell, however.

The other class feature that clerics benefit from is the ability to turn undead. By channeling the power of their faith through their holy symbols, clerics can repel undead creatures. At higher levels, clerics can even destroy undead through the power of their faith. Clerics can attempt to turn undead a number of times per day equal to their Charisma modifier plus three. A cleric with a +1 Charisma modifier, for example, can make four turn undead attempts each day.

Other classes

The DUNGEONS & DRAGONS game features 11 core classes. We concentrate on the four most basic classes for this book, but you should know that there are other choices available. Chapter 3 in the *Player's Handbook* details all of these classes. Here's a brief rundown so you know what else is out there:

- ✔ **Barbarian, paladin, and ranger:** These are the combat-oriented classes that can take on the same roles as the fighter.

- ✔ **Bard and monk:** These are the classes that can fill some of the same roles as the rogue.

- ✔ **Wizard:** This is the arcane spellcasting class other than the sorcerer.

- ✔ **Druid:** This is the divine spellcasting class other than the cleric.

When you're ready for a bigger challenge, or when you just want to try something different, take a look at these classes in the *Player's Handbook*.

Chapter 12

Figuring Out Your Character's Ability Scores

*E*very DUNGEONS & DRAGONS character — on paper, at least — consists of a number of key statistics that begin with a character's ability scores.

Class, race, and equipment help to refine and develop a character concept, but when you create a new character, you begin by determining that character's ability scores. The *Player's Handbook* and *Dungeon Master's Guide* describe a variety of methods for generating ability scores. We discuss two methods for determining ability scores in this chapter: the random generation method and the elite array.

In this chapter, we examine what the ability scores are used for and how to generate the best scores for the character you want to create. We also talk about what to do when the dice don't roll exactly in your favor. Afterward, we look at the choices available and help you best assign ability scores to make the character you envision — or at least make the character viable and fun to play.

You can find out more about ability scores and ability score generation methods in Chapter 1 of the *Player's Handbook* and Chapter 6 of the *Dungeon Master's Guide*.

How the Ability Scores Work

Each character has six abilities — Strength, Dexterity, Constitution, Intelligence, Wisdom, Charisma. *Ability scores* rate a character, painting a broad picture of how strong, dexterous, and intelligent (and so on) that character is. Ability scores form the foundation upon which a character of myth and legend grows.

A character has six abilities. Three are physical abilities and three are mental abilities, as follows:

- **Strength (Str):** This score gauges your character's physical might. How much equipment can he or she carry? Can he or she force open a heavy door? Arm-wrestle a bugbear? Swing a greatsword? Bash open a locked chest? A strong character is better at melee combat than a weaker one. A character with the fighter class wants a high score in this ability.

- **Dexterity (Dex):** This score measures your character's reflexes and agility. How good is he or she with a ranged weapon, such as a sling or bow? Can he or she use speed and coordination to avoid being hit and taking damage? Can he or she use skills that require a great deal of hand-eye coordination? A dexterous character is better at ranged combat than a less agile one and has a better Armor Class (AC) thanks to quick reactions. A character with the rogue class wants a high score in this ability.

- **Constitution (Con):** This number expresses your character's overall physical health and stamina. How long can he or she hold his or her breath? How well does his or her body deal with physical damage? How much punishment can he or she take before falling unconscious? These are the types of things measured by your character's Constitution score. All characters want at least a minor bonus from this ability because of its bonus to hit points.

- **Intelligence (Int):** This score gauges your character's ability to learn and use deductive reasoning. How many languages does your character know? Can he or she disarm the trap without setting it off? What does your character know about the monster he or she is facing? The history of the dungeon? The uses for the arcane ingredients found in the necromancer's vault? A smart character is better at finding answers than a less intelligent one.

- **Wisdom (Wis):** This score measures your character's perception and willpower. Does he or she notice the gnolls lurking in the shadows? Can he or she hear the dragon breathing in the dark cave ahead? Does he or she have the strength of will to withstand the vampire's hypnotic gaze? A wise character is better at taking advantage of insight and intuition than a less wise character would be. A high score also provides a cleric with bonus spells. A character with the cleric class wants a high score in this ability.

✔ **Charisma (Cha):** This number represents your character's personal magnetism and physical attractiveness. Can he or she get the castle guard to look the other way with convincing words or a well-timed bribe? A charismatic character is better at being suave or subtle when the situation calls for it than a less charismatic one is. A high score also provides a sorcerer with bonus spells and helps determine what level of spells a sorcerer can cast. For these reasons, a character with the sorcerer class wants a high score in this ability.

When you create a character, you generate ability scores and assign them to the abilities as you see fit. How you assign the scores depends on what kind of character you're creating. If you're making a sorcerer, for example, you would assign a high score to Charisma, whereas if you're making a fighter, you would assign a high score to Strength. (See Table 12-2, later in this chapter, for more information.)

An average score is 10 or 11. Scores of less than 10 are below average, while scores of 12 or better are above average. In general, ability scores range from 8 to 18 when you first create the character. The score provides a modifier, either a bonus or a penalty that is tied to certain types of actions in the game, as described in Table 12-1. In general, ability scores relate to actions in the following way:

✔ Low ability scores (9 and lower) provide penalties to actions they are associated with.

✔ High ability scores (12 and higher) provide bonuses to actions they are associated with.

Table 12-1		Ability Modifiers	
Score	*Modifier*	*Score*	*Modifier*
1	−5	12–13	+1
2–3	−4	14–15	+2
4–5	−3	16–17	+3
6–7	−2	18–19	+4
8–9	−1	20–21	+5
10–11	0		

Remember the Core Game Mechanic (described in Chapter 1):

- Roll a d20
- Add a modifier (bonus or penalty)
- Compare the result to a target number

So bonuses (such as +1) are always better, because they help make your d20 result higher and increase the chance of success at a given action. Penalties (such as –1) lower your d20 result and make the chance of failure more likely.

A low score in a physical ability means that the character faces difficult challenges as a front-line warrior; a high score, on the other hand, doesn't guarantee success in that field.

In the following list, we describe each of the six abilities and their effects on character actions in the game:

- **Strength (Str):** The modifier provided by the character's Strength score is applied to melee attacks, damage rolls, and physical skill scores (Climb, Jump, and Swim).

- **Dexterity (Dex):** The modifier provided by the character's Dexterity score is applied to ranged attacks, Reflex saving throws, the character's AC, and to Dexterity-based skill scores (such as Balance, Open Lock, and Tumble).

- **Constitution (Con):** The modifier provided by the character's Constitution score is applied to his or her Hit Die to determine the character's hit points (hp) every time he or she gains a level. The Constitution modifier also applies to Fortitude saving throws and the Concentration skill score (which is important to spellcasters such as the sorcerer and cleric).

- **Intelligence (Int):** The modifier provided by the character's Intelligence score is applied to the number of languages he or she can know as a 1st-level character, the number of skill points he or she gains at every level, and to Intelligence-based skill scores (such as Disable Device, Knowledge, Search, and Spellcraft).

- **Wisdom (Wis):** The modifier provided by the character's Wisdom score is applied to Will saving throws and Wisdom-based skill scores (such as Listen, Spot, and Survival).

- **Charisma (Cha):** The modifier provided by the character's Charisma score is applied to Charisma-based skill scores (such as Bluff, Diplomacy, and Intimidate) and to a cleric's checks to turn undead creatures.

Generating Ability Scores

Some people approach the game knowing exactly what kind of character they want to create and play. Others prefer to generate their ability scores first, see what they get in the way of bonuses and penalties, and then create the best character they can around those scores. Either way, at some point early in the process, you need to figure out what your character's ability scores are. Check with your Dungeon Master to see if he or she has a preferred method for determining ability scores. In this section, we examine the two most popular methods — the random generation method and the elite array — and discuss how to get the most out of them when creating a new DUNGEONS & DRAGONS player character.

The random method

D&D is a game of dice rolling. It's no wonder, then, that most D&D players create their characters by rolling ability scores randomly. The *Player's Handbook* describes this method in detail. There's just something about rolling dice that gets the blood pumping. It's exciting to see what happens. This method provides a chance for the highest scores possible — as well as for the lowest. It all depends on luck and how the dice fall.

With this method, you can generate scores between 3 and 18. This means that it's possible to do much better or much worse than by using the elite array to generate your character's ability scores. Of course, that's what makes this method so appealing. When the dice fall right, you can create a character that might have a score of 16, 17, or even 18. When the dice fall badly, though, you could wind up with a score of less than 8, and that's not good.

This method for generating ability scores has some safeguards built in. If you roll really poorly, for example, established rules allow you to scrap your results and roll again. This is detailed under the "Rerolling" section in the *Player's Handbook*. The game defines a poor set of rolls as follows:

- ✔ The sum of the ability modifiers is 0 or lower.

  or

- ✔ The highest score is 13 or lower.

So don't let the randomness of this method scare you. Instead, embrace the excitement of watching the dice fall and hope for some really high scores!

To use the random method to generate six scores and assign those scores to your character's abilities, follow these steps:

1. **Roll four six-sided dice (4d6). Discard the die with the lowest roll. Total the three remaining dice. Jot down the number. (You'll wind up with a number between 3 and 18.)**

   For example, you might roll 4 and 5 and 3 and 3. You discard one of the 3s and add the others. Your total for this roll is 12.

2. **Repeat five more times.**

   Suppose that you get the following results:

   4 and 5 and 3 and 3 = 12

   5 and 6 and 6 and 4 = 17

   5 and 6 and 5 and 2 = 16

   5 and 4 and 4 and 4 = 13

   3 and 4 and 4 and 1 = 11

   3 and 2 and 4 and 3 = 10

3. **Assign each score to one ability, pairing up number and ability to best create the kind of character you want to develop.**

   For instance, if you want to make a character with the fighter class, you could assign the example scores as follows:

   Str 17, Dex 13, Con 16, Int 10, Wis 11, Cha 12

   By placing the best score in Strength, you create a very strong fighter with a +3 bonus to melee attack and damage rolls. The second highest score goes in Constitution to pile on the hit points the character gets at every level. You place small bonuses of +1 in Dexterity to improve your character's Armor Class (AC) and Charisma, leaving you with two average scores to plug into the remaining mental statistics of Intelligence and Wisdom. No bonus for these stats, but no penalty, either.

   If you were looking to make a sorcerer, you might assign the example scores this way:

   Str 10, Dex 13, Con 16, Int 12, Wis 11, Cha 17

   Placing the best score in Charisma gives your sorcerer a distinct advantage as far as spellcasting is concerned, as this is the ability that governs bonus spells and maximum spell level for this class. Because Constitution grants extra hit points and factors into important Concentration skill checks, you opt to place the second highest score here. Small bonuses go into Dexterity and Intelligence to improve your character's AC and give him or her extra skill points. This just leaves the average scores, which provide neither a bonus nor a penalty. You slot them into Strength (because you don't plan on having your sorcerer get up close and personal during combat) and Wisdom (the character can be charismatic and smart, but you decide that the character isn't especially perceptive or wise).

The elite array

The potential highs and lows of the random method make it the method of choice for most Dungeon Masters and players, and that's why it was set up as the default method for generating ability scores in the *Player's Handbook*. We like this method best and recommend that you use it unless you have a very specific character concept in mind and would feel better having a little more control over the results. That's where the elite array comes in.

This method of ability score generation provides a solid group of set numbers that you can assign as you see fit. That's right — the elite array always uses the same numbers. You have more control with this method because you always know exactly what scores you're going to get. The dizzying heights or the disappointing lows that you get with random rolling are not part of this method, and that's kind of the point. The elite array provides a set of numbers that combines decent bonuses with one average score and one penalty thrown in for good measure. The elite array looks like this:

15, 14, 13, 12, 10, and 8

The benefits of using the elite array are speed and consistency. This set of scores allows you to quickly create a character that has at least a decent score (a score that produces a bonus) in every ability important to the class you want to play. The disadvantages are that you don't have the possibility of generating a score of 16 or higher (as you can, if you're lucky, with the random method) and that you lose out on the excitement of rolling the dice.

When you're in a hurry or when you want to guarantee a selection of bonuses so you can better create the character concept you've got in mind, go with the elite array. We used the elite array to create all of the ready-to-play characters in Part I.

Assigning Ability Scores by Class

For every class, certain abilities are more important than others and provide a key to a character's success. We define these important abilities for each class in Table 12-2. For each class, we show where to place the highest score (++), the other bonus-generating or average scores (+), and the penalty-generating scores (–). The fighter is presented as having either a melee or a ranged combat focus. In addition to the standard cleric, we present a cleric with a melee focus to round out that class. You see examples of these different types of fighters and clerics in Chapter 3 and 6.

Table 12-2	Ability Scores by Class					
Class	*Str*	*Dex*	*Con*	*Int*	*Wis*	*Cha*
Fighter, melee	++	+	+	–	–	–
Fighter, ranged	+	++	+	–	–	–
Rogue	–	++	+	+	+	–
Sorcerer	–	+	+	–	–	++
Cleric	–	–	+	–	++	+
Cleric, melee	+	–	+	–	++	+

Chapter 13

Picking a Race

. . . .

In This Chapter

▶ Examining the fantasy races

▶ Picking the right race for the job

▶ Checking out other race options

. . . .

*N*o fantasy world is complete without a selection of mythical races to join humans in the struggle against monsters and Evil with a capital "E." These distinct races usually have their own homelands, but everyone comes together in the larger human towns and cities. There, those with adventurous spirits join up and head out to banish threats and undertake quests that might be personal or world-altering in nature.

In this chapter, we look at the fantasy races available for use as player characters in the DUNGEONS & DRAGONS game. We concentrate on four of those races — humans, dwarves, elves, and halflings — discussing the benefits each brings to the table and why you'd want to play a character of that race. You can play any race and class option you want, but keep in mind that some races are predisposed to perform better in certain classes, as discussed in this chapter.

At the end of the chapter, we provide a quick overview of other races available in the D&D game.

Chapter 2 of the *Player's Handbook* goes into greater depth on character races and the benefits and disadvantages of each. Check it out after you read through this chapter.

Humans

Humans in D&D worlds are more or less just like humans in the real world, except stronger, more heroic and daring, and usually better looking. They come in all the usual human shapes, sizes, and colors. They range in height from about 5 feet to just over 6 feet tall. They reach adventuring age somewhere between their 16th and 20th birthdays. Human adventurers are adaptable, flexible, and extremely ambitious. They tend toward no particular alignment or deity, and they have a habit of championing causes and ideals over people or places.

Play a human character if you want to have a lot of maneuverability for your character as he or she advances in level. Although humans don't get any special abilities or statistical adjustments, they do gain extra skill points and an extra feat to reflect their racial tendency toward versatility and capability at mastering new tasks.

Ability adjustments

Human characters get no ability adjustments. Assign the ability scores you generated to specific abilities and you're done.

Special traits

Humans start play with one extra feat at 1st level, and 4 extra skill points at 1st level. With every level gained, a human character gets 1 extra skill point.

Best class

Humans do equally well with all of the classes, and they are suited to be good at any adventuring careers they set their minds to.

A word about gender

DUNGEONS & DRAGONS characters can be either male or female. Playing a male or female character is a personal choice, and to keep it that way, the game sees no difference in characters of different genders. In D&D worlds, female adventurers are the equals of their male counterparts.

Dwarves

Dwarves are short and extremely broad, standing about 4 feet tall and weighing about the same as much taller humans. Hailing from vast underground or mountainous kingdoms, dwarves excel at warfare, mining, and construction. Longer lived than humans, dwarves have great patience and take pride in hard work done well. Dwarf adventurers tend to be lawful (and usually good) in their alignment, seeking quests that will bring honor to their clans, respect from their friends, and treasure beyond their wildest imaginings.

Play a dwarf character if you want to focus on combat. Dwarves also have special abilities that favor underground and dungeon adventuring, such as the ability to see in the dark. If courage, loyalty, and a love of strong ale appeal to your sense of heroics, the dwarf race is a good choice for you.

Ability adjustments

After you've assigned the ability scores you generated to your abilities, make the following adjustments:

- ✔ Add 2 points to your Constitution score. Dwarves are stout and tough.
- ✔ Subtract 2 points from your Charisma score. Dwarves are gruff and reserved.

Special traits

Dwarves have the following racial traits:

- ✔ Due to their size and build, dwarves have a base speed of 20 feet (4 squares). However, they retain this speed even when wearing medium or heavy armor, or when carrying a medium or heavy load.

- Dwarves have darkvision, which allows them to see up to 60 feet in the dark.
- Dwarves gain a +2 racial bonus on Search checks to notice unusual stonework.
- Dwarves treat dwarven waraxes as martial weapons, rather than exotic weapons.
- Dwarves are extremely stable. They gain a +4 bonus on ability checks to resist bull rushes and trip attacks.
- Dwarves are hardy. They receive a +2 racial bonus on saving throws against poisons.
- Dwarves have an innate resistance to magic spells. They receive a +2 racial bonus on saving throws against spells and spell-like effects.
- Due to special training, dwarves gain a +1 racial bonus on attack rolls against orcs and goblinoids.
- Due to special training, dwarves gain a +4 dodge bonus to Armor Class when fighting giants (including ogres, trolls, and hill giants).
- Dwarves receive a +2 racial bonus on Appraise checks made to determine the value of stone or metal items.
- Dwarves receive a +2 racial bonus on Craft checks related to stone or metal.

Best class

Dwarves are especially suited to the fighter class, thanks in large part to their Constitution adjustment and their innate combat skills. Cleric is a good second choice for a dwarf character. While dwarves can excel at any class, they have a harder time with the arcane spellcasting classes due to their innate magic resistance.

Elves

Elves are slender and graceful, standing about 5 feet tall, with pale, otherworldly skin, dark hair, large, almond-shaped eyes, and pointed ears. Elven home-lands lie deep in the forests and woodlands, where the elves learn swordplay, archery, and magic. With a love for nature and a talent for the arts, elves have a unique outlook on life. They have amazingly long life spans, which tend to make them appear amused and curious — they rarely show the extremes of emotion that humans regularly demonstrate. Elf adventurers love freedom and variety, which makes them lean toward the gentler aspects of chaos, usually neutral or good. For elves, the call to adventure comes from an inborn wanderlust, though they can become focused and relentless when a particular quest catches their interest.

Play an elf character if you want to focus on magic or ranged combat. Elves have special abilities that make them indispensable for wilderness adventuring. If playing a hauntingly beautiful, somewhat alien and magically inclined character appeals to you, consider selecting the elf race for your character.

Ability adjustments

After you've assigned the ability scores you generated to your abilities, make the following adjustments:

- Add 2 points to your Dexterity score. Elves are quick and graceful.
- Subtract 2 points from your Constitution score. Elves are frail and less hearty than other races.

Special traits

Elves have the following racial traits:

- Elves are immune to magic sleep effects, and elves receive a +2 racial bonus on saving throws against enchantment spells and effects.
- Elves have low-light vision, which allows them to see twice as far as a human in poorly illuminated conditions.
- Elves receive the Martial Weapon Proficiency feats for the longsword, rapier, longbow, and shortbow as bonus feats.
- Elves have keen senses. They gain a +2 racial bonus on Listen, Search, and Spot checks.

Best class

Elves make great arcane spellcasters, so the sorcerer class is a good choice for them. While elves can excel at any class, be careful with the combat-oriented classes due to their reduction in Constitution.

Halflings

Halflings are about half as tall as humans, with slender, muscular frames and nimble features. Halflings are nomads, wanderers with no homelands to call their own. Clever and capable, cunning and resourceful, halflings constantly seek ways to avoid boredom and complacency. Halfling adventurers tend to take a neutral stance when it comes to alignment, and they watch for ways to use their skills to attain wealth and status. Although all halflings have a bit of thief in them, most follow their curiosity and have learned how to get into and out of trouble better than any of the other races.

Play a halfling character if you want to focus on stealth and skill use. Halflings have special abilities that let them excel at avoiding danger. If curious, fun-loving, good-hearted thieves appeal to your sense of adventure, consider selecting the halfling race.

Ability adjustments

After you've assigned the ability scores you generated for your abilities, make the following adjustments:

- Add 2 points to your Dexterity score. Halflings are quick, agile, and athletic.
- Subtract 2 points from your Strength score. Halflings are weaker than the other races due to their small size.

Special traits

Halflings have the following racial traits:

- ✔ Halflings are Small creatures. Due to their size, halflings gain a +1 size bonus to Armor Class, a +1 size bonus on attack rolls, and a +4 size bonus on Hide checks. However, they must use smaller, less effective weapons and have a base speed of 20 feet (4 squares).

- ✔ Halflings gain a +2 racial bonus on Climb, Jump, and Move Silently checks.

- ✔ Halflings are naturally good at avoiding danger. They gain a +1 racial bonus on all saving throws.

- ✔ Because they let their curiosity overpower their sense of fear, halflings gain a +2 morale bonus on saving throws against fear.

- ✔ Due to special training and natural athleticism, halflings gain a +1 racial bonus on attack rolls with thrown weapons and slings.

- ✔ Due to keen hearing, halflings gain a +2 racial bonus on Listen checks.

Best class

Halflings make great rogues. They do less well as melee fighters, but they can excel as fighters that specialize in ranged attacks.

More Races to Choose From

The *Player's Handbook* features additional races for player characters. These include the gnome (a small race whose members make good bards), the half-elf (whose features include human adaptability combined with elven special features), and the half-orc (who is geared toward combat, especially as a barbarian).

Beyond the core books, the D&D game is full of fantasy races suitable for use as player characters. The *Eberron Campaign Setting*, for example, introduces four new races that offer new options for creating cool player characters. Start by playing the races from the core books, and then look for new options with which to expand your play experience.

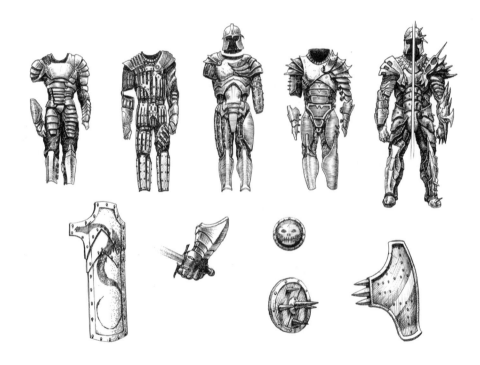

Chapter 14

Selecting Feats

*N*ot all fighters fight the same. Some slice their foes to pieces with skillful swordplay, some overpower their enemies with brute strength and a big axe, and still others pincushion the bad guys with a barrage of arrows. Each of these fighters learns different tactics and special maneuvers, or *feats,* to master his or her chosen style of combat. Choosing your character's feats is a key step in differentiating your fighter from every other fighter in the game.

Every character gets to take advantage of feats; they're not just for fighters. Sorcerer characters can gain feats that make them especially good at casting certain types of spells, or casting spells in combat, or crafting unique magic items that will help them in their adventures. Clerics can learn feats that make them extremely good at turning and destroying undead monsters such as skeletons, ghouls, or vampires. And rogues can take feats that make them stealthier, quicker, and deadlier in combat.

In this chapter, we tell you how your character gains feats and how you can use feat selections to power up your character with great combat moves, special edges, and hidden strengths. We also show you a set of handy shortcuts (we call 'em feat ladders) to steer you through selecting your character's first few feats.

What's a Feat?

Feats are specific combat maneuvers or unusual advantages that customize your character's capabilities and performance. They range from relatively simple feats like Iron Will (which makes your character exceptionally hard to affect with mind-controlling magic) to spectacular combat combinations like Whirlwind Attack (which enables a character to launch a flurry of attacks against all enemies within reach of his or her weapon).

Sample feats

Here are three quick examples of some feats you'll find in the *Player's Handbook*. (You'll need to visit the *Player's Handbook* to find the definitions of the feats we mention throughout this book, as well as to see the entire range of feats available to characters.)

IMPROVED INITIATIVE [GENERAL]

You can react more quickly than normal in a fight.

Benefit: You get a +4 bonus on Initiative checks.

Special: A fighter may select Improved Initiative as one of his or her fighter bonus feats.

POWER ATTACK [GENERAL]

You can make exceptionally powerful melee attacks.

Prerequisite: Strength 13.

Benefit: On your action, before making attack rolls for the round, you may choose to subtract a number from all melee attack rolls and add the same number to all melee damage rolls. This

number may not exceed your base attack bonus. The penalty on attack rolls and bonus on damage rolls applies until your next turn.

Special: If you attack with a two-handed weapon, instead add twice the number subtracted from your attack rolls.

A fighter may select Power Attack as one of his or her fighter bonus feats.

STEALTHY [GENERAL]

You are particularly good at avoiding notice.

Benefit: You get a +2 bonus on all Hide checks and Move Silently checks.

The bracketed [General] after each of these feats tells you what sort of feat you're looking at. In each of these cases, the feat is a General feat, which means that any character can take it. You may notice that Power Attack has a special requirement: Your character must have a Strength score of 13 or better in order to choose it.

Over the course of your character's career, you eventually build up a collection of feats. Taken together, your character's feats form a suite or library of special edges, useful talents, and combat tricks that make him or her different from any other character of the same class and level. The higher your character's level, the more feats he or she knows, and the more feats known, the more unique and powerful your character becomes.

You can find the definitive word on feats in Chapter 5 of the *Player's Handbook*. Table 5-1 on page 90 lists every feat you'll ever need.

The Basics of Acquiring Feats

Here's the bad news about feats: They're great, but your character never learns very many of them. Characters get one feat at 1st level, plus one feat for every three levels they reach (which gives characters a total of two feats at 3rd level, three feats at 6th level, four feats at 9th level, and so on).

The three key exceptions to this rule are that

- ✔ Humans begin with one bonus feat at 1st level as a racial advantage.

- ✔ Fighters gain bonus feats at certain levels as a class feature.

- ✔ Other classes (for example, the monk, ranger, and wizard) or prestige classes (such as the eldritch knight) may offer bonus feats as a class feature. For the lowdown on character classes, see Chapter 11.

If you want to maximize the number of feats you can acquire, you should create a human fighter character. No other race/class combination in the game picks up feats faster.

Table 14-1 shows the number of feats acquired by character level. The Nonhuman Fighter and Human Fighter columns show this as the sum of level-based feats and fighter bonus feats; for example, a 3rd-level human fighter knows three feats for being a human and having three levels of a character class, plus two bonus feats for being a 3rd-level fighter.

Table 14-1	Feats Known by Character Level			
Level	*Nonhuman Nonfighter*	*Nonhuman Fighter*	*Human Nonfighter*	*Human Fighter*
1	1	1+1	2	2+1
2	1	1+2	2	2+2
3	2	2+2	3	3+2
4	2	2+3	3	3+3
5	2	2+3	3	3+3
6	3	3+4	4	4+4
7	3	3+4	4	4+4
8	3	3+5	4	4+5
9	4	4+5	5	5+5
10	4	4+6	5	5+6

Meeting feat requirements

As much as you might like to pick Whirlwind Attack for your character's first feat choice, you can't do it. Most feats have one or more requirements that your character must meet before you can add them to his or her arsenal. For example, your character must have a Strength score of 13 or better to take the Power Attack feat. The best feats require that your character first learn a whole string of feats and meet a number of requirements. In the case of Whirlwind Attack, your character must have a Dex of 13 or better, Int of 13 or better, a base attack bonus of +4 or better, and four additional feats (Combat Expertise, Dodge, Mobility, and Spring Attack). Wow!

The good news for beginning characters is that a number of feats have requirements that are easily met by even a 1st-level character (or no requirements at all), so you're pretty much guaranteed of finding something your character can use right from day one. Some of the best beginning feat choices for each character class are summed up in Table 14-2.

Table 14-2	Key 1st-Level Feats
Class	*Good Beginning Feat Choices*
Fighter	Exotic Weapon Proficiency, Power Attack, Weapon Focus
Cleric	Extra Turning, Improved Turning, Martial Weapon Proficiency
Rogue	Dodge, Improved Initiative, Point Blank Shot
Sorcerer	Combat Casting, Spell Focus, Toughness

Understanding feat types

Feats are organized into a number of different types, but there are four types you need to know about in order to choose feats that are useful and effective for your character. And they are

- ✔ **General feats:** These are feats that any character can learn. Your character might need to meet some difficult requirements — some so hard that some characters are effectively excluded from learning them. A fighter can learn Whirlwind Attack by 6th level, but a sorcerer gets fewer feat choices and couldn't manage it until 12th level at the earliest. Most feats are general feats.

- ✔ **Item creation feats:** These are reserved for spellcasters. If your character can't cast spells, he or she can't learn an item creation feat. That's the way it is. Item creation feats are feats that let your character learn how to manufacture various sorts of magic items, ranging from potions and scrolls, on up to rings, wands, and staffs.

Item creation feats are hard to use in play, especially for a beginning player. We recommend you steer away from them until your character is a spellcaster of at least 6th level and you've checked with your DM to make sure he or she will give you the opportunity to use an item creation feat.

✔ **Metamagic feats:** These are feats that let your character change the way his or her spells work. They're also reserved for spellcasters only. These feats make your character's spells more powerful, harder to resist, longer-lasting, or suitable for casting even in the heaviest armor. If your character is a cleric or a sorcerer, you're going to want to pick up a metamagic feat sooner or later in the character's career — but they're almost useless for 1st-level spellcasters, so don't be in a hurry to pick one up.

✔ **Fighter bonus feats:** These are the bonus feats of the fighter class. They do not constitute a feat *type,* per se — every feat in this category is a general feat — but they share one important characteristic: If your character is a fighter, these feats are easy to acquire in the course of his or her career.

Climbing up feat trees

Feats are often organized in specific *feat trees* or paths. For example, the Improved Bull Rush, Cleave, Great Cleave, and Improved Sunder feats are part of the Power Attack family. Your character needs to learn Power Attack first, and then you can go on to choose feats that have Power Attack as a prerequisite. The best feats may require your character to climb all the way to the top of a feat tree, sticking with it for level after level. In the case of Improved Bull Rush, Cleave, or Improved Sunder, this is easy; when your character knows Power Attack, you can use his or her next available feat selection to choose any one of those feats. But Great Cleave is farther up the tree. To learn Great Cleave, your character first must learn Power Attack, and then learn Cleave. He or she can't learn Great Cleave without mastering these two preceding feats first.

The major feat trees in the *Player's Handbook* are all named after the first feat in the tree. They are

✔ Combat Expertise

✔ Dodge

✔ Improved Unarmed Strike

✔ Mounted Combat

✔ Point Blank Shot

✔ Power Attack

✔ Two Weapon Fighting

✔ Weapon Focus

Making Your Choices Simpler with Feat Ladders

Your feat choices are pretty daunting because there are so many to choose from. So, what we do here is provide you with three basic feat ladders to consider for each character class. The goal of a feat ladder is to chart your way through your future feat picks at higher levels so that you get the feats you want for your character as soon as possible. The *Player's Handbook* doesn't say a word about feat ladders, but most experienced players designing characters often make a point of planning several levels ahead in feat acquisition.

If you're not sure which feats are the best choice for your character, you can use these feat packages as a basic plan for making a sound (if not particularly creative) set of feat choices for your character as he or she rises in level and gains more feat choices.

Try the following process when evaluating your feat choices:

1. **Determine the number of feat choices you have to make (see Table 14-1, earlier in this chapter).**

2. **Identify your character's class, and then decide which specialty or function you want your character to master within that class.**

   A master swordsman, for example, needs to learn different feats from a muscle-bound axe-wielder, even though they are both fighters. See Table 14-3 for a listing of these specialties and their descriptions.

Table 14-3	Specializations
Master This Specialization . . .	*So That Your Character Can . . .*
Fighter specializations (also good for barbarians, paladins, and rangers)	
Melee fighter	Deal out damage in close combat
Skill fighter	Outmaneuver the enemy
Ranged fighter	Be the best archer around
Rogue specializations (also good for monks and rangers)	
Melee rogue	Get close in order to make lots of sneak attacks in melee combat with foes
Sneaky rogue	Choose to strike once with surprise on your character's side, and not get bogged down in a slugging match
Ranged rogue	Be the fastest draw in the dungeon

Master This Specialization . . .	So That Your Character Can . . .
Cleric specializations (also good for druids and paladins)	
Melee cleric	Be the best fighting cleric your character can be, and do most fighting with a mace instead of with spells
Turn expert	Obliterate undead monsters
Spellcasting cleric	Do most fighting with spells instead of a mace
Sorcerer specializations (also good for bards and wizards)	
Attack sorcerer	Use maximum magical offense
Team buff sorcerer	Use spells to help allies fight better
Survival sorcerer	Cover your character's weaknesses and avoid getting killed early in his or her career

3. **Consult the feat ladder appropriate for your character's class and chosen path (for descriptions of these ladders, see the sections that follow), or design your own feat ladder.**

   After you've played the game for a while and you've made up a few characters, experiment with building feat ladders that exploit feat trees our feat ladders here don't make use of.

4. **Make any extra feat selections you have coming to you, such as the bonus feat that human characters get at 1st level.**

5. **Record your feat selections on your character sheet.**

The feat ladders presented in this chapter don't account for a human character's bonus feat. In most cases, you can use the bonus feat to buy your way up the ladder even faster, but watch out for feats with tough requirements. For example, if you're following the skill fighter ladder on Table 14-4, you simply can't buy the Spring Attack feat before your character reaches 4th level, because Spring Attack requires a +4 base attack bonus. Try using your character's human bonus feat to pick up Iron Will, Improved Initiative, Great Fortitude, or Toughness. These feats are good for any character.

Fighter feat ladders

For the purpose of choosing feats, we're going to make you decide if you want your fighter character to be a _melee fighter,_ a _skill fighter,_ or a _ranged fighter,_ described in Table 14-4. (See Table 14-3 for a description of these specialties.) You can also use the melee fighter ladder for barbarians or paladins, or the ranged fighter ladder for rangers. (Rangers gain a small number of bonus feats in their chosen combat style, so check out the ranger class description in the *Player's Handbook* to see which of these feats your character can learn for free.)

Table 14-4	Fighter Feat Ladders		
Level	Melee Fighter	Skill Fighter	Ranged Fighter
1	Weapon Focus (bastard sword), Exotic Weapon Proficiency (bastard sword)	Weapon Focus (longsword), Combat Expertise	Weapon Focus (composite longbow), Point Blank Shot
2	Power Attack	Dodge	Precise Shot
3	Cleave	Mobility	Rapid Shot
4	Weapon Specialization (bastard sword)	Spring Attack	Weapon Specialization (composite longbow)
5	—	—	—
6	Improved Sunder	Whirlwind Attack	Manyshot
7	—	—	—
8	Improved Critical (bastard sword)	Weapon Specialization (longsword)	Improved Critical (composite longbow)
9	Greater Weapon Focus (bastard sword)	Improved Disarm	Dodge
10	Great Cleave	Improved Trip	Mobility

Melee fighter

The basic plan for a melee fighter character is to run up to the monsters and just beat the tar out of them with a sword, an axe, a warhammer, or whatever implement of mayhem that catches your fancy. If you ever find that you don't know what you want your character to do, have him or her *hit something!* You want your character to deal out horrible amounts of damage in the shortest time possible.

The melee fighter needs a Strength score of 13 or better to make this feat ladder work. Your character is going to be a sword-and-shield or axe-and-shield fighter. Use the Exotic Weapon Proficiency feat to choose either the bastard sword or dwarven waraxe, because they dish out the most damage for one-handed weapons.

The Power Attack feat doesn't do that much for your character early in his or her career, but what it does do is help the character meet the requirements for Cleave — a very nice feat that will give your character extra chances to deal damage. And the melee fighter is all about dealing damage, remember?

Skill fighter

A skill fighter character is built to move to the exact spot where he or she can do the most good and then slice the enemy to pieces with panache. A skill fighter is especially good at fighting defensively and moving around the battlefield, so he or she shouldn't waste time scuffling with the rabble — the skill fighter identifies the key member of the opposition and goes after him, her, or it. Your character is willing to give up some damage-dealing potential in order to keep a lot of options on the table.

This is not an easy ladder to climb. Your character needs a Dexterity of 13 and an Intelligence of 13 to progress here. Again, your character should be a sword-and-shield fighter; the longsword is the best bet. You may also want to keep your character out of heavy armor in order for him or her to be as mobile as possible.

When you select the Spring Attack and Whirlwind Attack feats, you will find that your character owns the battlefield. Stick and move, stick and move! If you wanted your character to stand still and pound on a single foe at a time, you should have created a melee fighter character.

Ranged fighter

Remember how Legolas shot everything that moved in the *Lord of the Rings* movies? That's a ranged fighter character. This feat ladder is designed to make your character into the most fearsome archer in the dungeon. Make sure you choose composite longbow for your character's Weapon Focus; he or she will be crippled if you select this feat path with a crossbow or a sling (but you can do okay with thrown daggers, if you don't mind having your character constantly running out of ammunition).

To get the best bang for your buck in this feat ladder, your character should have a Dexterity of at least 13. A Dex of 17 (or higher) is better, because you can't select the Manyshot feat without it. If your character doesn't have a high enough Dexterity for Manyshot, buy Dodge early, and then pick up Mobility when your character reaches 10th level (you'll be well on your way to the feat Shot on the Run, which you can select at 12th level).

Rapid Shot and Manyshot form a perfect pair of tactical options. If you intend to have your character stand still for the round, use Rapid Shot. If you want your character to move, use Manyshot. If your character isn't shooting three arrows per round by 6th level, your heart's just not in it.

Rogue feat ladders

As a rogue, your character is not going to be buried in feat choices like the fighter. You don't get any bonus feat choices just for having a rogue character, and that means feat choices are rare and precious.

The three paths we show you in Table 14-5 are the *melee rogue,* the *sneaky rogue,* and the *ranged rogue.* (See Table 14-3 for a description of these specialties.) The melee rogue ladder works okay for monks, and the ranged rogue ladder is useful for a ranger (although a ranger will move up this ladder a lot faster than a rogue).

Table 14-5	Rogue Feat Ladders		
Level	*Melee Rogue*	*Sneaky Rogue*	*Ranged Rogue*
1	Improved Initiative	Stealthy	Improved Initiative
2	—	—	—
3	Weapon Finesse	Improved Initiative	Point Blank Shot
4	—	—	—
5	—	—	—
6	Two-Weapon Fighting	Weapon Finesse	Rapid Shot
7	—	—	—
8	—	—	—
9	Weapon Focus (rapier)	Dodge	Manyshot
10	—	—	—

Melee rogue ladder

A melee rogue character is built to get into a scrape and dish out as much sneak attack damage as he or she can. When one of your character's allies engages a foe in a toe-to-toe fight, your character gets behind the bad guy as quick as possible to set up a flanking situation and then makes as many attacks as he or she can.

Your character needs a Dexterity of 15 or higher to optimize this strategy, because that's what you need to select the Two-Weapon Fighting feat. (Then again, every rogue should have a Dex of at least 15, really.) A good Strength score will help your character dish out the damage.

Improved Initiative is key for any rogue, because you want your character to go first in a fight in order to maximize opportunities for dealing sneak attack damage. Selecting the Weapon Finesse feat allows your character to use his or her Dexterity bonus on melee attacks — this little trick will let a rogue keep pace with the fighter's melee attack ability better than any other non-fighter. And Two-Weapon Fighting gives your character extra attacks. When your character has a dangerous sneak attack, the more opportunities he or she gets to score a hit, the better.

Sneaky rogue ladder

Characters who spend a lot of time right next to the bad guys get hurt, so the sneaky rogue character wants no part of that. A sneaky rogue is the master of not being seen in the first place. If your character has to fight, you want to make sure he or she gets the drop on foes and leads off with a deadly strike from hiding.

You can get by if your character has a Dexterity of 13 in this feat ladder, but a higher score is better. A high Dexterity helps your character to win initiative and makes him or her harder to hit, and both are highly desirable for any rogue.

The Stealthy feat helps you to choose which fights your character gets into and to surprise enemies by adding to Hide and Move Silently skill checks. Improved Initiative helps your character to get the drop on enemies when he or she strikes. Eventually, you should buy into the Dodge-Mobility-Spring Attack feat tree, because a rogue's best defense against a monster's attack is to not be standing next to it when its turn comes up.

Ranged rogue ladder

Your ranged rogue character is a gunslinger. Your character strikes first and dishes out an enormous amount of damage before anyone else has even started to move. In fact, your character might be a better ranged combatant than even the ranged fighter. Sure, a ranged fighter will have a slightly better attack bonus and deal a little more damage than your ranged rogue character can do most of the time, but the rogue makes up for that by owning the first round of combat.

Make sure your character has a Dexterity score of 17 or better in order to pick up Manyshot quickly — it's the favorite feat for a ranged rogue character. You'll also want to pick up Precise Shot as soon as you have a feat to spare (human characters have an edge here because of their bonus feat choice), because you'll find your character shooting into melee quite often, and you don't want your character to take that attack penalty if he or she doesn't have to.

As with the ranged fighter, you'll find that your character constantly uses Rapid Shot and Manyshot. When your character is dealing sneak attack damage, you want him or her to make as many separate attack rolls as possible. Maximizing your character's rate of fire is your goal.

Sorcerer feat ladders

You have an entirely different set of feat choices to weigh for a sorcerer character than for a fighter or rogue. You want to choose feats to enhance your character's magical prowess and to master useful spellcasting tricks, not study the arts of swordsmanship and archery.

The three paths we describe in Table 14-6 are the *attack sorcerer,* the *team buff sorcerer,* and the *survival sorcerer.* (See Table 14-3 for a description of these specialties.) All three of these ladders work just as well for wizards as they do for sorcerers.

Table 14-6	Sorcerer Feat Ladders		
Level	*Attack Sorcerer*	*Team Buff Sorcerer*	*Survival Sorcerer*
1	Spell Focus (Evocation)	Improved Initiative	Toughness
2	—	—	—
3	Improved Initiative	Craft Wondrous Item	Great Fortitude
4	—	—	—
5	—	—	—
6	Greater Spell Focus (Evocation)	Extend Spell	Lightning Reflexes
7	—	—	—
8	—	—	—
9	Spell Penetration	Spell Focus (Evocation)	Still Spell
10	—	—	—

Attack sorcerer ladder

An attack sorcerer character is an eggshell armed with a hammer. Your character's philosophy is to beat down the monsters with his or her magical power so fast that they don't have an opportunity to hit back, because he or she simply can't stand up to any kind of punishment. Attack sorcerers count on teammates to keep them alive so that their spells can decide the battle.

Your character doesn't have any requirements to worry about in climbing this feat ladder, but it works best if your sorcerer has the highest Charisma score you can manage. This strategy is all about maximizing your character's offense, so you want your sorcerer to be the best raw spellcaster possible before you begin choosing feats.

The Spell Focus feat should be designed for the school of magic in which you expect your character to cast most spells. (See Chapter 17 for more information on choosing sorcerer spells.) Your best bets are enchantment, evocation, or transmutation, because these schools offer attack spells that work better when you maximize the difficulty of the saving throws your character forces his or her enemies to make. Of these paths, Spell Focus (evocation) is probably the best bet for a new player (but make sure you remember to choose evocation spells that require saving throws when you learn spells, or else you won't get any benefit for your Spell Focus feat!).

Team buff sorcerer ladder

A team buff sorcerer character is the master of spreading arcane power around the adventuring party (or "buffing" allies, hence the name): Your character uses his or her spells and abilities to dramatically enhance companions' fighting abilities. You've got to be a little patient to play a successful team buff sorcerer, because your character will often be giving up a chance to dish out some direct damage against the monsters in order to make his or her companions better able to serve up (and withstand) much more damage than they otherwise could.

As with the attack sorcerer, you don't have much in the way of specific requirements to watch out for when choosing feats for your character. However, you can afford for your character to not have the best Charisma score possible, because you won't need to make your character's spells especially difficult to resist — team buff sorcerers will be casting most of their spells to help their allies, not harm their enemies.

Craft Wondrous Item is going to be your character's signature feat on this path, because it will allow him or her to build cheap and effective magical items to share with everyone in the adventuring party. However, you may want to sound out your Dungeon Master ahead of time and make sure he or she will give your sorcerer a chance to use this feat as the campaign plays out. Sometimes DMs run games that offer characters little downtime, and if your sorcerer never has a chance to take a week off from adventuring and work on making a magic item or two, you'll never get to make use of the Craft Wondrous Item feat.

Survival sorcerer ladder

To put it bluntly, many sorcerers don't make it past 1st level. The sorcerer has the worst hit points and Armor Class of any character in the game, and any monster with the faintest glimmer of intelligence probably identifies the sorcerer as an enticing combination of Potentially Very Dangerous and Easily Killed If I Act Now. The survival sorcerer ladder is all about buying time for the character to grow old and powerful.

Once again, you don't have any real feat or ability requirements to worry about when choosing feats for your character. Make sure your sorcerer has the best Dexterity and Constitution scores you can afford to go along with his or her high Charisma. These abilities help keep a sorcerer alive.

The feats on this ladder are quite simple — they allow you to add to your character's hit points and saving throws as much as you can. The Still Spell feat requires a word of explanation, though. Still Spell lets your character cast spells in armor with no chance of spell failure. So a decent strategy for helping out your character's Armor Class is to pick up a good light armor (magic studded leather armor or a mithral chain shirt are good choices) and then keep Still Spell in reserve for those occasions when you decide your character just can't afford any chance of spell failure.

Cleric feat ladders

Unlike most other characters, clerics don't have any immediate needs that they have to meet with thoughtful feat selections. You don't have to buy into a school of fighting the way you do with a fighter character or play catch-up with a shortfall in feats you'd like to have for a rogue character. You don't even have to cover your character's weaknesses or maximize offense like with a sorcerer.

Our three recommended paths for the cleric are the *melee cleric,* the *turn expert,* and the *spellcasting cleric,* described in Table 14-7. (See Table 14-3 for a description of these specialties.) Paladins can use the turn expert ladder fairly well, and druids do well with the spellcasting cleric ladder.

Table 14-7		Cleric Feat Ladders	
Level	*Melee Cleric*	*Turn Expert*	*Spellcasting Cleric*
1	Martial Weapon Proficiency (longsword)	Improved Turning	Combat Casting
2	—	—	—
3	Weapon Focus (longsword)	Extra Turning	Spell Focus (Conjuration)
4	—	—	—
5	—	—	—
6	Combat Casting	Extra Turning	Augment Summoning
7	—	—	—
8	—	—	—
9	Craft Magic Arms and Armor	Spell Penetration	Spell Penetration
10	—	—	—

Melee cleric ladder

A melee cleric character likes mixing it up, and he or she wants to get some swings in. Your character will never be as good at melee combat as the fighter is, but with the right spells, your character can come close for a short time, and he or she has the added advantage of being able to buff friends and heal the wounded when needed.

You don't have any difficult requirements to worry about in following this ladder, although you'll find that a good Strength score will help your character fight well in melee combat.

You should use the Martial Weapon Proficiency so your character can learn to use a longsword, warhammer, or battleaxe. Those are the best martial weapons that let your character use a shield. At higher levels, Craft Magic Arms and Armor allows your character to customize weapons and defenses, both for personal use and for his or her allies.

If you want to play a melee cleric, make sure that you take the War domain when you're choosing domains and spells for your character. (For more about the cleric's spell domains, see Chapter 17.) The special power of the War domain is a free Martial Weapon Proficiency. That means you can spend your character's 1st-level feat choice on something else (Combat Casting is a good choice) and move your character up this ladder that much faster.

Turn expert ladder

You've decided to maximize your character's turn undead abilities. *Turning undead* is a special class ability of the cleric that allows him or her to repel monsters of the undead type, such as skeletons, ghouls, ghosts, or vampires. Your cleric can even destroy relatively weak undead outright by using his or her turn ability. (See Chapter 11 for more on a cleric's turning ability.) Some cleric domains offer your cleric the ability to turn or control other types of creatures besides undead, so if you choose this path, think about selecting a domain that will let your character use his or her good turning abilities against as many foes as possible.

Key feats for other classes

Although these feat ladders give you serviceable clerics, fighters, rogues, and sorcerers, you might wonder which feats you should consider if your character happens to be a member of one of the other classes in the game. Here's a quick and dirty set of suggestions for each of the classes we don't cover at length:

✔ **Barbarian:** Try the Power Attack feat tree or Two-Weapon Fighting feat tree. You want your character to be able to use his or her enraged Strength score to dish out tons of damage, and fighting with a two-handed weapon and Power Attack or fighting with a weapon in each hand is the best way to do that.

✔ **Bard:** Skill Focus is a dog of a feat for anybody else, but Skill Focus (Perform) will do wonders for your character's bardic music abilities.

✔ **Druid:** Natural Spell is a tremendously good feat for your character once he or she hits 6th level, because it lets him or her cast spells while in a wild shape form. You should also consider taking Spell Focus (Conjuration) and Augment Summoning because your character will always have plenty of *summon nature's ally* spells at his or her command thanks to the druid class's spontaneous casting ability.

✔ **Monk:** Like the fighter and the ranger, your character gets a number of bonus feats. You should take Weapon Focus (unarmed strike) early in your character's career because he or she will be throwing a lot of punches and kicks. If your character's Dexterity is better than his or her Strength, Weapon

Finesse is a good choice too. Seriously consider choosing the Dodge-Mobility-Spring Attack feat tree, because a monk is so much faster than anyone else that your character will be able to make an attack and then retreat out of an opponent's reach round after round.

✔ **Paladin:** With your character's high Charisma score, a paladin is a natural for Extra Turning and Improved Turning. However, these feats come at a cost: If you want your character to keep pace with the fighter or the barbarian, you'll need to pick up the basic attack feats (Weapon Focus or Exotic Weapon Proficiency) early on. Power Attack is handy for a paladin because your character can use the elegant trick of combining his or her smite evil ability with the Power Attack feat to hand out great big helpings of holy hurt on the bad guys.

✔ **Ranger:** The ranger's combat style class ability provides your character with a number of free feats. You've got two choices: two-weapon combat or archery. If you follow the archery path for your ranger, you can use the ranged fighter feat ladder described earlier in this chapter. If you decide you want your character to be a dual-weapon ranger, try picking up Weapon Focus in a weapon your character can use two of easily (short swords are the best for this trick).

✔ **Wizard:** Your character is essentially in the same boat as a sorcerer, but a wizard gets a modest number of item creation or metamagic feats for free. Refer to the sorcerer feat ladders for good wizard feat progressions.

As with other cleric feat ladders, your character doesn't need to meet many special requirements to follow this ladder. However, you'll want your character to have the best Charisma score you can manage to go along with a high Wisdom and other key scores. A high Charisma bonus will help with every turning attempt your character makes.

Extra Turning is a feat you can take as often as you like; your character gains four additional turn attempts per day each time you select this feat. If you are going to try this feat ladder, you may want to search out other DUNGEONS & DRAGONS supplements (such as *Complete Divine*) that include special feats known as divine feats. These aren't in the *Player's Handbook*, but they're driven by uses of your cleric's turn undead ability, and some of them are very powerful.

Spellcasting cleric ladder

A spellcasting cleric character wants to be the most powerful and efficient divine spell-caster possible. Your character has some decent direct-attack spells, but he or she is no sorcerer; most of your cleric's "attacks" come in the form of spells that enhance his or her companions' fighting abilities and defenses.

Your character doesn't have any ability require-ments or feat trees to climb, but you will want your character to have the best Wisdom score you can manage. You want your character to be able to cast as many spells as possible, and you want those spells to be difficult to resist.

As a spellcasting cleric, your character's best offensive strategy may lie in the various *summon monster* spells. Here, at least, your character is every bit the equal of a sorcerer. By choosing the Augment Summoning feat, your character will get the most out of each monster-summoning spell he or she casts. But before you pick up the Augment Summoning feat, you need to choose Spell Focus (Conjuration), which is the prerequisite for Augment Summoning.

Chapter 15

Picking Skills

In This Chapter

▶ Getting a handle on skills

▶ Buying skills for your character

▶ Quick picks: Using skill packages

Regdar the fighter and Kerwyn the rogue are fleeing from a rampaging umber hulk when they come to a dangerous-looking rope bridge sway- ing over a bottomless underground chasm. Kerwyn darts across the bridge with ease, but Regdar picks his way over the obstacle hand-over-hand, only one small slip away from a terrifying plunge. If you're wondering how Kerwyn made it look so easy, the answer is simple: skills. Kerwyn the rogue is trained in balancing, tightrope walking, tumbling, and other such tasks. Crossing a rope bridge is a piece of cake for him.

In this chapter, we tell you how characters learn and use skills, and we show you a set of quick skill packages that will make buying skills for your charac- ter fast, easy, and effective.

All about Skills

Skills represent your character's training in tasks that don't involve fighting or spellcasting. The DUNGEONS & DRAGONS game has almost 50 distinct skills in the *Player's Handbook*, ranging from Appraise to Use Rope.

The amount of training your character has in any particular skill is measured by the number of *skill ranks* he or she possesses in that skill. For example, a 1st-level fighter might have 4 ranks in Climb, 2 ranks in Jump, and 1 rank in Spot. This character is pretty good at climbing, can manage a jump when he or she needs to, and has a little edge in spotting ambushes or hard-to-see objects. The character has 0 ranks in all other skills, because he or she is just not trained in those tasks.

The number of skill ranks your character can spend depends on his or her class, Intelligence score, and level. Some character classes gain more skills than others — for example, rogues and rangers rely on their skills, while fighters rely on combat ability and sorcerers rely on magic. And, as you might expect, smart, high-level characters have more skills than not-so-smart, low-level characters. We explain the skill selection process later in this chapter, in the "Choosing your character's skills" section.

Every skill is associated with a *key ability,* which is simply the ability score that modifies any checks with that skill. Balance, for instance, is a Dexterity-based skill — the reasoning is that if you have great dexterity, you're good at balancing, and if you've got a crummy dexterity (like the authors), you're terrible at it. Sometimes a great ability score can easily count for more than a minimal amount of training. A character with 1 rank in Balance and a Dexterity modifier of +0 is not as good at balancing as another character with 0 ranks in Balance and a Dexterity modifier of +3.

A sample skill

Here's an example of a skill description from the *Player's Handbook,* Chapter 4. (You can find descriptions of all the other skills in the game there.)

OPEN LOCK (DEX; TRAINED ONLY)

You can pick padlocks, finesse combination locks, and solve puzzle locks. The effort requires at least a simple tool of the appropriate sort (a pick, pry bar, blank key, wire, or the like). If you use masterwork thieves' tools, you gain a +2 circumstance bonus on the check.

Check: The DC for opening a lock varies from 20 to 40, depending on the quality of the lock, as given on the table below.

Lock	DC
Very simple lock	20
Average lock	25
Good lock	30
Amazing lock	40

Action: Opening a lock is a full-round action.

Special: If you have the Nimble Fingers feat, you get a +2 bonus on Open Lock checks.

Untrained: You cannot pick locks untrained.

The information following the name of the skill tells you that this is a Dexterity-based skill, so your character's Dexterity modifier applies to Open Lock attempts. *Trained Only* means that you can't try to use this skill unless your character has at least 1 rank in Open Lock. The information under *Check* tells you what sort of Difficulty Class various applications of this skill have; this is the target number you'll have to hit with a roll of 1d20 + your skill ranks + your Dex modifier in order to open a lock of that sort. *Action* tells you how long it takes to use the skill, and *Special* lets you know about special modifiers or circumstances that affect the skill.

Using skills

To use one of your character's skills, you make a *skill check*. A skill check is a twenty-sided die (d20) roll modified by your character's skill ranks, the key ability score for the skill, and any special modifiers that might apply. The most common special modifier is an *armor check penalty* — a negative modifier to certain movement-based skills for wearing heavy armor. If a skill is affected by the armor check penalty, the skill description will clearly state so. In addition, a number of spells and magic items improve certain types of skill checks, and there may be various circumstance modifiers the DM decides to apply.

Your character doesn't always have to have training in a skill to try to use it. In fact, it's not uncommon at all for you to have to make an untrained skill check. Any character can try to climb a wall, balance on a narrow ledge, or make a jump, even if he or she doesn't have a single rank in the Balance, Climb, or Jump skills. You simply have no skill ranks to add to the skill check, and so you have to live with whatever modifier your character's ability score, magic, or circumstances provide. You might succeed with the skill check despite your character's lack of training, provided the task is relatively easy or you get lucky with your d20 roll.

Skill Check = d20 + skill ranks + ability modifier + special modifiers (if any)

Your skill check yields a result that might range from less than 0 (you rolled poorly on a skill that your character had few or no ranks in and significant negative modifiers) to 30 or better (you rolled well on a skill in which your character has a lot of ranks or significant positive modifiers for his or her ability scores and magic).

The DM compares your skill check result to a *Difficulty Class (DC)* or target number appropriate to the task your character is trying to accomplish. Difficulty Class works a lot like Armor Class — it's a target number you're trying to reach or exceed by rolling a d20 and adding the appropriate modifiers. For something easy, the DC might only be 5 or 10. For something fiendishly hard, the DC might be 35, 40, or even higher. In fact, it might be completely impossible for your character to succeed at some tasks; no human is going to leap a 100-foot wide crevasse (a DC 100 Jump check, in case you're wondering) without a lot of magical help.

The skill descriptions in the *Player's Handbook* list specific DCs for all sorts of things you might have your character try to do with that skill. Your DM uses these skill descriptions to set the DC for any specific skill use you want your character to attempt. Sometimes your DM just has to take a best guess at how hard something is, because you can try almost anything in a D&D game. If you want your character to leap down from a rooftop and land astride a galloping horse streaking by below, it's a Jump check of some kind, but you won't find "jump into the saddle of a galloping horse" on the DC table in the Jump skill. That's why you have a Dungeon Master, so someone can take a shot at adjudicating things the rules don't cover.

Table 15-1 shows some sample DCs.

Table 15-1	Sample Skill DCs
DC	**Example of a Task**
5	Climb a knotted rope with the Climb skill
10	Disable a simple trap with the Disable Device skill
15	Stabilize a dying character with the Heal skill
20	Balance on a surface less than two inches wide with the Balance skill
25	Leap 25 feet with the Jump skill
30	Notice a well-hidden secret door with the Search skill

Chapter 4 of the *Player's Handbook* has long descriptions of every skill, including a number of sample DCs for tasks in each skill.

Choosing your character's skills

When you create a 1st-level character, you gain a certain number of skill points you can use to buy skill ranks. The number of skill points you gain depends on your character's class, your character's Intelligence bonus, and whether or not you're playing a human — humans gain more skill points than characters of other races. As your character gains levels, you gain additional skill points to add to existing skills or to buy entirely new skills.

After you know the number of skill points you've got to spend, you're ready to buy your character's skills. There's one more thing you need to know before you start buying skill ranks: Some skills cost double. Take a look at Table 4-2 in the *Player's Handbook*, page 63. You'll see that each skill is coded as "C" or "cc" for each character class. This stands for class skills (C) and cross-class (cc) skills. When you buy a class skill, you get 1 rank for every skill point you spend. When you buy a cross-class skill, you must pay 2 skill points for 1 skill rank.

This distinction between class skills and cross-class skills also governs the maximum number of skill ranks your character is allowed to have in a single skill at any given time.

✔ For a class skill, you're allowed to have a number of ranks equal to your character's level +3. For example, a 1st-level character can have up to 4 ranks in any one class skill; a 6th-level character could have up to 9 ranks in any one class skill.

✔ For cross-class skills, your character can have only half as many ranks as with class skills. For example, 1st-level character can have 2 ranks in a cross-class skill, and a 7th-level character can have 5 ranks in a cross-class skill.

Six key skills

Not all skills are created equal. While skills such as Heal or Use Magic Device *sound* like they should be pretty important in the game, in practice you'll fall back on your character's class abilities and spells to deal with most situations involving those skills. Here's a short list of six skills with key game effects that you won't want to ignore:

✔ **Bluff:** Rogues can use the Bluff skill to manufacture sneak attack opportunities with the Feint in Combat skill application. It's also a great skill for your character to use to talk his or her way past suspicious guards or getting into places he or she shouldn't be.

✔ **Concentration:** If your character is a spellcaster, you should buy up the Concentration skill as high as you can for the first ten levels or so of your character's career. Concentration lets spellcasters safely cast spells while enemies are standing right next to them; without this skill, spellcasters could find themselves in situations where they don't dare to try to cast spells in the middle of big fights.

✔ **Diplomacy:** This is a great catch-all skill for convincing nonplayer characters (NPCs) to help your character out, leave him or her alone, or give your character something he or she needs.

✔ **Hide:** There are two sneaking-up-on-people skills: Hide and Move Silently. Hide is probably the more useful of the two. If you're playing a rogue, you can use your character's Hide skill to set up sneak attack opportunities (or avoid fights altogether, if you prefer).

✔ **Spot:** There are two I'm-hard-to-sneak-up-on skills: Listen and Spot. Spot is probably the more useful one. If you don't like monsters surprising your character, take some ranks in Spot so your character will see 'em coming.

✔ **Tumble:** This might be the best skill in the game. If your character has a lot of ranks in Tumble, he or she can move around a raging battle with impunity, rolling and leaping right past enemies who otherwise would get a lot of free attacks on your character. Rogues who like to sneak attack their enemies find that Tumble is essential for flanking their enemies and making sneak attacks possible. It's also a great technique for getting away from trouble.

Here's the quick summary of the skill purchasing process:

1. **Determine the base skill points per level for your character class, as follows:**

   - 2 skill points/level: Cleric, fighter, paladin, sorcerer, wizard

   - 4 skill points/level: Barbarian, druid, monk

   - 6 skill points/level: Bard, ranger

   - 8 skill points/level: Rogue

2. **Modify your base skill points per level by your character's Intelligence score modifier.**

   For example, a wizard with an Intelligence score of 15 gains 4 skill points per level: 2 skill points per level for being a wizard, +2 skill points per level for his or her 15 Int. You never get less than 1 skill point per level, even if your character is dumb as a post. You can find this information in Table 15-2, in the Skill Points/Level row for your character's Intelligence score.

3. **Add 1 skill point per level if your character is a human.**

4. **Calculate your character's starting skill points.**

   Your character's starting skill points at 1st level are equal to 4 times the number of skill points per level. For example, if in the last step you calculated that your character would receive 4 skill points per level, you multiply this by four to determine you have 16 skill points to spend on your character's skills at 1st level. (You can find this information in Table 15-2, in the Starting Skill Points row for your character's Intelligence score.)

   At 2nd level and each following level, your character gains skill points equal to his or her class's skill points per level, modified as described above for Intelligence score and race.

5. **Buy your character's skills.**

   Check our quick-pick skill packages (later in this chapter) for a fast set of reasonable skill picks. Or, if you prefer, go skill-shopping on Table 4-2: Skills on page 63 of the *Player's Handbook*.

   You pay 1 skill point per skill rank for class skills, and 2 skill points per skill rank for cross-class skills. Remember that the maximum number of skill ranks your character can have in any one skill is equal to his or her level +3 (or half that number for a cross-class skill).

Table 15-2	Starting Skill Points and Skill Points per Level				
Int Score		*2 Skill Points/ Level*	*4 Skill Points/ Level*	*6 Skill Points/ Level*	*8 Skill Points/ Level*
6–7	Starting skill points	4 (8)	8 (12)	16 (20)	24 (28)
	Skill points/level	1 (2)	2 (3)	4 (5)	6 (7)
8–9	Starting skill points	4 (8)	12 (16)	20 (24)	28 (32)
	Skill points/level	1 (2)	3 (4)	5 (6)	7 (8)
10–11	Starting skill points	8 (12)	16 (20)	24 (28)	32 (36)
	Skill points/level	2 (3)	4 (5)	6 (7)	8 (9)
12–13	Starting skill points	12 (16)	20 (24)	28 (32)	36 (40)
	Skill points/level	3 (4)	5 (6)	7 (8)	9 (10)
14–15	Starting skill points	16 (20)	24 (28)	32 (36)	40 (44)
	Skill points/level	4 (5)	6 (7)	8 (9)	10 (11)
16–17	Starting skill points	20 (24)	28 (32)	36 (40)	44 (48)
	Skill points/level	5 (6)	7 (8)	9 (10)	11 (12)
18–19	Starting skill points	24 (28)	32 (36)	40 (44)	48 (52)
	Skill points/level	6 (7)	8 (9)	10 (11)	12 (13)

(...) The number in parenthesis shows how many skill points a human character of that Intelligence score and class earns.

If you ever want to figure out how many skill points a higher-level character has available, you don't have to add them up level by level. Try this simple formula:

Total skill points = (level +3) × (modified skill pts/level)

For example, say you're creating a 5th-level human fighter with an Intelligence of 13. That character's total skill points available equals (5+3) × (2+1 Int modifier +1 human bonus), or 32 skill points.

Be warned: This technique doesn't work if your character's Intelligence changes over the course of the levels in question. For example, wizards often choose to increase their Intelligence scores at every opportunity, so you'll need to be more careful when figuring out how many skill points that character has.

Quick Picks: Using Skill Packages

The Skills table in the *Player's Handbook* is intimidating. In order to help you separate the useful from the distracting, we've created a set of skill packages for each class.

To use these packages, you need to determine how many skill points per level your character gains; refer to the "Choosing your character's skills" section, earlier in this chapter. Tables 15-3 through 15-6 sum up the skill packages. The 1st-Level Skill Buy column is what you use to spend your character's 1st-level skill points. The Skill Improvement column offers some advice on how to spend skill points your character receives as he or she gains levels.

Fighter skill package

A fighter is one of those characters who just doesn't care that much about skills. Your character lives or dies by fighting ability, not skill checks. However, your character does receive a small number of skill points to spend, and there's no reason not to spend them intelligently. Table 15-3 gives you some examples of useful skills to choose for a fighter.

Table 15-3	Fighter Skill Package	
Modified Skill Points per Level	**1st-Level Skill Buy**	**Skill Improvement per Level**
1	Climb 1, Ride 1, Spot 1*	Climb 1, Ride 1, or Spot ½*
2	Climb 2, Ride 2, Spot 2*	Spot ½* and Climb 1 or Ride 1
3	Climb 2, Jump 4, Ride 2, Spot 2*	Climb 1, Ride 1, and Spot ½*
4	Balance 2*, Climb 2, Jump 4, Ride 2, Spot 2*	Climb 1, Jump 1, Ride 1, and Spot ½*
5	Balance 2*, Climb 4, Jump 4, Ride 4, Spot 2*	Balance ½*, Climb 1, Jump 1, Ride 1, and Spot ½*

* Cross-class skills cost 2 skill points per rank.

The Ride skill is important only if you think you might eventually be interested in exploring mounted combat. If your game is strictly confined to dungeons, or if you prefer to simply have your character jump off his or her horse at the first sign of trouble, you won't ever need to put any ranks in Ride. Try buying more ranks in Climb or Jump instead (or, if you're already planning on maxing out your character's Climb and Jump skills, pick up a skill like Intimidate).

Spot is useful for avoiding ugly surprises, such as monster ambushes. Even though this is a cross-class skill for a fighter and you'll pay 2 skill points per rank, you should make an effort to improve your character's Spot skill over time. It's one of the few skills that might actually mean the difference between life and death.

Speaking of life and death, Balance and Swim are not bad skills to have a couple of ranks in. A fighter doesn't often have to make Balance or Swim checks, but these tend to be skills that come up in all-or-nothing situations. In other words, the consequences of failing a critical Balance check (to cross a swaying rope bridge over a bottomless pit, for example) might be lethal. If your character has some skill points to spare, it's worth a small investment.

Rogue skill package

As a rogue, your character is the master of skills. They are absolutely essential to your success in playing a rogue character. You should take some time and bone up on the Skills chapter in the *Player's Handbook*, because your familiarity with your character's skills will directly impact how well you are playing that character. You'd expect someone playing a sorcerer to know something about his character's spells — if you're playing a rogue, you should be just as conversant about your character's skills. Table 15-4 shows a selection of useful skills for a rogue.

Table 15-4	**Rogue Skill Package**	
Modified Skill Points per Level	*1st-Level Skill Buy*	*Skill Improvement per Level*
7	Climb 4, Disable Device 4, Hide 4, Move Silently 4, Open Lock 4, Search 4, Tumble 4	All skills +1 rank per level
8	Climb 4, Disable Device 4, Hide 4, Move Silently 4, Open Lock 4, Search 4, Spot 4, Tumble 4	All skills +1 rank per level
9	Climb 4, Disable Device 4, Hide 4, Listen 4, Move Silently 4, Open Lock 4, Search 4, Spot 4, Tumble 4	All skills +1 rank per level

(continued)

Table 15-4 *(continued)*

Modified Skill Points per Level	1st-Level Skill Buy	Skill Improvement per Level
10	Balance 4, Climb 4, Disable Device 4, Hide 4, Listen 4, Move Silently 4, Open Lock 4, Search 4, Spot 4, Tumble 4	All skills +1 rank per level
11	Balance 4, Bluff 4, Climb 4, Disable Device 4, Hide 4, Listen 4, Move Silently 4, Open Lock 4, Search 4, Spot 4, Tumble 4	All skills +1 rank per level
12	Balance 4, Bluff 4, Climb 4, Disable Device 4, Hide 4, Listen 4, Move Silently 4, Open Lock 4, Search 4, Sleight of Hand 4, Spot 4, Tumble 4	All skills +1 rank per level

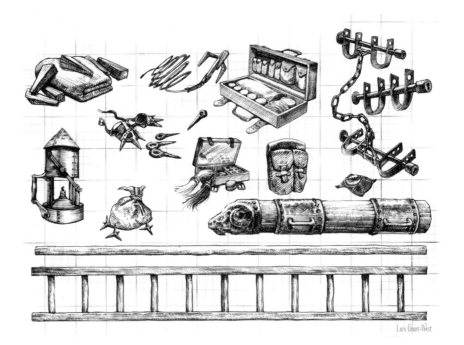

Lars Grant-West

Rogues can do three things that no other class can really manage: find traps, disable traps, and open locked doors. Consequently, our recommendation is that you max out your rogue's skill ranks in Search, Disable Device, and Open Lock. If your rogue isn't covering these important functions for the adventuring party, no one is. Most other tasks can be handled by other characters with the right spells or the right tactics, but these skills are very hard to fake. Spend the skill points and get good at them.

After those three key skills, you have a lot more discretion. Hide and Move Silently are important skills for your character to have, because a rogue is expected to be able to sneak into places without being seen or heard. Spot and Tumble are important for setting up fights and tactical movement during a battle. For the rest of your character's skills, you should decide early on if you want to play a fast-talker or a ninja, as follows:

✔ Fast-talking rogues spend skill points on people skills such as Gather Information, Intimidate, Sense Motive, Diplomacy, or even Use Magic Device. Those are very useful in many out-of-dungeon encounters and investigations, but don't bother with this track unless your character's Charisma score is 10 or better. If you've got a less-than-charismatic character, don't sink skill points into making him or her more likable.

✔ Ninja wannabes are those rogues who totally give up on interaction skills and instead choose getting-into-places skills such as Climb, Balance, Jump, and Swim. If you'd rather not talk to the bad guys, or if your character's Charisma is pretty crummy, spend the skill points on movement skills instead.

Sorcerer skill package

Skills? Bah! Sorcerers have magic. Skills are merely an afterthought for a sorcerer, with the exception of the Concentration skill. You will want to improve your character's Concentration as much as you can. Table 15-5 provides a selection of useful skills for a sorcerer.

Table 15-5	Sorcerer Skill Package	
Modified Skill Points per Level	*1st-Level Skill Buy*	*Skill Improvement per Level*
1	Concentration 4	Concentration 1; or Spot ½*
2	Concentration 4, Spot 2*	Concentration 1 and Spellcraft 1; or Spot 1*

(continued)

Table 15-5 *(continued)*

Modified Skill Points per Level	1st-Level Skill Buy	Skill Improvement per Level
3	Concentration 4, Spellcraft 4, Spot 2*	Concentration 1, Spellcraft 1, and Spot ½*
4	Bluff 4, Concentration 4, Spellcraft 4, Spot 2*	Concentration 1, Knowledge (arcana) 1, Spellcraft 1, and Spot ½*
5	Bluff 4, Concentration 4, Knowledge (arcana) 4, Spellcraft 4, Spot 2*	Bluff 1, Concentration 1, Knowledge (arcana) 1, Spellcraft 1, and Spot ½*

* Cross-class skills cost 2 skill points per rank.

Other than Concentration, which is clearly your first skill priority, your character really doesn't *need* any skills at all. Spend those skill points as you like.

Spot is useful for not getting surprised at the beginning of a fight, so if you don't know what else to do with your character's skill points, you could do worse than to buy up the Spot skill. Bluff is an opportunistic skill for a sorcerer; because your character has a great Charisma score (he or she is a sorcerer, after all), you might as well add a few ranks in Bluff, and look for chances to put your character's high Charisma to work.

Knowledge (arcana) and Spellcraft are generally expected of a sorcerer, because he or she is an arcane spellcaster. If your character doesn't know anything about these skills, no other character in the party will. But you don't need to buy those skills if you don't have many skill points to spare.

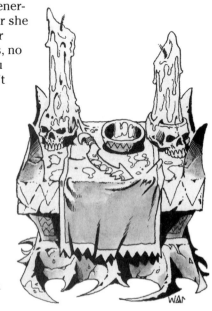

You may want to invest in Diplomacy and Gather Information if you have the skill points to spare. Even though these aren't class skills for your character, it's not unusual for a sorcerer to serve as the spokesperson for the adventuring party (again, that high Charisma comes in handy). If your character is the one the party will expect to persuade the frost giant chieftain to let them go instead of cooking them for dinner, you may want to pad that skill check with a little training in sweet-talking.

Cleric skill package

Like the sorcerer, a cleric doesn't rely much on skills. A cleric prefers to use spells and combat to solve problems, and skills are just the finishing details of your character. Don't be afraid to spend some skill points on things that just strike your fancy, because your cleric doesn't need to be good at very many skills. Table 15-6 describes the skills most useful for a cleric.

Table 15-6	Cleric Skill Package	
Modified Skill Points per Level	**1st-Level Skill Buy**	**Skill Improvement per Level**
1	Concentration 4	Concentration 1 or Knowledge (religion) 1
2	Concentration 4, Knowledge (religion) 4	Concentration 1 and Knowledge (religion) 1
3	Concentration 4, Knowledge (religion) 4, Spot 2*	Concentration 1, Knowledge (religion) 1, and Spot ½*
4	Concentration 4, Diplomacy 4, Knowledge (religion) 4, Spot 2*	Concentration 1, Diplomacy 1, Knowledge (religion) 1, Spot ½*
5	Concentration 4, Diplomacy 4, Knowledge (religion) 4, Spellcraft 4, Spot 2*	Concentration 1, Diplomacy 1, Knowledge (religion) 1, Spellcraft 1, Spot ½*

* Cross-class skills cost 2 skill points per rank.

Because your character is a spellcaster, Concentration is a key skill — perhaps even more so than it is for the sorcerer, because a cleric is expected to be in the thick of the fight from time to time. Your second skill priority is Knowledge (religion), at least until your character reaches 5 skill ranks in that skill. The reason for this is that 5 ranks of Knowledge (religion) confers a +2 synergy bonus on checks to turn undead. It's not often that a skill can provide a concrete benefit to a combat action like turning undead.

You may be tempted to take a lot of ranks in the Heal skill, because everybody knows that clerics are the master healers in the game — but you don't need to do that unless you really have spent all the other skill points you want to. Most of the time, your character can cast the *cure minor wounds* and *cure light wounds* spells to automatically stabilize dying characters, and that's the task the Heal skill is most useful for.

As with any other character, you'll do well to buy a rank or two in Spot if you can, but don't feel like you have to. Because your character is a cleric, he or she probably has a high Wisdom score, and that means he or she will be pretty good at Spot checks even if you didn't put any ranks in Spot.

Finally, you may want to pay for a couple of ranks in Balance, Jump, Swim, or Tumble. Most clerics wear heavy armor and don't have much in the way of a Dexterity score, which means that fairly easy Balance checks are murderously hard for them. The consequences of a failed Balance check or Swim check might be catastrophic, so you may want to invest a few skill points in these movement skills against the day your character will need to make a key check or die horribly.

Chapter 16

Choosing Armor, Weapons, and Gear

In This Chapter

▶ Choosing the optimal weapon

▶ Suiting up with the best armor

▶ Picking out adventuring gear

▶ Improving your character's weapons and armor

You've picked out your character's race, class, feats, and skills. You know who your character is and what he or she can do. But there's one more component your character needs — stuff. Just because a character knows how to swing a dire flail doesn't mean that he or she is going to start out walking around with one. All the training in the world won't do your character any good if you don't actually take a few minutes to equip him or her for adventuring.

In this chapter, we tell you about the considerations you should keep in mind when choosing your character's equipment, and we show you some quick optimal weapon and armor picks so that you can make good starting choices and begin playing fast.

Chapter 7 in the *Player's Handbook* tells you everything you could possibly want to know about your choices in mundane adventuring gear, ranging from weapons and armor to handy things like rope, grappling hooks, lanterns, and spell component pouches. Magic items are defined in the *Dungeon Master's Guide*, Chapter 7.

Going Shopping

You've got two basic options for equipping your character: Choose a starting package, or do it yourself. Taking a *starting package* — a list of preselected gear and weapons — is the quick and easy way to go. If you'd like to try this option, go to the *Player's Handbook*. Each of the character class descriptions in Chapter 3 of the *Player's Handbook* ends with a starting package.

On the other hand, if you want to do it yourself, you have to peruse the various tables in Chapter 7 of the *Player's Handbook*, deciding what you want. You start with a sum of money based on your character's class (see Table 7-1 on page 111 of the *Player's Handbook*), equal to 150 gold pieces (gp) for a fighter, 125 gp for a cleric or rogue, or 75 gp for a sorcerer. These amounts are average. Frankly, picking out equipment yourself can be a little tedious, and many of the minor details, such as rations and bedroll, are things that are never going to matter in many normal DUNGEONS & DRAGONS games.

If possible, you should make sure that you buy the following equipment for your character:

- A melee weapon (for example, a sword, mace, or dagger)
- A ranged weapon (bow or crossbow)
- The best suit of class-appropriate armor you can afford
- A shield (if you're playing a cleric or fighter)
- Class-specific items (a holy symbol, spell component pouch, or set of thieves' tools)
- A light source such as torches, lantern and oil, or a sunrod
- A backpack with rope, rations, waterskin, and anything else you think your character would need

The starting packages provide a serviceable set of gear for each class, but you may want to customize your selection somewhat. For example, the fighter starting package provides a greatsword and scale mail. The greatsword's a perfectly fine weapon, but it's a two-handed weapon, which means your fighter is passing up on the opportunity to use a shield. You may prefer for your character to have a little less offense and a little more defense. So trade down if you like. If you look on Table 7-5: Weapons in the *Player's Handbook*,

Money in D&D

The basic unit of currency in D&D is the *gold piece*, abbreviated as gp. When you see something that costs 15 gp, that's 15 gold pieces. Beneath gold pieces are silver pieces (sp); one gold is worth ten silver pieces. Under silver pieces are copper pieces (one silver is worth ten copper pieces), but by that point you really shouldn't care. Not many players actually keep track of how many copper pieces are in their characters' pockets. Try this little mnemonic: Gold pieces are dollars, silver pieces are dimes, and copper pieces are pennies. So if you have 4 gp, 6 sp, and 15 cp, it's like $4.75.

Equipping higher-level characters

If you are creating a higher-level character to join an existing game, you'll find that the agonizing decisions of the typical impoverished 1st-level character are simply a thing of the past. High-level characters typically have thousands of gold pieces worth of equipment, including magic weapons, armor, potions, and other such wondrous possessions.

To equip a higher-level character, you should ask your DM how much money your character has to spend. Then ask for the DM's help in picking out suitable magic items for your character. Remember, if your character doesn't have a magic weapon or magic armor, you'll need to pick out nonmagical gear to serve. Make sure that you review the bulleted list in the "Going Shopping" section and equip your character with magical or nonmagical versions of everything on the list.

---

you'll see that the greatsword costs 50 gp. You can trade down to a longsword, which only costs 15 gp, then go to Table 7-6: Armor and buy a heavy steel shield for 20 gp. Take everything else in the package, and you'll have 15 gp left in change.

Choosing the Right Weapon

For most characters, choosing the right weapons is an important part of building your combat strategy and creating an unforgettable character. Weapons have three important characteristics, as follows:

✔ **Proficiency:** This characteristic describes how complex the weapon is to use. Weapons are organized into simple, martial, or exotic categories. *Simple weapons* are weapons that characters of almost any class can swing without penalty, *martial weapons* require some training (for example, being a fighter), and *exotic weapons* are weapons that no character is proficient in without taking an Exotic Weapon Proficiency feat to learn to use that weapon. (The exception is that certain classes and races gain the ability to use specific exotic weapons as a class or race feature; for example, as a class feature, rogues are proficient with hand crossbows.)

✔ **Type:** Type describes the weapon's basic role and use. Weapons are divided into melee weapons and ranged weapons; melee weapons are divided again into light, one-handed, and two-handed weapons. A character can use a light weapon or one-handed weapon in one hand and still use a shield, but your character can't use a shield and a two-handed weapon at the same time.

✔ **Damage:** This is the fun part. Weapon damage is derived from two components: the weapon's base damage, which is a number ranging from 1d3 to 2d6, and its critical range and multiple. You want a weapon that has a high base damage, a wide critical range, and a high critical multiple. A wide critical range such as 18–20 or 19–20 means that you'll score critical hits more often. A high critical multiple, such as ×3 or ×4, means that when you do score a critical hit, you'll triple or quadruple the damage you deal.

In general, exotic weapons are better than martial weapons, which are better than simple weapons. And two-handed weapons deal out a lot more damage than one-handed weapons. Table 16-1 sums the best weapon choices, depending on your character's class, whether you're after a one-handed or two-handed weapon, and whether you are willing to spend a feat on a weapon proficiency or not.

Table 16-1	Optimal Melee Weapon Choices	
Class	*One-Handed Weapons*	*Two-Handed Weapons*
Fighter	Longsword (no feat required), bastard sword (Exotic Weapon Proficiency feat required), or dwarven waraxe (Exotic Weapon Proficiency required, unless the character is a dwarf)	Greatsword (no feat required) or spiked chain (Exotic Weapon Proficiency feat required)
Rogue	Rapier (no feat required) or longsword (Martial Weapon Proficiency feat required, unless the character is an elf)	Greatsword (Martial Weapon Proficiency feat required)
Sorcerer	Heavy mace (no feat required) or longsword (Martial Weapon Proficiency feat required, unless the character is an elf)	Spear (no feat required) or Greatsword (Martial Weapon Proficiency feat required)
Cleric	Heavy mace (no feat required) or longsword (Martial Weapon Proficiency feat required, unless the character is an elf or chooses the War domain)	Spear (no feat required) or Greatsword (Martial Weapon Proficiency feat required, unless the character chooses the War domain)

Dwarves enjoy some special advantages with weapon choices. For dwarves, the dwarven waraxe and dwarven urgrosh (a spearlike weapon) are treated as martial weapons, not exotic weapons. That means that a dwarf fighter can choose the dwarven waraxe — a weapon every bit as good as a bastard sword — without spending an Exotic Weapon Proficiency feat. Similarly, a dwarf cleric, rogue, or sorcerer who takes a Martial Weapon Proficiency feat might as well choose the dwarven waraxe instead of the longsword.

Elves also have an edge with weapon choices. All elves, regardless of class, are proficient with the longsword, rapier, longbow, and shortbow. If you're playing an elf fighter, this doesn't help at all. But if you're playing an elf rogue, sorcerer, or cleric, you should definitely choose longsword and longbow for your character's weapons. It doesn't even cost a feat.

Fighter weapons

A fighter pretty much has the pick of weapons. Fighters are proficient with almost every weapon, and the fighter class has the feats to spare if you decide you want your fighter to become proficient in something exotic.

If you don't spend an Exotic Weapon Proficiency feat, the best choices are the longsword (if you want your character to fight one-handed and keep another hand free for a shield or second weapon) or greatsword (if you want your character to deal more damage at the cost of some defense). The battleaxe and warhammer are good replacements for the longsword, if you prefer. The greataxe or falchion (a big two-handed scimitar, in case you're wondering) are reasonable substitutions for the greatsword.

If you're willing to spend a feat on weapon proficiencies, buy an Exotic Weapon Proficiency for the bastard sword or spiked chain. The bastard sword effectively gives +1 damage above the longsword. The spiked chain deals less damage than the greatsword, but your character will gain *reach* — the ability to strike foes who aren't standing next to him or her. That's a huge tactical advantage. The spiked chain also can be used for a number of fancy maneuvers such as trip attacks.

For a ranged weapon, buy a composite longbow as soon as you can, and get one sized for your character's Strength bonus. No other missile weapon in the game comes close in terms of rate of fire and damage potential to the composite longbow.

Barbarians, paladins, and rangers all have access to the same weapons as the fighter, and these classes face the same decisions.

Rogue weapons

A rogue's weapon choices are somewhat limited compared to the fighter's choices, but that's okay. Rogues have some decent weapons available to them, and to be honest, whatever weapons rogues employ in battle aren't anywhere near as important as their sneak attack capability. When your character is dealing 20 points of damage from a sneak attack, the difference between a weapon that averages 3 points a hit or 4 points a hit just isn't that important.

If you don't want to spend a feat on your rogue's weapon choices, go with the rapier. If you're playing a melee-oriented rogue, you'll probably want your character to fight with rapier and dagger pretty quickly, so don't tie up his or her second hand on a mediocre weapon such as a spear.

If you're willing to pick up a Martial Weapon Proficiency feat, learn to use the longsword. It's the most efficient and effective one-handed weapon. If your rogue happens to be an elf, he or she can just use the longsword right from the start; all elves, regardless of class, know how to use the longsword.

For a ranged weapon, your choices are the light crossbow or shortbow. At higher levels, the shortbow will give your character a better rate of fire than a light crossbow.

Cleric weapons

Weapons are tough for clerics. As a cleric, your character wants to be handy in a fight, but he or she begins with proficiency only in simple weapons. A mace, morningstar, or spear just doesn't deal the same damage that a similarly sized sword or axe deals, so you're a little bit behind the eight-ball in your character's weapon selection. You should seriously consider using a feat so your cleric can become proficient in a better weapon.

If you don't want to spend a feat, choose the heavy mace for a one-handed weapon or the spear for a two-handed weapon. You'll probably be happier with a shield and a one-handed weapon. If you choose to buy a Martial Weapon Proficiency feat, the longsword is your best choice.

If you want a free weapon boost, choose the War domain as one of your clerics two domains (see Chapter 17 for more about domains and spells). Choosing the War domain grants your cleric a free proficiency in his or her deity's favored weapon (along with a free Weapon Focus feat in that weapon, too!)

Take a light crossbow for a ranged weapon, but don't expect to get much use out of it. Most clerics have better things to do in combat than take potshots with a crossbow.

Sorcerer weapons

Sorcerers are restricted to a pretty short list of weak weapons. But you know what? You don't care if you're playing a sorcerer. Most of a sorcerer's actions will be taken up with casting spells, so toting around an effective melee weapon just isn't necessary for this class.

If you really want to, you can take a Martial Weapon Proficiency feat to get your character's hands on a better weapon, but here's the deal: A sorcerer is never going to make melee attacks, so don't waste a feat on this. (If you happen to be playing an elf sorcerer, though, your character is proficient with the longsword as a racial advantage — so your character might as well carry one.)

Take a light crossbow for a ranged weapon. Early in their careers, sorcerers might find it useful to hang back from a fight and shoot when they run out of spells. Hopefully, your character will have magic wands for that job after he or she gains a level or two.

Wizards have the same weapon choices as sorcerers.

Choosing Armor

The other important decision you need to make in equipping your character is what sort of armor you intend him or her to wear. Unlike weapons, you'll have an easier time changing your mind about armor — there are no feats that require you to choose a specific type of armor to be good at.

There are two basic decisions you need to make when considering your choice of armor: shield or no shield, and speed versus protection.

Shield or no shield?

If you're playing a cleric or fighter, you need to decide if you want your character to carry a shield or not. Shields are a great way to improve Armor Class by a couple of points, but by carrying a shield, your character is giving up some offense. Instead of carrying a shield, your character could be swinging a two-handed weapon or even fighting with a weapon in each hand. Many of the most combat-effective character builds revolve around fighting with two weapons.

There really isn't a right answer here. As they say, the best defense is a good offense; building your character to dish out damage instead of taking it means that he or she will kill enemies faster and give them fewer chances to put damage on him or her. On the other hand, you'll find that even 1 or 2 points of extra Armor Class often results in a disproportionate reduction in the amount of damage your character takes from enemy attacks. It's really up to you.

Speed versus protection

Heavy armor slows your character down, but protects him or her better from attack. When you're weighing armor choices, you need to decide if you care about having your character's movement reduced by wearing heavy armor.

Once again, this is largely a matter of personal choice. However, there is an important factor you should consider: Heavy armor limits the defensive value of a high Dexterity score. This is reflected in the armor's Max Dex value. If your character has a high Dexterity, you should think twice before you choose a suit of armor that slows your character down and prevents him or her from getting the full advantage of that high Dexterity score. Similarly, if your character has a poor Dexterity score, you might as well choose the heaviest armor you can find, because your Dexterity won't be helping your AC anyway.

Table 16-2 provides an overview of the best armor choices by class. The rows for beginning characters assume that you only have 50 gp to spend on armor. After your character has had a successful adventure or two, he or she can afford better armor, so you should upgrade to the armor choices listed in the advanced character rows.

Table 16-2	Optimal Armor Choices	
Class	*Fast Armor*	*Slow Armor*
Beginning characters		
Fighter	Studded leather	Scale mail
Rogue	Leather	—
Sorcerer	None	—
Cleric	Studded leather	Scale mail
Advanced characters		
Fighter	Chain shirt	Full plate
Rogue	Chain shirt	—
Sorcerer	None	—
Cleric	Chain shirt	Full plate

Fast armor choices are types of armor that don't penalize movement. *Slow* armor choices reduce movement to ⅔ or ¾ normal; if you're playing a human, your character's base speed is 30 feet per move, but if the character is wearing heavy armor, he or she can only cover 20 feet per move. (Halflings and gnomes are reduced from 20 feet to 15 feet.)

Armor choices for everyone else

Players who have characters of other classes have some different choices to weigh when picking out armor. Here are a few quick guidelines:

✔ **Barbarian:** Choose the fast fighter option.

✔ **Bard:** Same as the rogue.

✔ **Druid:** Druids should choose leather armor or hide armor, depending on whether you

want your character to be fast or slow (but better protected).

✔ **Monk:** Don't wear armor, it interferes with a monk's special abilities.

✔ **Paladin:** Same as fighter.

✔ **Ranger:** Choose the fast fighter option.

✔ **Wizard:** Same as sorcerer.

If you're playing a dwarf, you don't care about the distinction between fast and slow armor types. Dwarves get to ignore the movement penalty for wearing heavy armor, so unless you're playing a dwarf with a very high Dexterity score, your character might as well wear the heaviest armor he or she can afford.

Everything Else Your Character Is Carrying

Your choices of armor and weapons are important, but they're not all that's involved in equipping your character. Dungeon exploration requires a lot of specialized gear, and you'll want to make sure that your character is carrying everything he or she will need to survive in the hostile environment of a monster-filled dungeon.

Don't forget that you've got a ready-made equipment package waiting for you in each character class description in Chapter 3 of the *Player's Handbook*. Even if you decide to shop for your character yourself in Chapter 7 of the *Player's Handbook*, you might want to take a look at the recommended equipment packages for your character as a source of ideas.

Watch out! You might not realize it, but your character class might demand specialized gear to accomplish its basic purpose. There are three prime examples of this:

✔ Clerics require a holy symbol (1 gp or 25 gp) in order to cast most of their spells.

✔ Rogues require a set of thieves' tools (30 gp) to avoid taking a penalty on Disable Device and Open Lock skill checks.

✔ Sorcerers require a spell component pouch (5 gp) in order to cast many of their spells.

At the very minimum, make sure your character's miscellaneous equipment includes the noted item if you're playing a member of that class. Not many DMs will check you on this, but if your DM does, you need to be able to prove that yes, your sorcerer is carrying the material components for the *jump* spell, and no, he or she is not going to get stuck on the wrong side of the chasm when the angry troll attacks.

Useful gear

These things won't make your character fight better, but they're darned useful for successful dungeon exploration. Every adventurer should carry a light source, a rope, and a useful tool or two such as a grappling hook, crowbar, hammer and pitons, flint and steel, and so on. Not everyone in the party needs to carry one of each of these things — divvy out these implements among the party.

A light source is particularly important, because most races can't see a thing in complete darkness. You've got four choices: torch, lantern, sunrod, or magic (a *light* spell, *daylight* spell, or *continual flame* spell). Magic is a good emergency measure, but unless you want your character to prepare a lot of *light* spells (and you don't — your character has better things to do with spells), you'll find that it just doesn't last long enough.

Of the nonmagical alternatives, torches are heavy and don't light up a very large area, but they're cheap. Lanterns are more expensive but provide better light and usually last longer. In addition, you can set all kinds of things on fire with a few flasks of lamp oil. Trust us. We've seen it done. Your best non-magical alternative is probably the sunrod. Sunrods are alchemical devices that provide a bright, long-lasting light without the need for oil. They're expensive (2 gp apiece) but give six hours of illumination at a time. You'll find them on page 128 of the *Player's Handbook*.

Oh, and one more thing: *Don't forget the rope.* Every member of the party should carry at least 50 feet, preferably 100 feet or more, of rope. Too many dungeons feature difficult vertical obstacles to skimp on the rope. With enough rope, only one character in the party needs to be a good climber — everybody else can follow the best climber after he or she fixes a rope in place.

Write it down and forget it

Ever been camping? If so, you've probably got half an idea of what your character likely goes through every day when he or she is off exploring vast wildernesses or delving for weeks into a fearsome dungeon. Anybody going away from civilization for a few days carries something to sleep on or in, food, water, camp tools, and so on.

So, just for form's sake, you should probably write a few things on your character sheet like, "backpack, bedroll, 3 days' rations, 2 waterskins, flint and steel." (Altogether, they cost 6 gp, 1 sp, and weigh 18 pounds.) There. That's all it takes. The vast majority of Dungeon Masters will never challenge you on this, and you'll never actually concern yourself with this mundane gear again. But you'll be able to say that your character has it.

You might be tempted to write down a whole general store worth of tools, rations, special items, and miscellaneous junk, but remember — your character needs to carry everything. Check page 162 in the *Player's Handbook*, and you'll see that characters have a finite limit on how much weight they can carry. Again, not many DMs will think to enforce this rule, but some do, so don't be embarrassed by being caught with 860 pounds of gear on your 13 Strength rogue.

Improving Weapons and Armor

Your character's equipment at 1st level is nothing remarkable. Your character hasn't yet found the great piles of treasure that will let him or her buy really good armor or powerful magic weapons. But within a level or two, you're going to want to upgrade your character's weapons and armor to the best arms he or she can afford to own. In DUNGEONS & DRAGONS, your character doesn't *keep* treasure; he or she spends it to buy better weapons and armor so that he or she can find even bigger treasures and buy even better weapons and armor.

Better armor

You've probably already picked the best nonmagical weapon for your character that he or she can afford, but 1st-level characters generally start with pretty crummy armor. With only 150 gp or so to spend, you just can't buy a decent suit of armor. Early in your fighter or cleric's career, you will want to trade in his or her scale mail (50 gp) for banded mail (250 gp). After that, buy into full plate armor (1,500 gp) or a mithral chain shirt (1,150 gp). (See the section, "Magical arms and armor," for more about mithral.)

Masterwork

Between normal weapons and armor and magical weapons and armor, you find *masterwork* items — non-magical weapons and armor of superior craftsmanship. Masterwork weapons cost 300 gp more than normal, but give a +1 on attack rolls. Masterwork armor costs 150 gp more than normal armor, but reduces the armor check penalty by 1 point. Depending on the type of armor your character is wearing, this may or may not be significant; you may want to simply wait and buy magical armor for your character when you can.

Magical arms and armor

The best way to improve your character's attack rolls and AC is to get his or her hands on a good magical weapon and a suit of magical armor. Magical weaponry is expensive stuff, but you'll find that you absolutely need it if your character is going to have a fighting chance of dealing with the game's more dangerous monsters. See Chapter 20 for more details.

Magical weapons carry a bonus to attack and damage rolls, ranging from +1 to +5 or more. So when you hear someone at the table boasting about his *+3 sword,* what he's saying is that his character has a sword that gives a +3 bonus on attack and damage rolls. That's a good sword. A +1 weapon costs 2,000 gp more than a masterwork version of that same weapon — so a *+1 greatsword* costs 2,350 gp (50 gp for the greatsword, 300 gp for masterwork, and 2,000 gp for the +1 enchantment).

Magical armor carries a bonus to AC ranging from +1 to +5 or more. So a suit of chainmail normally provides an AC bonus of 5, but a suit of *+2 chainmail* gives an AC bonus of 7. Magic armor with an enhancement bonus of +1 costs 1,000 gp more than a masterwork suit of armor of that same type — so a suit of *+1 chainmail* costs 1,300 gp (150 gp for chainmail, 150 gp for masterwork armor, and 1,000 gp for the bonus).

In addition to magical armor, your character can have armor made out of *mithral,* a superior alloy that is strong as steel but much lighter. It's not magical, but it's darned handy. Mithral armor counts as armor one category lighter than normal, and it reduces armor check penalties by 2. So a mithral chain shirt provides a +4 AC bonus, with an armor check penalty of 0. Many characters wind up with magical mithral chain shirts, because it's simply the best light armor your character can buy. A mithral chain shirt costs 1,150 gp, and a *+1 mithral chain shirt* costs 2,150 gp. See page 284 of the *Dungeon Master's Guide.*

Chapter 17

Choosing Spells

. . . .

In This Chapter

▶ Learning sorcerer spells

▶ Picking out your sorcerer's spell path

▶ Choosing cleric domains

▶ Selecting cleric spell loadouts

. . . .

Spells are the lifeblood of characters who use magic. Just like a skilled fighter might master a particular weapon or defeat his or her foes with a deadly combination attack, a sorcerer or cleric quickly learns to use spells as his or her weapons. A fighter naturally invests a lot of time and thought in picking out the right weapon for his or her style of combat. Likewise, a spell-caster has to pick out spells with just as much care and forethought.

In this chapter, we tell you about the various opportunities and restrictions you face in choosing your character's spells. We also show you some basic sorcerer spell paths (sets of spells your sorcerer can acquire as he or she gains levels) and some sample cleric spell *loadouts* (suites of spells your cleric can prepare for the day's adventuring).

If you're playing a fighter or rogue, you can skip this chapter. Your character doesn't cast spells, so you don't need to make any decisions here.

Casting Spells as a Sorcerer

As a sorcerer, spells are 90 percent of your character's strengths. A sorcerer can't fight well, can't take a lot of damage, and feat and skill selections just aren't that impressive. But your sorcerer might be the most powerful character in the game, because no other characters have the sorcerer's ability to defeat a super-tough monster or a whole roomful of bad guys with a single well-timed blow.

Sorcerer spells are organized into spell levels, ranging from 0 to 9. As your character rises in level, he or she gains access to ever more powerful spells — and your character can use them more often, too. For example, a 1st-level sorcerer can cast five 0-level and three 1st-level spells per day, but a 6th-level sorcerer can cast six 0-level, six 1st-level, five 2nd-level, and three 3rd-level spells per day. (You might notice that your character level, also referred to as caster level, does not correlate to the maximum spell level; remember to keep character level and spell level separate. They're not the same thing.)

You'll find the spells-per-day progression on Table 3-16, on page 52 of the *Player's Handbook*. On page 54 of the *Player's Handbook*, Table 3-17 tells you how many spells of which spell levels your sorcerer knows, based on experience level. Finally, don't forget to check back to Table 1-1 on page 8 of the *Player's Handbook* to see whether or not your character's Charisma score entitles him or her to bonus spells per day. A sorcerer with a high Charisma gets to cast more spells per day than a sorcerer with a mediocre Charisma.

To use a spell in game play, you simply tell the DM that your character is casting a spell. In combat, you'll have to wait for your character's turn to come up. As your sorcerer casts spells, he or she uses up spell slots of the appropriate level. So, if you're playing a 6th-level sorcerer and you have your character cast *lightning bolt* twice in a fierce battle, you've used up two of your character's three 3rd-level spells for the day — you only have one use of *lightning bolt* left. You can't refresh spell slots until your character has an opportunity to rest for eight hours. Usually, this means the party retreats from the dungeon and circles the wagons for a time while your character recharges his or her magic for the next day.

Learning spells

Playing a sorcerer has two advantages over playing a wizard: Your sorcerer gets more spells per day than a wizard, and you don't have to fix spell selection in advance. In other words, your sorcerer can use a 3rd-level spell slot to cast any 3rd-level spell he or she knows; you don't have to decide in advance which of your character's 3rd-level spells you want to be available for the day.

The downside to playing a sorcerer is that your character's total repertoire of spells will be much more limited than a wizard's. A 6th-level wizard might know a dozen 3rd-level spells, and then choose to memorize the two he deems most likely to be useful for any particular day. A 6th-level sorcerer will be able to use three 3rd-level spells in the same day, but she knows only one 3rd-level spell. Sorcerers have no ability to adapt their spell capacity to the particular challenges they face today.

The upshot of all this is that you will want to pick your character's spells with care. At 1st level, your sorcerer knows only four 0-level spells and two 1st-level spells. Every time your character gains a level, he or she gains a small number of new spells known.

Sorcerer or wizard?

When you decide to try out some of the harder character classes, you'll find that the wizard's spellcasting ability is very similar to the sorcerer's. Here's a quick look at the key differences:

✔ Wizards know many more spells; in fact, they're not limited in the number of spells they know. However, they can only prepare (or memorize) a few spells of each spell level per day.

✔ Wizards must commit each spell slot to a particular spell at the beginning of the day. Wizards can't choose to reuse the same spell over and over unless they plan ahead by preparing that spell multiple times.

✔ Wizards gain access to more powerful spells faster than the sorcerer. However, sorcerers can use their spells more often.

Most experienced players feel that a wizard is a stronger spellcaster than a sorcerer. There's no doubt that the wizard is more flexible and has many more options at his or her fingertips. However, for a beginning player, a wizard is a very daunting choice, especially if you're starting off in a mid-level game. On the other hand, even a relative neophyte can manage a mid-level sorcerer with little trouble. And sorcerers have a superior ability to dish out attack spell after attack spell, if the situation calls for it. At the end of the day, the two choices are reasonably well balanced; go with whichever character class appeals to you more.

You'll find a complete list of sorcerer (and wizard) spells on page 192–196 of the *Player's Handbook.* Sorcerers and wizards make use of the same spell list.

Building your sorcerer's spell selection

Every sorcerer builds his or her own spell selection level by level. Want to play a fire sorcerer? Take a lot of fire spells. Want to play a mind-bending enchanter? Take a lot of enchantment spells. It's really up to you. However, for the sake of illustrating a couple of the possible paths you might choose, we provide three sorcerer spell paths — sets of level-by-level spell picks that can serve as a guide for choosing your own sorcerer's spells.

Like the feat ladders we discuss in Chapter 14, the spell paths require you to make a basic decision about what kind of spellcaster you want to play. There are dozens of good answers to this question, but we focus on three:

✔ **Blaster:** A sorcerer whose spell repertoire is geared toward dealing damage to enemies. The blaster is the simplest sorcerer to play. Choose a lot of spells that simply deal damage, and select defensive spells and utility spells only after you've established good offense at each spell level.

✔ **Buffer:** A sorcerer who learns a lot of spells that *buff* (or power up) his or her teammates. You give up a little of your character's offensive potential to dramatically increase the capabilities of everyone around your sorcerer.

> ✔ **Trickster:** A sorcerer who chooses spells that provide versatility, creative approaches to defeating encounters without fighting, and general confusion and frustration to the enemy. Trickster spells tend to be all-or-nothing; either they win the encounter outright, or they prove ineffective.

Most sorcerers will have some ability to "jump tracks" in the course of a fight. For example, every sorcerer should have some damage-dealing spells, so every sorcerer can be a blaster for a fight if need be.

To use the spell paths in Tables 17-1 through 17-3, all you have to remember is that your sorcerer knows every spell given for his or her character level, plus all the spells for all previous levels. In other words, the lists are cumulative; if you're playing a 5th-level sorcerer, your character knows every spell listed for sorcerer levels 1 through 5.

The blaster

The advantage of playing a blaster is that all your character's efforts directly contribute to the monster's defeat. Most of your character's spells (see Table 17-1) deal out damage by reducing hit points, just like the fighter's sword and the rogue's sneak attack. Everyone in the party is working toward the same goal, which is to reduce the monster's hit points to zero as fast as possible. The disadvantage of being a blaster is that there are much better ways to defeat some monsters than by plowing through their hit points, and your sorcerer is not going to be able to explore those alternatives.

Table 17-1	Blaster Sorcerer Spell Path
Character Level	*Sorcerer Spells Known*
1st	0 — *daze, detect magic, disrupt undead, read magic;* 1st — *mage armor, magic missile*
2nd	0 — *touch of fatigue*
3rd	1st — *burning hands*
4th	0 — *light;* 2nd — *scorching ray*
5th	1st — *grease;* 2nd — *invisibility*
6th	0 — *mage hand;* 3rd — *fireball*
7th	1st — *ray of enfeeblement;* 2nd — *web;* 3rd — *fly*
8th	0 — *message;* 4th — *Evard's black tentacles*
9th	2nd — *see invisibility;* 3rd — *displacement;* 4th — *wall of ice*
10th	0 — *dancing lights;* 5th — *cone of cold*

Your first and foremost spell choice is *magic missile.* Your sorcerer will be throwing *magic missile* throughout his or her whole career. At 4th level, your character can learn 2nd-level spells, and the best damaging spell at 2nd level is *scorching ray.* However, you could probably choose something else and pick up *scorching ray* later, because *scorching ray* isn't noticeably better than *magic missile* until your character reaches 7th level.

At 6th level, your sorcerer's power ramps up tremendously when he or she gains access to his or her first 3rd-level spell. *Fireball* simply destroys a lot of low-level encounters that used to give your character trouble. Your sorcerer wipes out whole roomfuls of orcs with *fireball.* This is one of the most significant power-ups any character in the game enjoys at any level, so make the most of it.

You'll find that there aren't many good direct-attack 4th-level spells. You may want to choose *polymorph, improved invisibility,* or *stoneskin* instead of *Evard's black tentacles;* it's your call. *Wall of ice* is a generally useful spell that can help your character control the battlefield and wall off foes so that your character or other party members can deal with them later.

Early in your sorcerer's career, you should choose the feat Spell Focus (evocation). You're going to want your sorcerer's *fireball* spells to be as effective as possible.

The buffer

The buffer path (see Table 17-2) is rarely used for most sorcerers. Clerics have a number of good buffing spells, and in most parties, your character can safely leave that job to a cleric buddy. But if you're playing the second sorcerer in an adventuring party, or your party doesn't have a cleric, you'll find that your sorcerer's spells can sometimes help his or her friends deal even more damage than your character might have dished out with a flash-bang spell like *fireball* or *lightning bolt.*

Table 17-2	Buffer Sorcerer Spell Path
Character Level	*Sorcerer Spells Known*
1st	0 — *detect magic, light, read magic, resistance;* 1st — *mage armor, magic missile*
2nd	0 — *daze*
3rd	1st — *enlarge person*
4th	0 — *touch of fatigue;* 2nd — *invisibility*
5th	1st — *protection from evil;* 2nd — *bull's strength*

(continued)

Table 17-2 *(continued)*

Character Level	Sorcerer Spells Known
6th	0 — *mage hand;* 3rd — *lightning bolt*
7th	1st — *ray of enfeeblement;* 2nd — *false life;* 3rd — *haste*
8th	0 — *message;* 4th — *improved invisibility*
9th	2nd — *scorching ray;* 3rd — *fly;* 4th — *stoneskin*
10th	0 — *dancing lights;* 5th — *teleport*

A buffer character begins with a spell selection similar to that of the blaster sorcerer, because every sorcerer relies on *magic missile. Mage armor* can be cast on your character's friends, so a rogue buddy (or maybe a monk, druid, or ranger, if one is in the party) would appreciate the no-encumbrance defense offered by that spell.

At 4th level, your sorcerer gains the ability to cast the spell *invisibility.* This offers a rogue friend a tremendous power up, because he can now manufacture a sneak attack opportunity almost at will. There are several other good buff spells at 2nd level that you should consider choosing, including *bull's strength, bear's endurance, cat's grace,* and *blur.* All are reasonable choices, but check to see if the cleric in your party intends to use *bull's strength* or *bear's endurance* a lot. There's no sense in wasting one of your character's precious spell choices on a spell the party will have regular access to anyway through the cleric.

When your sorcerer reaches 6th level, you've got a hard choice to make: Do you pick up *haste* right now, or do you shore up your character's offense with a spell like *fireball* or *lightning bolt* first? In the path we provide in Table 17-2, we recommend beefing up your character's offense first, because it's been neglected a bit — but *haste* is a very good choice too.

At 8th level, your sorcerer gets his or her first 4th-level spell. Your best choices are *polymorph, stoneskin,* or *improved invisibility. Stoneskin* buffs your character's fighter friends, but rogues just love *improved invisibility* — and so does your sorcerer, for that matter, because he or she gets to cast spells and remain invisible. Go with *improved invisibility* first.

Because your sorcerer will often be casting spells of a limited duration, you might want to consider choosing the Extend Spell metamagic feat. You'll want those power ups to stick around as long as possible.

The trickster

In many ways, the trickster spell path (see Table 17-3) is the strongest sorcerer build. These spells are devastating in effect. But there is a downside: When the blaster sorcerer hits a foe with a *lightning bolt,* he's guaranteed to do some damage. If a trickster sorcerer tries *suggestion* on that same foe and the enemy succeeds on his saving throw, nothing happens. In effect, the trickster is trying to beat the encounter all on his own. He's not cooperating with the fighter and rogue to eliminate the target's hit points; he's *competing* with them to see who knocks out the monster first.

Table 17-3	Trickster Sorcerer Spell Path
Character Level	*Sorcerer Spells Known*
1st	0 — *daze, detect magic, ghost sound, read magic;* 1st — *magic missile, sleep*
2nd	0 — *mage hand*
3rd	1st — *charm person*
4th	0 — *dancing lights;* 2nd — *invisibility*
5th	1st — *grease;* 2nd — *minor image*
6th	0 — *message;* 3rd — *summon monster III*
7th	1st — *ray of enfeeblement;* 2nd — *web;* 3rd — *suggestion*
8th	0 — *open/close;* 4th — *polymorph*
9th	2nd — *knock;* 3rd — *lightning bolt;* 4th — *improved invisibility*
10th	0 — *touch of fatigue;* 5th — *hold monster*

As with the other spell paths, it's hard not to start with *magic missile. Sleep* is potentially the best 1st-level spell in the game, because it offers your sorcerer a chance to take down a whole 1st-level encounter in one easy spell.

There aren't many good offensive 2nd-level spells, so your 2nd-level choices focus on delaying, confusing, and hindering the enemy. *Invisibility* offers tremendous opportunity for mischief, and a rogue friend likes it, too.

When your sorcerer can cast 3rd-level spells, you have a great wealth of spells to choose from. We like *summon monster III* and *suggestion* for the trickster. The *summon monster* spells offer a great amount of versatility in picking out the exact right monster to call for the situation your character is in; chances are good you'll find something on the list that will help your sorcerer in almost any fight. *Suggestion* is a devastating weapon in the hands of a creative player; you can have your sorcerer entice foes to surrender, leave, give up their stuff, or even fight each other with a little clever wording.

Feat ladders and spell paths

You might be wondering how these spell path-ways coincide with the feat ladders discussed in Chapter 14. Here are the best interactions of feats and spell paths to remember:

✔ **Attack sorcerer:** Choose the blaster or trickster spell paths.

✔ **Team buff sorcerer:** Choose the buffer spell path.

✔ **Survival sorcerer:** Choose any spell path.

At 8th level, your character picks up the single most useful spell in the game, *polymorph*. There is no end to the utility of this spell. It's offense, defense, mobility, and disguise all in one spell.

Casting Spells as a Cleric

Building your sorcerer's spell selection takes a little forethought, but then runs quickly and easily in play. Unfortunately, the cleric is the exact opposite. You don't have to make many decisions about which spells you'll gain on a level-by-level basis, because your character knows *all* cleric spells. But you have to decide which spells you want available to your cleric each day. And, to complicate things even more, your cleric has the ability to ditch a pre-pared spell and revert to a healing spell any time you like. So, you must constantly evaluate your character's current spell selection and decide which spells to use up and when to use them.

Just like sorcerer spells, cleric spells are organized into spell levels, ranging from 0 to 9. As your cleric gains levels, he or she has access to ever more powerful spells, which he or she can use more often than before.

You'll find the cleric's spells per day progression on Table 3-6 (page 31 of the *Player's Handbook*). If your cleric has a good Wisdom score (12 or better), your character gains bonus spells per day based on his or her Wisdom score; see Table 1-1 on page 8 of the *Player's Handbook*.

2+1 isn't 3?

You might wonder why the cleric spell table lists things like "2+1" as spells per day instead of just 3. There's a reason: This is a reminder that you must choose one spell per spell level from your cleric's domain spells, while you can select the remaining spells at that spell level from the general cleric spell list. So, if your character knows 2+1 2nd-level spells, you pick two 2nd-level cleric spells and one 2nd-level spell from either of your character's two chosen cleric domains.

Choosing domains

At 1st level, you must make a couple of fundamental choices that will forever dictate your cleric's spell access. You pick two cleric domains from which your character will be able to cast spells. You will always have access to the general list of cleric spells, but you have to decide which two (of the 22 available) domains your character will be able to cast from in addition to the general cleric spell list.

There are two ways to go about picking domains. You can choose a deity for your cleric from Table 3-7 on page 32 of the _Player's Handbook_ and then select two of the domains listed for that deity (see Table 17-4 for our suggested domains for each deity), or you can go straight to the list of domains in Chapter 11 of the _Player's Handbook_ (pages 185–189) and pick any two domains you think go together well.

Choosing a domain gives your cleric a modest special power of some kind, and access to a number of spells — some of which may only be available to clerics who choose that domain, others of which may also be available to druids, sorcerers, and wizards, or might appear in the general cleric spell list.

Table 17-4	Recommended Cleric Domain Choices	
Deity	**Alignment**	**Suggested Domains**
Heironeous, god of valor	Lawful good	Good, War
Moradin, god of the dwarves	Lawful good	Earth, Protection
Yondalla, goddess of the halflings	Lawful good	Good, Protection
Ehlonna, goddess of the woodlands	Neutral good	Animal, Sun
Garl Glittergold, god of the gnomes	Neutral good	Protection, Trickery
Pelor, god of the sun	Neutral good	Good, Sun
Corellon Larethian, god of the elves	Chaotic good	Protection, War

(continued)

Table 17-4 *(continued)*

Deity	Alignment	Suggested Domains
Kord, god of strength	Chaotic good	Luck, Strength
Wee Jas, goddess of death and magic	Lawful neutral	Death, Magic
St. Cuthbert, god of retribution	Lawful neutral	Destruction, Strength
Boccob, god of magic	Neutral	Magic, Trickery
Fharlanghn, god of roads	Neutral	Luck, Travel
Obad-Hai, god of nature	Neutral	Animal, Fire
Olidammara, god of thieves	Chaotic neutral	Luck, Trickery

Preparing cleric spells

Preparing your cleric's spells requires two steps. First, you choose your character's general cleric spells from the list on pages 183–185 of the *Player's Handbook*. Then, you choose which domain spells you want your character to prepare for the day. Clerics only get a single domain spell at each spell level per day, so the fact that your character has access to two domains means that you will need to compare the two domains in question spell level by spell level to decide which one you want your cleric to take a spell from that day. You'll find the domain spell lists on pages 185–189 of the *Player's Handbook*.

Clerics and healing spells

Clerics have a special ability called *spontaneous casting*. Whenever clerics are about to cast a spell, they can choose to ditch the spell they had prepared in that spell slot and substitute a *cure* spell of the same level or lower. For example, say that your cleric had *spiritual hammer* prepared as one of his or her 2nd-level cleric spells. You can simply strike this spell off your cleric's list of readied spells, and your character can then cast *cure moderate wounds* or *cure light wounds* instead. Only clerics of good or neutral alignment can do this; evil clerics use spontaneous casting to convert to *inflict wounds* spells instead.

What this means is that your cleric doesn't ever have to actually prepare *cure* spells. Any spell your cleric has prepared for the day is a potential *cure* spell. You simply decide on the fly which of your cleric's prepared spells you want to lose in order to power up some healing for your character or other party members.

For example, say that your cleric has the Good and War domains. At 2nd level, the Good domain spell is *aid,* while the War domain spell is *spiritual weapon.* You can use your cleric's domain spell slot (the odd "+1" on the cleric class table) to prepare either *aid* or *spiritual weapon,* but not both.

Now, here's where it gets really crazy: Many spells on the domain lists *also* appear on the base cleric spell list. In the example above, *aid* and *spiritual weapon* are both spells that are also found in the general list of 2nd-level cleric spells. You are free to use your cleric's general spell slots (the 1, or 2, or 3 before the +1 on the table) to select these spells, if you like. So, your cleric could conceivably prepare *spiritual weapon* three, four, or five times in a single day — once from his or her domain list, and the rest from his or her general spell slots.

Cleric spell loadouts

To help you quickly choose a set of useful cleric spells, we've created three separate spell loadouts, described in the following sections. Unlike the feat ladders or sorcerer spell paths, these loadouts are not exclusive paths — when you're playing a cleric, you can choose which spells you want your cleric to prepare for that day. If you want your cleric to be ready for a lot of melee combat one day, pick the combat monster loadout. If you want your cleric to be ready to fix any imaginable predicament his or her friends get into the next day, drop the combat monster loadout and go with the master healer suite of spell choices instead.

To use the loadout, simply select the spells indicated for your cleric's level (and all spells from previous levels, as well) when you choose which spells your cleric will prepare for the day.

The loadouts do not account for high Wisdom scores and bonus spells. Your cleric is certain to get some amount of bonus spells, but you should use those bonus slots to pick any darn spell you want. Similarly, these loadouts don't account for the domain spell at each spell level. Don't forget to choose your cleric's domain spells in addition to general cleric spells.

Combat monster cleric spell loadout

Choose to have your cleric prepare the selection of spells in Table 17-5 if you want your character to wade into the fight with his or her mace swinging. The spells on this path work especially well with the melee cleric feat ladder (see Chapter 14), but any cleric can become a dangerous melee opponent with a few of the right spells.

Table 17-5	Combat Monster Cleric Spell Loadout
Character Level	*Cleric Spells Prepared**
1st	0 — *detect magic, light, read magic;* 1st — *magic weapon*
2nd	0 — *guidance;* 1st — *shield of faith*
3rd	2nd — *spiritual weapon*
4th	0 — *resistance;* 1st — *divine favor;* 2nd — *bull's strength*
5th	3rd — *summon monster III*
6th	2nd — *align weapon;* 3rd — *searing light*
7th	0 — *light;* 1st — *protection from evil;* 4th — *divine power*
8th	3rd — *dispel magic;* 4th — *air walk*
9th	2nd — *lesser restoration;* 5th — *flame strike*
10th	4th — *summon monster IV;* 5th — *righteous might*

* Does not include domain spells or bonus spells for high Wisdom score.

Your cleric's key battle spells are *shield of faith, divine favor,* and *divine power.* If your cleric can prepare for a fight by casting one or two of these spells, you'll find that your character fights as well as (or even better than) his or her fighter comrades.

With domain spells or bonus spells for your character's Wisdom score, you may want to choose some good "fixing" spells such as *remove fear* or *lesser restoration,* or spells to buff your character's allies — *greater magic weapon* is an excellent, long-lasting spell that can significantly help comrades' attacks. Don't be afraid to use your cleric's extra spells to take multiple iterations of key spells; if your character gets into several fights in the course of one day of adventuring, he or she may cast *shield of faith* or *divine favor* in each one.

If you like this spell loadout, you'll find that the Strength and War domains offer the most useful domain spells. The Destruction domain is also worth considering.

Master healer cleric spell loadout

The spell loadout in Table 17-6 is designed to counter many of the various afflictions that can befall an adventuring party fighting monsters armed with poison, ability drain, and various supernatural and magical attacks. Any cleric can help his or her allies get hit points back, but fixing someone who's lost a few points of Strength or Constitution to a nasty poison of some kind requires some advance preparation. As the master healer, your character is going to keep the rest of the party operating at peak efficiency.

Clerics who follow the Turn Expert or Spellcasting Cleric feat ladders generally do well with this spell loadout. However, don't rule it out if you're playing a melee-oriented cleric; the trick with this slate of spells is that you don't know if or when your cleric will use them, so he or she should have a good offensive capability (such as beating foes silly with a mace) to fall back on if he or she doesn't find much opportunity for healing.

To be honest, you have to be a special kind of player to be happy with focusing your efforts on helping your character's friends, as opposed to battling the monsters with your character. If you choose to play a healing-heavy cleric, you will find that you have few discretionary actions in the course of the game. Many of your turns will be sucked up in tending to your character's allies' injuries. Other players will often take it for granted that you're willing to give up your turn in order to keep their characters in the fight. If that doesn't sound like fun to you, then you should take the combat monster or battle caster loadouts for your cleric instead.

Table 17-6	Master Healer Cleric Spell Loadout
Character Level	*Cleric Spells Prepared**
1st	0 — *detect magic, light, read magic;* 1st — *remove fear*
2nd	0 — *guidance;* 1st — *sanctuary*
3rd	2nd — *lesser restoration*
4th	0 — *resistance;* 1st — *protection from evil;* 2nd — *remove paralysis*
5th	3rd — *dispel magic*
6th	2nd — *status;* 3rd — *protection from energy*
7th	0 — *light;* 1st — *shield of faith;* 4th — *neutralize poison*
8th	3rd — *remove blindness/deafness;* 4th — *death ward*
9th	2nd — *bear's endurance;* 5th — *raise dead*
10th	4th — *dismissal;* 5th — *break enchantment*

* Does not include domain spells or bonus spells for high Wisdom score.

You should adjust your spell selection to account for the enemies you expect your cleric to face. For example, if you know that your cleric is going to enter a temple haunted by shadows (monsters that drain Strength), you should certainly pick extra *lesser restoration* spells in order to fix up Strength-damaged friends.

With bonus spells and domain spells, your cleric should probably prepare some offensive or team-buff spells, such as *searing light, greater magic weapon,* or *shield of faith.*

Domains that naturally steer your cleric toward the master healer spell loadout include Healing (naturally) and either Luck or Protection.

Battle caster cleric spell loadout

The selection of spells in Table 17-7 allows your cleric to stand back and deal damage from a distance. In general, a sorcerer will beat a cleric at simply handing out damage with spells, but with the right spell selections, a cleric can be nearly as effective as a sorcerer in spell duels.

Clerics who follow the Spellcasting Cleric feat ladder will do well with this spell loadout.

Table 17-7	Battle Caster Cleric Spell Loadout
Character Level	*Cleric Spells Prepared**
1st	0 — *detect magic, light, read magic;* 1st — *command*
2nd	0 — *guidance;* 1st — *shield of faith*
3rd	2nd — *hold person*
4th	0 — *resistance;* 1st — *protection from evil;* 2nd — *spiritual weapon*
5th	3rd — *searing light*
6th	2nd — *silence;* 3rd — *summon monster III*
7th	0 — *light;* 1st — *divine favor;* 4th — *summon monster IV*
8th	3rd — *blindness/deafness;* 4th — *dismissal*
9th	2nd — *lesser restoration;* 5th — *flame strike*
10th	4th — *air walk;* 5th — *summon monster V*

* Does not include domain spells or bonus spells for high Wisdom score.

The one place where the cleric's offensive potential matches that of the sorcerer is with the various *summon monster* spells. They take a long time to cast, but they offer tremendous tactical flexibility, and they allow your cleric to take control of the battle by swamping the battlefield with more allies. This strategy is especially effective if your character has the Augment Summoning feat.

Spell selections for other characters

Three other character classes are spellcasters from the get-go: the bard, the druid, and the wizard. Here are a few quick tips for spell selection if you choose to play a character of one of these classes:

✔ **Bard:** Your character learns spells like the sorcerer — you choose a small number of spells that your character knows, but he or she can use them any time he or she has spell slots available. As a 1st-level bard, your character only knows 0-level spells: We suggest choosing *daze, detect magic, mage hand,* and *read magic.* At 2nd level, your character gains access to 1st-level bard spells, which are much more interesting. You get to choose two of these for your character; *disguise self* and *sleep* are pretty good choices.

✔ **Druid:** Your character uses spells like the cleric — he or she has access to all the spells on the druid list and can customize his or her picks every day. However, druids don't use domains, and they can't spontaneously convert to healing spells. Instead, they can lose prepared spells to cast *summon nature's ally* spells, so your character always has an offensive option to fall back on. The druid's best 1st-level spells are *cure light wounds, charm animal, produce flame,* and *speak with animals.*

✔ **Wizard:** Your character begins with a small subset of the 0-level and 1st-level sorcerer/wizard spells in his or her spellbook. Each day, he or she prepares spells from the spellbook. Good 1st-level spells to have in your character's spellbook include *charm person, mage armor, magic missile, shield,* and *sleep.*

Lars Grant-West

Use domain spells and bonus spells to pick up some miscellaneous defenses, such as *resist energy* and *shield of faith*. Your cleric can easily share these spells with fellow adventurers, and the efficient distribution of magical power from clerics and sorcerers to rogues and fighters is one of the secret success strategies for the game.

A number of cleric domains lend themselves to the battle caster spell load-out. Some of the better ones include Death, Destruction, Fire, Good, Sun, and Water. (Water is especially sneaky; few players recognize how good its spells are at higher levels, because no one ever takes the Water domain.)

Chapter 18

Advancing Your Character

. . . .

In This Chapter

▶ Discovering how your character earns experience points

▶ Examining what happens when your character gains a level

▶ Understanding multiclassing

▶ Exploring prestige classes

. . . .

Characters in the DUNGEONS & DRAGONS game are not static. They grow and develop the longer you play the game. That's one of the key aspects of the game — like the heroes of a novel, movie, or television series, your characters learn, grow, and are influenced by past and present events.

In this chapter, we explore the concept of experience points (XP) and gaining levels, examining how and in what ways your character improves. We also look at multiclassing, an option that allows your character to experiment with different class features by taking levels in another class. Finally, we look at prestige classes, the pinnacle that every character can strive to achieve.

Chapter 3 of the *Player's Handbook* goes into greater depth on experience points and multiclassing. Check out pages 58–60 of the *Player's Handbook* after you read through this chapter. Page 36–41 of the *Dungeon Master's Guide* provides the tables and reward options that DMs use to award XP. Finally, you can find a collection of prestige classes in Chapter 6 of the *Dungeon Master's Guide*.

Gaining Experience Points

Experience points, or *XP*, measure a character's accomplishments. They represent both training and learning by doing. In the fantasy worlds of D&D, experience has a direct correlation to power. Characters earn experience points by defeating opponents and otherwise overcoming the challenges that the Dungeon Master places before them. When a character has earned a specific number of XP, as detailed on Table 3-2 on page 22 of the *Player's Handbook* (a portion of the table is shown in Table 18-1, as well), he or she gains a new level.

Table 18-1	XP and Your First Few Levels
You Need This Many XP . . .	*. . . To Reach This Level*
0	1st level
1,000	2nd level
3,000	3rd level
6,000	4th level

Where does XP come from?

Every monster and opponent in the game has a Challenge Rating (CR). This CR is a rating of how easy or difficult a monster is to overcome. Every monster stat block includes the monster's CR. Traps and other obstacles can also be assigned CRs, as described in Chapter 2 of the *Dungeon Master's Guide*. The Dungeon Master can adjust the CRs (and thereby the XP award) based on circumstances and unusual situations.

The DM decides when a challenge has been overcome. Usually, this means when a battle has been won or a trap disarmed, but clever players can come up with all kinds of ways for their characters to overcome the challenge of the moment. If the party successfully slips by the hobgoblins guarding the corridor by using stealth and clever distractions, the DM can determine that the characters have overcome this challenge and reward them experience points accordingly.

All characters that take part in an encounter should gain XP for that encounter. Remember that encounters come in three forms: a challenge, a combat, or a roleplaying encounter that is integral to the plot of the adventure. If a character

What is a Challenge Rating?

Every monster or obstacle the player characters have to deal with in an adventure has a Challenge Rating (CR). The CR suggests the average level of a party of adventurers for which one creature of a particular CR would make an encounter moderately difficult. In other words, with reasonable luck and a bit of skill, an average party should overcome a creature or obstacle of their CR with some damage and expenditure of resources.

When we talk about an average party, we mean four player characters. (Your gaming group, of course, might make up a larger or smaller adventuring party.)

A 4th-level party, for example, should be able to get through an encounter with a CR 4 monster or trap a little beat up and a few resources expended but without suffering any casualties.

dies or is knocked out prior to the start of an encounter, he or she earns no XP, even if the rest of the party successfully overcomes the encounter. DMs usually award XP at the end of an adventure, though granting awards at the end of encounters or game sessions works too, as long as level advancement happens between adventures.

For the Dungeon Master

The DM usually awards experience points at the end of an adventure, but some DMs dole out awards at the end of a game session. Training and advancement, however, should still take place between adventures (see the "Advancing a Level" section). To determine the XP award for an encounter, follow these steps (which are described more fully in Chapter 2 of the *Dungeon Master's Guide*):

1. **Determine each player character's level. Remember to include only those characters that took part in the encounter.**

2. **Determine each defeated monster's Challenge Rating (CR).**

3. **Cross-reference one character's level with the Challenge Rating for each defeated monster on Table 2-6 on page 38 of the *Dungeon Master's Guide* to find the base XP award.**

4. **Divide the base XP award by the number of characters in the party. The result is the amount of XP that one character receives for helping to overcome the monster.**

5. **Add up all the XP awards for all the monsters the character helped defeat.**

6. **Repeat this process for each player character that participated in the encounter.**

Advancing a Level

Your character can advance to the next level when your XP total reaches the minimum amount needed, according to Table 3-2 in the *Player's Handbook*. Regdar, for example, can go up from 1st to 2nd level when he accumulates at least 1,000 XP. Going up a level provides a number of immediate benefits that demonstrate that the character has learned and improved in some way.

Imagine that your character spends time between adventures training, studying, and practicing his or her skills. Even if your character achieves the necessary XP milestone, he or she can't go up a level in the middle of an adventure. In game terms, this means that you have to wait until the adventure or game session ends before you can level up your character; in the D&D world, your character has to return to a safe place to train before he or she can make use of the knowledge and experience gained in the course of adventuring.

How high can you go?

How high can your character advance in level? That depends. The core Dungeons & Dragons rulebooks provide for 20 levels of play. For those who want to explore adventures beyond 20th level, check out the *Epic Level Handbook*. How far you advance really comes down to the type of campaign your Dungeon Master wants to run. Some campaigns continue for years, with characters advancing to 20th level and beyond. Others run for a few months, reach a satisfying conclusion, and then the DM kicks off something new. This gives everyone an opportunity to try new character and class options, and for the DM to try a new world on for size.

Every class has a table that describes class features and statistics that become available and increase as your character advances in levels. Refer to the tables in Chapter 3 of the *Player's Handbook*. When your character has earned the necessary XP to go up a level, grab your character sheet and your *Player's Handbook*, and follow these steps:

1. **Choose the class in which to apply your new experience level.**

   When your character qualifies for a new level, decide which class you're going to take that level in. Most players select their characters' class during character creation and stick with it for the rest of their characters' adventuring careers. The best fighter, for example, takes all his or her levels in the fighter class. However, you may have other reasons for diverging as your character advances levels. (See the section called "Multiclassing," later in this chapter, for more information.)

2. **Adjust your base attack bonus modifiers.**

   If the new class level indicates that your base attack bonus increases, record this on your character sheet and adjust your attacks accordingly.

3. **Adjust your base save bonuses.**

   If the new class level indicates that your base saves increase, adjust your character sheet accordingly.

4. **Adjust your ability score.**

   When your character attains 4th, 8th, 12th, 16th, and 20th character level (as opposed to class level — see the nearby sidebar, "Character level versus class level"), choose an ability and increase its score by 1 point. Check Table 1-1 on page 8 of the *Player's Handbook* to see if modifiers or scores associated with that ability need to be adjusted.

5. Increase your hit points.

Roll the Hit Die indicated for your class, add your character's Constitution modifier, and add the total to your hit points. Your character will always gain at least 1 hit point upon level advancement, even if a Constitution penalty and a low roll would indicate otherwise.

6. Increase your skill points.

You get an allotment of skill points based on class and Intelligence modifier. (And humans always get 1 bonus skill point every level.) Remember that you can buy class skills for 1 point per rank, but 1 skill point only buys ½ rank in cross-class skills. Your maximum rank in any class skill is your character's level +3; for cross-class skills, it's half that number.

7. Choose your new feat.

When your character attains 3rd, 6th, 9th, 12th, 15th, and 18th character levels, you gain one feat of your choice. Make sure that your character meets any prerequisites the feat may require.

8. Get your new spells.

Spellcasting characters gain the ability to cast more spells as they advance. In Chapter 3 of the *Player's Handbook*, check the Spells per Day section of your character's class table to see if your character can now cast more spells per day. If you're playing a sorcerer or bard, also check the Spells Known table to see if your character can learn new spells.

9. Acquire your new class features.

Finally, check your class table (in Chapter 3 of the *Player's Handbook*) to see if the new level provides any new class features. These might include bonus feats, special attacks, or new powers.

Character level versus class level

Character level refers to the total number of levels in all classes. Character level is used to determine when feats and ability score improvements become available.

Class level is your character's level in a particular class. For a single-class character, character level and class level are the same. When Regdar is a 4th-level fighter, he's also a 4th level character.

However, for a multiclass character that is a 2nd-level fighter/2nd-level rogue, that character is a 4th-level character with two class levels of fighter and two class levels of rogue. Such a character would have more options for dealing with obstacles, but would never equal Regdar's pure power as a fighter.

Multiclassing

As your character advances in level, you get to decide what class to advance your character in. Most player characters stick with a single class throughout their careers, because sticking with one track provides the easiest and most rapid power advancement. You can, however, select a new class and combine its features with those of your previous class. This is called *multiclassing*. Multiclassing makes your character more versatile, but weakens your focus and puts your character behind the power curve as compared to characters that stick with a single class.

Page 59 of the *Player's Handbook* describes multiclass characters and how to add a second class. For more on multiclassing, see Chapter 22 of this book.

Prestige Classes

Prestige classes offer a special kind of multiclassing for characters of higher levels. Prestige classes are specialized, focused classes that have requirements that characters must meet before they can take levels in them. Requirements can include a specific base attack bonus, a specific number of ranks in a specific skill, a specific race, a specific alignment, or a specific feat. Prestige classes are purely optional and must be approved by the Dungeon Master before you decide to take levels in them. Some prestige classes might not fit into certain campaigns, for example.

The *Dungeon Master's Guide* provides 17 prestige classes to choose from, including the arcane archer, the blackguard, and the loremaster. See Chapter 6 of that volume for more information. Other D&D supplements also feature prestige classes that you might want to add to your campaign.

Part III
Playing Your Best Game

The 5th Wave   By Rich Tennant

"Is there <u>really</u> a monster called a cursed nose hair, Janet, or are you trying to tell me something?"

In this part . . .

DUNGEONS & DRAGONS is a complex game that presents
your character with an infinite variety of challenges.
In this part of the book, you graduate from the basics of
how to play and how to create a character into the study of
how to play the game *well*. You can play the game at a basic
level (see the monster, hit the monster) and have plenty of
fun, but if you want to find out how to take on the toughest
opponents and win, how to forge your adventuring party
into a tight team of specialists who can take on any challenge, and how to immerse yourself in the imagination and
fun of the game, this part is for you.

Chapter 19

Handling Yourself in a Fight

- -

In This Chapter

▶ Picking the right way to beat the monsters

▶ Building a combat strategy

▶ Using advanced tactics

▶ Maximizing your attacks

▶ Adapting your tactics to your foes

- -

The point of the DUNGEONS & DRAGONS game is to have fun, be creative, and engage in a little healthy escapism. But D&D is a game, and just like any game, you can play it well or you can play it poorly. Many people have a great time making bad choices and exploring those consequences, but we're guessing that you want to play to *win* — or at least do your best to maximize your character's impact on the game.

There are two good ways to play the game smart: Build effective characters (we talk more about that later in this book), and fight your best fight. Any character can shine for a battle with some lucky combat rolls, but if you consistently select the best and most efficient actions for your character round after round, you won't need lucky die rolls to excel.

In this chapter, we tell you about the right way to approach battles and encounters, and we show you how to come up with a winning strategy for almost any fight.

Choosing the Right Weapon for the Job

This doesn't mean carrying around a *bag of holding* full of magic weapons and pulling out the most effective one for each foe. This means finding your enemy's weakness and targeting it. This strategy goes all the way back to Sun Tzu: Don't throw strength at strength if there's a better option available. Your high-powered fighter might be able to cut his or her way through a roomful of frost giants, but melee combat is what frost giants do *best.* You would be better off to use magic to immobilize or defeat the frost giants, because giants generally can stand up to a lot more physical abuse than magical attacks.

The four basic strategies for defeating foes in the D&D game are hit point damage, save-or-die spells, maneuver, and diplomacy.

Killing 'em slowly: Attacking hit points

Use melee attacks, ranged attacks, and damage-causing spells such as *magic missile* or *lightning bolt* to reduce your opponents' hit points to zero as fast as possible. This strategy works best against foes with low hit points or foes who don't have much ability to hurt your character while the party chips away at their hit points. It's a bad strategy to use against beaters (big strong monsters who frankly are seeking to mix it up with your party).

This is the default strategy for almost any monster; if you don't know what else to do, make attacks and knock down your enemy's hit points. Sooner or later, you'll win.

Swinging for the fences: Save-or-die spells

Many spells are affectionately referred to as *save-or-die spells*. If a save-or-die spell works, your character will screw up the enemy so bad he might as well be dead even if the spell itself doesn't kill him. Spells such as *deep slumber, hold person, disintegrate,* or *finger of death* certainly fall into this category.

Most save-or-die spells don't actually work well with hit point ablation, because if your character drops a monster that a fighter ally has been attacking for a round or two, you've effectively rendered the fighter's earlier attacks pointless. If you're going to paralyze the troll on round 4, why spend any actions at all hitting it in rounds 1, 2, and 3? So if you're using all-or-nothing spells in a fight where your comrades are beating down the monsters the hard way, at least make sure that you target fresh, "un-hit-yet" monsters for your save-or-die effects.

Save-or-die spells work best on monsters with a significant saving throw vulnerability that you can exploit. The *Monster Manual* is the place where you can study up on what works best on each particular monster. For example, giants usually have poor Will saves but great Fortitude saves. Don't use *finger of death* on a giant; you're likely to waste the spell. Use *hold monster* instead.

Beating 'em with footwork: Maneuver

Many foes can be avoided through an artful maneuver, especially if your character or another in the party has potent magic at hand. If nothing else, you might be able to maneuver your character into a position from which he or she can attack a foe with no chance of being hit back. For example, if the opponent is a powerful melee basher with no ranged attacks (say, a gray render or purple worm), your character might be able to take to the air and attack it safely with ranged weapons and spells.

The true coup of maneuver, of course, is to simply bypass a fight you don't need to fight. If the evil lord surrounds his castle with a moat of giant fiendish crocodiles, why would you slog your way through the monsters when you might go around, over, or through them without fighting? Spells such as *dimension door, teleport,* and *fly* are obvious mechanisms for winning an encounter through maneuver, but don't overlook the rogue's knack for sneaking through dangerous places, or spells that disguise or hide your whole party from your foes.

Maneuvering works best on enemies who are stuck in place. (There's not much point in avoiding a pack of hell hounds if they'll just follow the party to the next room and attack them there.) It's also the best way for dealing with enemies who are simply too dangerous to fight.

Winning with a smile: Negotiation

Sometimes you can simply talk your way past an obstacle. If your character is facing a roomful of orc warriors, he or she might be able to convince them that the adventuring party is far too dangerous to attack with a display of astounding bravado (and a good Bluff or Intimidate check). Or your character might persuade them that it's in their own best interest to let the party continue through the dungeon unmolested so that the party can deal with a rival gang of monsters the orcs might want out of the way — a good use of the Diplomacy skill.

Magic can be very helpful in getting your foot in the door with the negotiation strategy. Spells such as *charm person, suggestion,* or *charm monster* can go a long way toward convincing someone (or something) to talk instead of fight.

Negotiation works best on intelligent adversaries, but don't rule out negotiation tactics against non-intelligent monsters. A druid's or ranger's wild empathy ability can easily get a party of adventurers past a dangerous and ill-tempered creature such as a dire bear or giant crocodile. And, even if you're not playing a druid or ranger, throwing a big haunch of meat to the evil warlord's fiendish dire wolf might serve as well as a bribe of gold would for an intelligent guardian.

Many Dungeon Masters will require you to attempt skill checks in skills such as Bluff, Diplomacy, Handle Animal, or Intimidate in order to carry off a negotiation strategy. However, some DMs will deliberately avoid using the skill rules to resolve these encounters: They want you, the player, to explain exactly what your character says, and then they'll decide if they think you were convincing enough for your character to succeed in his or her efforts to talk to the monsters. Other DMs combine skill checks with roleplaying, letting good rolls bolster weak roleplaying or vice-versa. Each method is a reasonable way for the DM to handle a negotiation — you'll just have to see which way your DM prefers to play encounters like this.

Bugging out: Knowing when to retreat

Even the best D&D players tend to forget that running away is an option. Very few challenges in the game are worth getting a player character killed for. If the situation is so grim that it seems likely that one or more characters will die, extricate the party from the battle and come back to fight another day — after all player characters have healed up and made the right magical preparations for dealing with whatever dangerous adversary forced a retreat.

Warning signs that you should watch out for include:

- ✔ One or more player characters rendered helpless.

- ✔ Two or more player characters reduced to 50 percent hit points or less, with no prospect of healing back up to full.

- ✔ Player character spellcasters down to 50 percent or less of their normal spell capability (half their spell slots or prepared spells have been used up).

- ✔ Three straight rounds go by in a fight where no player character damages an adversary.

Whether or not you heed these warning signs is up to you. Sometimes, retreat is simply not an option. Other times, you might need to fight on past the warning signs because you'll put your character at greater risk in trying to retreat than you would by trying to win the fight.

Putting It All Together: Developing Your Combat Strategy

Every time your character gets into a scrape, you should have an idea of what you're trying to accomplish and how you're going to go about it. That means formulating a combat strategy early in the fight. Here's a quick and dirty primer on combat strategy for you to use:

1. **Define the situation:** Identify what sort of fight you're facing by figuring out if anyone is surprised and what sort of terrain you're fighting on.

   When you're determining surprise, you must figure out who got the jump on whom. Do you even have a choice about this fight? Here are some guidelines to keep in mind:

   - **We got ambushed:** The bad guys jumped out of the darkness and attacked your party without warning. Your first step should be to limit the damage the monsters are dealing to the party by drawing back or using defensive magic. Only when you're sure that your character or another player character in the party is not going to get killed do you turn to serious offense.

   - **We just ran into them:** Neither side has an advantage. These situations are dangerous, because you might not realize how much trouble the party is in until you're several rounds into the fight and you don't have any good escape options open. Fight defensively until you know that it's safe to shift over to offense.

   - **They're in our way:** The monsters are obstacles the party has to get past, but you've got time to get ready for a fair fight. Use your spellcaster's buffing-up spells and try to make the fight distinctly unfair by turning allies invisible, summoning monsters, or creeping up to start the battle with a sneak attack.

   - **We ambushed them:** You've got time to hide and set up a surprise attack of your own. Lay down as much hurt as you can as fast as you can, so that the monsters don't get any real chance to fight back.

   Where are you fighting? Does the ground favor your party or the other side? Does the party have an easy way to get out if things go bad? Terrain affects combat in myriad ways. Here are some guidelines:

   - **Obstructed:** You're fighting in tight spaces or with little room to maneuver. Make sure that you control the battlefield by using walls and obstacles to keep enemies from getting around your character or other characters in the party.

   - **Wide open:** There's no place to hide. If your party is faster than the monsters, don't let them close with the party until you're ready. If your party is slower, try to bog down your foes in melee combat.

   - **Grossly unfair:** Your party is hanging on a cliff, fighting against harpies, fiendish giant eagles, or something else with wings. Back off and try it again when you've taken steps to make it a fair fight.

2. **Evaluate your foes:** Study the monsters you're facing and determine if they're battlers, ambushers, magic users, special attack users, or multiple threats. Don't forget to take a quick head count and determine if your party is outnumbered. Take special note of the following characteristics:

- **Battlers:** They're big, strong melee machines. Gangs of orc warriors, evil fighters, ogres or trolls, or solitary hulks like gray renders or stone giants are battlers.

- **Ambushers:** The monsters are dangerous when they catch your party by surprise, but aren't much for a stand-up fight.

- **Magic users:** The monsters attack with magic. Evil clerics or mad wizards are clearly magic users, but so are monsters such as demons and devils with dangerous spell-like abilities.

- **Special attack users:** The monster has a signature special attack that does most of the damage. The medusa with its petrifying gaze is a good example. Others include stirges (blood drain), many undead (ability or energy drain), or harpies (beguiling song).

- **Multiple threat:** The monsters do several things well. Dragons are both battlers and special attack users. Most demons and devils are battlers and magic users.

- **No threat:** The monsters aren't a real threat to your party. They might outnumber the party, but they're individually too weak to hurt anyone in the party.

3. **Choose the right tactic:** Decide what method will give you the best odds of victory, depending on your foes, such as:

   - **Battlers:** Maneuver is your best ploy. You don't want to give a battler a fair fight, that's what it excels at. Try save-or-die spells if a character in the party has them, because it'll be easier than wading through a ton of hit points.

   - **Ambushers:** Assuming your party was ambushed, it's too late for maneuver or negotiation. Use your save-or-die spells, or just deal damage.

   - **Magic users:** Many magic-using monsters tend to be vulnerable in close combat. Using spells and spell-like abilities is dangerous when enemies are close by, so get close and reduce their hit points with melee attacks.

   - **Special attack users:** Most special-attack users tend to be soft in hit points, but dangerous to get close to. Try dealing damage at range with damaging spells or archery, or use maneuver to make the fight safer.

   - **Multiple threat:** Monsters of this sort usually have high saving throws and are frequently very maneuverable, so avoid save-or-die spells and complicated maneuver plans. Try to beat multiple threats through dealing damage or with negotiation.

   - **No threat:** Save the cleric's and sorcerer's spells, and take out the monsters with melee attacks and archery.

4. **Rethink your assumptions:** At the end of every round, you should reassess the battle and figure out if any of your basic assumptions about the fight have changed. Did the monsters get reinforcements? Have you found a spot of good terrain that gives your character an advantage? Were the monsters no real threat at all? Was this a fight you needed, to run away from? Rethink your assumptions every round to make sure you're still fighting the right fight.

Using Advanced Tactics

If all you ever do is pick the right target for your character's spells, attack efficiently, and consider the occasional tactical retreat, you're already better off than a significant number of experienced players. You might have noticed that the preceding advice is fairly generic. In this section, we talk about a few specific artifacts of the D&D rules that you can master in order to play your best game.

Flanking

This is the first and easiest of the advanced tactics you should put to work for you. If your character and your allies are fighting the same foe, make sure that someone gets on the monster's opposite side. Now your character and your flanking buddy each gain a +2 bonus to melee attacks, and better yet, every attack your character and your ally make is a potential sneak attack (assuming that one or the other of your characters is a rogue).

Flanking is described on page 153 of the *Player's Handbook*.

Using the Tumble skill is a great way to slip around the monster without getting mauled by attacks of opportunity (more about those later in this chapter).

Beating the initiative order

The novice player assumes that it's always better to take his or her turn as early as possible in the round. We're working on making you smarter than that. Sometimes you can manufacture significant tactical advantages by readying actions or delaying your character's actions. These two tactics are known as *special initiative actions*.

Special initiative actions let you change the initiative order and time your character's attacks for maximum effect.

You find special initiative actions on page 160 of the *Player's Handbook*, right at the end of Chapter 8.

Some specific examples of ways to use the ready and delay actions to your advantage include:

- **Waiting for a flank:** Your character is toe-to-toe with the ogre, but your buddy hasn't taken his turn yet. Delay your character's action until your friend's character moves up to flank the ogre. When your ally attacks, he'll get the flanking bonus because your character is already in position. Then, your character attacks after your friend goes, and your character gets the flanking bonus also. If you had just had your character attack on your turn before your friend's character was in place on the other side of the monster, your character wouldn't have been flanking.

- **Waiting for a spell:** You're about to have your character go charging into melee against a troll, but the cleric has a spell to buff your character for the fight. You can have your character run off and make an attack right now without the benefit of the spell — or, you can delay your character's action until after the cleric bestows the spell on him or her, and then make an attack with the help of a comrade's magic.

- **Interrupting enemy actions:** Instead of blasting away at your foe on your turn, ready an action to attack or cast a spell on an enemy as soon as he does something you don't like. Instead of putting the damage on your foe on your turn, you wait until it's his turn — and the damage your character does may cause his action to fail.

- **Fighting enemies your character can't reach:** If you're dealing with a flying monster that swoops in to attack your character and then finishes its turn well out of reach, ready an action to strike at the monster the instant it comes within sword-reach. When it attacks, so does your character, and you don't spend round after round with your character getting hit and not being able to strike back.

Charging and full attacks

We'll admit it; if there's a monster in sight when your turn comes up for the first time in a fight, it's awful tempting to have your character run right up and begin whaling away. But there's a key mechanic in the game that you need to keep in mind: If your character moves more than 5 feet, you get only one attack. If your character stands still or moves 5 feet or less, you can use the full attack action to strike or shoot multiple times, provided your character is fighting with two weapons or has a base attack bonus of +6 or better.

The same rules apply for monsters. Consider this example: You're facing a high-level evil fighter, and your turn comes up before his or hers. If you have your character run up to the fighter, you'll only make one attack — but when his or her turn comes up, the evil fighter doesn't have to move to reach the target, because your character is already there. He or she gets to make a full attack, and possibly attack your character three or four times. If you hadn't had your character run up to face the fighter, there's a good chance he or she might have chosen to use an action to come up to you. The fighter would be the one making one attack, and your character would get to unload on him or her with a full attack on your next turn.

If you're playing a low-level character, you probably don't have any way to attack more than once per turn in any event. So you might as well move and attack at the same time, because you don't get an advantage by making the monsters and villains come to you.

Charging is a special attack action that enables your character to move up to twice his or her speed and make an attack at the end of the move. If you need to reach a foe and attack him fast, charging is a good answer. Your character also receives a +2 attack bonus when charging — but he or she also suffers a –2 penalty to Armor Class.

Charging is described on page 154 of the *Player's Handbook*. Full attacks are described in the "Full-Round Actions" section on page 143.

To sum up the key points of charging and full attacks:

- ✔ If the enemy is farther away than your character's speed, but not more than twice your character's speed, you can charge and attack. For example, if your character's speed is 20 feet, he or she could charge a foe up to 40 feet away.

- ✔ If the enemy is not farther away than your character's speed, your character can move and attack (or your character can charge in order to gain the attack bonus, as long as he or she is at least 10 feet away). If your character's speed is 20 feet, your character can move up to 20 feet and charge or attack the enemy.

- ✔ If the enemy is next to your character or only 5 feet away, your character can stand still or take a 5-foot step and make a full attack, striking with all weapons or gaining multiple attacks with a single weapon if his or her base attack bonus is +6 or better.

Avoiding attacks of opportunity

Attacks of opportunity are free, instant attacks anyone gets when someone who's *threatened* (close enough to get hit with a melee weapon) undertakes a complicated or risky action. Things that provoke attacks of opportunity include casting spells, trying to start a grapple, ignoring a foe in order to move through multiple squares he or she threatens, and a whole host of other things.

You can read all about attacks of opportunity on page 137 of the *Player's Handbook*.

Basically, you don't want to provoke attacks of opportunity. It's not smart to give the monsters free extra attacks against your character, because sometimes those attacks will hit, and your character will wind up taking more damage than necessary. Worse yet, maybe the monster will get really lucky, roll a critical hit, and take your character out of the fight with one swing — when it's not even the monster's turn.

That said, sometimes players go to extreme lengths to avoid insignificant attacks of opportunity. If you're playing a cleric with an AC of 22 who's fighting a goblin warrior with an attack bonus of +2, the goblin's only going to hit your cleric on a roll of 20. Ninety-five percent of the time, you can safely disregard the threat the goblin poses and ignore him or her. Be conservative in deciding when a foe can be ignored, though.

You've got four good ways to have your character maneuver around monsters and foes without giving them attacks of opportunity:

- ✔ **5-foot step:** You can limit your character's movement to a 5-foot step. If your character only takes a 5-foot step, he or she doesn't provoke attacks of opportunity just for moving through an enemy's threatened squares. You can also just have your character step back from a foe in order to get room to cast a spell or use a magic item safely.

- ✔ **Tumble:** The Tumble skill lets your character move safely through squares threatened by a foe. It's a great way to make risky moves that otherwise might get your character pounded by your enemies.

- ✔ **Using up the monster's attacks:** The vast majority of monsters and characters can only make one attack of opportunity per round (the exceptions are those creatures and characters who have the Combat Reflexes feat). After an ally has provoked the creature's attack of opportunity, your character is safe to ignore it — until the monster's turn comes up again, and its capability for attacks of opportunity resets. You might try callously throwing away a weak ally in order to draw off the foe's attacks of opportunity. For example, if you use a *summon monster* spell to conjure a fiendish wolf, you might be able to direct that wolf to do things that deliberately provoke attacks of opportunity. You don't care if the wolf gets killed because it's only a summoned monster. But it might be very useful to you for your minion to draw an opponent into using up his or her attacks of opportunity.

- ✔ **Withdraw:** If you need to get away from an enemy without that enemy getting a "parting shot," use the withdraw action (see page 143 of the *Player's Handbook*). Your character won't be able to do anything else this turn, but at least he or she won't get killed just for leaving.

Fighting defensively

Sometimes your best move is to play for time. Most players believe that the best defense is a good offense; if you want to avoid getting hit, take down the monster so fast it doesn't get many chances to hurt you.

Consider this scenario: You're playing a cleric with few combat spells left, fighting alongside a raging barbarian friend who's got his Strength cranked up to 25 and is cutting hill giants in half with every swing of his greataxe. Your cleric's mace attack just isn't going to make that much difference in taking down the monsters, but there are significant advantages to staying in the melee. First of all, your cleric will draw some number of attacks away from the barbarian; when he's raging, his Armor Class might be a 16 or 17, while your cleric's is well above 20. Second, your cleric is close to the barbarian so that your cleric can heal him up quickly if necessary. Finally, your cleric can maneuver to give your raging barbarian buddy a flanking bonus and improve his attack capability even more.

In a situation like this, you might try fighting defensively. You take a penalty on your attack rolls to improve your character's AC and reduce his or her chances of getting hit. Fighting defensively also works well when you're dealing with an enemy that your character can hit pretty much automatically (giving up some attack bonus in that case costs you nothing). And, if your character is fighting someone that he or she can only hit if you roll a 20, well, you might as well give your character the best AC possible while you wait for a lucky roll.

Here are some good ways to fight defensively:

- **Fight defensively:** Take a −4 penalty on your attack rolls, and get a +2 dodge bonus to your character's AC for the round.

- **Go totally defense:** If you don't want your character to make even a token swing at the monster, use the total defense option. You have to use a standard action, so you can't have your character attack or cast a spell in the same round that you use total defense, but you gain a +4 dodge bonus to your character's Armor Class.

- **Use the Combat Expertise feat:** The Combat Expertise feat allows you to fine-tune your attack rolls and your character's Armor Class by voluntarily taking a penalty of −1 to −5 to improve AC with a dodge bonus equal to the penalty you took. So you could take a −2 attack penalty to get +2 dodge bonus to AC. You'll find the full description of this feat on page 92 of the *Player's Handbook*.

- **Take advantage of cover:** Try to put something big and solid between your character and the monster. Cover generally offers your character a +4 bonus to Armor Class. You may or may not suffer a penalty to attack the monster, depending on where your character is in relation to the monster and the object that's providing cover. Cover is described in detail on page 150 of the *Player's Handbook*.

Most of these special combat rules can be found in Chapter 8 of the *Player's Handbook*. Fighting defensively is described on page 140. Total defense is described on page 142, and cover is described at length on page 150. Finally, you'll find the rules for the Combat Expertise feat on page 92.

Maximizing Your Character's Attacks

Your single most precious commodity in the game is the number of turns you get in the course of the day. The typical D&D battle lasts about five rounds, and you can expect your character to be in about four battles per day of adventuring — so your character only has 20 turns per day to beat down bad guys and make a difference in the adventure. Getting the most out of every turn you take is absolutely vital.

Setting up attacks of opportunity

If actions are your most valuable asset, then any tactic that lets your character get more opportunities to damage the enemy without costing any actions is worth a closer look. Attacks of opportunity offer your character the chance to make extra attacks when it isn't even your turn; if you can manufacture even one attack of opportunity per five rounds of combat, you're cramming six rounds of actions into five rounds of fighting. You'll be 20 percent more effective than the player who didn't position his or her character to take advantage of the opening when it came up.

Manufacturing lots of attacks of opportunity requires three things: A weapon with reach, the Combat Reflexes feat, and some tactical acumen. In the first two cases, you need to deliberately design your character to get lots of attacks of opportunity. But, as for the last, all you have to do is play a little smart.

Character building for the bloodthirsty

If you like your character to make lots of attacks, here are some character design tips you can try out:

- **Carry a reach weapon:** Choose a weapon with reach as your character's primary weapon. A reach weapon lets your character threaten far more of the battlefield than a weapon that he or she can only use against someone adjacent to him or her. The best choices are the longspear (simple), glaive (martial), or spiked chain (exotic). Longspears and glaives have a big drawback — they can *only* attack with reach, so your character can't use one to attack someone standing right next to him or her. The spiked chain doesn't have that disadvantage, but it takes an Exotic Weapon Proficiency feat to master the spiked chain.

✔ **Take the Combat Reflexes feat:** Buy the Combat Reflexes feat as early in your character's career as possible. Be warned: Unless your character has a Dexterity score of 13 or better, you don't get much benefit from taking this feat. But a spiked chain wielder with Combat Reflexes and a Dex of 14 or better can cover a *lot* of ground and make up to three attacks of opportunity *each round.*

Tactics that go for the throat

In addition to some clever character design, you can also use some hard-nosed tactical play to put your character in a position to gather up every attack of opportunity that might come his or her way:

✔ **Controlling territory:** Put your character in a spot where the enemy has to go past your character to get at other party members (or to get away from other party members). Look for tactical chokepoints in the fight where your character can block a hallway or a door and get a free hack on anyone trying to go through.

✔ **Menacing everyone:** Move your character up to put as many foes as possible within reach of his or her weapon, especially if they are spell-casters (or monsters who use spell-like abilities, which also provoke attacks of opportunity). This strategy is a little risky, because it's some-times not a great idea to go get your character surrounded, but the more enemies within reach of your character's weapon, the more likely it is that one of them will do something stupid and give you a free shot.

✔ **Tripping the light fantastic:** Use trip attacks or spells that knock people down in order to knock your foes prone. Standing up provokes an attack of opportunity — and crawling away provokes one too. The best combo for tripping is the spiked chain in conjunction with the Improved Trip feat, but there are other ways to manufacture trip attacks. Dogs, wolves, and wolf-like monsters usually have a trip ability, so choose something canine for your character's animal companion if you're playing a ranger or druid, or make a point of summoning such creatures with *summon monster* spells if you're playing a spellcaster.

Hitting hard: Power Attack 101

One of the best ways to maximize your character's attacks is to get the Power Attack feat and use it cleverly. First of all, the Cleave feat is part of the Power Attack feat tree (see Chapter 14 for more about feat trees), so buying Power Attack puts you on the road to a feat that generates extra attacks for your character — and, as we already noted earlier in this chapter, extra attacks are all good. But, even more than that, Power Attack allows you to convert "overkill" attack bonus into a big-time damage bonus. The trick lies in determining how much you can safely take off your character's attack bonus and still have a good chance of hitting the target.

In any given situation, you want the best expected damage value you can get. Your *expected damage value* is equal to your character's chance of hitting times your average damage roll. For example, say that your character has an attack bonus of +8 and he or she deals 1d10+4 points of damage on a success-ful hit. Against a target with an AC of 17, your character hits on a roll of 9 or better (a 60 percent chance to hit) and deals an average of 9.5 points of damage (the average value of a d10 roll is 5.5). The expected damage for that attack is 5.7 points. Your character's average hit deals more than that, of course, but you have to factor in the 40 percent of attacks in which your character swings and misses.

Now, say that you use 3 points of Power Attack. Your character's attack bonus drops to +5, but your average damage increases to 1d10+7. Against this same AC 17 foe, your character hits on a 12 or better (45 percent chance) and deals an average of 12.5 points of damage. The expected damage value is 12.5 × 0.45, or 5.625 points. Your Power Attack didn't help you at all.

But . . . if your character uses a two-handed weapon, the Power Attack feat gives you twice the damage bonus. Taking a –3 on your attack roll gives you a +6 on damage. So now your average damage increases from 1d10+4 to 1d10+10 (15.5 points). Your expected damage value is 15.5 × 0.45, or 6.975 points. Even though your character will miss more often, the extra damage makes using the Power Attack feat worth it against this AC 17 enemy.

Most experienced players with a character built for Power Attack do all this math ahead of time, so that they can make an educated guess at the oppo-nent's AC and quickly determine if they want to Power Attack, and how much they want to Power Attack for. Here's a quick primer on "easy" Power Attack situations:

- ✔ **Charging:** You get a +2 attack bonus, so you can roll this into Power Attack and get a damage boost without changing your normal attack bonus.

- ✔ **Flanking:** Ditto. You get a +2 attack bonus when your character is flank-ing, so you can roll it straight into Power Attack.

- ✔ **Smiting:** When a paladin or cleric of the Destruction domain makes a smite attack, he or she gets an attack bonus. Roll this into Power Attack.

- ✔ **Very soft targets:** If your opponent has a crummy AC, you can Power Attack for a lot and still hit him.

- ✔ **Very hard targets:** If you can only hit on a 20, you might as well Power Attack for all you're worth.

Adapting Your Tactics to Your Foes

The earlier sections of this chapter give you the medieval equivalent of a Ph.D. in Hurt — in the rest of the chapter, we show you some specific tactical situations that come up all the time in game play. It's rare that you participate in an adventure that doesn't feature at least one or more of the following scenarios.

Beating spellcasters

Enemy spellcasters are dangerous because they can either put damage on a number of party members at once with a spell such as _fireball_ or take out one of your comrades per turn with an all-or-nothing spell such as a _hold person_ or _disintegrate_. However, the most dangerous spellcasters (sorcerers and wizards) tend to be soft targets (enemies with low Armor Class and poor hit points). Hit them fast and hard.

Here are three nasty tricks you can try the next time your party comes across an evil wizard:

- **Suppressive fire:** If you're having your character use a ranged attack (a bow or spells of his or her own), don't attack when your turn comes up. Instead, ready an action to take a shot (or cast a spell) on the enemy spellcaster's turn, as soon as he or she begins to cast a spell. If your character lays some damage on the enemy wizard when he or she is casting a spell, the wizard will have to make a Concentration check to complete the spell. If your character had just shot him or her on your turn, the wizard wouldn't have to do that. Your character will end up dealing the same damage to the enemy that he or she was going to deal the wizard by shooting on your turn, and you'll also give the wizard a chance to muff his or her spell.

- **Box and menace:** The classic response to an enemy wizard is to put an angry fighter in his or her face. Charge or run past any obstacles in the way to reach the wizard. If he or she casts a spell while threatened by your character, he or she will have to either cast defensively or step away from your character in order to cast safely. If you can get an ally on the other side of the enemy wizard, you can box him or her so that he or she can't move or cast a spell without giving your character an attack of opportunity. The downside of this tactic is that many enemy spellcasters have great Concentration skill modifiers, allowing them to cast defensively with a fair amount of confidence.

- **Grapple:** This is our favorite, because for some reason DMs just don't think it can happen to their master villains. Run up to the enemy wizard and start a grapple. Wizards are usually very poor grapplers and often don't even bother to keep a weapon in hand to foil your character's grapple attempt. The best part is that spellcasting in a grapple is virtually impossible.

Handling numerous foes

The good news about being outnumbered is that you're probably dealing with foes who are individually weaker than your character. D&D is heroic fiction, and in heroic fiction, you can mop the floor with whole gangs of numerous bad guys who can't hit the broadside of a barn. If you find your character outnumbered by foes who are as tough (or tougher) than your character, then *run!* Your character is going to get creamed.

The following list offers some helpful tactics to try when your character is outnumbered and surrounded by enemies:

- ✔ **Concentrate the damage:** Don't have your character hit one orc in one round, and then attack a different orc in next round. In D&D, enemies don't lose any offensive potential until they drop dead, so slowly wearing down multiple foes at once simply means that you're giving more enemies opportunities to hurt your character before they go down. Pick on one or two foes at a time and drop them before starting on the next enemies.

- ✔ **Control the battlefield:** Look for ways to divide and conquer foes. Have your character retreat into a narrow passage where enemies can only come at him or her a couple at a time. Use terrain-altering spells such as *grease* or *wall of ice* to isolate some of your enemies from their pals. If nothing else presents itself, just move. When your character is standing still on open ground, you're making it easy for your foes to surround your character and attack from all sides. If you keep your character moving, you won't find your character in the middle of three or four bad guys all taking full attacks on him or her every round.

Fighting monsters your character can't hurt

Lots of monsters have defenses that are very difficult to overcome, but usually *someone* in the party has a weapon that works. The sorcerer's *magic missiles* hurt almost anything, if all else fails.

The basic strategy for fighting a monster most of the party can't hurt is to protect and support whichever characters *can* hurt the monster. Everybody else simply buys time for the effective character or characters to wear down the foe, and does their best to make sure the character doing the hard work stays healed up and in the thick of the fight.

High-AC foes

Enemies with superior Armor Class may be virtually impossible for your character to hit with melee or ranged attacks. Fortunately, your character can hit anything if you roll a natural 20 on your attack roll, so if nothing else, you can simply have your character flail away at the enemy until you get a lucky roll. Here are some different ideas:

- ✔ **Tackle the monster:** Grapple your enemy. Grapple attacks ignore Armor Class, and if your character can wrestle the creature to the ground, you can gain control of the situation. But don't try to grapple really big monsters: Large monsters have high Strength scores, as well as an inherent bonus to grapple checks that your character will have a hard time beating. Check out the "Grapple" section, which starts on page 155 of the *Player's Handbook.*

- ✔ **Flank and aid another:** If your foe is nothing you want your character to wrestle with, surround it to get the +2 attack bonus for flanking . . . then have as many characters as possible use the aid another action in order to provide the character with the best chance of hitting extra attack bonuses.

- ✔ **Maximize one character:** Have your party's buffing spellcasters power up the most effective character with spells such as *bless, enlarge person,* or a bard's song, whatever it takes. You can usually manufacture a boost of at least +4 to +6 or more on one character's attack rolls.

High-DR foes

DR, or damage resistance, can be very hard to fight through. When the iron golem is ignoring the first 15 points from every hit each of the player characters hands it, the party is not going to wear it down very fast at all. Assuming that you can't solve the problem by having your character cast a spell such as *align weapon* or switching to a secondary weapon such as a silver dagger stuck in a boot, you're in for a hard fight.

The following tactics work well against monsters with a high damage resistance:

- ✔ **Power Attack:** It's ugly, but it works. If your character has the Power Attack feat, take a big penalty on your attack roll in order to crank up the damage your character deals with each hit. If your character is wielding a two-handed weapon, you can take a –5 attack penalty in order to deal +10 damage . . . which is certainly enough to make a dent in even the best DR. Because you're giving up your character's chance of scoring a hit, you should then use some of the tactics described in the "High-AC foes" section, earlier in this chapter, in order to restore as much of your attack roll as you can.

- **Sneak attack:** The rogue's sneak attack is also useful for getting through DR, because a good sneak attack (say, +4d6 or +5d6) can turn a 5-point hit into a 20- or 25-point hit. Once again, you'll want to do everything in your power to make sure the rogue makes a lot of sneak attacks with the most help you can provide him or her.

  Watch out for monsters that have a good DR and are also immune to sneak attacks, such as golems or undead. This tactic won't work on them.

- **Magic:** Make the sorcerer work for a living. Almost all spells ignore damage reduction. Let your party's spellcasters beat the monster with damaging spells or save-or-die spells.

Elusive foes

Some enemies are hard to hurt because they're simply not there for your character's attacks. Good examples are incorporeal creatures such as specters or shadows that can attack through the walls, or evil monks who use high movement rates and Spring Attacks to whack your character and then bound away before your character can reply.

Try the following strategies when your character is facing an elusive foe:

- **Ready an attack:** Ready an action to whale on your adversary whenever he or she comes within reach. Even if your foe's movements and attacks don't normally provoke attacks of opportunity, a readied attack isn't an attack of opportunity; your character can get a swing at the enemy when he or she moves in to attack. It works better than standing around waiting to get hit.

- **Get the right help:** Cast *summon monster* or *summon nature's ally* to bring in an ally better suited for fighting the foe than your character. For example, most animals have the Scent ability; they're much better at attacking invisible foes than your character is. A fiendish dire wolf does wonders to keep invisible enemies honest.

Chapter 20

Making the Most of Magic

Although every adventuring party needs a fighter or two to stand up and dish out the physical damage to the monsters, the majority of combat encounters in the DUNGEONS & DRAGONS game are decided by the use of magic. A *fireball* drops the evil wizard's orc bodyguards; an *improved invisibility* spell on the party's rogue lets him or her launch a dizzying barrage of lethal sneak attacks; the attacking mummies are simply incinerated by the cleric's *flame strike* spell. The D&D experience has been summed up as simply as "the game where you fight monsters with magic," and that says it all.

In this chapter, we tell you about the fine arts of picking the right spell for the right job, casting effective spells in battle, and maximizing any character's power with the acquisition of the right magic items. We also show you some baseline magic item purchases to quickly equip higher-level characters.

Selecting Spells for the Adventure

Beyond the basic division of arcane and divine spellcasters, there's another important categorization for characters who wield magic: *spontaneous casters* and *prepared casters*.

Bards and sorcerers are spontaneous casters. Any spell that they know, they can use at any time, so long as they still have spell slots left. Spontaneous casters generally don't know very many spells; finding versatile spells or spells with more than one application is a big part of being a successful spontaneous caster. Bards and sorcerers can only add to the spells they know when they gain a character level; they can't adjust their magic capabilities to the specific mission at hand.

On the other hand, clerics, druids, and wizards (and paladins and rangers too, for that matter, although they don't really cast enough spells to matter) must prepare their spells. They can choose from much broader spell lists than the bard and sorcerer, but once they fix their spell choices in place, they generally can't alter those choices on the fly. The good news is that their spell lists can change drastically from day to day, allowing you to focus your character's spell selection for very specific missions.

The differences between each spellcasting character class's ability to prepare or spontaneously cast some or all of their spells give you some basic guidelines to choosing your character's spells, as follows:

- **Bard:** As a spontaneous caster, you can't adjust your bard's spell selection for the adventure. When your character gains new spells at each experience level, select spells that provide versatility, such as *silent image, summon monster,* and *charm person* or *charm monster.*

- **Cleric:** The cleric's ability to spontaneously convert prepared spells into healing spells means that you should not include a *cure* spell of any sort in your cleric's prepared spells. Instead, prepare offensive spells such as *spiritual hammer* or *searing light.* You can convert them to *cure* spells at a moment's notice. Also, don't forget to prepare one domain spell per spell level.

- **Druid:** The druid's ability to spontaneously convert prepared spells into *summon nature's ally* spells means that you should never assign any *summon nature's ally* spells to your druid's available spell slots. Instead, prepare various *cure* spells and other defensive spells; you can switch them to offense at a moment's notice by turning them into *summon nature's ally* spells.

- **Sorcerer:** The sorcerer doesn't have the ability to adjust spell selection in mid-adventure, because he or she is a spontaneous caster. If you're playing a sorcerer, you want your sorcerer's known spell list to include spells that can be used in a number of different ways. Such spells include illusion spells, *summon monster* spells, and transmutation spells such as *alter self* or *polymorph.* If your character knows a few of these spells, you can quickly generate offense, defense, or utility as you need it.

- **Wizard:** The wizard has the greatest flexibility of all the spellcasting classes. If you're playing a wizard, you can reinvent your wizard as an entirely new character every time you decide which spells you want your character to prepare. In general, you should prepare about 40 to 60 percent of your wizard's available spell slots as attack spells of some kind, but that depends on what you're up against in the game. Check out the spell selection process described in the following steps for more specific guidance.

Here's an easy process to follow when you're considered which spells you want your character to prepare for the day's adventuring:

1. **Consider the scenario:** What are you trying to do? Is the party going monster-hunting? Select spells to find and kill monsters. Is the party going to explore a trap-filled tomb? Take spells that will let the party get around or through traps. Is the party trying to infiltrate an evil thieves' guild? Take spells of disguise, enchantment, and subterfuge.

2. **Review what you know:** What do you know about the obstacles you expect to meet in the adventure? If the party has learned that the evil warlord's castle is guarded by ogre berserkers, you can expect to run into lots of ogres. Chances are good that *charm person* or *dominate person* spells won't help much, because ogres are giants, not humanoids. If you discover you don't have any information at all, perhaps you should make gaining information your mission for the day (see Reconnaissance, below), and then go in with guns blazing tomorrow, after you know a little bit more.

3. **Choose your mission:** How do you want to accomplish your goals in the current adventure? Do you expect to have your character directly attacking the foes with magic? Will you have your character use magic to help friends move through difficult terrain or around dangerous enemies? Or do you want your character to be ready to support friends with buffing and healing spells? Here are some of your choices:

   • **Direct attack:** Your character's role for the day is to provide magical firepower for the party of adventurers. Prepare offensive spells such as *magic missile, sleep, web, fireball, confusion,* or *hold monster.* If you're playing a cleric, consider the combat monster or battle caster cleric spell loadouts described in Chapter 17.

   • **Maneuver:** Your character is going to help the party get to where it can do the most good. *Fly, water breathing, teleport,* and *resist energy* are typical spells that allow the party to go somewhere they otherwise couldn't go. Prepare however many spells of the right sort that you'll need to make your plan work.

   • **Reconnaissance:** Your character is going to gather information pertaining to the mission. Spells such as *charm person, invisibility, clairaudience/clairvoyance, scrying,* or even *summon monster* may be useful in allowing your character to efficiently question captured foes, slip into places he or she is not supposed to be, or scout out dangerous locales before the party walks into a deadly ambush.

   • **Support:** Your character is going to help the party stand up to damage and fight better. Prepare spells that buff comrades and generally contribute versatility and extra options. *Mage armor, invisibility, dispel magic, polymorph, stoneskin,* and *teleport* are all good options for this kind of role. If you're playing a cleric, consider the master healer cleric spell loadout.

4. **Leave a slot open?** If you're playing a wizard, you don't have to fill all your character's spell slots with prepared spells. You can choose to leave some slots "empty," ready to be filled with just 15 minutes of study time (see "Spell Preparation Time" on page 178 of the *Player's Handbook*).

Leaving a few spell slots open is an extremely powerful tool for a wizard. The wizard is the only spellcaster who has the ability to examine an obstacle or opponent and then study a spellbook to find the exact right spell to deal with it. If you don't know what your character is going to meet in the adventure, and you've got a lot of spell slots to fill, consider leaving a handful of slots empty. Don't leave too many slots empty, though — you might need those spells in a fight!

Casting Effectively in Combat

You can have your character use spells to secure all the advantages you like before entering the dungeon, but sooner or later, your character is going to have to fight the monsters. If you're playing a sorcerer or a wizard, your character has no weapon worth speaking of other than magic. Bards, clerics, and druids have more options in a fight, but by the time a cleric is 7th or 8th level, he should be spending most of his actions in a battle casting spells to aid his allies and hinder his foes. A high-level cleric might as well leave his mace at home, because he never gets a chance to swing it.

As a spellcaster, your character should stay away from sword fights. The last place you want your character to be is right in front of the monsters or villains, where they can pound on your character with their melee attacks. Unfortunately, this decision is not always up to you. Sometimes spellcasters get caught off-guard or trapped in tight quarters, and the monsters are in their faces before they can get out of the way.

Getting caught in a melee is bad for two reasons. First of all, your character is exposed to the enemies' best and most dangerous attacks. No sane sorcerer wants to be anywhere near an angry ogre with a big spiked club. Second, the great majority of spells your character casts in melee provoke attacks of opportunity (see Chapter 19 of this book for more info). Even if your character survives the free attack he or she just gave the bad guy, each hit your character takes while casting a spell forces him or her to make a Concentration skill check or lose the spell outright. So, not only is your character exposed to direct attack, you're putting your character in a situation where he or she might not be able to safely use the best weapon at his or her disposal: spells.

Fortunately, there are a few ways to slither out of this difficult position:

✔ **5-foot step:** Your character can step one square away from the foe threatening him or her without provoking an attack of opportunity for moving. If you then find that your character is no longer threatened, he or she can then safely cast spells. Be careful about trying this on large opponents such as ogres or giants, though — your character might back off one square but still be within the area these monsters threaten due to their great melee reach.

✔ **Cast defensively:** Your character can attempt to cast a spell defensively with a successful Concentration check. The DC of the check is 15 + spell level. For instance, if you want your character to cast *lightning bolt,* all he or she has to do is pass a DC 18 Concentration check. If your character has a lot of ranks in the Concentration skill (or has the Combat Casting feat), it's pretty easy to make this check.

✔ **Find cover:** If you can get some kind of cover in between your character and the monster threatening him or her, you prevent the monster from making an attack of opportunity on your character. Even hiding behind an ally works. If your character can't take a 5-foot step away from the monster, see if you can find a square nearby where your character will have something (a wall, another character, a big rock, almost anything) in between him or her and the antagonist.

✔ **Use a wand:** A number of magic items replicate the effects of various spells but don't provoke attacks of opportunity. Staffs and wands are two of the most common. If you find your character in a situation where casting a spell will draw an attack of opportunity, you can fall back to using a wand or other magic item to cast a spell instead.

Powering Up with Magic Items

The spells your character commands represent only a portion of the magical power available to the typical adventuring party. The other half of the equation is the party's collection of magic items. For example, the fighter carries a magic sword and wears magic armor; the rogue has a *ring of invisibility;* the wizard has a wand of *lightning bolt;* and the cleric wears a *helm of brilliance.* Spells are just for spellcasters, but any character can carry a powerful magic item.

When you create a 1st-level character, that character begins with low-grade, nonmagical gear and a handful of pocket change. But as your character has successful adventures, he or she recovers staggering amounts of wealth and magic items of great and terrible power. Your character's collection of magic items is just as much a part of him or her as the choice of class, skills, and feats. A fighter who owns *winged boots* is a very different character from a fighter who owns a *scarab of protection.*

Types of magic items

Magic items come in a variety of different forms, ranging from mighty magic swords, to life-saving potions, to artifacts of godlike power. By the time your character gets a few experience levels under his or her belt, you'll probably have a good array of magic items to choose from.

Here's a quick tour of the types of magic items you're likely to find or purchase:

- ✔ **Armor:** Magic armor (and magic shields) work much like normal armor, except better. Magic armor has an enhancement bonus (or a "plus") associated with it, so you might find a suit of *+2 scale mail* or a *+4 heavy steel shield.* The value of the bonus is added to the AC bonus provided by the armor. So, for example, normal scale mail gives a +4 armor bonus to AC, but *+2 scale mail* adds 6 points to AC.

- ✔ **Weapons:** Magic weapons work a lot like magic armor; they've got an enhancement bonus (a "plus") that you add to each attack and damage roll your character makes with the weapon. For example, a 4th-level fighter with a Strength of 16 and a longsword has an attack bonus of +7 (+4 for the character's fighter levels and +3 Strength modifier) and deals 1d8+3 points of damage. If the same character fights with a *+2 longsword,* the attack bonus becomes +9, and the fighter deals 1d8+5 points of damage per hit.

- ✔ **Potion:** A potion is a one-use spell your character drinks. When your character drinks it, the potion's magic takes effect for a short time, and the potion is used up. Almost any low-level spell can be found in the form of a potion, but some of the most common are potions of *cure light wounds, bull's strength, invisibility,* and *fly.*

- ✔ **Scroll:** A scroll is a one-use spell that a trained spellcaster can read. It lets your character cast the spell on the scroll without using up any of his or her own spell slots for the day. Potions work for anybody, but only a character of the right class (sorcerer or wizard for a scroll with a sorcerer/wizard spell, cleric for a cleric spell scroll, and so on) can use a scroll. (However, if your character has some ranks in the Use Magic Device skill, a successful skill check enables your character to break that rule.)

- ✔ **Ring:** Well, we all know about magic rings now, don't we? Don't worry, not every ring is The One Ring to Rule Them All. Magical rings range from minor protective devices such as a *+1 ring of protection* (which adds a +1 deflection bonus to AC) to powerful items such as the *ring of wizardry* (which doubles your character's spell slots at a particular spell level). Some rings have charges that eventually run out, but others provide benefits that last as long as a character wears the ring.

✔ **Wand:** A wand simply holds a single spell with 50 uses. So a wand of *magic missiles* holds the *magic missile* spell, and your character can use it 50 times before the wand is burned out. Like a scroll, a wand can only be used by a character of the right spellcasting class. Wands are set at a certain caster level when they're created, and you can't change that. So, even if you're playing a 10th-level wizard, a wand of *magic missiles* (caster level 1st) only produces a single missile each time it's used. Once your character spends that last charge, he or she might as well throw away the wand — it's nothing but a stick now.

✔ **Staff:** A staff is like a wand, except that it usually holds several different spells. Your character can use the staff's charges to cast any spell the staff holds. A staff also allows you to use your character's own caster level to cast those spells, if your character's caster level is higher than the staff's caster level. If you're playing a high-level spellcaster, this is a significant advantage.

✔ **Rod:** Rods are weird. They're devices that incorporate strange powers that aren't easily replicated by existing spells. Many rods also serve as weapons, too — for example, the *rod of thunder and lightning* serves as a *+2 light mace,* if your character just wants to beat somebody with it.

✔ **Wondrous item:** Most other magic items are lumped together in the wondrous items category. Wondrous items range from magical articles of attire, such as a *hat of disguise, boots of speed, belt of giant's strength,* or *cloak of resistance,* to useful devices such as a *flying carpet* or *crystal ball.* We just can't offer much in the way of generalizations about wondrous items, because they're all diverse and unique. But here are four basic types of wondrous items that are exceptionally common:

- **Ability adders:** Many wondrous items increase your character's ability scores. For example, *gauntlets of ogre power* gives a character a +2 enhancement bonus to his or her Strength score as long as the character is wearing them — any fighter would love to have a pair of these. Other ability adders include the *belt of giant strength, gloves of Dexterity, headband of intellect, periapt of Wisdom, amulet of health,* and *cloak of Charisma.*

- **AC adders:** Characters who can't wear armor turn to magic items to improve their Armor Class. *Bracers of armor* add an armor bonus ranging from +1 to +9, depending on how good they are. The *amulet of natural armor* adds a natural armor bonus ranging from +1 to +5.

- **Save adders:** Several items add a bonus to one or more of your character's saving throws. The most common is the *cloak of resistance,* which adds a +1 to +5 resistance bonus to all your character's saves.

- **Spell users:** Finally, a variety of items give your character the ability to use one or more spells. These may be disposable items (a *necklace of fireballs* may hold as few as three fireballs) or items that give your character the ability to use the spell a limited number of times per day (the *circlet of blasting* lets your character use the spell *searing light* once per day).

Acquiring magic items

Magic items sound great, don't they? You might think that every character should have some, and in the vast majority of D&D games, they do. But here's the downside: Your character's acquisition of magic items is entirely in the hands of your Dungeon Master. If your DM doesn't include magic items in the treasure stashes of the monsters the party defeats, well, your character won't find many. And if your DM decides that magic items just aren't bought and sold in his or her campaign, you won't be able to turn big piles of gold into a wand of *lightning bolt* and a flaming sword. You've got to live with what your DM lets your character have.

Finding items

Monsters often guard hoards of staggering wealth, including long-lost devices with mighty enchantments. Champions of evil are usually armed and armored with powerful magic items, which are there for the taking after the party has defeated the previous owner. In fact, a knowledgeable player often goes out of his or her way to battle against villains such as dark knights and evil wizards, because these NPCs (nonplayer characters) are great sources of magic items your character can "turn to the service of good" (which sounds better than "loot from their bloody corpses," but a rose by any other name . . .).

The best way to quickly determine if there's some interesting booty at hand is to cast the *detect magic* spell. Most 0-level spells are pretty worthless, so you might as well fill up those slots with *detect magic* spells. Or, if you don't mind making a minor investment in looting technology, buy a wand of *detect magic*. It's only 375 gp, and your character can use it 50 times before it runs out of charges.

The difficulty with items your character finds in monster hoards or on the persons of defeated villains is that they don't often come with name tags and instruction manuals. Many DMs don't waste much time on making you guess what magic items your character is carrying, because nothing is more annoying than listening to a player constantly say things like, "Okay, I rolled an 18 for my attack roll . . . plus whatever the bonus on this sword is, so maybe it's a 19 or a 20. So did I hit or what?" But some DMs are sticklers for this, so be prepared.

The surest way to figure out what item your character has is to cast an *identify* spell (or arrange to have such a spell cast, if no one in your party of adventurers can do it). *Identify* isn't cheap; it costs 100 gp each time you cast it, because the spell requires a pearl worth 100 gp. Save *identify* spells for things you really can't figure out otherwise.

Clever guessing with detect magic

All magic items possess a magical aura, which can be detected by means of a *detect magic* spell. The *detect magic* spell can often provide some dead-giveaway clues as to an item's use or function, because the spell tells you how strongly the item in question is enchanted. You're also allowed to make a Spellcraft check to determine the school of magic of the item. (The schools of magic are abjuration, conjuration, divination, enchantment, evocation, illusion, necromancy, and transmutation.) Different types of items make use of different magic schools. Here are some quick tips on using *detect magic* to make a quick and accurate assessment of a magic item:

- ✔ **Armor and weapons:** If the aura is faint, you're looking at a weapon or armor with a +1 magical enhancement. If it's moderate evocation, the item probably has a +2 or +3 enhancement.

✔ **Potions:** If the aura is conjuration, it's probably a *cure light wounds* or *cure moderate wounds* potion. There are other potions based on conjuration spells, but *cure light wounds* potions are by far the most common.

✔ **Bracers:** If the aura is moderate conjuration, they're *bracers of armor*.

✔ **Cloaks:** A cloak with a faint abjuration aura is probably a *cloak of resistance*.

Buying and selling items

The other way to acquire magic items is to simply buy them. If your character loots a dragon's hoard and finds 20,000 pieces of gold, you've got 20 grand to spend. In D&D, the point of gaining wealth is so that you can spend it on the biggest, most impressive magic items you can find for your character, and then go get even *more* treasure so you can buy even *better* magic items.

Buying magic items works in both directions, of course. When your character finds a *+3 flaming adamantine longsword,* that old *+2 longsword* doesn't look so useful anymore. You can sell items, too — but you usually only get 50 percent of the purchase price. Your character may acquire a dozen *+1 rapiers* when the party raids the drow outpost; the best thing to do is to keep one and sell the rest, so that your character can turn some of that loot into magic items that are more useful to him or her.

In general, your character needs to find a good-sized city in order to buy or sell an expensive magic item. The reasoning is that no one in a flea-speck-sized village way off in the middle of nowhere has a *+3 sword* to sell. The bigger the town, the better the odds of finding good magic items to buy. A word of advice: A lot of DMs are old school on the topic of buying magic items. In earlier editions of the D&D game, magic items just weren't bought; your character could only find or steal them. Ask your DM how he or she wants to handle this in the game.

Defining the magic item baseline

Heads up! The D&D game *assumes* that your character has a selection of magic items appropriate to his or her class and level. The Challenge Rating of monsters is based on this assumption. You may think it's absolutely snazzy for your 10th-level fighter to walk around with a *carpet of flying,* but if your fighter doesn't have a magic weapon by 10th level, you're going to find that it's hard to hold up your end in a fight.

In this section, we show you a typical path for collecting magic items for each of the four base classes (fighter, rogue, cleric, and sorcerer). These are summed up on Tables 20-1 through 20-4.

These tables are based on the character wealth assumptions stated on Table 5-1, page 135 of the *Dungeon Master's Guide.* The tables in the *Dungeon Master's Guide* are there to give a Dungeon Master an idea of how much treasure a character of a certain level ought to have, which is useful when creating new characters at higher than 1st level or for pacing the rate of treasure acquisition the DM provides in his or her game. However, your character is not *entitled* to treasure and magic items of the stated amount. Your character's acquisition of treasure is entirely in the hands of your Dungeon Master. You may lag behind drastically for a long time, only to score an epic hoard by slaying a mighty dragon. Or your character might get lucky and find particular items that are significantly more than he or she might normally be able to afford, based on these assumptions.

That said, it's a fairly common practice for DMs, when a player is starting with a character above 1st level, to tell that player, "Make up a 5th-level character and equip him or her appropriately. You've got 9,000 gp for gear." Definitely check with your DM before you start shopping in the magic items chapter of the *Dungeon Master's Guide.*

One more thing: In Tables 20-1 through 20-4, we use three conventions you should know about. First, the abbreviation "MW" stands for "masterwork." (Masterwork items are described on page 122 and 126 of the *Player's Handbook.*) Second, the names of magic items are italicized. Third, your character might have a fair amount of cash unspent at particular levels. You can use that cash to pick out additional gear for your character or save it for a rainy day; it's up to you. If the cash balance includes an "**or,**" that's because the table presents you with two options at that level that have different costs — if you choose the more expensive option, you'll have less cash available.

The tables all list specific potions to buy, but feel free to swap the suggested potions for any other potions of similar price.

Magic item descriptions begin on page 215 of the *Dungeon Master's Guide.* You'll find the scoop on mithral armor on page 284.

Fighter magic items

If you're playing a fighter, your primarily concern is finding good weapons and armor. The better your character's armament, the better he or she fights. The items given in Table 20-1 also work well for barbarians, paladins, and rangers — but if you're playing a barbarian or ranger, make sure you stick with the lighter armor. Table 20-1 lists the fighter's magic items by level.

Table 20-1	Typical Fighter Magic Items by Level		
Level/Total Wealth	**Weapons**	**Armor**	**Other Gear**
1st	As starting package	As starting package	As starting package
2nd/ 900 gp	MW longsword (315 gp), composite longbow (+1 Strength) (200 gp)	Banded mail (250 gp) **or** chain shirt (150 gp); large steel shield (20 gp)	Potion of *cure light wounds* (50 gp), cash (65 **or** 165 gp)
3rd/ 2,700 gp	MW longsword (315 gp), composite longbow (+2 Strength) (300 gp)	Full plate armor (1,500 gp) **or** mithral chain shirt (1,100 gp); MW large steel shield (170 gp)	Potions of *bull's strength* (300 gp) and *cure light wounds* (50 gp), cash (65 **or** 465 gp)
4th/ 5,400 gp	*+1 longsword* (2,315 gp), composite longbow (+2 Strength) (300 gp), 10 *+1 arrows* (460 gp)	Full plate armor (1,500 gp) **or** mithral chain shirt (1,100 gp); MW large steel shield (170 gp)	Potions of *bull's strength* (300 gp), 3 *cure light wounds* (150 gp), cash (205 **or** 605 gp)
5th/ 9,000 gp	*+1 longsword* (2,315 gp), MW composite longbow (+3 Strength) (700 gp), 20 *+1 arrows* (920 gp)	*+1 full plate armor* (2,650 gp) **or** *+1 mithral chain shirt* (2,100 gp); MW large steel shield (170 gp)	*+1 cloak of resistance* (1,000 gp), potions of *fly* (750 gp), *bull's strength* (300 gp), and 3 *cure light wounds* (150 gp), cash (45 **or** 595 gp)
6th/ 13,000 gp	*+1 longsword* (2,315 gp), MW composite longbow (+3 Strength) (700 gp), 20 *+1 arrows* (920 gp)	*+1 full plate armor* (2,650 gp) **or** *+1 mithral chain shirt* (2,100 gp); MW large steel shield (170 gp)	*Gauntlets of ogre power* (4,000 gp), *+1 cloak of resistance* (1,000 gp), potions of *fly* (750 gp), *cure moderate wounds* (300 gp), and 3 *cure light wounds* (150 gp), cash (45 **or** 595 gp)

Level/Total Wealth	Weapons	Armor	Other Gear
7th/ 19,000 gp	*+2 longsword* (8,315 gp), MW composite longbow (+3 Strength) (700 gp), 20 *+1 arrows* (920 gp)	*+1 full plate armor* (2,650 gp) **or** *+1 mithral chain shirt* (2,100 gp); MW large steel shield (170 gp)	*Gauntlets of ogre power* (4,000 gp), *+1 cloak of resistance* (1,000 gp), potions of *fly* (750 gp), *cure moderate wounds* (300 gp), and 3 *cure light wounds* (150 gp), cash (45 **or** 595 gp)
8th/ 27,000 gp	*+2 longsword* (8,315 gp), *+1 composite longbow* (+3 Strength) (2,700 gp), 10 *+2 arrows* (1,660 gp)	*+2 full plate armor* (5,650 gp) **or** *+1 mithral breastplate* (5,200 gp); *+1 large steel shield* (1,170 gp)	*Gauntlets of ogre power* (4,000 gp), *+1 cloak of resistance* (1,000 gp), potions of *fly* (750 gp), *cure moderate wounds* (300 gp), and 3 *cure light wounds* (150 gp), cash (1,305 **or** 1,755 gp)
9th/ 36,000 gp	*+2 longsword* (8,315 gp), *+1 composite longbow* (+3 Strength) (2,700 gp), 10 *+2 arrows* (1,660 gp)	*+2 full plate armor* (5,650 gp) **or** *+1 mithral breastplate* (5,200 gp); *+2 large steel shield* (4,170 gp)	*Boots of striding and springing* (5,500 gp), *gauntlets of ogre power* (4,000 gp), *+1 cloak of resistance* (1,000 gp), potions of *fly* (750 gp), *cure moderate wounds* (300 gp), and 3 *cure light wounds* (150 gp), cash (1,805 **or** 2,255 gp)

(continued)

Table 20-1 *(continued)*

Level/Total Wealth	Weapons	Armor	Other Gear
10th/ 49,000 gp	+3 longsword (18,315 gp), +1 composite longbow (+3 Strength) (2,700 gp), 10 +2 arrows (1,660 gp)	+2 full plate armor (5,650 gp) **or** +1 mithral breastplate (5,200 gp); +2 large steel shield (4,170 gp)	Boots of striding and springing (5,500 gp), gauntlets of ogre power (4,000 gp), +2 cloak of resistance (4,000 gp), potions of fly (750 gp), cure moderate wounds (300 gp), and 3 cure light wounds (150 gp), cash (1,805 **or** 2,255 gp)

The table assumes that your character is using a longsword and composite longbow, but if you prefer a different weapon (say, a bastard sword, greatsword, or crossbow), just substitute the right weapon, and make a note of the difference in price. For example, a nonmagical greatsword costs 50 gp to a non-magical longsword's 15 gp, so a *+2 greatsword* is 35 gp more expensive than a *+2 longsword.* If you prefer to have your character fight at a distance, make a bow your character's primary magic weapon, and pick up an enchanted melee weapon at the point where the table recommends a magical bow.

Magic weapons often have really interesting special abilities that are paid for by adding to the weapons' plus value. For example, a flaming weapon deals an additional 1d6 points of fire damage with each hit, but the flaming ability costs a +1 bonus. In other words, a *+2 longsword* and a *+1 flaming longsword* have the same monetary value: 8,315 gp. The flaming longsword effectively has a –1 penalty on attack rolls when compared to the +2 weapon, but it deals an average of +2.5 points of extra fire damage with each hit. If you have the opportunity to buy or otherwise pick out for yourself the magical gear your character owns, don't overlook the cool special abilities available for weapons and armor; you'll find them on page 223 of the *Dungeon Master's Guide.*

Regarding armor, you'll notice that we present two basic options on this table — a heavily armored fighter in full plate or a fast and maneuverable fighter wearing a chain shirt. Don't go with the light-armor option unless your character's Dexterity score is 14 or better, because a fighter needs a high Dexterity bonus to offset the fact that full plate armor has an armor bonus 4 points higher than a chain shirt. If your fighter doesn't use a shield, put the extra money into a *+1 ring of protection* (it costs 2,000 gp) or *+2 amulet of health* (a +2 bonus to your character's Constitution for only 4,000 gp).

Some of the simplest and most useful magic items in the game are "ability adders" — items that increase your character's ability scores. For example, *gauntlets of ogre power* add a +2 bonus to your character's Strength score. That gives your character a +1 bonus on melee attack rolls and damage rolls compared to the unenhanced Strength score, so clearly it helps a character to fight better. You'll also get a lot of benefit out of an *amulet of health* (which improves your character's Constitution score) or *gloves of Dexterity* (which add to your character's Dex score). Our fighter baseline in the preceding table assumes that you acquire *gauntlets of ogre power* as quickly as possible, but if you get the chance, upgrade to a *belt of giant strength +4* (16,000 gp) or *+6* (36,000 gp). You'll use that extra Strength every time your character makes an attack.

Rogue magic items

A rogue wants to acquire good magic weapons as much as the fighter does, but a rogue also wants to pick up interesting and useful magic items for avoiding detection and getting around in the dungeon. These items are reasonably good choices for bards as well as rogues, although a bard would substitute a masterwork musical instrument for the thieves' tools. Table 20-2 lists the rogue's magic items by level.

Table 20-2	Typical Rogue Magic Items by Level		
Level/Total Wealth	**Weapons**	**Armor**	**Other Gear**
1st	As starting package	As starting package	As starting package
2nd/ 900 gp	MW rapier (320 gp), composite shortbow (+1 Strength) (175 gp)	MW studded leather armor (165 gp)	Potion of *cure light wounds* (50 gp), MW thieves' tools (100 gp), cash (90 gp)
3rd/ 2,700 gp	MW rapier (320 gp), MW composite shortbow (+1 Strength) (475 gp)	Mithral chain shirt (1,100 gp)	MW thieves' tools (100 gp), potions of *cat's grace* (300 gp), *invisibility* (300 gp), and *cure light wounds* (50 gp), cash (55 gp)

(continued)

Table 20-2 *(continued)*

Level/Total Wealth	Weapons	Armor	Other Gear
4th/ 5,400 gp	*+1 rapier* (2,320 gp), MW composite shortbow (+1 Strength) (475 gp), 10 *+1 arrows* (460 gp)	Mithral chain shirt (1,100 gp)	MW thieves' tools (100 gp), potions of *cat's grace* (300 gp), *invisibility* (300 gp), and 3 *cure light wounds* (150 gp), cash (195 gp)
5th/ 9,000 gp	*+1 rapier* (2,320 gp), MW composite shortbow (+1 Strength) (475 gp), 20 *+1 arrows* (920 gp)	*+1 mithral chain shirt* (2,100 gp)	*Cloak of elvenkind* (2,500 gp), MW thieves' tools (100 gp), potions of *invisibility* (300 gp) and 3 *cure light wounds* (150 gp), cash (135 gp)
6th/ 13,000 gp	*+1 rapier* (2,320 gp), MW composite shortbow (+1 Strength) (475 gp), 20 *+1 arrows* (920 gp)	*+1 mithral chain shirt* (2,100 gp)	*Gloves of Dexterity +2* (4,000 gp), *cloak of elvenkind* (2,500 gp), MW thieves' tools (100 gp), potions of *invisibility* (300 gp) and 3 *cure light wounds* (150 gp), cash (135 gp)
7th/ 19,000 gp	*+2 rapier* (8,320 gp), MW composite shortbow (+1 Strength) (475 gp), 20 *+1 arrows* (920 gp)	*+1 mithral chain shirt* (2,100 gp)	*Gloves of Dexterity +2* (4,000 gp), *cloak of elvenkind* (2,500 gp), MW thieves' tools (100 gp), potions of *invisibility* (300 gp) and 3 *cure light wounds* (150 gp), cash (135 gp)

Level/Total Wealth	Weapons	Armor	Other Gear
8th/ 27,000 gp	*+2 rapier* (8,320 gp), MW composite shortbow (+1 Strength) (475 gp), 20 *+1 arrows* (920 gp)	*+2 mithral chain shirt* (5,100 gp), *+1 ring of protection* (2,000 gp)	*Gloves of Dexterity +2* (4,000 gp), *cloak of elvenkind* (2,500 gp), *Heward's handy haversack* (2,000 gp), MW thieves' tools (100 gp), potions of *fly* (750 gp), 2 *invisibility* (600 gp), and 3 *cure light wounds* (150 gp), cash (85 gp)
9th/ 36,000 gp	*+2 rapier* (8,320 gp), MW composite shortbow (+1 Strength) (475 gp), 20 *+2 arrows* (3,320 gp)	*+2 mithral chain shirt* (5,100 gp), *+1 ring of protection* (2,000 gp)	*Boots of striding and springing* (5,500 gp), *gloves of Dexterity +2* (4,000 gp), *cloak of elvenkind* (2,500 gp), *Heward's handy haversack* (2,000 gp), MW thieves' tools (100 gp), potions of *fly* (750 gp), 2 *invisibility* (600 gp), and 3 *cure light wounds* (150 gp), cash (1,185 gp)
10th/ 49,000 gp	*+2 rapier* (8,320 gp), *+1 composite shortbow (+1 Strength)* (2,475 gp), 20 *+2 arrows*	*+2 mithral chain shirt* (5,100 gp), *+1 ring of protection* (2,000 gp)	*Boots of striding and springing* (5,500 gp), *gloves of Dexterity +4* (3,320 gp) (16,000 gp), *cloak of elvenkind* (2,500 gp), *Heward's handy haversack* (2,000 gp), MW thieves' tools (100 gp), potions of *fly* (750 gp), 2 *invisibility* (600 gp), and 3 *cure light wounds* (150 gp), cash (185 gp)

As before, substitute your own preferred weapons if you don't like the rapier or shortbow. For example, if you're playing an elf rogue, your character should use a longbow instead of a shortbow because it deals more damage and has a better range.

Unlike the fighter, the rogue has no real decision to make about armor — at the earliest opportunity, your rogue should pick up a mithral chain shirt. It's the best light armor available, and it has no armor check penalty to get in the way of a rogue's attempts to be stealthy, graceful, or athletic. Magic studded leather armor is a passable second choice.

For a rogue character, Dexterity is the ability you want to boost through the roof. It helps with AC, Reflex saves, signature skills such as Hide and Move Silently, and ranged attacks. If your rogue has the Weapon Finesse feat (and most rogues should), it also helps with melee attacks. No other character can get as much benefit from improving only one ability score, so we recommend buying the best pair of *gloves of Dexterity* that you can afford.

One more bit of advice to file away for later: Sooner or later, you'll want to acquire a *ring of invisibility* (20,000 gp). Turning invisible is one of the easiest and most effective ways to generate sneak attack opportunities as well as sneak into places you aren't supposed to be, and any rogue worth his salt relishes both applications of the item. Until you can pony up the 20 grand, make do with potions of *invisibility,* or get on the good side of a sorcerer with the right spells.

Cleric magic items

Like the fighter, the cleric is also interested in picking up good magic weapons and magic armor to stand up to anything the monsters might throw at him or her. A cleric is also capable of using items that store divine spells, such as wands, scrolls, and other such devices. Table 20-3 lists the cleric's magic items by level.

You can use this table for druids as well, but you'll need to make a few substitutions. Use a scimitar in place of a mace and a sling in place of a crossbow, and substitute hide or leather armor and wooden shields instead of the cleric's selection at that level.

Table 20-3	Typical Cleric Magic Items by Level		
Level/Total Wealth	Weapons	Armor	Other Gear
1st	As starting package	As starting package	As starting package

Level/Total Wealth	Weapons	Armor	Other Gear
2nd/ 900 gp	MW heavy mace (312 gp), light crossbow (35 gp)	Banded mail (250 gp), light steel shield (9 gp)	Silver holy symbol (25 gp), potion of *cure light wounds* (50 gp), scroll of *hold person* (150 gp), cash (69 gp)
3rd/ 2,700 gp	MW heavy mace (312 gp), MW light crossbow (335 gp)	MW full plate armor (1,650 gp), light steel shield (9 gp)	Silver holy symbol (25 gp), potion of *cure light wounds* (50 gp), scroll of *hold person* (150 gp), cash (169 gp)
4th/ 5,400 gp	*+1 heavy mace* (2,312 gp), MW light crossbow (335 gp)	MW full plate armor (1,650 gp), light steel shield (9 gp)	Silver holy symbol (25 gp), wand of *cure light wounds* (750 gp), scroll of *hold person* (150 gp), cash (169 gp)
5th/ 9,000 gp	*+1 heavy mace* (2,312 gp), MW light crossbow (335 gp)	*+1 full plate armor* (2,650 gp), *+1 light steel shield* (1,159 gp)	Silver holy symbol (25 gp), wand of *cure light wounds* (750 gp), scroll of *neutralize poison* (700 gp), *+1 cloak of resistance* (1,000 gp), cash (69 gp)
6th/ 13,000 gp	*+1 heavy mace* (2,312 gp), MW light crossbow (335 gp)	*+1 full plate armor* (2,650 gp), *+1 light steel shield* (1,159 gp)	*Periapt of wisdom +2* (4,000 gp), silver holy symbol (25 gp), wand of *cure light wounds* (750 gp), scroll of *neutralize poison* (700 gp), *+1 cloak of resistance* (1,000 gp), cash (69 gp)

(continued)

Table 20-3 *(continued)*

Level/Total Wealth	Weapons	Armor	Other Gear
7th/ 19,000 gp	*+1 heavy mace* (2,312 gp), MW light crossbow (335 gp)	*+1 full plate armor* (2,650 gp), *+1 light steel shield* (1,159 gp)	*Periapt of wisdom +2* (4,000 gp), silver holy symbol (25 gp), wand of *cure light wounds* (750 gp), scrolls of *raise dead* (6,125 gp) and *remove disease* (375 gp), *+1 cloak of resistance* (1,000 gp), cash (269 gp)
8th/ 27,000 gp	*+2 heavy mace* (8,312 gp), MW light crossbow (335 gp)	*+1 full plate armor* (2,650 gp), *+1 light steel shield* (1,159 gp), *+1 ring of protection* (2,000 gp)	*Periapt of wisdom +2* (4,000 gp), silver holy symbol (25 gp), wand of *cure light wounds* (750 gp), scrolls of *raise dead* (6,125 gp) and *remove disease* (375 gp), *+1 cloak of resistance* (1,000 gp), cash (269 gp)
9th/ 36,000 gp	*+2 heavy mace* (8,312 gp), MW light crossbow (335 gp)	*+2 full plate armor* (5,650 gp), *+2 light steel shield* (4,159 gp), *+1 ring of protection* (2,000 gp)	*Periapt of wisdom +2* (4,000 gp), *gauntlets of ogre power* (4,000 gp), silver holy symbol (25 gp), wand of *cure light wounds* (750 gp), scrolls of *wind walk* (1,650 gp) and *remove disease* (375 gp), *+2 cloak of resistance* (4,000 gp), cash (744 gp)

Level/Total Wealth	Weapons	Armor	Other Gear
10th/ 49,000 gp	*+2 heavy mace* (8,312 gp), MW light crossbow (335 gp), wand of *searing light* (caster level 6th, 13,500 gp)	*+2 full plate armor* (5,650 gp), *+2 light steel shield* (4,159 gp), *+1 ring of protection* (2,000 gp)	*Periapt of wisdom +2* (4,000 gp), *gauntlets of ogre power* (4,000 gp), silver holy symbol (25 gp), wand of *cure light wounds* (750 gp), scrolls of *wind walk* (1,650 gp) and *remove disease* (375 gp), *+2 cloak of resistance* (4,000 gp), cash (244 gp)

If you're playing a cleric, you are interested in improving your character's defense as much as you can by acquiring good armor. Your secondary goals are keeping up your cleric's melee attacks and helping your cleric's spellcasting. Because clerics usually don't have great Dexterity scores, we've taken the liberty of putting them in full plate armor. Your cleric should stick with light shields instead of heavy shields, because a light shield allows a character to hold another object in the shield hand — for example, your cleric's holy symbol, which is required for most spellcasting.

Because clerics are skilled spellcasters, your character has the ability to use scrolls and wands with divine spells. After your cleric has gotten past 5th level or so, these are probably even more important to you than the quality of your cleric's melee weapon, because a cleric will spend more of his or her combat actions casting spells than thumping bad guys with a mace. A wand of *cure light wounds* costs only 750 gp and holds 50 uses of that spell — which means it only costs 15 gp per use! Compare that to the normal cost of 50 gp for a single potion of *cure light wounds*. The downside about the wand is that it takes a long time to heal someone of 30 or 40 points of damage, but as long as your character is not in combat, you shouldn't mind taking some extra time to heal characters on the cheap, without using up your cleric's own spell slots.

There are two good strategies for making the most out of your cleric's ability to use scrolls: Buying scrolls that are "over your head," and buying scrolls of "scrollbait" spells, as follows:

✔ **Over-your-head scrolls:** If you're playing a 4th-level cleric, your character can't cast 3rd-level spells yet. However, your cleric can use a scroll with a 3rd-level spell on it. Scrolls are extremely cheap (at least compared to

> potions or wands), so it's a good strategy to look at the spells about one level above what your character can normally cast and get a scroll or two to cover spells that you think your character might need. Usually, these will be spells that fix problems your character can't otherwise fix at his or her current level, such as *neutralize poison, remove disease,* or *raise dead.*
>
> ✔ **Scrollbait scrolls:** Many spells are only useful in very specific situations. For example, it's usually a waste of time to prepare the spell *water breathing.* What are the odds that any given dungeon adventure is going to require the party to adventure underwater? But, if you find that you need it, you *really* need it.

Spellcasters get just as much benefit from ability-improving items as fighters and rogues. In the case of the cleric, you want to improve your character's Wisdom score, because a high Wisdom score means that his or her spells are harder to resist and that he or she gains more bonus spells. The *periapt of Wisdom* is a must-buy for any cleric who can afford it. After you've boosted your cleric's Wisdom score with a magic item, look for opportunities to improve your character's Strength and Constitution scores (*gauntlets of ogre power, belt of giant strength,* or *amulet of health* are the relevant wondrous items). A better Strength score increases melee attack power, and a higher Constitution gives your character more hit points and a better Fortitude save.

Sorcerer magic items

Unlike every other character, a sorcerer has no real use for magic weapons or armor. Spells are the weapons of choice for a sorcerer, and a sorcerer can't wear armor anyway. However, sorcerers are very interested in finding items that help defend them from physical attack; most of their defense comes from their choice of magic items. Sorcerers also have the ability to employ deadly magical weaponry in the form of scrolls, wands, and other spell-storage devices. Table 20-4 lists the sorcerer's magic items by level.

Wizards can use this table just as well as sorcerers, but you may want to change the emphasis on the particular scrolls and wands you choose. Sorcerers should pick scrolls and wands that diversify their powers, allowing them to get around their limitation in the small number of spells they know. Wizards should pick up magic items that allow them cheap and disposable offense, so that they've got attack magic to fall back on during extended battles.

Table 20-4	Typical Sorcerer Magic Items by Level		
Level/Total Wealth	*Weapons*	*Armor*	*Other Gear*
1st	As starting package	As starting package	As starting package

Level/Total Wealth	Weapons	Armor	Other Gear
2nd/ 900 gp	Spear (2 gp), MW light crossbow (335 gp)	None (hope you know the *mage armor* spell!)	Potions of 3 *cure light wounds* (150 gp), scrolls of *invisibility* (150 gp) and *web* (150 gp), cash (113 gp)
3rd/ 2,700 gp	Spear (2 gp), MW light crossbow (335 gp), wand of *magic missile* (caster level 1st, 750 gp)	*+1 bracers of armor* (1,000 gp)	Potions of 3 *cure light wounds* (150 gp), scrolls of *invisibility* (150 gp) and *web* (150 gp), cash (163 gp)
4th/ 5,400 gp	MW spear (302 gp), MW light crossbow (335 gp), wand of *magic missile* (caster level 1st, 750 gp)	*+1 bracers of armor* (1,000 gp)	*+1 cloak of resistance* (1,000 gp), *pearl of power* (1st-level spell, 1,000 gp), potions of 3 *cure light wounds* (150 gp), scrolls of *fireball* (375 gp) and *haste* (375 gp), cash (113 gp)
5th/ 9,000 gp	MW spear (302 gp), MW light crossbow (335 gp), wand of *magic missile* (caster level 3rd, 2,250 gp)	*+1 bracers of armor* (1,000 gp), *+1 ring of protection* (2,000 gp)	*+1 cloak of resistance* (1,000 gp), *pearl of power* (1st-level spell, 1,000 gp), potions of 3 *cure light wounds* (150 gp), scrolls of *fireball* (375 gp) and *fly* (375 gp), cash (213 gp)
6th/ 13,000 gp	MW spear (302 gp), MW light crossbow (335 gp), wand of *magic missile* (caster level 3rd, 2,250 gp)	*+2 bracers of armor* (4,000 gp), *+1 ring of protection* (2,000 gp)	*+1 cloak of resistance* (1,000 gp), *pearl of power* (1st-level spell, 1,000 gp), potions of 3 *cure light wounds* (150 gp), scrolls of *charm monster* (700 gp), *polymorph* (700 gp), and *fly* (375 gp), cash (188 gp)

(continued)

Table 20-4 *(continued)*

Level/Total Wealth	Weapons	Armor	Other Gear
7th/ 19,000 gp	MW spear (302 gp), MW light crossbow (335 gp), wand of *magic missile* (caster level 3rd, 2,250 gp)	*+3 bracers of armor* (9,000 gp), *+1 ring of protection* (2,000 gp)	*Cloak of Charisma +2* (4,000 gp), potions of 3 *cure light wounds* (150 gp), scroll of *fly* (375 gp), cash (588 gp)
8th/ 27,000 gp	MW spear (302 gp), MW light crossbow (335 gp), wand of *magic missile* (caster level 5th, 3,750 gp)	*+3 bracers of armor* (9,000 gp), *+1 ring of protection* (2,000 gp)	*Cloak of Charisma +2* (4,000 gp), *amulet of health +2* (4,000 gp), potions of 3 *cure light wounds* (150 gp), scrolls of *summon monster V* (1,125 gp) and *teleport* (1,125 gp), cash (1,213 gp)
9th/ 36,000 gp	MW spear (302 gp), MW light crossbow (335 gp), wand of *magic missile* (caster level 7th, 5,250 gp)	*+4 bracers of armor* (16,000 gp), *+1 ring of protection* (2,000 gp)	*Cloak of Charisma +2* (4,000 gp), *amulet of health +2* (4,000 gp), potions of 3 *cure light wounds* (150 gp), scrolls of *summon monster V* (1,125 gp) and *teleport* (1,125 gp), cash (1,713 gp)
10th/ 49,000 gp	*+1 spear* (2,302 gp), MW light crossbow (335 gp), wand of *lightning bolt* (caster level 5th, 11,250 gp)	*+4 bracers of armor* (16,000 gp), *+2 ring of protection* (8,000 gp)	*Cloak of Charisma +2* (4,000 gp), *amulet of health +2* (4,000 gp), potions of 3 *cure light wounds* (150 gp), scrolls of *summon monster V* (1,125 gp) and *teleport* (1,125 gp), cash (713 gp)

For sorcerers, one of their biggest weaknesses is their inability to wear armor. That means you should acquire magic items that provide bonuses to your sorcerer's Armor Class as soon as possible. The most obvious way to do this is with *bracers of armor;* you'll find that *bracers of armor +3* are just as good as studded leather armor (but unfortunately, they're far more expensive). Other magic items that offer some defense include:

- ✔ **Ring of protection:** A *ring of protection* adds a deflection bonus to your character's AC. Minor rings (+1 or +2) are pretty common in the game; better rings are prohibitively expensive.

- ✔ **Amulet of natural armor:** An *amulet of natural armor* provides a natural armor bonus. Just like *rings of protection,* minor amulets (+1 or +2) are fairly commonplace, but more powerful amulets are quite expensive.

- ✔ **Robes of the archmagi:** These magic robes give your sorcerer a +5 armor bonus to AC, in addition to a host of other cool magic powers. The downside: They're quite pricey at 75,000 gp. But you can always dream, can't you?

Like the cleric, the sorcerer's ability as a spellcaster allows your character to use scrolls, wands, and staffs with great skill. In fact, there's not much point in carrying a crossbow around by the time your character gets to 3rd level or so, because he or she ought to be toting a wand of *magic missiles* for a primary ranged attack.

The ability-adding item you are most interested in is the *cloak of Charisma.* With a higher Charisma score, your sorcerer's spells get harder to resist, and your character also gains more bonus spells. However, the sorcerer has to pay a heavy price for his or her signature ability-boosting item. All other characters can use a *cloak of resistance,* which improves their saving throws with a relatively inexpensive item purchase. Characters can't wear two cloaks at the same time, so you'll have to decide what's more important: offense or defense. (If you're playing a wizard, you dodge this bullet — you want to increase your character's Intelligence score, not Charisma, so you need to buy a *headband of intellect,* which means your wizard can still use a *cloak of resistance.*)

Chapter 21

Roleplaying and Working Together

*W*e spend most of this book immersed in the nuts and bolts of character creation and the mechanics of game play. But DUNGEONS & DRAGONS isn't just a game of statistics and rules. It's also a game of *imagination.* When you take control of your D&D character, you can pretend for a short time that you're someone else entirely — a mighty swordsman, a dangerous wizard, a sly and cunning rogue — and that all the evil in the world can be beaten senseless with a broadsword or a wand of *lightning bolt.* In fact, for a lot of people, roleplaying (the process of pretending you're someone else) is the whole reason they play the game. Character statistics and game rules just help you figure out what happens next.

In this chapter, we tell you about the art of roleplaying and show you how to breathe personality, life, and purpose into your character. We also take a look at ways you can make yourself appreciated by everyone else at the table, both as a character and a player.

Roleplaying with Style

D&D is very entertaining as a pure tactical exercise; many players are perfectly content to view the game as consisting of puzzles to be solved, many of which involve fantastic combat scenarios. But the game really shines when you make an effort to get out of your own skin and put yourself in the place of the character you've brought to the table. After all, in real life, you'd run screaming from a howling, blood-maddened werewolf intent on ripping your throat out and tearing you limb from limb. But your dashing rogue Saros can stand his ground calmly, rapier in hand, and even make a quip about his fear-some foe. It's not that much more of a leap to think about how Saros might respond to other sorts of challenges and situations.

Choosing your character's alignment

One of your best guides for roleplaying your character is a fundamental rule of the game: Every character (as well as NPCs and intelligent monsters) in the game has an alignment. *Alignment* is a quick summary of what your character stands for and how he or she tries to live life. Your choice marks your character as a good guy or a bad guy, and alignment allows you to quickly determine how other folks in the world see your character — and how you should see others. For example, you can see at a glance that a lawful good dwarf probably has nothing kind to say to a chaotic evil orc, and vice versa.

Alignment consists of two intersecting scales. The first is ethos: lawful, neutral, or chaotic. The second is morality: good, neutral, or evil. Someone who is lawful good chose the good component on the morality scale and the lawful component on the ethos scale. Here's a quick primer on these five components:

- ✔ **Good:** You are generally unwilling to hurt others to get ahead. You are altruistic, protect innocent life, and believe in the dignity of all beings. You're willing to make personal sacrifices to help others.

- ✔ **Evil:** You feel free to hurt, oppress, or kill others if it suits your ends. Maybe you lack compassion or maybe you think moral conventions shackle you and keep you from taking what's yours. Or maybe you wallow in the vile, the despicable, and the depraved, celebrating evil gods and hurting others for the sheer pleasure of it.

- ✔ **Lawful:** You believe that you are bound to uphold the codes, laws, and standards of behavior of your culture and society. You voluntarily subjugate your personal gain to the rules and expectations of the society you live in.

- ✔ **Chaotic:** You believe that individual freedom is the greatest virtue a society can offer. You think that rules are made to be broken, and that notions such as honor codes or even sacred oaths should be discarded if they get in the way of common sense. Society exists to exalt the individual, not the other way around.

- ✔ **Neutral:** You haven't taken a stand on one, the other, or both of the alignment scales. If you're neutral with regard to good and evil, you might be a person who tries to accomplish good ends but is willing to use evil means to achieve them. If you're neutral with respect to law and chaos, you have a normal respect for authority but don't feel any real compulsion to follow rules or break them.

This system results in nine possible alignments: lawful good, neutral good, chaotic good, lawful neutral, neutral, chaotic neutral, lawful evil, neutral evil, and chaotic evil.

Your character's code of behavior and personal standards should reflect his or her alignment. For example, if your character is chaotic good, he or she acts as his or her conscience dictates to help people, without caring about what other people expect of him or her. The character especially hates it when people try to intimidate others and tell them what to do. On the other hand, a lawful evil character plays by the rules, but has no mercy or compassion. He or she seeks power and wealth, and doesn't care who gets hurt on his or her way up — but he or she adheres to the codes, laws, or standards of his or her race or society, using these as tools to further his or her own ends.

You can read more about how your character's alignment influences his or her approach to life on pages 104–106 of the *Player's Handbook.*

What alignment you choose is generally up to you, but keep in mind that a number of character classes have specific alignment requirements. For example, paladins must be of lawful good alignment, while barbarians cannot be lawful (they're not much for following rules). Your Dungeon Master may warn you that your character's actions are not conforming to his or her chosen alignment. If you have your character act in an evil manner, your DM may rule that your alignment is, in fact, evil — evil is as evil does, after all. If your character's alignment changes, he or she may lose some class benefits. Check your character class's description to see if you need to have your character stick to a particular alignment.

Be careful about playing an evil character. Many DMs prefer that all the characters in the party be good or neutral in alignment. It makes a lot more sense for good or neutral characters to take up adventures about protecting the innocent or stopping the depredations of evil monsters. It's also easier for good or neutral characters to cooperate within the party. The game works fine no matter what alignment you choose, but you should check with the DM before you decide on an evil alignment for your character.

Building a persona

Alignment is a pretty broad brush to paint with. It tells you something about what your character stands for and how he or she thinks the universe ought to run, but it doesn't tell you much about his or her personality. Consider the lawful good paladin: You're just a goody two-shoes, right? Well, you might play that paladin as a saintly martyr, a beatific and blameless agent of good who goes willingly to face nigh-certain death in the service of his or her deity. Or the character might be a grim crusader, tireless and unswerving in his or her determination to bring justice to evil wherever it lurks. Or you might even play that paladin as a great captain, a bold and courageous leader who urges on his or her companions with never-say-die cheerfulness and confidence. How you play that character is up to you.

Personas tend to evolve in play; your character ought to learn from his or her adventures and experiences, just like a real person does. But, as a place to get started, take a look at the traits below and decide where your character falls on the scale between each extreme:

> Arrogant – Humble
>
> Avaricious – Ascetic
>
> Blunt – Tactful
>
> Brave – Not so brave
>
> Devious – Straightforward
>
> Driven – Lackadaisical
>
> Flexible – Stubborn
>
> Flippant – Serious
>
> Naïve – Cynical
>
> Pleasant – Irascible
>
> Reckless – Cautious
>
> Sincere – Duplicitous
>
> Talkative – Taciturn
>
> Trusting – Suspicious

Pick two to four character traits, and in conjunction with your character's alignment, race, and class, you should have enough to craft a reasonably unique character. Some traits may be a little hard to reconcile with some alignments, but maybe those traits are weaknesses or failings — places where your character doesn't quite measure up to his or her self-imposed standards.

Creating mannerisms

Now that you know what your character stands for and what sort of personality he or she has, think of ways that you can portray that easily and consistently at the gaming table. You don't have to view each D&D session as a trip to the Renaissance Faire in full costume, but if you can think of a couple of memorable "hooks" to use at the table, you'll find that the other players have an easier time envisioning who your character is and what he or she stands for.

Habitual sayings

Does your character have any distinctive trademark phrases or battle cries? If you can't think of any, look to your character's choice of deity. Dwarves usually worship Moradin, the god of the dwarves. If you're playing a dwarf, you could do worse than to swear, "By Moradin's beard!" or "Moradin's hammer, what a bad idea that was!"

Voice or speech pattern

Take on a unique character voice or way of speaking that you can manage so easily you forget you're doing it. If you're playing a dwarf, growl and splutter and talk like you are angry. If you're playing a half-orc with a low Intelligence score, frown seriously and speak slowly, like you're working hard to sort out what you're trying to say. If you're playing a pretentious sorcerer or imperious wizard, refer to yourself in the third person (like "Leon" in the Budweiser commercials), or even use the "royal we." Maybe your chivalrous paladin even uses a few "thees" and "thous." If Thor can shout, "I SAY THEE NAY!" in Marvel comics, it'll work for you at the gaming table.

Gestures

This is a little harder, because there's only so much you can do while seated at a table. But maybe your pious cleric Jorune steeples his fingers in front of his chest when he speaks, while your devious rogue Shadow rubs her hands together avariciously, or your intellectual wizard Evard strokes his beard (or chin, if you lack the necessary facial hair) and casts his eyes up toward the ceiling while he contemplates a decision. Facial expressions are good ground for role playing, too. You can scowl or glower, stare stupidly with a slack-jawed expression, or squint crookedly and mutter to yourself. (We just sort of hope you don't do those things normally, so that your friends can actually detect that your efforts are roleplaying.)

Favored tactics

Here's an easy one that doesn't require any out-of-your-skin acting at all: Pick a couple of things your character likes to do, and make those your favored tactics. If your barbarian recklessly charges into battle and always Power Attacks for the maximum possible on the first round of combat, that's a distinctive hook — everybody at the table will start looking for you to try it in every fight. Maybe your sorcerer loves electricity spells, and so uses *lightning bolt* in preference to any other spell. Look for trademark maneuvers and try to put your own distinctive stamp on them.

Knowing when to stop

Believe it or not, it's possible to have too much of a good thing. Different D&D groups have different standards for how much roleplaying is the right amount; we've played in very entertaining game sessions in which no dice were rolled at all, because the nights were taken up with tense negotiations or tricky sets of investigations and interviews, all resolved purely in "character voice." But sometimes you need to stop talking and start rolling the dice. If D&D had referees who kept an eye on your roleplaying, here are three things that would draw penalty flags:

- **Delay of game:** Sometimes a dungsweeper is just a dungsweeper. Don't expect that you have to engage in meaningful conversation with every nonplayer character (NPC) your character happens upon. We've seen people spend 30 minutes of real-time haggling with a shopkeeper over the price of a pick and shovel. For goodness' sake, just have your character throw a couple of gold pieces on the counter and get on with the real adventure! You might not have noticed the other players at the table gnawing off their own ears because you won't give it a rest.

- **Excessive roleplaying:** A little bit of real-world acting goes a long way. Talk in a funny accent, scowl and glare a lot, use acidic sarcasm (hopefully not directed at other players), but don't take it too far. We've seen a player who insisted on perching on her chair and screeching unintelligibly for hours on end because her druid character was wildshaped into an eagle. When you freak out or annoy the other players, you're roleplaying excessively.

- **Intentional grounding:** Try not to have your character take stupid or counterproductive actions because you think that's what your character *should* do. For example: "Well, Kerro is scared of undead, so I guess I'll spend this round yammering in terror. Oh, I know I made my saving throw. But I think it's what Kerro would do." Be a little helpful to the rest of the party, and roleplay Kerro overcoming his fright enough to swing a sword or cast a spell, even though he's shaking in his boots. Your friends will like Kerro much better that way.

Working Together

Every character in the D&D game is the best at something, but no character can be the best at everything. What that means is simple: Good teamwork is a skill of vital importance to a D&D party. Learning how to cooperate with the other players at the table and work together effectively is important.

The first rule of working together is building a balanced adventuring party. Every character class has strengths and weaknesses; for example, if everyone in the group plays wizards, all the characters will be terribly vulnerable to monsters fast enough to reach them before they can drop the monsters with their spells. A party of nothing but fighters has no way to get past a 20-foot-wide pit in a corridor, but a rogue might be able to climb across, or a wizard might be able to overcome the obstacle with a simple low-level spell such as *jump* or *spider climb*.

The second rule of working together is making sure that everybody has the opportunity to do what he or she does best. For example, don't put the party's rogue in the position of being a front-line combatant; make sure the fighter in the party is standing in front of the bad guys, so that the rogue has the opportunity to maneuver for a flank attack.

The third rule of working together is staying on top of what your allies are trying to do. If your party's wizard is about to unleash a *fireball* spell, don't have your fighter run right into the middle of the orc warriors to launch an attack — the wizard won't be able to throw him or her spell without endangering your character. Don't be afraid to engage in a little "table-talk" and ask other players what they're planning. Most DMs don't mind a reasonable amount of table-talk, as long as you don't start designing ten-step battle plans in the middle of combat.

Cooperating in a fight

As you might expect, the most important place to use good teamwork and cooperative tactics is in a fight. When you fail to cooperate outside of combat, the result is usually not too much more serious than a delay of some kind. When you fail to cooperate in a fight, you're likely to get somebody's character killed. Death is not a permanent career-ender in D&D, but it's no fun, either. It costs a lot of gold pieces, experience points, or both to bring a character back from the dead, so it behooves everybody at the table to work hard to make sure that nobody's character gets killed.

Cooperative tactic #1: Flanking

The first tactic everybody should use is flanking. *Flanking* involves catching monsters directly in between two allies. If you and your buddy can work together to flank a monster, you each get a +2 bonus on your attack rolls. Moreover, if one or the other of you happens to be playing a rogue, the player will also get your bonus sneak attack damage against the flanked foe.

If you don't have enough friends available to flank a monster (or it's just too dangerous to move to a flanking position), a spellcaster can manufacture a flanking situation by casting a *summon monster* spell. By placing a conjured monster on the opposite side of a foe as the fighter or rogue in the party, the fighter or rogue will fight better due to the flanking bonus, even if the summoned creature isn't all that powerful. (Don't worry, the summoned monster is strictly on your side.)

Cooperative tactic #2: Aiding another

When you're fighting an enemy who is very hard to hit, or you need to give a character in trouble the best defense possible against an attack, consider using the aid another action. (You'll find a description of this action on page 154 of the *Player's Handbook*.) Instead of making an attack against your foe, you can make a melee attack against an AC of 10. If you succeed, your friend gains either a +2 attack bonus or a +2 Armor Class bonus.

Here's an example: Say two characters are fighting an opponent with an Armor Class of 24. One character has an attack bonus of +5 and deals an average of 5.5 points of damage per hit (using a *+1 longsword*), and the other has an attack bonus of +8 and deals an average of 11 points of damage per hit (*+1 greatsword* with 14 Strength). If they both just attack, the expected damage is 2.75 plus 0.55, or 3.3 points of damage per round. If the weaker character aids the better, there's an 80 percent chance the average damage output jumps to 3.85, because the weaker character successfully aids another on a roll of 5 or higher. (There's a 20 percent chance the damage output drops to 2.75, too.) That averages out to an expected damage output of 3.63 instead of 3.3 for attacking separately.

Cooperative tactic #3: Delaying

It's only natural to jump up the instant your turn comes around and whack the bad guys. But sometimes, the smartest way to play is to be a little patient. If you think that you've got an ally who will move before the monster does, you can delay your action and wait for your ally to get into position. By waiting, you might give yourself and your friend the benefit of making a flanking attack when that opportunity didn't exist before.

Delaying is also a good tactic when you've got spellcasters on your side who have spells that might help everyone attack. If the cleric in your party is about to cast a *bless* spell, you can simply wait to make your attack until *after* the cleric casts his or her spell. Now you've got a free +1 morale bonus on your attack roll that didn't exist before the cleric took her turn. Obviously, if the cleric's turn comes up *after* the monster(s) take their turn, you might not want to wait. But keep an eye on the initiative order in the fight, and look for opportunities to coordinate your actions for the greatest effect.

Buffing: Making your character and the team better

Spellcasting characters have a direct and obvious way to work cooperatively: They can cast buffing spells. The term *buffing* means improving a character with magic or special abilities, so that he or she can fight better. A spell such as *bull's strength* is a perfect example of a buffing spell — the character on the receiving end of this spell temporarily gains a +4 Strength bonus, which translates into a +2 bonus to the recipient's attack and damage rolls. Little bonuses go a long way in a D&D game. Table 21-1 lists some great buffing spells.

Table 21-1		Top Buffing Spells	
Spell	*Level*	*Cast By*	*Effect*
Bless	1st	Cleric	All allies get +1 attack bonus
Magic weapon	1st	Cleric, sor/wiz	One ally gets +1 attack and damage bonus and beats damage reduction
Shield of faith	1st	Cleric	One ally gets +2 (or better) AC bonus
Barkskin	2nd	Druid	One ally gets +2 (or better) AC bonus
Bear's endurance	2nd	Cleric, druid, sor/wiz	One ally gets +4 bonus to Con (which gives +2 hp per Hit Die, +2 on Fort saves)
Bull's strength	2nd	Cleric, druid, sor/wiz	One ally gets +4 bonus to Str (which gives +2 melee attack and damage bonus)
Cat's grace	2nd	Druid, sor/wiz	One ally gets +4 bonus to Dex (which gives +2 AC, Ref saves, and ranged attacks)
Invisibility	2nd	Sor/wiz	One ally turns invisible; sets up rogue's sneak attack
Haste	3rd	Sor/wiz	All allies get extra attacks, +30 feet speed, and +1 bonus to attacks, AC, Ref saves

Some characters have innate abilities that work just as well or even better than spells to buff other characters. The bard is the master of buffing his or her friends, because several of the most powerful bard song effects grant bonuses to all the bard's allies. Similarly, the paladin has an aura of fearlessness that grants any character standing within 10 feet of the paladin a bonus on saves against fear effects.

The real trick in managing your buffing spells and effects lies in finding effects that *stack* — that is, two or more bonuses of different types that work in combination to give an even greater benefit. In general, effects of the same type don't add together. For example, *gauntlets of ogre power* provide a +2 enhancement bonus to Strength, and the *bull's strength* spell provides a +4 enhancement bonus to Strength. Because these bonuses are of the same type, you only use the best one. In other words, it's inefficient to throw your *bull's strength* spell on the character wearing the gauntlets, because he or she will get a smaller benefit from the spell than another character would.

Armor Class is another good example of where you want to be careful to make sure that magical items and buffing spells will stack. The *barkskin* spell adds a natural armor bonus to the recipient, while *shield of faith* adds a deflection bonus. You can throw both these spells on the same character, and he or she will get full benefit for both. But watch out for a *ring of protection* or an *amulet of natural armor* — the *shield of faith* won't stack with the ring, and *barkskin* won't stack with the amulet, because the spells and items give the same type of bonus to AC. Usually, dodge bonuses and *untyped* bonuses (a bonus not assigned any descriptive term) are the only AC bonuses that stack with each other.

Saving downed characters

Sooner or later, it's going to happen: Some character in the party is knocked to 0 or negative hit points by a monster's attack. (A character is disabled at 0 hit points, a character is dying when his or her hit points are –1 to –9, and a character dies when his or her hit points reach –10 or less. For more details, see the "Injury and Death" section in Chapter 8 of the *Player's Handbook*.) Getting that character back into the fight requires some real cooperation and clever play, especially if the fight's still going on. What do you do when one of the other characters drops?

You have two ways to fix a character sitting in negative hit points: Stabilize him or her with the Heal skill, or use a *cure wounds* spell (or potion) of some variety (which automatically stabilizes the dying character and may bring him or her back to positive hit points, depending on how many points of damage are cured). The Heal skill is by far the inferior approach; use curing magic if you have any at all.

Try this short checklist the next time a character goes down in your game:

- ✔ **Is the character beyond help?** If your companion's been reduced to –10 hit points or less, there's no hurry. The character is dead, and he or she won't get any deader.

- ✔ **Is the character in immediate danger of dying?** A character reduced to –1 or –2 hit points won't die right away. You might be able to wait for the right chance to aid him or her. However, watch out if there are monsters standing around with nothing better to do than finish off a helpless character.

- ✔ **Can you help the character?** If you have no healing potions or spells, and can't use the Heal skill worth a darn, you might not be able to do much good anyway. You can stand over your fallen friend and keep a monster from finishing him or her off, but that's about it.

✔ **Can you reach the character?** You might have no way to actually get to a dying comrade. If you're threatened by dangerous enemies and might cause your own character's death by trying to reach your buddy, you might only complicate the situation by trying to help.

✔ **Can you afford the action to help this round?** Usually, it's good play to try to get your friends back into a fight. But if spending your turn going to your fallen friend's aid will give the monster or villain the opportunity to wreak even more damage, you might not be able to afford the luxury of ignoring the bad guys to aid your friend. For example, if you've got the dragon down to just a couple of hit points, you might be smarter to try to finish it off than to let it take another turn.

✔ **Will you make the character a target by healing him or her?** Generally, intelligent monsters don't waste actions pounding on adventurers who are already down as long as there are others still on their feet and fighting. If you're battling a frost giant berserker who lays out 40 points of damage with each swing of his or her axe, the safest place for your wounded friend might be lying helpless in the low- to mid-negatives. When you heal your friend up to 10 or 15 hit points, you place him or her in the very dangerous position of being easy to kill outright with just one more attack. Make sure the frost giant's got something better to do than cut your friend in half when he or she stands up.

Minding Your Table Manners

So far in this chapter, we talk about a lot of things you do to breathe life into your character and to play your character constructively with the other players at the table. Now we broach a somewhat awkward topic: Your behavior as a *player*, not just a person controlling a character in the game.

Most D&D games are regularly occurring social gatherings of a group of friends who share a common interest. Just like weekly poker games, or PlayStation slugfests, or bar crawls, or whatever it is you do for fun with your friends, it's just good manners to be a considerate guest or a pleasant host. You want to have fun and help everyone else have fun; you don't want to be the guy or gal who's making everyone else miserable.

The following sections take a quick look at five things you can do to contribute to everyone's gaming experience, and five things you ought to avoid if you want everyone to have fun.

Five dos

It would be easy to give you a long list of things to avoid, but we don't think that's as helpful as pointing out some positive steps you can take right from the get-go to make game night more fun for everyone:

✔ **Think about what you want to do on your turn while other people are taking their turns:** Time is the single most precious commodity at the gaming table. Most D&D sessions run about three or four hours. If you take ten minutes to figure out what your perfect move is during each round of every combat you get into, you're taking more than your share. Instead of everybody getting a chance to bash through five or six exciting encounters in the course of that session, you might limit them to half that many. Plan ahead so that your turns don't take forever, and everyone gets to play more D&D.

The minute your turn ends, start thinking about what you're going to do on your next turn. If you're playing a spellcaster, figure out which of your spells you're likely to use when your turn comes up again. If you're playing a fighting character, think about which foe you're going to attack, and whether or not you need to maneuver or use any special feats. Sometimes your plans will get spoiled by things that happen when it's not your turn — but sometimes they won't, and you'll give everybody at the table a little more D&D for their time.

✔ **Do the math ahead of time:** By the third or fourth time you've attacked with your longsword, you ought to know what your attack bonus is. Ditto for the save DC on that *fireball* spell you cast three or four times a night. Don't figure these things out from scratch each time you pick up the dice — be proactive and organized. Look at the actions you undertake all the time, and add up your bonuses and modifiers before you come to the table. No one minds too much if you don't know your character's grapple check modifier off the top of your head, but you shouldn't have to figure out your Armor Class each and every time some monster takes a swing at you.

Part of this tip involves figuring some numbers before you come to the game, but the other part of this tip is hard for some folks: Write things down in places where you can find them easily. It doesn't matter if you figure out your complete Power Attack options for every conceivable monster AC you might face if you lose your notes at the table. We suggest using a standard character sheet for this sort of thing; you can find one in the back of the *Player's Handbook,* pick up the D&D *Deluxe Character Sheets* pack, or check out a thousand variations by poking around the Internet. Wizards of the Coast provides free character sheets in PDF format, which you can download and print out, at `www.wizards.com/default.asp?x=dnd/welcome` (click Character Sheets on the left side of the page to see the list of downloadable PDFs). (Check out Chapter 10 for an example of a character sheet.)

✔ **Exercise some common courtesy:** If you told your buddies you were going to meet them at 7 o'clock to go out to the movies, you wouldn't expect them to be happy with you if you wandered in at quarter past eight. The same thing applies for a D&D game. Show up on time so your buddies don't have to wait for you before they start playing. If you find you can't be on time, use a phone and call somebody to let 'em know you'll be late. At least that way your friends can decide whether to wait for you or to start the game without you.

Miss Manners is right more often than she's wrong at the gaming table. Throw in some cash for the pizza. Bring the chips and soda (at least some of the time). Be a good guest. Heck, you know this stuff. Just be considerate.

✔ **Stay on target, stay focused, stay in the game:** Every D&D game we've ever attended featured at least some amount of senseless cutting up and Monty Python movie quotes for no particular reason. Gaming is fun; it's a social activity. Part of the reason you're at the table is because you enjoy the company of the people you're gaming with, and you want to socialize. But try to recognize when people are trying to move the game along and get somewhere, and when people are kicking back and shooting the breeze.

When the game's on, pay attention to what's going down. If the Dungeon Master is talking, pay attention! Nothing is more annoying than a DM giving a crucial encounter set-up, adventure background, or key bit of NPC conversation, only to have one of the players pipe up and say, "Huh? I was looking at my spells."

✔ **Help your friends to shine:** This one's a little tough. When you have the chance to grab the spotlight, it's natural to want to do exactly that. But sometimes it's actually more rewarding to let another player at the table have that moment in the sun.

Try to look out for situations that a particular character is suited for, and defer to that other character if you can. For example, if you're playing an armor-plated fighter, and the party needs to scout out a side passage that might lead into a monster's lair, you might say, "I'm the toughest guy, I'll go look." Or you might look over to your friend who's playing the stealthy rogue and say, "Steve, Kerdigard's no good at scouting. I'll follow your lead on this." Every character at the table is the best at something, so let your friends show off at the things their characters do best.

Five don'ts

Now for the flip side — here are some things you should try to avoid doing at the table:

- **Don't hog the spotlight:** If there are four players and a DM at the table, you should assume that you're entitled to about one-quarter of the DM's time. If you insist on being the character who scouts every tunnel, tackles every puzzle, talks to every NPC, and dictates the strategy for every fight, you're being a bore. You're not the star of the show; D&D is a movie with an ensemble cast, so you have to expect that sometimes other players will get good lines too.

  It's usually okay to take point on something that your character is the best at, or roleplay a long conversation that's of vital interest to your character, but remember that you've got the spotlight, and it's good to share it.

- **Don't disrespect the other characters:** Back in the Dark Old Days of gaming, many players understood D&D to be a fiercely competitive game. Squabbling over the best magic items in treasure hoards, stealing from inattentive allies, or even bullying lower-level characters were accepted behaviors in some games. None of that old-school garbage flies these days. Who wants to use their leisure time to play in a game where their characters get picked on, shoved around, or stolen from? We'd rather go back to grade school.

  So don't slip the DM notes saying that your 10th-level rogue is going to pick the fighter's pockets when he isn't looking. Don't threaten to vaporize your allies with a *disintegrate* spell if they don't let you have the *+4 ring of protection* the evil wizard was wearing. Don't sneer at people, or run down their characters, or generally go out of your way to let them know how stupid you think they are for being in the same game with you. It doesn't play well in real life, and it's just as unwelcome at the gaming table.

- **Don't be a poor loser:** It's natural to want to be successful in the game. When things don't go your way, try not to take it personally. Sometimes your character's going to get killed in horrific and spectacular ways. It happens.

  We've seen more than a few players absolutely enraged, embittered, or brought to the point of tears by the death of a beloved character. If you play a long-running campaign and get attached to your alter ego in the DM's world, it's only natural to feel disappointed when the game doesn't go your way. Try to remember, if your character's never in any real danger, there isn't all that much excitement to any game. On occasion, you're going to have a character get mauled, because the other 90 percent of the time, it's way more exciting to be worried about what's going to happen next.

Usually, characters get killed in one of two ways: You did something stupid and it didn't work out, or a monster just got lucky. When an ogre crits your 2nd-level sorcerer and deals out 33 points of damage, well, the ogre got lucky. Why get mad about it? The vast majority of DMs don't start an encounter with the intent of killing a specific character, so don't blame the Dungeon Master! That's just the way the dice fell. Besides, truly horrific character deaths make for great "war stories."

✔ **Don't disrespect the supporting cast:** Most D&D adventures are populated with a whole host of "supporting cast" — nonplayer characters the DM uses to populate the places your character visits. Sometimes these NPCs are patrons or employers who give your character directions to the adventure. Sometimes they're sources of information, folks who might know interesting rumors or who can point you toward useful resources. And sometimes they're nothing more than window dressing, a little bit of color the DM uses to give you a chance to roleplay your character. It's bad form to make the DM feel stupid for putting a "talky" encounter in front of you instead of something your character can just kill.

So how do players abuse NPCs? One classic bit is acting like a thug or putting on a show of sneering superiority because you're pretty sure your character is a few levels higher than the poor schmuck he or she is talking to. We don't know why some players enjoy the pretend-bullying of imaginary people, but they do. Another common tactic is the "outrageous insult and take-back." It runs like this: "I shove my wand of *lightning bolts* up the baron's nose and ask him if he'd like his brains all over the ceiling. Ha, ha! No, I don't do that. I *disintegrate* a hole in his castle wall, and then tell him he'd better get his daughters down here for me to check out, or he's gonna learn how to fly real quick! No, I don't really do that."

The point of all this is that there's *constructive* roleplaying, and there's *destructive* roleplaying. While you're slapping around the town guards because you're playing a 10th-level character and they're 1st-level NPCs, the clock's running on the real adventure, and the DM isn't having any fun. You want to keep the DM happy and show his or her game world some respect.

✔ **Don't argue with the DM:** The Dungeon Master is not infallible. Sometimes he or she will remember a rule wrong, or forget that you are holding your action, or overlook an obvious plot hole in the adventure. But it's accepted gaming etiquette to let the DM run the game as he or she sees fit. The DM is the guy or gal who's putting in a lot of extra work to make the game fun for everybody else. Cut him or her some slack.

That said, you're within your rights to ask a DM to check a rule that you think he or she got wrong. If the DM says, "Joe, your fighter Kerdigard is charmed by the evil wizard, so you have to attack your buddies," you can point out that you agree that Kerdigard can't attack the evil wizard, but you're not sure if the *charm person* spell automatically turns you against your friends. If the DM insists he or she is right, the best thing to do is let it slide, and go along with the way the DM wants to play it. That way you don't stop the game altogether and leave the other players sitting around waiting for the argument to resolve. You can always take up your point later on, after the game session is over.

If the DM is spectacularly wrong, spitefully inconsistent, uses NPCs to bully your characters (see the previous bullet), or refuses to be questioned, you're dealing with a pocket tyrant. You'll have to decide if you can submit to playing the game by the, ah, unique rules the DM uses for his or her game, or if you'd rather not let this person tyrannize your gaming time. If the DM is a great storyteller, maybe you can put up with his or her butchery of the rules. But if he or she runs a bad game all around, maybe someone else at the table would be a better DM.

Lars Grant-West

Chapter 22

Character Building for Experts

. . . .

. . . .

Many players are perfectly happy choosing a character class and sticking to it, spending their character's whole career getting better at the path laid out in the *Player's Handbook*. However, some players are fanatics about building the toughest, most capable, most specialized character they can come up with. In fact, thousands of D&D players constantly debate the virtues of various *character builds* (combinations of race, class, feat, and spell choices) and share their efforts with each other in hundreds of message boards and mailing lists. When you factor in the zillions of additional options for classes, feats, and other such things available in other D&D supplements (for example, *Complete Warrior*, *Races of Stone*, or the FORGOTTEN REALMS *Campaign Setting*), your character building options are effectively infinite.

In this chapter, we discuss the art of extreme character building and show you how to use some advanced tactics to maximize your character's strengths and minimize weaknesses.

Min-Maxing Your Character

D&D is a tough game on your character. Fierce orc berserkers try to hack him or her into quivering chunks of meat with huge axes. Giants try to stomp a character into bloody paste. Dragons want to incinerate a character like flamethrowers with wings. And, as if that weren't enough, a character spends most of his or her time stumbling through dismal dungeons with fun features like hidden pits full of rusty spikes and the occasional yawning gate leading directly to the infernal planes. To survive and thrive in this admittedly hostile environment, you need to build the strongest character you can put together.

The art of optimizing your character is known (somewhat derogatorily) as *min-maxing.* When you min-max, you're looking for corners in the game rules. You're trying to make sure that you're getting the most you possibly can out of your character design.

Here's an example: Say you're trying to build a rogue who's good in melee combat. Your rogue character has a Strength score of 12 and a Dexterity score of 16. At 1st level, your character's attack bonus with the rapier is +1 (+0 for your base attack bonus, +1 for your Strength bonus). You'd like to choose the feats Weapon Focus or Weapon Finesse to improve your character's attack with the rapier, but both of these feats require a base attack bonus of +1, so your 1st-level character can't choose either one yet. When your character reaches 2nd level, your attack bonus with the rapier improves to +2 (base attack bonus +1 for a 2nd-level rogue, +1 for Strength as before) — but your character *still* can't take Weapon Focus or Weapon Finesse, because he or she doesn't get a feat selection at 2nd level.

The min-maxer, on the other hand, doesn't take a level in the rogue class when his or her character advances a level. Instead, he or she has the character take a level in the fighter class. (This is called multiclassing — we discuss it later in this chapter.) By choosing to be a 1st-level rogue/1st-level fighter, the min-maxer's character still has a base attack bonus of +1, just like the 2nd-level rogue. But the fighter class offers a bonus feat at 1st level. The min-maxer chooses Weapon Finesse at 2nd level. This gives the character an attack bonus with the rapier of +4 (+1 for base attack, +3 for Dexterity bonus). Compare that to the +2 bonus a 2nd-level rogue would have. As you can see, some creative and informed character building can pay off big.

Character optimization resources

You can build a bewildering variety of competent, min-maxed characters using just the core rulebooks — the *Player's Handbook, Dungeon Master's Guide,* and the *Monster Manual.* But wait, there's more! If you like exploring various character builds and assembling the best characters you can imagine from the material at hand, you'll find that other D&D supplements offer tons of additional options. Check out *Races of Stone, Races of the Wild, Complete Warrior, Complete Divine, Complete Arcane,* and *Complete Adventurer* just for starters.

In addition to looking for new options in other D&D supplements, you'll find that thousands of D&D fans discuss their favorite character-building tricks with each other every day. If you want to find good character builds fast, we recommend a visit to the official D&D message boards, hosted by Wizards of the Coast, the folks who publish the DUNGEONS & DRAGONS game. You'll find the message boards at www.wizards.com. Another good source of ideas is *Dragon Magazine,* a monthly publication chock full of good D&D tidbits; you can find a copy at your local gaming store.

Min-maxing strategies

There are three basic courses you can follow when optimizing your character:

- ✔ **Maximizing strengths:** Pick something you do well and throw every resource available into getting even better at it. A highly specialized character is generally far more dangerous in a fight than a character whose abilities aren't as tightly focused. So, if your character is already a good archer, maximize him or her by choosing archery-friendly feats at every opportunity. Buy the best magical bow you can afford. Improve your character's Dexterity score as much as possible. Yes, your character will be a bit one-dimensional, but if he or she is part of a balanced adventuring party, you're smart to specialize; your versatility lies in the fact that you are part of a team.

- ✔ **Covering weaknesses:** Make choices that patch holes in your character. For example, fighters have terrible Will saves. Choose the Iron Will feat or buy a *cloak of resistance* to cover that weakness. Wizards are fragile in melee; choose spells, magic items, or feats that improve your Armor Class and/or Constitution score, so that your wizard can stand up to more punishment than normal.

- ✔ **Increasing versatility:** Broaden your horizons by making choices that provide you with access to a variety of class features. For example, take advantage of multiclassing (discussed in the "Multiclassing: Maxing Out Your Choices" section, later in this chapter) to get access to a whole new list of class features. If you're playing a spellcaster, choose spells that have multiple uses. If you're playing a fighting character, take up a new feat tree that makes you good at an entirely different set of tactics.

Although all of these are decent strategies for optimizing a character, many experienced players believe that maximizing strengths is the way to go. Here's the reason: When you maximize your character's strengths, you generally get to decide when to use them. If you're playing a fantastic archer, you're in control of whether or not you shoot or don't shoot in any given combat round. On the other hand, when you cover a weakness, you aren't able to control whether or not your efforts will matter. If you build a fighter who is great at resisting magic, you don't get much benefit out of an encounter in which your fighter isn't threatened by magic.

Exploiting good interactions

The real art of character optimization lies in finding good interactions between your character's subsystems. Anybody can make good choices about which feats to learn, or what equipment to carry, or which spells to keep handy. We're going to look at making choices that synergize with each other.

Try this at home!

We don't have enough room in this book to detail all the possibilities for great character builds, but here are a few particularly good combinations you might want to try with your next character:

- **Spiked chain fighter:** Start with a good Dexterity score, and take the feats Exotic Weapon Proficiency (spiked chain), Combat Reflexes, and Weapon Finesse. Raise your Dexterity through the roof. The extra reach granted by the spiked chain means that your character threatens more of the battlefield, and the more area your character threatens, the more likely it is foes will give your character chances for attacks of opportunity.

- **Axe murderer:** Start with a good Strength score, take a level of barbarian, and pick up the feat Power Attack. Choose a big two-handed weapon such as a greatsword or greataxe for your weapon of choice; you get to add 1½ times your character's Strength bonus to damage rolls with a two-handed weapon. Flying into a barbarian rage temporarily increases your character's Strength by +4, which translates into a +2

attack bonus and +3 damage bonus with a two-handed weapon. When you use the Power Attack feat with a two-handed weapon, you deal +2 damage for every –1 you take on the attack roll. You can deal huge damage fast with this build.

- **Armored wizard:** Arcane spellcasters normally can't afford to wear heavy armor, because the chance of spell failure is too high. But try this: Learn the Still Spell feat, and then take the Armor Proficiency feat (or better yet, multiclass and take a level of fighter). When your character uses the Still Spell feat, spells no longer have a somatic (gesture) component, and therefore, you bypass the chance of spell failure for wearing armor. Another tactic for a sorcerer or wizard who wears armor is to take the Scribe Scroll or Craft Wand feats and make a number of these magic items. Scrolls and wands get around the armor restriction, too. If you're willing to throw your character's spells a little less efficiently, there's no reason your sorcerer or wizard can't stomp around in full plate armor and carry a heavy shield.

That may sound like a lot of gobbledygook to you, so we provide an example. Say that you like the Combat Reflexes feat. To get the most out of this feat choice, you should probably take the spiked chain as your weapon of choice in order to give your character the extra reach to manufacture opportunities for the Combat Reflexes feat to work. And, when you consider spells or magic items that will help this character, take a look at effects that increase your character's Dexterity score, such as a *cat's grace* spell or *gloves of Dexterity*. The higher your character's Dexterity, the more bonus attacks of opportunity you get to make using the Combat Reflexes feat. And, if you're going to have a great Dexterity score, you should consider the Weapon Finesse feat so that you can use your character's Dexterity bonus on attacks with the spiked chain. So, as you can see, your choices in three distinct game subsystems — feats, equipment, and spells or magic items — all work together to make this character far more effective with the Combat Reflexes build than he or she would be if you made the feat choice in isolation and didn't follow up with complementary choices in the other game systems.

Here's a quick checklist of game systems that you can mesh together to make your character a true Frankenstein monster of min-maxing:

- ✔ **Ability scores:** Can you find a way to exploit your character's highest ability score(s)?

- ✔ **Character class:** Do your character's ability scores make sense for his or her class? Is there another class your character's ability scores make him or her well suited for? If so, that might be a good class to multiclass into.

- ✔ **Feat selections:** Do your feat selections make use of your character's best ability score?

- ✔ **Equipment choices:** Do you have the right armor and weapons for your character's ability scores and your choice of character class?

- ✔ **Spells known:** If you're playing a spellcaster, does your character know (or prepare) spells that make the best use of his or her key ability score?

- ✔ **Magic items:** Are there magic items that can help your min-maxing strategy? Would a more powerful weapon allow your min-maxing plan to work better? What about a magic item that improves your character's most important ability score?

Multiclassing: Maxing Out Your Choices

Perhaps the single best tool at your disposal for optimizing your character is multiclassing: Starting your adventuring career as a character of one class, and then switching over to another class after you gain a level or two. For example, your character might start out as a 1st-level rogue, which gives you a bunch of skill points and a little sneak attack right at the start of your career. But after your character gains a level or two, you might decide you want to get better at fighting, so when your character reaches the next level, you stop taking rogue levels and instead start taking fighter levels. Your character might eventually become a 2nd-level rogue/4th-level fighter, or a 3rd-level rogue/8th-level fighter, or even something as crazy as a 2nd-level rogue/4th-level fighter/5th-level ranger.

You'll find the rules on multiclassing on pages 59–60 of the *Player's Handbook.*

There are some downsides to multiclassing. When you decide that you want your character to become a 3rd-level rogue/1st-level fighter instead of being a 4th-level rogue, you have to give up 4th-level rogue abilities in order to acquire 1st-level fighter abilities. This is especially painful for characters who are primarily spellcasters. Very few classes look as good at 1st level as your wizard's 5th, 7th, or 9th level looks, because at those levels, your wizard gains access to new spell levels. You may also paint yourself into a corner by making it nearly impossible to reach important goals down the road. For example, if you think the Improved Critical feat is the best feat in the game, you'll have a hard time getting it if you take a lot of nonfighter levels, because Improved Critical requires a base attack bonus of +8. You can buy this feat at 8th level as a straight fighter, but if you multiclass, you'll need to wait until at least 9th level, because no other class gets a bonus feat at 8th level.

That said, multiclassing is the min-maxer's dream. By combining the best class features from two (or more) classes, you can build extremely powerful and capable characters. Of course, this takes time — you can't reach the good features in two or more classes until your character is at least 5th or 6th level overall. However, you're generally better off putting most of your effort into your character's primary class — the thing you really want to do, whatever that is — and just dip into another class for a level or two. This kind of character building is called *cherrypicking*. For example, if you're playing a 2nd-level rogue/8th-level fighter, you've cherrypicked two levels of rogue, but you're mostly a fighter.

Different classes have good breakpoints for cherrypicking, as shown on Table 22-1. The Key Level column indicates just how many levels you'd like to have of the class to get the best benefit for your cherrypicking.

Table 22-1		Cherrypicking	
Class	*Key Level*	*What You Get*	*Comments*
Barbarian	1st	+1 base attack, fast movement, rage, proficiency with martial weapons, light armor, medium armor, and shields	Barbarian is very good for cherry-picking, because taking 1 level of barbarian gives you the fast movement and rage class abilities. While you will only be able to rage once per day, it's still a great way to pump yourself up for a climactic battle.

Class	Key Level	What You Get	Comments
Bard	1st	Bardic music, 0-level bard spells, good Reflex and Will saves, 6 skill points per level	Bard isn't a good cherrypicking option. You get 2 good saves and a few skill points, but those aren't worth diverting a level from your primary career.
Cleric	1st	1st-level cleric spells, good Fortitude and Will saves, proficiency with all armor types shields	Cleric is a little better than bard, simply because cleric spells are generally more useful. You also gain the ability to use cleric spell-trigger items, so by taking a level of cleric, you gain the ability to use wands of *cure wounds* spells — one of the best ways to carry extra healing power for your party.
Druid	3rd	2nd-level druid spells, good Fortitude and Will saves, animal companion, woodland stride	Druid is better as your primary career choice. If you do decide to take a little druid, stick it out until 3rd level, because 2nd-level druid spells are pretty good (especially *barkskin,* one of the best low-level defensive spells in the game).
Fighter	4th	+4 base attack, three bonus feats, opportunity to take Weapon Specialization feat, proficiency with all armor types and shields	Fighter is good for almost anybody. Getting 4th level as a fighter makes you eligible to learn the feat Weapon Specialization, one of the better feats in the game. But you won't be unhappy just to take 1 or 2 levels in fighter because of the fighter's bonus feats.
Monk	2nd	Good Fortitude, Reflex, and Will saves, two bonus feats, unarmed strike, flurry of blows, evasion	Monk offers lots of interesting abilities and a great boost to all saving throws, but it's tough to cherrypick, because many monk abilities require you to forego wearing armor and using weapons. Few martial characters want to give up their gear in order to make use of the monk's abilities.

(continued)

Table 22-1 *(continued)*

Class	Key Level	What You Get	Comments
Paladin	3rd	+3 base attack, detect evil, smite evil, divine grace, lay on hands, aura of courage, divine health	Paladin presents some difficulty, because once you stop taking levels in paladin, you can't go back and take more. But the low-level paladin abilities are very enticing, especially the divine grace ability (it allows you to add your Charisma bonus to all of your saving throws). If you stay in for 3 levels, you pick up aura of courage (immunity to fear) and divine health (immunity to disease).
Ranger	2nd	+2 base attack, good Fortitude and Reflex saves, Track, combat style, favored enemy, 6 skill points per level	Ranger is an excellent class for cherrypicking. You get 2 good saves, a lot of skill points, and some bonus feats. Stay with it for 2 levels so that you get your first bonus feat for your chosen combat style (archery or two-weapon fighting).
Rogue	2nd	Sneak attack +1d6, trapfinding, evasion, 8 skill points per level	Rogue is another good class for cherrypicking. Sneak attack is a very useful class ability that almost any character can get some benefit from, and 8 skill points per level make you competent in a lot of skills quickly. If you stick with rogue for 2 levels, you also pick up evasion, a very good defensive feature that helps you avoid damage from area-effect attacks.
Sorcerer	1st	1st-level sorcerer/wizard spells	Sorcerer is tough for cherrypicking. Sorcerer/wizard spells are nice, but unless you want to stay a sorcerer for a long time, you won't get past 1st-level spells, and they're just not worth a long diversion from your primary class.

Class	Key Level	What You Get	Comments
Wizard	3rd	2nd-level wizard spells, Scribe Scroll feat	Wizard is a little better than sorcerer, just because you achieve higher-level spells significantly quicker than sorcerers do. Go with 3 levels of wizard in order to get 2nd-level wizard spells; spells such as *invisibility* and *web* are useful for almost anybody.

Choosing a Prestige Class

The pinnacle of multiclassing is taking a prestige class. *Prestige classes* are classes that are *only* available through multiclassing. In fact, prestige classes have special requirements that your character must meet before you can take a level in that class. Any character can take a level of fighter or ranger at any point, but if you want to take a level of dwarven defender, your character needs to know the feats Dodge, Endurance, and Toughness; have a base attack bonus of +7; and be a dwarf of lawful alignment. Until all those things are true for your character, you can't take a level of the dwarven defender prestige class.

You'll find prestige classes hidden away in the *Dungeon Master's Guide*, beginning on page 176. Most DMs treat these prestige classes as "in play" in their games — you won't have to argue with your DM about whether or not your character can make use of one. Prestige classes are also a major component of many other D&D supplements.

Table 22-2 provides a quick overview of the prestige classes found in the *Dungeon Master's Guide* and describes the quickest way to make your character qualified for the class. Your character will have to meet some specific feat and skill requirements too — the Quickest Entry column simply tells you what classes to take in order to breeze through the requirements.

In terms of what specific prestige classes offer, there are a few things you want to look out for:

✔ **Attack progression:** If a prestige class offers full base attack progression, it's increasing your base attack bonus (BAB) by +1 per level. That's good for characters who want to indulge in physical combat.

✔ **Spellcasting progression:** If a prestige class offers full spellcasting progression, it allows your character to cast spells as if you had kept on advancing as a cleric, or wizard, or whatever your character used to be. That's critically important for players who want their characters to remain good spellcasters.

✔ **Sneak attack progression:** If a prestige class offers sneak attack progression, it makes your character better at sneak attack as you take levels. This is useful for anybody, but especially good for rogues who don't want to miss out on big sneak attacks.

✔ **Special abilities:** Many prestige classes offer a variety of interesting or powerful special abilities. Sometimes it's worth trading off some base attack or spellcasting progression in order to get the prestige class's special abilities. You'll have to decide that on a case-by-case basis.

Table 22-2	*Dungeon Master's Guide* Prestige Classes	
Prestige Class	*Quickest Entry*	*What You Get*
Arcane archer	Elf or half-elf, 1 level of sorcerer or wizard, and 6 levels of fighter or ranger	Full base attack progression, 2 good saves, every arrow you shoot is a magic arrow. Best for rangers.
Arcane trickster	Nonlawful alignment, 3 levels of rogue, and 5 levels of wizard or 6 levels of sorcerer	2 good saves, your sneak attack damage and arcane spellcasting both continue to progress at the same time as you take more levels in arcane trickster. Best for rogue/wizards.
Archmage	13 levels of wizard	Full arcane spellcasting progression, ability to trade some of your spell slots for powerful special abilities known as high arcana. Best for wizards.
Assassin	Evil alignment, 5 levels of bard, monk, rogue, or ranger	Full sneak attack progression, ability to make death attacks and use poison, assassin spells. Best for rogues.

Prestige Class	Quickest Entry	What You Get
Blackguard	Evil alignment, 6 levels of ranger (or 1 level of rogue and 6 levels of fighter, paladin, or ranger)	Full base attack progression, blackguard spells, a variety of cool (but evil) special abilities. Best for fighters.
Dragon disciple	5 levels of sorcerer (but you're better off with 1 level of sorcerer and 4 levels of fighter or something else that fights well)	d12 Hit Die, two good saves, cleric/rogue base attack progression, extra Str, Con, and natural armor. Best for fighters.
Duelist	1 level of bard, rogue, or monk, and 6 levels of fighter	Full base attack progression, you can use your Int bonus on your AC. Best for fighters or rogues.
Dwarven defender	Dwarf, lawful alignment, 7 levels of fighter or ranger	d12 Hit Die, two good saves, full base attack progression, ability to use a defensive stance that grants big combat bonuses. Best for fighters.
Eldritch knight	1 level of fighter and 5 levels of wizard (or 6 levels of sorcerer)	Full base attack progression, almost full arcane spellcasting progression. Best for fighter/ wizards.
Hierophant	13 levels of cleric	Give up spellcasting progression in order to choose from powerful special abilities. Best for clerics.
Horizon walker	5 levels of ranger (bard and wizard work too, but aren't as good in the class)	Full base attack progression, special abilities related to terrain. Best for rangers.
Loremaster	7 levels of cleric or wizard	Full spell progression, ability to acquire interesting secret lore abilities. Best for wizards.

(continued)

Table 22-2 *(continued)*

Prestige Class	Quickest Entry	What You Get
Mystic theurge	3 levels of cleric and 3 levels of wizard	Full spell progression in both arcane and divine spellcasting ability. Best for cleric/wizards.
Red wizard	Human, nongood alignment, 5 levels of wizard	Full arcane spellcasting progression, special abilities that make your spells more powerful. Best for wizards.
Shadowdancer	7 levels of bard, ranger, or rogue	Ability to hide in plain sight and use shadow and darkness powers. Best for rogues.
Thaumaturgist	7 levels of cleric	Full spellcasting progression, special abilities that make you a better monster summoner. Best for clerics.

Part IV
The Art of Dungeon Mastering

The 5th Wave   By Rich Tennant

"So tell me about this new feat you invented."

In this part . . .

The single most important factor in a successful D&D game is the Dungeon Master. Every player gets to concentrate on playing one character at a time and exploring the fantastic world around his or her character, but the DM plays a cast of thousands and in fact creates the world that the other players explore. Being a DM is like being a novelist whose characters are completely out of his control — because you don't know what the heroes of the story are going to do and how they're going to interact with the adventure and the game world, you're just as surprised by the shape of unfolding events as the players are. With a good DM, the D&D game is filled with excitement, wonder, intrigue, humor, suspense, and unforgettable moments players will talk about for years afterwards.

Chapter 23

Running the Game

The first and most important ingredient of a DUNGEON & DRAGONS game is a good Dungeon Master. The DM serves as referee, judge, storyteller, supporting cast, scenery builder, villain creator, monster player, and dungeon crafter. Without the DM's efforts, all the other players are left with interesting characters but nothing to do with them. We can't stress this one enough: You need a DM to run the D&D game, and the better your Dungeon Master, the better the game is going to be.

Ideally, you should learn how to be a DM by observing an experienced and talented Dungeon Master work his or her magic — preferably by playing in that DM's game. However, we can't always promise that you will be able to start your D&D gaming experience by landing in the hands of a talented DM. If you and your friends are all pretty new at the game, someone at the table will have to step up and do the DM's job, and it might as well be you. Although it's challenging to be the DM, and it takes some extra time and preparation, you'll also find that it can be very rewarding. When you realize that everyone else at the table is going to remember *your* dungeon for years afterwards, reliving their characters' triumphs (and failures) over and over again, you'll understand what we're talking about.

In this chapter, we discuss the basics of being a Dungeon Master. We tell you all about the role of the Dungeon Master in running the D&D game, and we show you how to administer the game with fairness, consistency, and an eye for dramatic tension. Before you know it, you'll be one of those great DMs that other folks hope to learn from.

DMing: The Best Job in the Game

If you're new to the game, you're probably wondering what in the world a Dungeon Master *does*. There isn't really a short answer to that question. As DM, you run the game. You narrate the story of the player characters. You play the monsters. You build the world. You design the dungeons. You hand out the treasure. You play the villains, and you give the other players in the game the opportunity to feel great about beating evil into paste with a broadsword or a *lightning bolt*. You're the director of this movie, and you're the guy or gal who's going to put people at the edge of their seats time and time again.

Because "You do everything," isn't a particularly helpful answer, in the following sections, we break down the big parts of the job and discuss them at more length.

Preparing an adventure

Are the heroes pillaging the long-lost Crypt of Azar-Malzz? Defending the town of Pommeville from a plague of werewolves? Stomping out the cult of Elemental Evil? Searching the depths of an old dwarven stronghold? When you're the DM, you decide what challenge the heroes are facing. You pick the monsters they'll fight, and you decide the stakes.

Preparing an adventure takes some extra work, usually between game sessions. You need to design your own adventure or pick up a published adventure from your hobby store (see the section, "Choosing an Adventure to Run," later in this chapter). You should read ahead so that you know what four or five encounters or situations the heroes are most likely going to encounter in each game session, and be ready to run those encounters on game night.

Building the world

So what's outside of the dungeon? Is there a spider-infested forest surrounding the place? Is there a town nearby? Who lives there? What sort of adventures can they point the player characters toward? What lies over the next range of hills? Who built that ruined castle, and who or what lives there now?

Running a D&D game gives you a perfect excuse to indulge yourself in the fine art of world building. You get to craft an entire kingdom for the players to explore when they decide to take a break from plundering whatever dungeon you put in front of them to start with. Sometimes you simply use your world building to provide your dungeons and monsters with a place to live. Other

Using a published campaign setting

A number of professionally designed campaign settings are available in your friendly local gaming store. A published campaign setting is a ready-to-use world for your D&D game, usually filled with countless ideas for adventures just waiting for you to bring to life. Two good options you'll find out there right now are the FORGOTTEN REALMS *Campaign Setting* and the *Eberron Campaign Setting*, both published by Wizards of the Coast, Inc. Whether you prefer to build your own world or use someone else's is up to you, of course. But even if you decide to create your own campaign, you can find lots of cool and interesting elements to borrow from in a published setting.

times, you're weaving an intricate and living setting to serve as the backdrop for the heroes' story. Whatever the case may be, your players expect you to know (or expertly make up on the fly) countless answers about what their characters see around them as they travel through the world.

You don't need to start by building a whole world at once; some of the best campaigns begin as tiny kernels, nothing more than a dungeon and a nearby town that the players shuttle back and forth between. Start small and answer the questions one at a time as they come up.

Playing NPCs

As a DM, anytime the player characters interact with another person or intelligent monster (also known as an NPC, or nonplayer character), you speak for that being. Many DMs feel that this is the most fun part of the job; you get to try out all kinds of parts, including power-mad dark overlords delivering villainous monologues, stammering stable boys, gruff innkeepers, shifty informants, imperious wizards, absent-minded sages, sinister dragons chatting with the heroes they expect to be their next meal, regal elf lords too proud to ask for help, or slow-witted ettins who take turns speaking with each head. The world is full of people and monsters for the heroes to talk to, and it's your job to figure out what they're going to say and deliver their lines.

Sometimes, this is pretty easy. When you're starting an adventure by having a mysterious wizard hire the party to accomplish a specific task, you've got a fair idea of what the wizard wants, how he's going to pay the party, and what he's willing to tell them about the perils they'll face on their mission. On the other hand, players (as their characters) sometimes strike up random conversations with people you never expected to have to know anything about. When the players ask the captain of the lord's guard if he likes working for Baron Duncastle, well, you've got to decide what the answer to that question is, whether or not the guard captain feels like sharing it, and how he'll do so.

Running monsters

Playing monsters is the other part of the job most DMs love. When the player characters get into a scrap with a ferocious monster or an evil villain, you run the bad guys in the fight. You decide what they're going to do — which of the heroes they attack, what tactics they use, and when they give up and surrender or run away. You roll their attack and damage rolls, make their saving throws, and keep track of their hit points (or any other damage they're taking).

Your goal when you run the bad guys in the fight is not necessarily to find the most efficient way to slaughter the player characters. You're trying to challenge the players and help to build a riveting and suspenseful story. You want each fight to feel distinctive and memorable, and you want to run the monsters and villains as intelligently (or unintelligently) as they really would fight. The key ideas are *excitement, suspense,* and *believability* — not just running up the body count.

Adjudicating results

Most of the time, the game rules are clear. This is especially true with attacks, spells, and physical skill uses like Balance, Climb, or Tumble. But part of the fun of a roleplaying game like D&D is that a player can have his or her character try anything he or she can think of — and a fair number of those spontaneous actions are things that the rules don't cover. The DM's got to make a call on the fly to decide whether these unusual actions succeed or fail.

For example, the heroes are fighting in an evil temple when one of the players tells you that his character Krusk is going to kick over a brazier full of glowing red coals so that it'll singe the skeleton he's fighting and kick up hot embers in its face. Sorry to say it, but there aren't any rules in the game for exactly what it takes to kick over a heavy, solid metal brazier and make the coals fly in the right direction. But it's a heroic move that sure sounds cool, so you want to reward your player for thinking outside the box. You'll have to decide what kind of roll Krusk ought to make, how much damage hot coals do, and whether the skeleton is even bothered by a face full of embers. (Off the cuff, we'd say have Krusk make a DC 15 Strength check, the skeleton takes 1d6 fire damage from the coals, and no, it doesn't care about embers in its face. But we're ruling on the fly, too.)

Keeping up with the characters

Last but not least, a good DM stays involved with each one of the players' characters. In a perfect world, you'll eventually get around to showcasing every character in an adventure that's tailored to that character's strengths, personality, and backstory. If your buddy Joe is playing Torvald, the paladin who's secretly an exiled prince of the kingdom of Erewhon, sooner or later it would be great to create an adventure that pits Torvald against the evil baron who arranged for his exile — and who now has his eyes on Erewhon's throne. You can't do that with every adventure, but it's a fine idea to run something "personalized" for your players once in every two to three adventures, spotlighting a different character each time you do it.

On the nuts-and-bolts side, you'll also want to keep up with the player characters' abilities and gear. It's important for you to know just how tough the player characters really are, whether they're ahead of the curve or behind the curve on arming themselves with great magic items, and what sort of feats and spells they have at their disposal. Specifically, you should be aware of which prestige classes your players are angling for and what their characters are going to need to get into those classes. Helping your players to realize characters that are cool, powerful, and distinctive is one of the real pleasures of DMing.

Choosing an Adventure to Run

Your first challenge as a new Dungeon Master is to figure out what kind of adventure you're going to serve up to the players. You've got two basic options:

- **Designing your own adventure:** We cover this extensively in Chapter 24 of this book. Basically, you collect a suitable array of monsters and challenges and create a good plot or story to involve the players. When you design your own adventure, you have the advantage of knowing exactly what your players are like and what characters they're going to bring to the game.

- **Using a published adventure:** With a little looking around, you can find literally hundreds of adventures published by various game companies. Check out your local hobby store or bookstore for starters. *Dungeon Magazine* is an outstanding resource that prints four or five great adventures every month. You can also find adventures online (check www.wizards.com), or locales suitable for developing into adventures in many roleplaying game supplements. This definitely saves you time and effort, but no game designer can know exactly how your gaming group works or what sorts of things your players are interested in doing.

When writing your own adventure or choosing a published adventure to run for your friends, keep your adventuring party's character level and class mix in mind. Ideally, most of the combat encounters in the adventure should have an Encounter Level equivalent to your party's average character level. Check out "Encounters" on page 48 of the *Dungeon Master's Guide*.

Task-Oriented DMing

As with many things, the best way to learn how to be a Dungeon Master is to just try it. Through trial and error, you'll eventually get the hang of what a Dungeon Master needs to do to make a game run. There's nothing like jumping in at the deep end, after all . . . but if you find this prospect a little intimidating, then read on. As best we can, we try to reduce the DM's job to a set of processes that we call *task-oriented DMing*.

Here's the theory: Most game play takes place in one of five basic tasks — talking, exploring, fighting, setting up, or free time. What you need to do as a novice DM is identify what kind of task you're currently engaged in, and follow the appropriate process. Table 23-1 describes each of the basic tasks.

Table 23-1	Guidelines for Identifying Your Task	
Task Type	**Sample Situations**	**Things You Might Hear or Say**
Talking	The player characters are questioning a patron or employer about the mission.	PC: "How many trolls are we talking about, Your Lordship?" PC: "So what'll you pay us to fix this troll problem for you?"
	The player characters are convincing someone to tell them something or do something for them.	PC: "If we agree to track down the orcs that have been killing animals in the forest, will the centaurs let us pass?"
Exploring	The player characters are deciding which way to go in a dungeon corridor.	DM: "You come to a T in the passage. You can go left down a set of slick, wet stairs, or you can turn right, where there's a door of oak bound with iron. Which way now?"
	The player characters are searching a room or investigating a scene.	PC: "I'll take a careful look down the well, shining my lantern that way." PC: "I search the big green face on the wall and see if there are any hidden buttons or compartments or anything around it."
Fighting	The player characters kick in a dungeon door and attack whatever monster they see in the room.	PC: "A troll? I charge!" DM: "Something *big* in that pile of garbage just moved. Roll initiative, everybody!"

Task Type	Sample Situations	Things You Might Hear or Say
	The player characters walk into an ambush.	DM: "Suddenly a centipede as big around as a barrel drops down from a crevice overhead and darts at Torvald! It's got surprise . . . Torvald, what's your flatfooted AC?"
Setting up	Telling the players what their characters know about the adventure or the mission at hand.	DM: "You are summoned to the baron's secret council chamber. He studies you for a long moment, and then says, 'Gentlemen, we've got a troll problem.'"
	The player characters prepare to go into the dungeon.	DM: "You're looking at the cave mouth. Any special preparations?" PC: "Before we leave town, I want to buy some magic arrows."
Free time	The player characters kill time in the game.	DM: "Nothing comes sniffing around your camp while you rest, and the night passes without event. It's morning, you're all rested, and you can pick out new spells if you like."
	The players are talking about which path of an adventure to follow next.	PC: "We can follow the map to the Caves of Doom, or we can follow these troll tracks we just found. What do you think, guys?"

It's not always going to be clear what task you're in at the moment. In fact, it's possible for one group to be engaged in multiple tasks at the same time. For example, if the heroes just won a fierce fight against a band of savage lizard-folk warriors, you might have the rogue searching the chamber for hidden treasure, the cleric busily healing up the fighter with *cure wounds* spells, and the sorcerer quietly questioning the two villagers the heroes just rescued from the clutches of the cruel lizardfolk.

Here's a quick primer on prioritizing tasks:

✔ **Free time ends as soon as you have something else to do:** Free time is usually "time out" from one of the other tasks. For example, if the party is exploring a cave system and winds up having a discussion about which way to go and how to use their magic to move safely and stealthily, you've put the exploration job on hold for a few minutes. There's nothing wrong with that; as soon as the players reach a decision, just pick up with the exploring again.

✔ **Set up is a lot like free time:** It also ends as soon as you have something else to do. Usually, you'll go from set up into exploration.

✔ **Exploration is the default condition:** If you're done with setting up but you haven't yet hit an obstacle or encounter of some kind, you're in exploration. Usually, PCs explore until they hit an obstacle to deal with (see the following section, "The exploration tasks"), a character to talk to, or a monster to fight.

✔ **Talking trumps exploration:** When you meet someone or something in the game, it's called an *encounter*. Many encounters take you straight to a fight, but some offer the possibility of talking in place of fighting. If there's a conversation going on, resolve that first before you move on to any other tasks. Of course, fights sometimes break out in the middle of conversations. When you finish your conversation, you go back to exploration mode.

✔ **Combat trumps everything else:** If there's a fight going on, everything else can wait. The fight continues until one side or the other runs away, surrenders, or dies (or is otherwise defeated). When the fight is finished, you usually will default back to exploration again.

The exploration task

Exploration is the default state of the game. When you're exploring, you're soliciting from the players some decision or direction about which way they're going and what they're looking for. Then you resolve that decision and continue until the heroes come to an obstacle, meet with an encounter of some kind, or reach another decision point. As a general rule, when running the activity of exploring, a DM follows these steps:

1. **Describe the options.**

   Tell the players what paths are available for their characters. For example: "The rubble-choked stairwell descends into a dusty old vault beneath the ruined monastery. There's a large, dark well shaft in one corner of the room with a low stone wall around it, a passage leading off toward the east, and an old wooden door in the north wall. What do you do?"

2. **Get the players to tell you what their characters are doing.**

   Sometimes this might be a group action — "We'll take the passage to the east," — or sometimes this may be an individual action, such as, "I'm going to search the door for traps."

3. Identify player responses.

Identify the action the player character is attempting to perform. Don't be afraid to ask your player to be more specific or helpful. If she tells you something like, "I'll go search the old well," you can ask, "Are you just leaning over the well to look down? Are you searching around the stone rim? Or are you going to climb down in there?"

If you're not sure how to resolve what the player character is trying to do, try the following:

- Is she trying to use a specific skill such as Disable, Open Lock, or Decipher Script?

- Is he trying to shove or move something? (A Strength check may be in order.)

- Is she just looking around? (A Spot check may be in order, if there's anything to see.)

- Is he seriously examining something? (A Search check may be in order.)

- Is she trying to move on, in, or through something? (Balance, Climb, Jump, or Escape Artist skill checks may be in order.)

4. Interrupt with obstacles or encounters.

If the player characters meet up with an obstacle, trap, or creature of some kind, interrupt the exploration and either tell the players what obstacle the characters have met with, resolve the trap, or move to a talking encounter or fighting encounter, as appropriate.

Some examples of this sort of interruption include:

- "The door's stuck. It won't open. If you want to try to force it open, you'll have to make a Strength check."

- "The inside of that well is smooth and slippery. You've got to make a DC 20 Climb check to descend safely."

- "When you step into the east passage, you hear a click and feel a pressure plate depress slightly under your foot, and then a hidden device shoots a steel dart at you! What's your flatfooted AC?" (You then roll to see if the trap hits and if so, how much damage it does.)

- "You hear a grinding, rumbling sound from the wall behind you, and suddenly a hulking bug-eyed monster the size of an ogre bursts through the wall and attacks! Roll initiative everybody!"

5. Advance to the next decision point.

Assuming that nothing jumps out and tries to kill the heroes, you can move to the next place where they need to make a decision. If the heroes follow a ten-mile long trail through the forest to the old ruins, and nothing in particular happens during that hike, you can just say, "You hike for about five hours, and then you reach a dark and dismal hollow in the middle of the forest, where an old broken tower stands in the gloom."

The conversation task

Many of the most important challenges in the D&D game don't involve any combat at all. Player characters can talk to anything they meet (especially after they get their hands on the *speak with animals* spell). Sometimes conversation is clearly not going to help; dungeons are full of big, hungry, stupid monsters who want nothing more than to eat anybody they meet, and can't or won't introduce themselves properly first. And other times, conversation is possible, but it just won't go anywhere; not every castle guard or innkeeper knows something that the players can use in their current adventure (or any adventure at all, for that matter).

Conversations in the game tend to fall into three categories: Avoiding fights, gathering information, and asking for help. As a general rule, when running conversation scenarios, a DM follows these steps:

1. **Describe the scene and the NPC.**

   Tell the players who or what their characters have met, what that person or monster looks like, and what he or she is doing.

2. **Decide what the NPC wants.**

   If you don't know already, take a moment and consider what this NPC wants to get from the player characters in the conversation that's coming up. It might be as simple as, "I want these people to go away and leave me alone." It might be more complicated: "I don't want anything in particular, but if they drop a bag of gold in my lap, I'd try hard to be helpful." It might be downright devious: "I want these people to go off to Grimdeath Keep and tell me when they're going, so that I can tell my evil master when to ambush them."

3. **Give an opening line.**

   A good way to signal that this is going to be a talking encounter is to have the NPC or monster speak first. Figure out what this NPC will say, how he, she, or it will say it, and then deliver your opening line. For example: "The ogre standing in the middle of the road squints at you and scratches his chin. 'This is Og's road!' He growls. 'But you give Og some gold, and Og be happy to let you use it.'"

   Don't be afraid to ham it up. Chances are you're not a professional actor, but who cares? Let it all out when you're speaking for your monsters and NPCs. You want the players to *remember* this person or monster and this conversation later, or you wouldn't be having a talking encounter now, would you?

4. **Pursue the conversation.**

   Let the players respond to your opening line (or have your monster or NPC respond to theirs), and then continue the conversation as long as necessary. If you need to, take a minute or two to think it over, and let the players know that you're trying to figure out what the NPC or monster says next.

5. **Say goodbye and hang up.**

   When the conversation's over, make sure you let the players know that this monster or NPC is done talking and that you consider the conversation to be at an end. For example, say something like, "Og counts the coins you gave him, which seems sort of hard for him. Then the ogre grins with a mouth full of crooked fangs and says, 'Have good trip on Og's road!'"

The combat task

Running a fight can be pretty complex, but here's the good news — there's little doubt about whether or not you're in a fight scene. If the player characters are trying to kill someone or something, or vice versa, your job is clear: You've got to get the battle resolved before anything else happens.

Here's the basic process for running the combat task:

1. **Fix everyone's position.**

   Figure out where the heroes and monsters are standing at the beginning of the hostile encounter. In a dungeon, this is pretty clear: If the heroes bust open the door to Room 7, the Armory, any monsters that your adventure notes as occupying Room 7 will be inside the room. If you don't know exactly where the monsters are in the room, take your best guess.

   If the battle is not in a dungeon, you may have to be more creative. In a wilderness setting, you'll want to determine the encounter distance based on how far away the heroes and the monsters are likely to spot each other. Refer to the terrain descriptions on pages 87–93 of the *Dungeon Master's Guide*.

2. **Is this an ambush?**

   If there's a chance that one side isn't aware of the other side when the encounter begins, figure out who sees who first by making Spot or Listen checks for the monsters and having players make Spot or Listen checks for their characters. See the "Starting an Encounter" section on page 22 of the *Dungeon Master's Guide*.

   There are four basic scenarios that you want to consider when deciding who might be ambushing who:

- **Heroes storm the room:** The PCs kick open a dungeon door and leap in, swords bared. Usually, no one should be surprised; the bad guys might be startled by the sudden appearance of the heroes, but the heroes don't know for sure that there's someone to fight in the room. Skip the surprise round and go to initiative.

- **Monster jumps out:** A monster is watching some place a hero might walk into or through, and leaps out to attack as soon as the hero appears. The monster is aware of the hero, but the hero might not see the monster before it attacks. Usually, it's fair to have the monster make a Hide check (maybe with a big bonus, if it's got a great place to lurk), and then allow the character under attack to make a Spot check to see the monster before it springs. If the character spots the monster, he or she is aware of it in the surprise round, so he or she can act. If the character doesn't spot the monster, the monster surprises him or her.

- **Heroes sneak up on the monster:** The heroes have a good idea that there's a monster someplace up ahead, and they try to take it by surprise. The heroes are aware of the monster, but the monster may not be aware of the heroes. Usually, you'll have the heroes doing the sneaking try their stealth skills (Move Silently, or possibly Hide) or use stealthy magic (like the *invisibility* or *silence* spells) to get close. The bad guys get the opportunity to make Spot or Listen checks to detect the heroes; if they fail, they're surprised. Otherwise, roll initiative normally.

- **Chance meeting:** The heroes and monsters blunder into each other. Maybe the heroes are walking along a forest trail when they meet a dire wolf out hunting, or maybe they're confronting a gang of ruffians in a bad part of town when someone draws a blade. Whatever the case, neither side has any special advantage over the other; the best thing to do is to just roll initiative and start the fight.

3. **Set out the battle grid.**

   Draw out the terrain or room outline on the battle mat, with one square on the mat equal to a 5-foot square on your map. Then place the figures or markers for the characters and the monsters in their appropriate positions. This will help players figure out where they can and can't move.

4. **Roll initiative.**

   Everybody on both sides of the fight rolls initiative to determine the initiative order for the fight. (However, surprised characters or monsters won't get to act in the surprise round.)

5. **Surprise round.**

   If only some of the monsters or heroes can act, they get to do so now. Only those characters or monsters who are aware of the enemy get to act in this round. They only get one standard action each. See the section, "The Surprise Round," on page 23 of the *Dungeon Master's Guide*.

6. **First round.**

   Now start resolving combat rounds:

   A. **Count down the initiative order.** Beginning with the highest initiative roll, resolve each character or monster's action for the round.

   B. **Monsters and villains act.** When you reach a monster or villain (some bad guy you're running, because you're the DM) decide what that bad guy is going to do this round. Resolve the action. See the section called, "Getting the Most out of Your Monsters," later in this chapter, for advice on running monsters in combat.

   C. **The heroes act.** When you reach a player-controlled character in the initiative order, tell the player that it's his or her turn and ask him or her what the character is going to do. Resolve whatever action the player character attempts.

   D. **Finish the round.** When everyone has acted, you've finished the round. This is a good place to pause and take stock of what's going on. Are there other monsters nearby that might hear the fight and come to investigate? Do the monsters decide to break off the battle and run for it? (They'll have to wait for their next action to begin running, of course.)

7. **Go to the next round.**

   After you reach the end of the initiative order in the first round, the round's over. Go back up to Step 6 and begin the second round.

A combat encounter lasts until one side or the other is dead, runs away, surrenders, or manages to call a truce.

The free time task

You'll find that you begin most adventure sessions and most new adventures with some DMing that isn't really "on the clock." For example, if you know that the players are about to go explore the Caves of Doom, you'll usually provide a little information about why their heroes are interested and how they got there. At a bare minimum, you ought to say something like, "You've heard of a great treasure hidden somewhere in the monster-haunted Caves of Doom, so you've hiked into the Dragonbone Hills. You're now standing in front of a gaping cave mouth in the side of a hill. Any special preparations before you go in?" (That's an extremely minimal set up, but most players will cut a new DM some slack and go along for now.)

Free time is also good for evaluating options and attending to tasks that take time, but don't need DMing. For example, if the heroes are going to rest up for a week in town, the player running the wizard might look at you and say, "While we're waiting, I'm going to scribe a couple of scrolls." You don't need to run through any real process for this. Just assess the cost and have the player pay up the gold pieces and XP that the character needs to make some scrolls. Similarly, debating the question of which way to turn next in an adventure, or what adventure to set off on, is also a good free time task.

Finally, even in the tightest-run games, there's a lot of screwing around. People sitting around the table will drop out of game mode and chat about movies they've seen, how things are going at work, or memorable scenes from old games. As DM, you're not in charge of all this. We only mention it because it's important for you to recognize free time when your players happen to stumble into it. Clam up for a few minutes, let your players gab or joke, make a trip to the bathroom or whatever, and then get back into the game when you think your players are ready.

Getting the Most out of Your Monsters

One of your most important jobs as DM is to run the monsters and bad guys in a fight. The first thing you need to do to run a monster in a fight is to learn where to find key information about the monster — getting a handle on the format in which monsters and villains are normally presented. When you know how to navigate a monster description or stat block, you'll want to learn how to make decisions for the monsters that make sense and suit the situation, without cutting the players too much of a break or being too tough on them.

Figuring out monster stats

Monsters have many of the same critical numbers that characters do. They've got hit points, Armor Class, attack bonuses, saving throws, skills and feats, even ability scores.

In most D&D supplements or adventures, monsters are presented in one of two basic formats: the *Monster Manual* entry, or the *stat block*. In order to run a monster in combat, you'll need to have an idea of how these two formats tell you crucial information about the monster or villain in question.

Take a look at the nearby sidebar, "Gargoyle (*Monster Manual*)," which shows the *Monster Manual* entry for the gargoyle.

You'll find the key for reading the *Monster Manual* entry on pages 5–7 of the *Monster Manual*. But just to help you out, here's a quick look at some of the more important pieces of information hidden in this format:

Gargoyle (*Monster Manual*)

Medium Monstrous Humanoid (Earth)

Hit Dice: 4d8+19 (37 hp)

Initiative: +2

Speed: 40 ft. (8 squares), fly 60 ft. (average)

Armor Class: 16 (+2 Dex, +4 natural), touch 12, flat-footed 14

Base Attack/Grapple: +4/+6

Attack: Claw +6 melee (1d4+2)

Full Attack: 2 claws +6 melee (1d4+2) bite +4 melee (1d6+1) and gore +4 melee (1d6+1)

Space/Reach: 5 ft./5 ft.

Special Attacks: —

Special Qualities: Damage reduction 10/magic, darkvision 60 ft., freeze

Saves: Fort +5, Ref +6, Will +4

Abilities: Str 15, Dex 14, Con 18, Int 6, Wis 11, Cha 7

Skills: Hide +7*, Listen +4, Spot +4

Feats: Multiattack, Toughness

Environment: Any

Organization: Solitary, pair, or wing (5–16)

Challenge Rating: 4

Treasure: Standard

Alignment: Usually chaotic evil

Advancement: 5–6 HD (Medium), 7–12 HD (Large)

Level Adjustment: +5

Freeze (Ex): A gargoyle can hold itself so still it appears to be a statue. An observer must succeed on a DC 20 Spot check to notice the gargoyle is really alive.

The Hide bonus increases by +8 when a gargoyle is concealed against a background of stone.

- ✔ **Medium:** The gargoyle's size. Most monsters range from Tiny to Huge. A monster's size influences several other stats.

- ✔ **Monstrous Humanoid (Earth):** The monster's type and subtype. A monster type is sort of like a character class — it dictates the type of Hit Dice, attack bonus, and saves the monster gets.

- **Hit Dice:** The number of Hit Dice the monster has, plus its bonus hit points based on its Constitution bonus and any feats like Toughness. Hit Dice are very much like a monster's level.

- **(37 hp):** The number of hit points an average gargoyle has.

- **Initiative:** The gargoyle's modifier for initiative rolls.

- **Speed:** The gargoyle's speed in one move action. If it charges or takes a double move, it can go twice this distance in one round.

- **Fly 60 ft. (average):** Gargoyles can fly. If the gargoyle stays on the ground, its speed is 40 feet. If it takes to the air, its speed is 60 feet, and its maneuverability is average. Maneuverability only matters if you're using the tactical aerial movement rules (they're on page 20 of the *DMG*).

- **Armor Class:** The gargoyle's AC. The touch AC is helpful information for spells (many use a touch attack, not a melee or ranged attack). The flat-footed AC is the gargoyle's AC when it can't use its Dex bonus.

- **Base Attack/Grapple:** Two numbers you won't use very often. Base attack is really only useful for a few monsters that have feats such as Combat Expertise. Grapple is more common; many monsters try to grab the heroes. Gargoyles aren't particularly inclined to grapple, but if a wrestling match breaks out in the middle of a gargoyle battle, its grapple modifier is +6.

- **Attack:** When the gargoyle can make only one attack (usually because it moved and attacked in the same round), this is its attack. The "+6 melee" tells you that it makes a melee attack with both claws with a +6 bonus (1d20+6), and the value in parenthesis tells you how much damage it deals if it hits (in this case, 1d4+2).

- **Full Attack:** When the gargoyle can use the full attack action (usually because it happened to begin its turn within five feet of a character it wanted to attack) it makes claw, bite, and gore attacks in a single round.

- **Space:** How much territory the gargoyle takes up on the battle map. In this case, it's just one 5-foot square.

- **Reach:** How far away the gargoyle can hit someone with its attack. This means it has to be in a square right next to the hero it wants to attack.

- **Special Qualities:** Any special abilities the gargoyle has are noted here. Damage reduction is a big one; this means that the gargoyle ignores the first 10 points of damage any opponent does with a physical attack, unless the opponent is wielding a magical weapon.

- **Saves:** The gargoyle's save modifiers for Fortitude, Reflex, and Will saves.

- **Abilities:** The gargoyle's ability scores.

- **Skills:** The gargoyle's skill modifiers. Monsters get skill points and spend them just like PCs do; if a skill isn't listed here, you can assume that the gargoyle has 0 ranks in it.

- **Feats:** The feats the gargoyle knows. (Multiattack is a feat from the *Monster Manual.*)

- **Environment:** The types of places you find gargoyles. Most monsters' habitats are a lot more specific, such as "cold forests" or "temperate hills."

- **Organization:** The number of gargoyles you're likely to run into at one time.

- **Challenge Rating:** The CR of a typical gargoyle. The DM uses this to determine if a monster is a good match for the party of player characters and to determine how many XP the players earn for beating that monster.

- **Advancement:** Don't worry about this. It's just a guideline for how you can customize a gargoyle if you want to make a super-tough one.

- **Level Adjustment:** If somebody wanted to play a gargoyle as a player character, you'd use its level adjustment to determine how to balance that against normal character race choices. Don't worry about it now.

See the nearby sidebar, "Gargoyle (stat block)," to take a look at how that same monster looks when you change it from the monster entry format to the stat block format.

A stat block may look pretty intimidating at first glance, but it's not as bad as it seems. Every abbreviation in the stat block format mirrors a line from the *Monster Manual* entry format. For example, "HD" stands for Hit Dice, "AC" stands for Armor Class, and "Grp" stands for Grapple. It's just a denser way of providing the same information.

Statistics blocks are discussed at length on page 85–86 of the *Dungeon Master's Guide.*

Gargoyle (stat block)

Gargoyle: CR 4; Medium monstrous humanoid (earth); HD 4d8+19; hp 37; Init +2; Spd 40 ft., fly 60 ft. (average); AC 16, touch 12, flat-footed 14; Base Atk +4; Grp +6; Atk +6 melee (1d4+2, claw); Full Atk +6/+6 melee (1d4+2, 2 claws) and +4 melee (1d6+1, bite) and +4 melee (1d6+1, gore); Space/Reach 5 ft./5 ft.; SQ DR 10/magic, darkvision 60 ft., freeze; AL CE; SV Fort +5, Ref +6, Will +4; Str 15, Dex 14, Con 18, Int 6, Wis 11, Cha 7.

Skills and Feats: Hide +7*, Spot +4, Listen +4; Multiattack, Toughness.

Freeze (Ex): A gargoyle can hold itself so still it appears to be a statue. An observer must succeed on a DC 20 Spot check to notice the gargoyle is really alive.

*The Hide bonus increases by +8 when a gargoyle is concealed against a background of stone.

Deciding what the bad guys do

After you've looked up a monster in the *Monster Manual* or created an evil NPC and you know what that monster or villain *can* do, it's natural to ask what it *will* do. Many monsters or villains are pretty complicated; they've got a list of attacks and special abilities as long as your arm. So how in the world do you figure out which of these abilities the monster is going to use in any particular round?

Any monster or villain should consider taking one of four basic actions each round. Not all monsters will be able to use all four choices; for example, an ogre doesn't command any magic or have any special attacks. Just ignore the choices that don't apply. The four basic choices for a monster's or villain's action in a given round are as follows:

> ✔ **Hit something:** If the monster or villain is standing next to one of the heroes, it can make a melee attack. Use the monster's melee attack, whatever that may be; you'll roll a d20, add the attack bonus, and see if you equaled or beat the player's AC. (If the monster has a good ranged attack — for example, a goblin with a crossbow — it can attack at range, of course.)

- ✔ **Move:** If the monster isn't standing next to one of the heroes, but needs to get next to a hero in order to use its melee attack, it probably ought to move and get into fighting range. A monster can move up to its speed and make a single attack in the same round. Or the monster can move up to twice its speed and make a single attack by taking a charge action (see page 154 in the *Player's Handbook*).

- ✔ **Use magic:** If the monster or villain can cast spells or has spell-like abilities, it can use one of its spells instead of making a melee or ranged attack. Use your discretion — if the monster has a great melee attack and only has a couple of low-level "fluff" spell-like abilities (say, something like *detect magic* or *burning hands*), the monster probably prefers to make melee attacks. But a powerful evil wizard will certainly use his magic every round that he or she can.

- ✔ **Make a special attack:** Finally, many creatures have special attacks like breath weapons, gaze attacks, sonic attacks, and so on. If a monster has a special ability, you should probably use it. What's the point of pitting the PCs against a medusa if you don't use its petrifying gaze?

Fighting smart, fighting dumb

Say you've got a half-fiend red dragon attacking the players. It's got a fiery breath weapon, awesome melee attacks, nasty evil spell-like abilities, and — oh yeah — it also casts a bunch of sorcerer spells, too. Which of its attacks will it use on its next round, and which character will be ground zero for all this dragon beat-down?

The first thing you want to do is take a look at your monster's Intelligence score. Is it a voracious, mindless brute like a huge monstrous centipede? If so, the most realistic thing for that monster to do is simply move toward the nearest character and try to eat him or her. That's what big, dumb bugs would do. Is it a clever and malicious opponent like a demon or devil? If that's the case, it fights with cunning and cruelty, switching easily from attack to defense and using patience and guile if necessary.

Here's some guidance on making your tactical decisions when you're running a monster or villain:

- ✔ **Intelligent foes *plan*, but dumb foes *react*:** A hobgoblin blademaster knows that the heroes' cleric can heal up the good guys as fast as the blademaster can carve them up, or worse yet, get off a lucky *hold person* spell, so he'll go after the cleric with a vengeance. A giant wolf is much more likely to whirl and snap at the last character who hurt it.

✔ **Lead with your best:** Most monsters don't save their best attack for last. An evil wizard doesn't go through a battle throwing 1st-level spells when he or she has higher-level spells to use. The game assumes that monsters use their best attacks; that's why they're assigned the Challenge Rating they've got.

✔ **Rolling to pick a target:** If you honestly don't know which character a monster is more likely to attack, there's nothing wrong with deciding the monster will randomly pick which PC to attack — simply roll a d6 and call evens for Joe the Fighter and odds for Bob the Cleric.

Chapter 24

Building a Dungeon

In This Chapter

▶ Exploring adventure creation

▶ Using a sample dungeon

*I*n the previous chapter, we examined the Dungeon Master's role in running a DUNGEONS & DRAGONS game. The game requires adventures, the framework through which players work together to create memorable tales of fantasy and adventure. An adventure can be an epic tale that spans multiple locations, but at its heart, an adventure focuses on the dungeon.

In this chapter, we examine the basics of adventure creation. We look at creating encounters, which are the building blocks of adventures. In the end, we get to the roots of D&D and provide you with a classic dungeon crawl to get you started.

Finally, we briefly examine the concept of the ongoing D&D campaign and how you can build a simple campaign by linking adventures in a series or an intricate campaign to rival anything ever published.

 Chapter 3 of the *Dungeon Master's Guide* goes into greater depth on creating D&D adventures. Use the material here as a guide and to see one way to construct an adventure, and then go to the core rulebooks for more details and advice.

Creating a D&D Adventure

The player who takes on the role of the Dungeon Master has a wealth of cool and intriguing ideas to share with others. We might not all have the discipline to write epic novels or the talent to paint vast vistas from our imaginations, but we can all find an outlet for creative expression and great fun as a Dungeon Master for a D&D game.

Bear in mind that when you create a D&D adventure, you don't have to fill in all the holes or connect all the dots. After all, the DM provides just one part of the adventure — the players provide the rest through the actions of their characters. The DM sets up the basic plot and structure of the adventure, but he or she doesn't come up with any of the conclusions. How does a specific scene end? Do the bad guys get defeated? Unlike writing a story, where the writer determines not only the beginning of the tale but the middle and the end, the DM just sets the scene. What happens is determined by how the player characters react and how the dice fall.

This leads to one of the great enjoyments of the game — surprise. The DM might know what monsters and scenes the adventure includes, but he or she doesn't know how things will turn out. The twists and turns of adventures are often as surprising to the DM as they are to the players.

Parts of an adventure

Adventure creation may seem like a daunting task. The best way to approach it is by examining the individual parts of an adventure. An *adventure* (sometimes called a *quest* or a *module,* which goes back to the days when the industry referred to published adventures as modules) is a collection of related encounters that offer a rudimentary storyline. An adventure promises a story, offers challenges that allow each player character to shine, and provides opportunities for action and roleplaying.

The DM needs to think in terms of beginnings, scenes, and situations that kick off action and offer players choices of behavior. "What does your character do now?" is a question DMs often ask players. Don't think in terms of endings, because you want your adventure to reach a conclusion through the actions and ideas of the players and their characters.

The premise

An adventure starts with a premise, a hook that catches the players' interests and involves their characters in some motivation-inducing manner. Think in terms of set up and build from there. The player characters can get involved in the premise, but they need a motivation to carry on. More than one motivation might suggest itself, and different PCs can have different motivations that drive them to take on an adventure. Character motivations include greed, fear, revenge, morality, curiosity, and need. Player motivation boils down to seeking to gain experience to improve a character and to having fun playing the game.

Here are some examples of an adventure premise:

- A hostile kobold tribe has claimed the abandoned manor and is using it as a staging area for raids on defenseless travelers using the nearby trade road.

✔ A scholar of ancient lore needs a group of brave adventurers to explore the haunted graveyard and find the tomb of Eldrup the Insane.

✔ A gang of orcs has taken Oleem, the beloved pet cat of the village elder's youngest daughter.

You can imagine how any of these premises can be turned into an adventure. You just need to sketch out a number of related encounters, populate them with monsters and other obstacles, and draw a map.

Encounters

Encounters are where the action and drama of every adventure take place. Every encounter is kind of like a miniature, concentrated version of the entire adventure. An encounter has a hook and a set up. It has a location. It has a goal that, when attained, ends the encounter and pushes the characters deeper into the adventure.

Encounter goals usually can be summed up by the verb that best describes the required action — *capture, defeat, discover, destroy, escape, find, negotiate, obtain, protect, rescue,* and *survive* are a few examples. In an encounter, characters might have to *capture* the master thief, *discover* the secret door, *negotiate* with the ogre mage, or *rescue* the merchant from the mind flayer's slave pen.

There are three types of encounters:

✔ **Challenge encounters** provide some kind of hazard, trap, or obstacle that the characters must overcome to attain the goal. Skills, spells, and ability checks are the tools that characters usually employ to overcome challenge encounters.

✔ **Combat encounters** feature creatures or opponents that the characters might have to battle in order to win the encounter. Combat abilities and spells see the most use in these kinds of encounters.

✔ **Roleplaying encounters** involve a DM-controlled character (also called a nonplayer character, or NPC) whom the player characters must interact with to attain the goal of the encounter. They might have to talk to, convince, bluff, bribe, trade insults with, seduce, negotiate, intimidate, beg, or otherwise interact with the NPC in order to advance the plot. A roleplaying encounter can lead to or become a challenge or combat encounter, depending on how things work out. Such encounters rely on roleplaying talents, and skill checks are only used sparingly to augment the roleplaying and to determine the reactions of the NPCs.

Encounters are typically keyed to areas on a map. Only when the player characters arrive at the specific map area can the encounter take place. When all of the encounters in an adventure take place within the confines of a specific location (such as a dungeon), the adventure is called a *site-based adventure*. This is the easiest type of adventure to create and run, because the whole story works off the map you draw and the encounters you key to it.

Site-based versus event-based adventures

The adventures discussed in this book are site-based adventures, meaning that they are set in a single location that is driven by exploration more than story or a complex plotline. Easy to create and easy to run, site-based adventures such as *The Tomb of Horrors* and *The Temple of Elemental Evil* are infamous among long-time D&D players for their simplicity and sheer genius.

A more challenging adventure to create is an *event-based adventure,* an adventure built around a series of events that the characters can influence through their actions. The characters have a complex goal or mission that they must accomplish, and the encounters that take place are a direct result of that effort. There may be maps for many of the encounters, but the events take place over a course of time or as triggered by previous events and keyed to a flowchart, timeline, or some combination of the two. Chapter 3 of the *Dungeon Master's Guide* provides more details on these sorts of adventures.

Adventure structure

Good adventures provide choices, points at which the players can make important decisions that have significant impact on what happens next. Choices can be as simple as providing the option to go right or left at an intersection in a dungeon corridor, or as complex as giving the characters the option to retrieve the *crimson wand of doom* or destroy it in the dwarven furnace of the undercity.

Good adventures combine the different kinds of encounters and vary the experiences they provide. Attack, defense, problem-solving, roleplaying, and investigation should all come into play in varying degrees.

Good adventures are exciting. They provide rising and falling tension, building action, increasing stakes, and fantastic locations that add to the ambience.

Finally, good adventures provide encounters that make use of the abilities of the player characters. If one of the players in your group has a rogue character, but you never provide that character with the opportunity to be stealthy and use his or her rogue skills, then that player will have less fun and few opportunities to shine.

Conversely, don't restrict character actions or lead the characters around by their noses just to make sure they get to see every detail of your adventure. Don't create situations where the PCs are spectators, watching NPCs accomplish all the important tasks. Beware of putting your PCs in situations where they must be saved by the intervention of others — that's just not heroic. And don't look for ways to countermand or foil what the characters are capable of. Design interesting encounters where they can employ their abilities to the best advantage or use them in new and clever ways.

The end

Each adventure eventually comes to an end. As an adventure designer, you should provide a set up for a climactic encounter, but how the adventure ends depends on the players' actions. The climactic encounter should take place in a suitably impressive location. It should feature the boss villain of the adventure, perhaps someone the characters met early on or someone they heard rumors of but don't meet until the final scene.

Sometimes an adventure finishes with a satisfying conclusion that wraps up all the loose ends. Sometimes the boss villain gets away to challenge the characters another day. And, once in awhile, the characters discover that the boss villain takes his orders from a secret, more powerful nemesis they will meet in the future.

Adventure-builder checklist

As a beginning Dungeon Master, stick to the site-based adventures until you feel you have the hang of the basics of adventure design. Here's a checklist to help you get started as an adventure designer:

- Brainstorm the premise of the adventure and the motivations of your player characters.

- Sketch a map of the adventure location(s) on a sheet of graph paper. Number each encounter site on the map.

- Choose the opponents that will populate the adventure, from the weakest minions to the most powerful boss villains. Use the Challenge Rating system (refer to page 48 of the *Dungeon Master's Guide*) and the *Monster Manual* to select opponents that will be an appropriate challenge for your party.

- Flesh out and key each encounter with notes, tactics, and statistics. Tables 3-1 and 3-2 in the *Dungeon Master's Guide* provide guidelines for determining the difficulty of encounters. In general, most of the encounters you create for a particular adventure should have Encounter Levels (EL) equal to or lower than the party's level. A few challenging encounters can have an EL that's one or two levels higher than the party, while the climax can have an EL that's three or four levels higher than the party. The Challenge Ratings (CRs) of all the opponents in the encounter determine the encounter's EL, as shown on Table 3-1 in the *Dungeon Master's Guide*. Use CRs and ELs in conjunction to create balanced encounters for your party. (The sample dungeon later in this chapter provides examples of this in play.)

- Check everything over and try to think like your players. Look for clever ways to overcome certain encounters that don't necessarily rely on combat.

Here's one final nugget of advice — you don't have to follow any set order when you create an adventure. You can start with a single cool encounter idea and build an adventure around it. You can sketch out a map and then fill in the details. Be creative, have fun, and don't sweat it.

Sample Dungeon: Hall of the Spider God

This section explores adventure creation by providing you with a finished sample that you can play and use as a model for your own adventures. It's designed for a party of four 1st-level adventurers — a fighter, a rogue, a sorcerer, and a cleric. Use the ready-to-play characters presented in Chapters 3 through 6. It will be somewhat tougher if your party has less than four characters, and a bit easier if the party contains more than four characters.

Adventure premise

The long-abandoned dungeon of the evil wizard Volnudar is rumored to lie in the hills overlooking the town of Briston. In recent days, seven townsfolk have disappeared and strange creatures have been seen lurking in the shadows of the hills. The town elders have come to the reluctant conclusion that something stirs in the hidden corridors that once reverberated with the arcane evil of Volnudar. Now the call goes out: The town elders will reward the party of adventurers who investigate the hills and learn the fate of the missing townsfolk. The wizard is long gone, but something evil still resides in the vile dungeon.

What threatens the town and lurks in the dungeon? A band of monsters, led by the bugbear Broot, have made the dungeon their home and have been launching small raids into the town. They worship an even worse monster that they discovered in the dungeon — a giant spider that Broot has named Sperrin!

Using the battle grid

One side of the fold-out battle grid included at the beginning of this book features a map of dungeon rooms and corridors. Use that map as Volnudar's hidden dungeon. The battle grid should be placed, map side up, on the table within reach of all of the players and the Dungeon Master.

Using the character and monster markers

This sample adventure makes use of all of the monsters provided as markers along the edge of the battle grid. The statistics for the monsters are provided later in this chapter. There are also markers that can be used to represent the adventurers, one for each of the four classes presented in this book.

Place the markers representing the adventurers in the corridor near the space marked "A" on the map. Let the players arrange the markers as they see fit, as long as all characters start out in the corridor squares to the far left side of the map. Remember that each character must occupy a space, and only one character can be in a square at any time.

Put the monster markers to the side. Don't place them on the battle grid until the adventure tells you to.

Adventure key

The Hall of the Spider God features five encounters. The key is numbered, but the encounters can occur in any order, depending on where the characters explore and when. Refer to the keyed locations when the characters approach or enter the numbered areas on the map (see Figure 24-1).

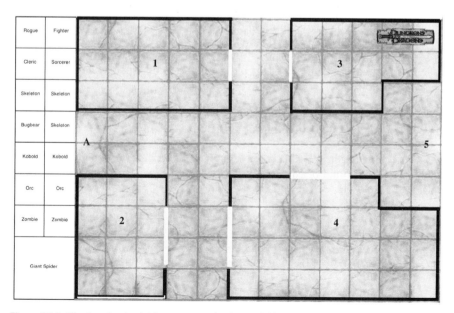

Figure 24-1: The key for the fold-out map at the front of this book.

Starting the adventure

After the players place the markers representing their characters, as described previously, the DM reads the following out loud:

> "You entered the hills above the town of Briston at the request of the town elders. Seven members of the town have mysteriously disappeared over the past few days, and the elders have offered a reward for their safe return or an explanation as to their fate. You have heard rumors that an evil wizard once called these hills his home, and that his dungeon remains somewhere beneath the hills. You also learned that mysterious creatures have been seen lurking in the hills, and the elders believe that these creatures might be the source of the trouble that has descended upon Briston.
>
> "After much searching, you discovered an opening in the hillside. Now you find yourselves in a dark corridor of shaped stone that must be part of the evil wizard's lost dungeon."

Encounter Area A

Encounter Level (EL) None: Not every encounter provides a challenge or obstacle. This one simply sets the stage for the rest of the adventure, and so it doesn't have a listed EL.

The dungeon corridor where the PCs enter has a dank smell of stale air and age. Lichen streaks the corridor walls, glowing with an eldritch light that provides shadowy illumination.

Ask the players to make Listen checks for their characters. To make a Listen check, each player rolls a d20 and adds his or her character's Listen skill modifier. The DC for the check is 20.

Failed Listen Check (result is less than 20): The character doesn't hear anything out of the ordinary in the dark corridor.

Successful Listen Check (result is 20 or better): The character hears the distant sound of snorts and guttural laughter. (This is coming from Encounter Area 5.)

Experience Points Award: Each character that makes a successful Listen check earns 25 XP.

Next: When the characters have looked around and made whatever preparations they want to, it's time to move deeper into the dungeon. If the characters stick to the corridor and head toward the sound, go on to Encounter Area 5. If they move toward one of the closed doors, go on to that encounter.

Encounter Area 1

Encounter Level (EL) 2: The opponent the PCs face in this encounter has a Challenge Rating (CR) of 2. Because there's only one opponent, in this case the CR and EL are the same.

When the characters approach the door to this room, read the following out loud:

> "The door ahead hangs open the smallest amount, revealing a narrow crack of torchlight in the room beyond. What do you want to do?"

This is a combat encounter. Ask the players what their characters are doing, based on the description of the scene you just read to them.

Inside the Room: The characters might swing open the door with wild abandon or send a rogue to sneak up and check things out first. Reveal the information about the room as you see fit, depending on how the PCs approach the area.

The room is lit by four torches spaced evenly on the walls of the chamber. A solid table and chair are near the door, and a tall, muscular, fur-covered bear-like humanoid sits there, drinking from a large stone mug and picking at the remains of an animal carcass. This is Broot, a bugbear who leads the orcs and kobolds that make up the band of marauders that have claimed this dungeon as their base. He has a morningstar (a spiked mace) and a wooden shield close at hand, and he can make a Listen check if the characters try to approach the room quietly.

Broot's followers believe that the giant spider that resides in Encounter Area 4 is a god. Broot thinks his followers are fools, but he goes along with them because at the very least, Broot's luck has changed for the better since meeting the spider. He has named the spider Sperrin, and he plans to feed townsfolk to it in order to keep his band happy and his luck running strong.

The far end of the room serves as a prison for the townsfolk that Broot and his band have captured. Currently, four townsfolk (three men and a woman) are tied up against the far wall opposite the door.

There is also a locked chest (Open Lock DC 15) near the table. It contains some of the loot that Broot and his band have recently collected. If the PCs open the chest, they find gems and gold pieces worth 600 gp among bloody clothes and dirty rags.

Initiative Check: As soon as the PCs notice Broot, or Broot spots the PCs, call for initiative checks. Everyone rolls a d20 and adds their initiative modifier to the result. The DM rolls for Broot. The rest of the encounter plays out in rounds, with characters and monster acting in initiative order.

Bugbear

Bugbears are savage creatures that stand 7 feet tall and are covered in coarse hair. They have long sharp fangs and flat noses, and they possess a keen love of both food and treasure.

Initiative	+1	Armor Class	17
Speed	6 squares (30 feet)	Hit Points	16
Morningstar	d20+5	Morningstar Damage	1d8+2
Throwing Javelin	d20+3	Throwing Javelin Damage	d6+2
Skills:	Listen +4, Spot +4		
Saves:	Fort +2, Ref +4, Will +1	Alignment:	Chaotic evil
Challenge Rating:	2		

Markers: Place the bugbear marker along the top wall of the room, two spaces from the wall with the door. The PC markers start in the corridor. There are no markers for the prisoners; feel free to use coins or some other items to mark the positions of the prisoners along the wall farthest from the door.

Broot: The bugbear is a violent, savage foe. He's extremely confident of his own abilities, however, and will attempt to defeat the intruding adventurers on his own, without calling for help. Use the statistics in the "Bugbear" sidebar for Broot.

The Prisoners: The characters must defeat Broot before they can deal with the prisoners or the locked chest they find in the room. They can easily free the townsfolk and point them to the way out after the bugbear falls.

The townsfolk seem grateful for being rescued but nervous and weary from their ordeal. If the PCs ask the townsfolk about how they got here or what else is in the dungeon, the townsfolk explain:

> "Each of us was captured by that bugbear's marauders — orcs and kobolds of the fiercest kind. One of the orcs came in and took Elar and Tob away about an hour ago. The bugbear laughed and told the orc something about making sure that Sperrin knew where her meal was coming from. When we were first brought here, there was a seventh captive, little Jammy the tailor's son. He slipped free of his ropes and ran off into the darkness. We haven't seen him since, but we've heard the bugbear asking about him every time some of his marauders entered this room."

The townsfolk don't know anything else that will help the PCs. One of them has been hiding a handful of *goodberries* that he will give to the party as a reward for rescuing them. There are five *goodberries*; each one cures 1 hit point of damage when eaten.

Experience Points Award: The party divides 600 XP for defeating Broot and rescuing the four townsfolk. In a party of four, each character receives 150 XP.

Next: The characters should attempt to find the rest of the missing townsfolk, little Jammy and the two prisoners taken to Sperrin.

Encounter Area 2

Encounter Level (EL) 1: The PCs face three opponents in this encounter, each with a CR ⅓. Table 3-1 in the *Dungeon Master's Guide* shows that three CR ⅓ creatures constitute an EL 1 challenge.

When the characters approach the door to this room, read the following out loud:

> "The door ahead is open wide. As you get closer, you can smell freshly turned dirt and hear a child crying. What do you want to do?"

This can be a combat encounter or a challenge encounter, depending on how the characters approach it. Ask the players what their characters are doing, based on the description of the scene you just read to them.

Inside the Room: The floor of this chamber, unlike the rest of this dungeon, consists of dirt instead of hewn stone. In the very center of the room stands a 5-foot wide circular stone platform. Atop the platform is a small, ruffled young boy — Jammy the tailor's son. Jammy appears tired and frightened, sitting curled in a ball and trying not to look at the room's other inhabitants.

Three skeletons surround the platform and Jammy. They stand almost completely still, swaying ever so slightly, the red lights smoldering in their otherwise empty eye sockets fixed menacingly on the small boy. Long ago, the evil wizard Volnudar used this chamber to experiment with spells designed to raise and control the undead. If any character casts a *detect magic* spell, the stone platform glows with an ancient magic that protects whoever stands upon it from the anger and hatred of undead creatures. That's all that keeps little Jammy safe from the animated skeletons.

The room is completely dark except for the tiny fires glowing in the skeletons' eye sockets. The skeletons ignore the characters unless they step into the room. So, if the players can figure out some way to get Jammy safely out of the room without stepping onto the dirt floor, their characters won't have to battle the skeletons. If the characters do enter the room, however, call for initiative checks. The skeletons move to attack and destroy any living creatures that enter the chamber. The only space in the room that is safe is atop the stone platform in the center.

Skeleton

Skeletons are the animated bones of humans that wear the tattered remnants of clothes and carry scimitars and shields. The only sign of life, other than the fact that they move with purpose and menace, is the malevolent red fire that glows in their empty eye sockets.

Initiative	+5	**Armor Class**	15
Speed	6 squares (30 feet)	**Hit Points**	6
Scimitar	d20+1	**Scimitar Damage**	1d6+1
Skills:	A skeleton has no skills		
Saves:	Fort +0, Ref +1, Will +2	**Alignment:**	Neutral evil
Challenge Rating:	⅓		

Special quality: Damage reduction 5/bludgeoning (damage dealt by most weapons is reduced by 5 points; skeletons take full damage from bludgeoning weapons such as quarterstaffs and maces)

Initiative Check: As soon as the PCs enter the room, call for initiative checks. Everyone rolls a d20 and adds their initiative modifier to the result. The DM rolls for the skeletons (one check covers them all, and all three act when their turn comes up in the initiative). The rest of the encounter plays out in rounds, with characters and monster acting in initiative order. Use the statistics in the "Skeleton" sidebar for all of the skeletons.

Markers: Place the three skeleton markers around the room's center square. The PC markers start in the corridor. Use a coin or some other item to mark the location of Jammy atop the platform in the center of the room.

Jammy: The characters must defeat the skeletons or otherwise get Jammy out of this chamber before they can have a meaningful conversation with him. He explains that the small lizard people chased him into the room, and he felt safe when they didn't follow him in. Then the skeletons rose up out of the dirt and surrounded him. He tells the PCs the following before they point him toward the exit, but only if they can calm him down with a DC 12 Diplomacy check:

> "There's something really bad in that room across the hall. Really, really bad." (Then, after a pause and in a whisper) "It eats people."

Experience Points Award: The party divides 300 XP for defeating the skeletons and/or rescuing little Jammy from the room. In a party of four, each character receives 75 XP.

Encounter Area 3 (Part 1)

Encounter Level (EL) 2: This is a challenge encounter that has a trap and a locked door.

When the characters approach the door to this room, read the following out loud:

> "The door ahead is closed. The heavy wood of the door features ornate carvings of strange symbols that seem to glow with a faint light. What do you want to do?"

This starts out as a challenge encounter, because the characters must find a way to get past the locked door. If they enter the chamber beyond, they face a combat encounter and the possibility of a magical reward.

The Locked Door: The PCs can check the door and determine that it is locked. Here are some options for dealing with the door:

Spot Checks: Call for Spot checks (DC 10) when the PCs start to examine the door. Any character that succeeds notices some scratches around the ancient lock. It looks like the marauders tried to gain entry into this chamber and failed.

Search Checks: A rogue character can Search (DC 20) the door for traps. If the check succeeds, the rogue finds indication of a resetting mechanical trap, which probably discouraged the marauders from further attempts to open the door. If the check fails, the door appears to be safe and trap-free as far as the rogue can determine.

Disable Device Check: If a rogue notices the trap (by making a successful Search check), he or she can try to disarm it. This requires a Disable Device check (DC 20). If the check succeeds, the trap is disarmed. If the check fails by 4 or less, the rogue can try to disarm it again. If the check fails by 5 or more, the rogue springs the trap (see the following option, *The Trap*).

Open Locks Check: A rogue can attempt to unlock the door. This Open Locks check has a DC 20. If the trap has been disarmed, there is no danger. If it hasn't been disarmed, any attempt to pick the lock (whether it succeeds or not) springs the trap (see *The Trap*). If the rogue successfully picks the lock, even if doing so sets off the trap, the door can be opened any time thereafter.

Bashing Down the Door: If the rogue's Open Lock check fails, or the party doesn't have a rogue, the door can be bashed open. This requires one character to make a DC 18 Strength check. This is an ability check; roll a d20 and add the character's Strength modifier. Here's a situation where a special action, *aid another,* can be used. One other character can help the acting character to try to bash open the door. The helping character also makes a Strength check, but the DC is 10. If the helping character succeeds, then the acting character receives a +2 bonus to his or her Strength checks. The characters can make as many attempts as they want to bash down the door. The first time a character tries to bash down the door, he or she sets off the trap (if it hasn't been disarmed). Each attempt to bash down the door, successful or not, makes a lot of noise. Make a Listen check (DC 15) for the orc in Encounter Area 5 each time a character makes a Strength check to bash down the door. If the orc successfully hears the racket, the creatures from Encounter Area 5 (see the later section, "Encounter Area 5") start to move toward Encounter Area 3.

The Trap: The door has a mechanical trap that, when triggered by an Open Lock or Strength check used on the door, shocks anyone touching the door or the lock for 1d4+1 damage. The trap resets after one hour.

Experience Points Award: The party divides 300 XP for disarming the trap and 300 XP for opening the door. If the trap is triggered but they manage to open the door, the reward is just 300 XP.

Encounter Area 3 (Part 2)

Encounter Level (EL) 1: The PCs face two opponents in this encounter, each with a CR ½. Table 3-1 in the *Dungeon Master's Guide* shows that two CR ½ creatures constitute an EL 1 challenge.

When the characters open the door to this room, read the following out loud:

"The door opens into a thick darkness. What do you want to do?"

Zombie

Zombies are the animated corpses of humans that shamble about as they follow the commands of their sinister creators. Half decayed and partially consumed by worms, zombies wear the tattered remains of their grave clothes and smell like putrid death.

Initiative	−1	**Armor Class**	11
Speed	6 squares (30 feet)	**Hit Points**	16
Club	d20+2	**Club Damage**	1d6+1
Skills:	A zombie has no skills		
Saves:	Fort +0, Ref −1, Will +3	**Alignment:**	Neutral evil
Challenge Rating:	½		

Special quality: Damage reduction 5/slashing (damage dealt by most weapons is reduced by 5 points; zombies take full damage from slashing weapons such as swords); zombies are slow and can only make one action in a round (move or attack, not both)

The PCs need some sort of light in order to explore this chamber effectively. After they light a torch or otherwise illuminate the scene, read the following out loud:

> "The chamber features rows of dusty shelves and strangely shaped crates. Cobwebs hang from the ceiling, and dust swirls in the air around you. Then you hear a disturbing sound from somewhere deep in the shadows: a moaning, threatening sound, and the shuffle of heavy feet slowly moving toward you. What do you do?"

Inside the Room: This was one of the ancient wizard's storerooms. Few of his most powerful items remain, but if the PCs can defeat the chamber's guardians, they can find some helpful items and treasure here.

Two human zombies guard this chamber. They were placed here long ago by Volnudar and continue to follow the last orders they were given — let no living creature enter this area and survive.

Initiative Check: As soon as the PCs light up the room or enter the chamber, call for initiative checks. Everyone rolls a d20 and adds their initiative modifier to the result. The DM rolls for the zombies (one check covers both of them, and both act when their turn comes up in the initiative). The rest of the encounter plays out in rounds, with characters and monster acting in initiative order. Use the statistics in the "Zombie" sidebar for both of the zombies.

Markers: Place the two zombie markers in the chamber, one near the center and one near the far wall. The PC markers start in the corridor.

Treasure: After the PCs defeat the zombies, they can examine the room. Among the crumbling scrolls and dusty vials, they find four *potions of cure light wounds*. If anyone decides to Search, the character that gets the highest result over 20 finds a magic weapon wrapped in cloth. The weapon matches the character's primary weapon, except that it is a +1 version of that weapon (meaning it has a magical +1 bonus on attack and damage rolls). For example, if Regdar rolls the highest Search result over 20, he finds a *+1 greatsword* that he can use instead of his mundane weapon.

Experience Points Award: The party divides 300 XP for defeating the zombies.

Encounter Area 4

Encounter Level (EL) 3: The PCs face three opponents in this encounter, each with a different CR. Table 3-1 in the *Dungeon Master's Guide* shows that one CR 2, one CR ½, and one CR ¼ creature constitutes an EL 3 challenge.

When the characters approach either of the doors that lead to this room, read the following out loud:

> "The door ahead is closed. You can hear chanting coming from beyond the door, but you don't understand the words. What do you want to do?"

Kobold

Kobolds are small, lizard-like humanoids about the size of halflings, with a tail, scaly hide, and a horned, doglike head.

Initiative	+1	**Armor Class**	15
Speed	6 squares (30 feet)	**Hit Points**	4
Spear	d20+1	**Spear Damage**	1d6–1
Sling	d20+3	**Sling Damage**	1d3 (roll a d6 and divide by two)
Skills:	Hide +6, Listen +2, Move Silently +2, Spot +2		
Saves:	Fort +2, Ref +1, Will –1	**Alignment:**	Lawful evil
Challenge Rating:	¼		

The doors into this room are not locked. The PCs can open them easily.

Inside the Room: The first thing the PCs notice upon opening the doors is that great pans of burning coals (called braziers) are situated to either side of both sets of doors, filling the room with firelight and smoke. The second thing they notice are the two creatures kneeling before a raised platform covering the left half of the long wall. One creature is an orc, the other a kobold. Atop the platform, tied up and obviously frightened, are the last two townsfolk — Elar and Tob. The third thing is that the entire right side of the room is covered in curtains of thick, clinging webs.

If the PCs enter quietly, they can surprise the orc and the kobold. That means that each of the PCs can perform one action (either a move or an attack) before the regular rounds of initiative begin.

When the battle is fully joined, Sperrin emerges from the webs to attack the intruders. Sperrin is a giant spider that the orcs and kobolds worship as a god. The townsfolk are meant to be a meal and a sacrifice for the giant spider.

Initiative Check: Everyone rolls a d20 and adds their initiative modifier to the result. The DM rolls once for the kobold (his check covers the kobold and the orc, who both act when their turn comes up in the initiative), and once for the giant spider. The rest of the encounter plays out in rounds, with characters and monsters acting in initiative order. Use the statistics in the "Orc," "Kobold," and "Giant spider" sidebars for the orc, kobold, and giant spider.

Markers: Place one orc and one kobold marker near the left side of the long wall. The PC markers start at whichever door they opened. Use a coin or some other item to mark the location of Elar and Tob atop the platform. The first time the giant spider gets to act, place its marker on the right side of the room.

Experience Points Award: The party divides 900 XP for defeating the orc, kobold, and giant spider, and rescuing Elar and Tob from the room.

Encounter Area 5

Encounter Level (EL) 1: The PCs face two opponents that constitute an EL 1 challenge.

An orc and a kobold start out in the part of the corridor marked "5" on the map. Place their markers there when one of the following takes place: The PCs step into a square more than halfway along the corridor, or the orc makes a successful Listen check when the PCs make noise trying to open the door to Encounter Area 3.

Use the kobold and orc statistics from Encounter Area 4 (see the "Orc" and "Kobold" sidebars in this chapter). These two creatures can be encountered alone, or they can join the zombies in Encounter Area 3 to make a more challenging encounter.

Initiative Check: Make initiative checks as you have been doing throughout this adventure.

Experience Points Award: The party divides 300 XP for defeating the orc and the kobold.

Orc

Orcs are aggressive humanoids with gray skin, coarse hair, and boarlike faces. They hate adventurers and seek to destroy them on sight.

Initiative	+0	Armor Class	13
Speed	6 squares (30 feet)	Hit Points	5
Falchion	d20+4	Falchion Damage	2d4+4
Throwing javelin	d20+1	Throwing Javelin Damage	d6+3
Skills:	Listen +1, Spot +1		
Saves:	Fort +3, Ref +0, Will −2	Alignment:	Chaotic evil
Challenge Rating:	½		

Giant spider

A giant spider is an aggressive predator that uses a poisonous bite to subdue and eventually consume prey.

Initiative	+3	**Armor Class**	14
Speed	6 squares (30 feet)	**Hit Points**	22
Bite	d20+4	**Bite Damage**	1d8+3 plus poison
Skills:	Climb +11, Hide +3, Jump +2, Spot +4		
Saves:	Fort +5, Ref +4, Will +1	**Alignment:**	Neutral
Challenge Rating:	2		
Special Quality:	Poison (DC 13 Fortitude save or take an additional 1d6 points of damage)		

Wrapping up the adventure

What happens after the PCs have successfully rescued the townsfolk? They should return to the town elders and claim their reward (1,000 gp to split among the party). They may want to return and fully explore the ancient dungeon. What lies in the corridors beyond what the PCs have already seen? That's up to you, as the DM, but you could use it as the basis of the first adventure you create from scratch. Try it and have fun!

Chapter 25

Keeping Your Players Happy

. . . .

. . . .

A great Dungeon Master doesn't just run a good DUNGEONS & DRAGONS game; he or she also tells a riveting story. The D&D game works fine as a series of tactical exercises and problem-solving puzzles, but a great storyteller behind the DM's screen can elevate the game to a whole other level. Building interesting story lines and villains for your adventures and presenting your players with the sort of challenges they want to face goes a long way toward making your game a memorable and long-lasting one.

In this chapter, we tell you about story-building and storytelling in the D&D game, and we show you some narrative, game pacing, and campaign building tips good for any D&D game.

Figuring Out Your Players

The first rule of any enterprise is to figure out what your customers want and give it to them. A D&D game is no different. If your players just want to kill monsters and not think too hard, they're not going to be happy with a subtle murder mystery or combat-light court intrigue. Similarly, if your players love to immerse themselves in their characters and enjoy the play-acting more than anything else, they won't be happy if you present adventures that don't give them opportunities to talk to the creatures and characters around them.

Most players fall into one of four basic categories:

✔ **Actors:** These are players who enjoy roleplaying for its own sake. Extreme actors would be just as happy to play D&D if it had no rules at all. Players who like this style of play often choose the bard, ranger, and rogue classes. They like adventures that have lots of opportunities to talk to NPCs (not just villains and monsters), and they tend to dislike adventures that offer nothing but combat encounters.

✔ **Puzzle-solvers:** This type of player loves figuring out riddles and challenges in the game. Extreme puzzle-solvers would be just as happy to play D&D without rules, just like the extreme actors. Puzzle-solvers often play clerics, rogues, and wizards. Puzzle-solvers don't mind combat encounters, because beating tactically challenging encounters (such as archers on a castle wall) is solving puzzles of sorts. They like adventures that offer chances to solve riddles and puzzles as players at the gaming table, and not just by rolling dice as characters in the game.

✔ **Hack-and-slashers:** These are players who just love to fight and beat up monsters. The bigger the fight, the happier they are. Hack-and-slashers live for dishing out the damage, and they're inclined to like the rules, because the game rules help them figure out how much damage they can deal out. Hack-and-slashers often play barbarians, fighters, and sorcerers. Obviously, they like adventures with plenty of monsters to fight, and they don't like adventures that involve too much talking.

✔ **Competitors:** These are those players who play for the thrill of winning in whatever form it might take. They're happy to fight big fights and win, but unlike the hack-and-slasher, they're just as happy to win by doing roleplaying or solving tough puzzles. Competitors tend to be heavily engaged with the rules, and they don't like to throw out the rulebooks. You can throw a variety of challenges at a competitor, and he or she is happy. Competitors often play clerics, fighters, and wizards.

Now, here's the tricky part: You probably have players of more than one type in your game. One player may like roleplaying, another might like combat, and a third player might be interested solely in beating the game. The best way to keep everybody happy is to simply alternate the types of encounters to cater to your players' various interests. Intersperse roleplaying encounters with combat encounters and challenge encounters, and you can make exciting adventures that feel varied and fresh where everybody gets the game he or she wants at least some of the time.

Table 25-1 summarizes some key adventure characteristics or features and which players are happiest with them.

Table 25-1	Player Preferences			
Adventure Characteristic	*Actor*	*Puzzle-Solver*	*Hack-and-Slasher*	*Competitor*
Big but tactically simple fights	Eh	Okay	Great	Good
Fights with difficult tactical challenges	Eh	Good	Okay	Great
Challenging traps that can be avoided with some thinking	Okay	Great	Eh	Good
Encounters that offer the chance to question NPCs or piece together different stories	Great	Good	Eh	Okay
Monsters who can be negotiated with, deceived, or bluffed	Great	Okay	Eh	Good
Simple choices; easy to determine the next move or course of action	Okay	Eh	Great	Good
Complex choices; many different ways to proceed	Good	Okay	Eh	Great
Rich background and story elements	Great	Good	Okay	Eh
Opportunities to act rashly, take ridiculous actions, show off, or declare yourself king or queen	Okay	Eh	Great	Good
Opportunities to get ahead by knowing the rules better than anyone else	Eh	Okay	Good	Great

If you're trying to keep everyone happy with the same adventure, try to include some "good" or "great" situations for each player at your table. You'll find that hack-and-slashers are a little difficult to entertain; they tend to be impatient and anxious to get to the next fight, and more than a few hack-and-slashers will look for ways to manufacture fights if none are at hand.

This table makes hack-and-slashers look like the worst players, but that's somewhat misleading. If most of the players at the table enjoy a lot of combat and view playing D&D as a way to let off steam by pretending to kill monsters, well, who's to say that's not the right way for them to play the game? Hack-and-slashers are often pretty knowledgeable about the rules, and tend to run decisive and effective characters. Sure, they're impatient to get to the fun, but a hack-and-slasher at the table can go a long way toward keeping the other players moving and motivated.

Narrating the Adventure

Knowing what your players like and catering to them is nothing more than good marketing. But a crummy movie with great marketing is still a crummy movie. What you need is some great writing and great directing to get an entertainment experience that will have your players on the edges of their seats. So what can you do to run a game that's fast-paced, exciting, emotionally charged, and makes your players feel like they can slay dragons and challenge gods?

Getting ready, getting organized

It's so simple we hesitate to mention it, but we will anyway: Be ready to run your game. Read ahead on the adventure you're running, visualize how you're going to set up the key encounters and decision points, and plan for what you're going to do when the players take a wrong turn. You shouldn't be seeing an encounter for the first time when the players kick open the door to Room 7 and storm inside.

The corollary to reading ahead is organizing your materials to run the game efficiently and effectively. Nothing brings a game to a crashing halt like the DM saying, "Uh, hang on guys, I gotta do some reading." Pausing for a moment to check your notes is one thing, but sticking your nose in the book to read for 10 minutes means that your players are sitting around doing nothing but watching you read. That ain't great entertainment.

Good ways to be prepared include the following tips:

- ✔ **Check the rules ahead of time:** If you see that you're likely to run an encounter involving a whole gang of basilisks, refresh your memory on how gaze attacks work and read the monster description the night before the game.

- ✔ **Make notes in your adventure:** Plan some actions or special moves for your monsters and villains ahead of time. Think about things that NPCs might say if the players wind up talking instead of fighting.

- ✔ **Keep a folder:** Organize your adventure notes and any records you're keeping (treasure the heroes find, NPCs they meet, and so on) so that you can quickly find information when you need it during play.

Creating evocative scenes

Your players are immersed in an imaginary world of soaring beauty, awesome magic, and horror beyond human endurance. It's your job to get this across with each scene you describe and every action your monsters and villains take. You don't have to stick three adjectives in front of every character or object you describe in the game, but you don't want to fall into the rut of droning, "The minotaur swings. He misses. The minotaur swings again. Uh, he gets an 18. Does that hit you?" Put some zip into it!

> **Boring:** "The room is 30 feet by 30 feet. There's a door in the north wall, and a stairway leading down. There's an ogre in here."

> **Better:** "The room smells dank and musty. It looks like an old cellar, with thick cobwebs in the blackened rafters. A towering creature with long arms and a crooked, fang-filled jaw glares at you, clutching a spiked club in its knotted fists. Behind it you think you see a battered old door in the north wall, and a set of stairs leading down into darkness."

> **Boring:** "The ogre charges and attacks. It rolls a 23. It hits you for 17 points of damage."

> **Better:** "The hulking monster throws back its head and howls in rage, and then it throws itself at you! It brings its spiked club whistling down in a deadly arc — that's a 23 to hit. Unnh! A mighty blow sends you reeling. You take 17 points of damage. 'Ha! I SMASH!' the creature bellows."

> **Boring:** "The hell hound breathes fire. You take 8 fire damage."

> **Better:** "The coal-black hound suddenly belches out a great blast of searing green flames. You take 8 points of fire damage."

Using the cut-scene

One handy trick for DMing multiple tasks at the same time is the cut-scene. Here's the idea: Give one player and whatever task he's involved in 5 to 10 minutes of your time, then put that situation on hold and switch over to work with another player on whatever she's doing. It's like a movie that hops between a couple of different characters doing different things. It's a great tool for pacing, because it lets you briefly "cliffhanger" a player in a challenging position (which builds suspense) while you involve another player who otherwise wouldn't be immediately involved in the scene (which keeps the players out of the key action from getting bored).

Cut-scenes work best when the party is split up. If some characters are fighting against assassins in a dark alleyway while other characters are trying to help the elven ambassador make her escape, you can easily switch back and forth between the two groups.

Cut-scenes also work on a smaller scale, when players are engaged in different tasks in the same area. For example, say that the PCs are searching through an evil wizard's laboratory. One might be searching for secret doors, another might be looking through the mysterious old tomes on the bookshelf for any interesting clues, and a third player might be talking to the wizard's captive, a human hero chained to the wall. You might start by DMing the player's conversation with the captive hero. Then when you reach a good break in the conversation, you switch over to tell another player what her rogue found when she searched the room. Then you switch over to the player whose character was looking at the books. As the DM, you're the director of the movie; you decide which player you're going to talk to, for how long, and where you're going to cut away to next.

Running a Fun Game

If you're creating interesting adventures for your players, and you're doing a good job of narrating and pacing the game, you're ahead of the eight ball. However, the game isn't all about the adventures you write and your ability to describe the action — you want to run a fun and entertaining game as much as a well-crafted one.

Using props

One great way to take your players from *listening* to *experiencing* is to introduce some props in your game. If the players defeat the sly rogue who's been carrying coded messages for the thieves' guild, make up a set of cryptic coded messages ahead of time, write them on a piece of paper, and crumple it up for effect — and if you stain the paper with tea or coffee, you might even get it to look a little like parchment. (If you don't want to mess with staining paper, you can find colored paper and parchment paper at any office supply store.) Not only will the puzzle-solvers in your group have a great time unraveling your code, but everyone else will like passing around a tangible object they can peer at and study, just like their characters would.

Old maps and secret messages are easy props to come up with. If you want to go a step further, try handfuls of old coins (especially foreign currency), tarot cards, books in foreign languages, and sketches or artwork. Anything that lets your players visualize the scene or item you're describing verbally is great. Not every encounter or challenge deserves a prop or handout, but a few here and there go a long way toward keeping your players interested and alert.

One prop you might not have thought of is a soundtrack. A little music played softly in the background as you play the game can be very evocative. You'll want to consider your music choice carefully, of course; the ideal piece is something that's orchestral, doesn't have many words or singing for the DM to compete with, and frankly just feels like it fits with the D&D game. Movie soundtracks can be great for this, especially from fantasy or science fiction movies — you could do worse than to play the soundtracks for the three *Lord of the Rings* movies, for example. Some companies actually produce soundtracks specifically to serve as roleplaying background music. Good choices include *Dungeons & Dragons the Official Roleplaying Soundtrack* (produced by Midnight Syndicate) and the *Shards of Eberron* CD soundtrack included with *Sharn: City of Towers* supplement.

Table rules

Every group of D&D players gradually evolves a set of *table rules* — conventions for starting new characters, looking up rules on the fly, urging other players to take specific actions, or simply whether to reroll or read as it lies when a die is cocked or falls on the floor. These rules really don't have much to do with the D&D game, because your table rules might conceivably apply to any number of other games you play with the same group of players. But it's a good idea to lay out your expectations on this sort of thing before an argument comes up about what is or isn't allowed at your table.

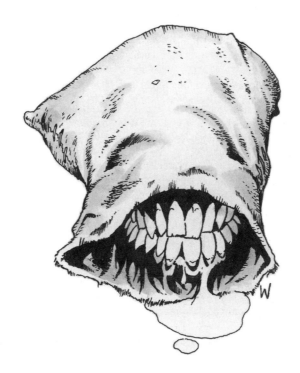

Some things you ought to clarify ahead of time include the following:

- ✔ What to do when a player can't make the game (specifically, is his or her character present in the party or not, and who controls the character if he or she is).

- ✔ Which rulebooks and supplements you allow players to refer to in play (many DMs prefer that players don't look up monsters in a *Monster Manual* while their characters are fighting the creature in question).

- ✔ Whether or not you'll allow "take backs" if a player figures out that his or her attack roll was really a 24 instead of a 21 after his or her action is over.

If you're a new DM running the game for an experienced group, you might want to simply adopt the table rules of the previous DM until you feel comfortable with instituting your own. You'll find a good discussion on table rules on page 11 of the *Dungeon Master's Guide*.

How honest should you be?

You're DMing a furious fight. Joe's paladin Baldror blows his Reflex save against the evil wizard's *lightning bolt* and gets knocked down to 7 hit points. Then the wizard's ogre henchman rolls a 20 against Baldror and scores a critical hit with his greataxe. Baldror's going to eat 2d8+8 damage, tripled for the crit — probably 40 or 50 points, easy. Do you let this lucky hit kill Baldror outright? Or do you fudge the result and tell Joe that Baldror got hit for 12, keeping the critical to yourself so that you don't kill Joe's character?

There isn't an easy answer to this one. Some DMs let the dice do their work, and they don't cut any breaks for the player characters or the bad guys. Other DMs feel that a character death is a pretty big occurrence, and it shouldn't happen "by mistake" — so, as long as the dice were rolled behind the screen and no players observed the result, it's okay to fudge by announcing a miss or two when a monster really would have hit.

Our recommendation for a beginning DM is to avoid fudging and to let your players know you're going to let the dice fall where they may. If you

do decide to fudge the dice behind the screen, don't announce it to the players and don't make it obvious. You shouldn't intercede to rescue every character on the threshold of death, because if your players realize that there's no chance for their characters to be killed, their enjoyment of the game will be diminished — no risk and no challenge means no suspense. And if the players attempted something that was obviously highly risky (or simply stupid), you shouldn't protect them from the consequences of their own poor decisions.

One more thing: Just because the DM may fudge the rolls every now and then, we strongly advise you not to try to do this as a player. When DMs "cheat," it's usually for the effort of improving the play experience of everyone at the table. If you cheat by pretending you didn't roll badly as a player, you're doing it to beat the game. It's only going to lead to a diminished experience for you, and may in fact cause a lot of trouble around the table if you're caught doing it. Most players can't abide a cheater, even one who's on their side.

Game balance

Keeping a game fun and interesting requires that you keep an eye on the balance of your game. Game balance basically comes down to two dimensions:

- ✔ **Risk versus reward:** This basically measures how dangerous your dungeon is compared to the payoff in treasure, experience, and the fun your players get out of the game session. If your adventures just cream party after party of PCs, or if you can't remember the last time you got a PC down to half his or her hit points, your game might be out of balance. It's not fun to lose all the time — and believe it or not, it's not really fun to win all the time, either. A healthy game features a sprinkling of setbacks and retreats that the players can learn from.

- ✔ **Player versus player:** The question of player versus player balance arises when one or more of the characters at the table is clearly better than another character. If you've got a party of four 8th-level characters and one 3rd-level character, how much fun do you think the player of the 3rd-level character is having? Trickier balance issues may arise when one player gets his or her hands on a magic item, feat, or spell that makes his or her character significantly more effective than the rest of the party.

To maintain good player versus player balance, consider the following pointers:

- Make sure that no character in the party really steps on another character. If players stick to segregated character roles, direct comparison is pointless. Of course, the cleric doesn't fight as well as the fighter, but the fighter can't cast all those cleric spells; both do different things and do them well.

- Think about how you handle character death and the introduction of new characters into the campaign. If you insist that everybody starts at 1st level, then clearly the player who joins your game as a 1st-level character when the 8th-level heroes are battling mind flayers and umber hulks is in for a hard time. Many DMs allow new characters to join a game at one or two levels behind the average level of the rest of the party.

- Watch out for magic treasure that is useful only for one character. If you put a *+4 flaming keen bastard sword* in your adventure, you have to figure that the fighter in the party will claim this 72,000 gp item. If the other choices in the monster hoard are a *+2 ring of protection* and a couple of potions of *cure light wounds,* somebody in the party just scored ten times better than everybody else. You can give unique and powerful treasures to characters, but you can't give those items to the same character every game session.

Part V
The Part of Tens

"I wouldn't waste a Rage Spell in this encounter. Save it for when we're driving home on the expressway."

In this part . . .

This part introduces you to Bill's and Rich's picks for the best spells, monsters, and resources to use to make your Dungeons & Dragons games even better. You can read about the best spells to add to any sorcerer's or cleric's spellcasting repertoire. You can peruse our selections for the top ten monsters, and why these creatures leap ahead of the pack. Check out the most-often used books on our DMing shelves, glance at the titles that fill our player shelves, and take a look at what we read when we want to relax and be inspired while away from the gaming table. Maybe you'll see something you just have to try or pick up or read for yourself. Enjoy!

Chapter 26

The Ten Best Sorcerer Spells

*Y*ou might think that sorcerers and wizards are pretty weak characters. They can't wear armor effectively, they have low hit points, and their saving throws aren't too good either. But what they do have is a lot of arcane spells — the most powerful and flexible spells in the game. Armed with these spells, sorcerers and wizards can easily come to dominate the game. There are few monsters or obstacles a high-level sorcerer or wizard can't easily defeat with the right spell. Of course, the trick lies in choosing the right spell, which is why we're covering this topic here.

Choosing the right spells is important for a wizard, but it's absolutely crucial for the sorcerer. The wizard will eventually have a spellbook filled with possibilities, but every spell choice the sorcerer makes excludes other choices. The *Player's Handbook* lists 39 1st-level sorcerer/wizard spells, but even the highest-level sorcerer only knows five of them.

Just so you know, we excluded spells of 6th level or higher from this list on purpose. Naturally, high-level spells are better than low-level spells; if we compiled a list of spells strictly by power level, we'd use ten 8th- and 9th-level spells. That's not so useful for a player of a low-level sorcerer struggling with the decision of which spells to learn now, which spells to wait for, and which to never learn. Think of this list as "the ten sorcerer spells that will help your character reach 10th level," not "the ten spells that a 10th-level sorcerer likes best."

For a full description of each spell (its effects, amount of damage dealt, duration, and so on) listed in this chapter, see Chapter 11 of the *Player's Handbook*.

10. Mirror Image

The list of 2nd-level spells contains some great spells; choosing the five that your sorcerer knows is tough. *Mirror image* competes with *blur, alter self,* and *web,* but we chose *mirror image* because nothing is as good at saving your bacon when your sorcerer is surrounded by three angry ogres. Even at higher levels, your character's *mirror image* spell is great for getting dangerous foes to waste attacks striking or blasting at nothing.

9. Hold Monster

We would have ranked *hold monster* higher, but the fact that it's a 5th-level spell means that you have to trudge through 8 or 9 levels of your sorcerer's adventuring career without it. *Hold monster* is a "save-or-die" spell that can paralyze anything susceptible to compulsion effects. Many monsters have an Achilles' heel in their Will saves, and *hold monster* allows your sorcerer to exploit that weakness and end almost any encounter in the first round.

8. Fly

The 3rd-level spell list includes so many good choices that it's hard to pick just one. Certainly, *dispel magic, haste,* and *suggestion* are very strong choices, too. But we're going with *fly* because it is a critical capability that any adventuring party needs to have available after reaching a certain level. Many monsters simply have no answer to a flying opponent, allowing you to win an encounter with ease. And *fly* lets your character breeze past almost any vertical obstacle in a dungeon or in the wilderness, such as a cliff, chasm, or pit.

(We would have chosen *dispel magic* for this slot, but here's the deal: Your cleric buddy can prepare *dispel magic* as a cleric spell, covering your party's dispelling needs. Your sorcerer has to save spell picks for spells the cleric can't replicate.)

7. Stoneskin

There are three 4th-level spells that just rock: *improved invisibility, polymorph,* and *stoneskin.* For this spot on the Top Ten, we're going with *stoneskin.* It is an extraordinarily effective defense against 99 percent of the monsters and villains your character will meet. Better yet, your sorcerer can cast it on friends; a fighter with *stoneskin* can stand in front of almost any monster and shrug off its attacks while he or she carves it to pieces.

6. Sleep

Many people feel that *sleep* is insanely good for a 1st-level spell. With one spell, your sorcerer might drop two, three, or four low-level opponents, destroying an encounter outright. It's true that *sleep* is just devastating against the right opponents — but we find that after your character reaches 2nd or 3rd level and starts fighting CR 2 or 3 monsters, the odds of clobbering a creature with a *sleep* spell drop off drastically. In fact, many players with sorcerer characters use their 4th-level spell swap to chuck *sleep* and learn something else. Still, for all that, *sleep* is a game-breaker for a 1st-level party. Nothing will help your sorcerer get to 2nd level faster.

5. Teleport

Like *fly* (#8 on the list), *teleport* is a crucial character capability that lets your sorcerer and other characters escape from even the direst situations. Choosing the right time to leave the dungeon saves more characters' lives than any other tactic, spell, or magic item. As long as your sorcerer has a *teleport* spell handy, the adventuring party is only one standard action away from a cold ale and hot dinner at their favorite tavern, no matter how bad things are getting in the dungeon.

We would have ranked this spell higher, but the fact that it's a 5th-level spell means that you have to wait a long time before your character is of a high enough level to get it.

4. Fireball

The best spells simply change the game when your character acquires them, and *fireball* is the perfect example. The ability to deal heavy damage to multiple foes at the same time is a major ramp-up in your sorcerer's power. Before you get *fireball,* you look at a roomful of enemies and resign yourself to taking out one, maybe two, with your sorcerer's first spell. After *fireball,* your sorcerer might clean out the whole encounter in one devastating shot. Better yet, unlike the *sleep* or *hold monster* spells, the damage from a *fireball* stacks with the damage the fighter and rogue are dishing out with their attacks. Even if your sorcerer doesn't wipe out all the monsters in one shot, you make the encounter easier for everyone else. (Remember to avoid frying your friends with the spell; if they're too close to the bad guys, they'll take damage, too.)

Lightning bolt is every bit as good as *fireball;* you could pick either one and do just fine.

3. Polymorph

The king of 4th-level spells is *polymorph.* The amount of versatility offered by the spell is just crazy. You want defense? Use *polymorph* to change your character into something with a good AC, like a hag. You want offense? Change your character into something with a high Strength and great natural attacks, like a dragon. Need to save a buddy from a cave-in? Find a monster with a burrowing speed and dig for him or her. Better yet, you can use this same spell to change other players' characters into whatever you need them to be. *Polymorph* rewards the player who knows the *Monster Manual* well, and it's just fun, too.

2. Invisibility

We probably would have dropped this a spot or two, but the fact that it's only a 2nd-level spell means that *invisibility* is one of the best options available in the game. It's a tremendously powerful defense against most monsters or villains if you choose to use this spell and not to attack directly. *Invisibility* lets your character flee from almost anything easily, and its usefulness for scouting and sneaking into places is obvious. Best of all, it works great when your sorcerer casts it on allies, too. The rogue loves being invisible to set up his or her sneak attack, and the invisible cleric is free to move around and heal up friends in the thickest of fights.

1. Magic Missile

And the best sorcerer/wizard spell is . . . *MAGIC MISSILE!*

We chose *magic missile* as the best because it's the spell your character is likely to cast more than any other spell — especially if you're playing a sorcerer. While its damage is not especially good (not at caster level 1 or 2, anyway), *magic missile* always hits. The ability to stick a few points of damage on the bad guys at will is tremendously useful. At 3rd level, *magic missile* gives an average of 7 points of damage; at 5th level, 10 points; at 7th level, 14 points; and at 9th level, 17 points. No saving throw, no attack roll, no energy resistance, no nothing. Just damage, pure and simple. Better yet, *magic missile* lets your character damage things that other characters have a very difficult time hurting, such as monsters with damage reduction or incorporeal (ghostly) monsters like shadows or wraiths.

So unfair we hesitate to mention it

Here's an especially dirty trick: Cast *invisibility*, and then skulk back out of the fight while using *summon monster* spells to attack the enemy. Believe it or not, this doesn't bust your invisibility, so your sorcerer can remain safe while summoned monsters do the fighting for him or her. While you're at it, you might as well place the summoned monsters to take up flanking positions that help your fighter and rogue buddies with their attacks. Other players won't be so quick to call you a coward if your sorcerer's summoned monsters are giving their characters +2 flanking bonus to hit.

Chapter 27

The Ten Best Cleric Spells

*U*nlike sorcerers or wizards, who find their spell choices constrained by the number of spells known or in the contents of their spellbooks, clerics get to peruse the whole cleric spell list every day when they prepare spells. Choosing the right spell is an important step toward a successful adventure.

As in Chapter 26, we're excluding spells of 6th level or higher from this list. We also exclude spells that only appear on the various cleric domain spell lists; although we like the *holy smite* spell a lot, the fact that it's not available to every cleric means that we didn't consider it for the Top Ten. Finally, we also left off the *cure wounds* spells because clerics of good or neutral alignment can use spontaneous casting to cast a *cure wounds* spell in place of any other prepared spell of the same level, making all of those spells are available to your cleric at any time, so there's no point in picking them in preference to other spells of the same level.

10. Air Walk

We agonized over this one, because there are a number of very good 4th-level cleric spells. If you're into melee combat, *divine power* is a very solid choice. And, in the right encounter, *freedom of action* or *neutralize poison* can save your bacon. But we went with *air walk* because getting airborne offers a character a tremendous tactical advantage against many monsters. Characters or creatures subject to the *air walk* spell aren't any faster in the air than they are on the ground (unlike the sorcerer's *fly* spell, which increases speed to 60 feet), but *air walk* lasts ten times as long as *fly*. Consider throwing *air walk* on your sorcerer buddy, and let him or her have the benefit of using his or her spells from the safety of altitude. Or throw it on your barbarian or monk friend, and watch him or her run circles around (and over) the bad guys.

9. Bull's Strength

The cleric has several interesting spells at 2nd level, but the one we like the second-best is *bull's strength*. It's the quintessential buff spell, a quick and easy way for your cleric to give up some spell power and hand one ally a +2 to attack rolls and damage rolls by temporarily increasing his or her Strength score. You can always choose to throw this spell on your own character, too.

Two other 2nd-level spells deserve some mention here: *lesser restoration* and *remove paralysis*. While *bull's strength* is a good offensive choice, you might do well to take a spell that counters a dangerous condition such as being held or poisoned. Clerics have a critical responsibility to be able to fix problems such as poison, paralysis, or ability score damage, because no other character in the party can. *Lesser restoration* and *remove paralysis* can literally be life-savers if the adventurers happen to run across monsters that use attacks such as these.

8. Summon Monster III

The various *summon monster* spells are the only ones that allow a cleric's offensive spell power to match that of the sorcerer's. *Summon monster III* happens to occupy a particularly sweet spot in the cleric's spell list because most other 3rd-level cleric spells are just not very sexy. In other words, if you're going to select a *summon monster* spell or two for your arsenal, then go with *summon monster III,* because you'll have a hard time turning down the other available 2nd- or 4th-level spells you'd have to pass up in order to take *summon monster II* or *IV.*

7. Death Ward

Some of the most dangerous monster attacks in the game are ability drain and energy drain attacks. *Death ward* is the spell that shuts them down. There aren't many spells that can pull the fangs out of an otherwise terrifying encounter in quite the same way. This spell is particularly good against the undead.

Although we like *death ward* for its comprehensive protection, we have to admit that there are many other fine 4th-level spells for clerics. We readily admit that unless you run into something undead, *death ward* is quite likely to wind up as the first 4th-level spell you chuck in order to convert to a *cure critical wounds* spell when you use your spontaneous casting class ability. But if you've got reason to expect your cleric might be facing undead, you've got no excuse not to prepare this spell.

6. Flame Strike

One of the best damage-dealing spells available to any character, *flame strike* is every bit as effective as the sorcerer's *cone of cold* at 5th level. Yes, it affects a much smaller area, but it's also far more precise; you rarely manage to catch more than two or three enemies in an area-effect spell anyway, so *flame strike*'s smaller footprint is rarely a real drawback. And the fact that half of *flame strike*'s damage is sheer divine power (that is, not fire, electricity, or any other kind of energy) means that any foe you hit with *flame strike* is guaranteed to take at least a little damage.

5. Dispel Magic

This is one of those key capabilities you really want to have available in the adventuring party by the time your character reaches 5th or 6th level. Many bad things can happen to your character or your allies through enemy magic — for example, one of your allies might be charmed, dominated, or slowed by an enemy spellcaster. *Dispel magic* gives your cleric a fighting chance to negate at least some of those effects. It's also a great offensive spell when your cleric is fighting a group of bad guys who are using "buffing" tactics, such as a band of orc warriors under the effect of a *haste* spell.

Sorcerers and wizards have access to *dispel magic* too, but it's generally better for the cleric to prepare this spell. The sorcerer doesn't want to devote a precious spell known slot to learning *dispel magic* if he or she can help it, and the wizard's 3rd-level spell slots offer many other attractive options, especially compared to the 3rd-level spells a cleric might take.

4. Divine Favor

If you're playing the sort of cleric who just loves to wade into battle and crack some heads with his or her mace, then *divine favor* is for you. By casting this spell, your cleric gets a +1 on attack and damage rolls. Better yet, the type of bonus conferred by the spell is a luck bonus, and luck bonuses apply no matter what other spells or effects your character is benefiting from; they always stack. The spell also scales up rapidly, so that the attack and damage bonus improve quickly as your cleric gains levels. With *divine favor*, a cleric built for melee combat can temporarily equal (or even surpass) the party fighter in ability to deal out damage with melee attacks.

Another 1st-level spell we like a lot is *shield of faith.* Together with *divine favor*, these spells form a great one-two punch, boosting your character's AC as well as his or her attack and damage rolls.

3. Protection from Evil

This excellent defensive spell gives your character a +2 bonus to Armor Class and a +2 resistance bonus to saving throws against attacks made by evil creatures. It also protects your character against the natural attacks of summoned monsters. No other 1st-level spell offers as many defensive benefits in one spell as *protection from evil*. And, better yet, your cleric can bestow this spell on one ally instead of keeping the benefit for him or herself. Buffing the party's fighter is an excellent strategy for beating many encounters, and a few extra points of AC goes a long way toward keeping a fighter in the fight.

The only real drawback to *protection from evil* is that the bonuses it confers (a deflection bonus to AC, and a resistance bonus to saving throws) replicate the effects of common magic items, such as the *ring of protection* and the *cloak of resistance*. By the time your character is about 5th level, he or she probably has one or the other of these items (if not both), which means you won't get as much benefit out of *protection from evil* as you used to. But until that time, it's an excellent spell choice.

2. Raise Dead

Nothing ruins the day like a character getting killed, but *raise dead* can fix that. It's not free — your character has to spend 5,000 gp on the material component, after all — but it lets the party pick up the adventure and continue with the fallen ally, instead of burying the poor sod and finding the party short a fighter, rogue, sorcerer, or whatever. Plus, it means that the player who was running that character doesn't have to start from scratch with a brand-new character or sit around for the rest of the game session doing nothing because his or her character is, well, dead.

Raise dead has three significant drawbacks. First, it's a 5th-level spell, so it won't help you when your character is still a novice adventurer. Second, the cost is significant. You don't want your character to cast this spell each day if you can help it. Finally, the character that's being raised comes back to life one experience level lower than he or she was before dying, so there's definitely a penalty for having gotten killed. But even with all that, *raise dead* is still an irreplaceable choice in any cleric's arsenal.

1. Hold Person

The top choice in cleric spells isn't as clear-cut as it is in sorcerer/wizard spells, but it's still a strong one: *Hold person* is a save-or-die spell that's only a 2nd-level spell for a cleric.

The big limitation on *hold person* is, of course, the fact that it only affects people — creatures of the humanoid type. It won't help you beat dragons, demons, or even angry ogres. But it is lethally effective against evil fighters, orc barbarians, bugbear ambushers, duergar raiders, or what-have-you. Most NPC villains are humanoids of some kind, which means that a disproportionate amount of the enemies your character faces will be vulnerable to a *hold person* spell.

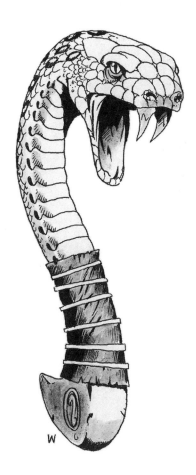

Chapter 28

The Ten Best Low-Level Monsters

*F*inish this sentence: "It ain't a great D&D game until we've fought a
_____." What's your answer? An orc? A dragon? An evil wizard?

In this chapter, we try to answer that question for low-level games. Although
it's true that big red dragons, mind flayers, and mummies are great D&D monsters, you can't really throw powerful monsters like that at a party of 1st-level
characters and expect them to survive. So, we split up this Top Monsters list
into a low-level version and a high-level version. This chapter tackles the low-
level monsters, of course.

We built this list by considering monsters of Challenge Rating 3 and lower,
although we slipped one CR 4 monster onto the list. (Don't tell anyone.) We
also made an effort to spread out our picks among creatures of different types
and different Challenge Ratings. (A creature's Challenge Rating tells you what
level of characters a single monster of that type is a suitable challenge for; for
example, a CR 2 monster is a good challenge for a party of 2nd-level characters.) Every monster also includes its Challenge Rating (or CR), so that you
brand-new Dungeon Masters out there can decide for yourselves whether
your players are ready for them.

10. Stirge (CR 1/2)

(*Monster Manual* page 236)

What's creepier than a giant mosquito that can suck a person dry? A whole
flock of giant mosquitoes, that's what. Stirges are fun because they introduce
players to the power of some monsters to drain ability score points. They
also fly and grapple. Yes, they're individually weak, but there's nothing quite
as horrifying for characters (and their players) as watching one of their comrades thrashing about with two or three stirges attached at the same time.

9. Hell Hound (CR 3)

(*Monster Manual* page 151)

Hell hounds make it onto the list because they're the first serious representatives of a class of monsters your players will be fighting against for their whole careers: evil outsiders. *Outsiders* are monsters like demons, devils, and such. They're from other planes of existence (the Nine Hells, in the case of the hell hound) and are therefore "outside" the normal world. Hell hounds are also interesting because they introduce players to monsters with an area-effect attack (their fiery breath) and the ability to deal extra fire damage with every bite.

8. Young White Dragon (CR 4)

(*Monster Manual* page 78)

We had to include a dragon, didn't we? It's in the name of the darned game, after all. But dragons generally aren't very good low-level monsters. The weakest dragons start at CR 2 or 3, in which case, the characters are fighting a *wyrmling* — a baby dragon just about fresh out of the egg. We think it's more satisfying for characters to battle against a dragon that's at least as big as a person, if not bigger. The young white dragon offers the best chance for this kind of fight, even if its Challenge Rating makes it the toughest of our top ten low-level monsters. Better yet, the young white dragon is one of the sample dragons that have already been assembled for you to use straight out of the *Monster Manual*. (You have to do a lot of work to assemble a dragon if you don't use one of the sample dragons provided.)

7. Large Monstrous Spider (CR 2)

(*Monster Manual* page 289)

A surprising number of low-level D&D monsters are big bugs. Monstrous spiders are the scariest and most representative of this crew, thanks to J.R.R. Tolkien. Who isn't creeped out by the notion of a spider the size of a horse? The large monstrous spider is good because it lets your players fight a Large-sized creature that's only CR 2. And it also introduces players to the poison rules . . . mwah hah hah hah.

6. Werewolf (CR 3)

(Monster Manual page 175)

The werewolf is a classic monster. Everybody understands the fear of letting out the beast within, the feral killer deep inside. Not only is the werewolf an iconic legendary monster, it's also interesting in the context of the D&D rules. It's the best illustration of a monster with damage reduction; unless characters have a silver weapon, they'll have a hard time hurting this creature. Werewolves are shapechangers, which means players can never be entirely sure whether that surly villager might indeed be the great black wolf who attacked their characters out in the forest. And best of all, werewolves carry the dreaded disease of lycanthropy; those heroes bitten by werewolves may become werewolves themselves.

5. Ghoul (CR 1)

(Monster Manual page 118)

Ghouls are undead creatures that haunt graveyards and crypts and feast on the dead . . . or, whenever they're handy, the living. Ghouls are terrifying to low-level heroes because one scratch of a ghoul's filthy claws may cause even the most resolute of heroes to freeze up in complete (but thankfully short-lived) paralysis. Fighting off a pack of ghouls requires the heroes to cooperate to defend friends who are temporarily helpless. And just like the werewolf, the ghoul's bite carries with it a supernatural disease that days later might weaken or kill those who survived the initial encounter.

4. Dire Rat (CR 1/3)

(Monster Manual page 64)

Low-level heroes often find themselves fighting various mundane animals as well as weird magical creatures or restless undead. Animals such as wolves, snakes, bears, and tigers are common opponents for beginning heroes, as are dire animals. *Dire animals* are animals that are unusually large, powerful, and foul-tempered versions of the normal creatures you're familiar with. Dire rats are the weakest and most common of these vicious animals. A dire rat can be 4 feet long and weigh more than 50 pounds. They're not terribly tough as far as monsters go, but they're rarely found alone; if you meet one, you can bet that a half-dozen more are somewhere nearby. Dire rats are one of those classic bits of "dungeon dressing" that just seem to turn up any time you've got a refuse pit, trash heap, or sewer to explore.

3. Ogre (CR 3)

(*Monster Manual* page 198)

The lowest-level giant in the game, an ogre can deliver quite a beating to a low-level party. An ogre pounds a target for 2d8+7 damage each time it hits with that big club, an average of 16 points per hit! One swing is usually enough to kill or incapacitate any 1st-level character, and an ogre that gets a little lucky can often drop a 3rd- or 4th-level character in one blow. An ogre teaches players about fighting big, powerful, stupid monsters, which is an iconic D&D experience. An ogre encounter just screams out for clever player tactics such as stealth, bluffing, or the use of magic; if characters just go right at the ogre and try to beat it at its own game of melee damage, they're going to get hurt.

2. Skeleton (CR 1/2)

(*Monster Manual* page 225)

Thanks to Ray Harryhausen, everybody knows just what fighting skeletons ought to look like. What's scarier and more fantastic than battling against silent, remorseless things made from the bodies of the dead? Like the ghoul, the skeleton introduces players to the special advantages and weaknesses of undead monsters; they're immune to the rogue's sneak attack, they're immune to critical hits, but they're vulnerable to the cleric's turn undead power. Skeletons also show off the damage reduction rules: Because they're just bone, they take 5 fewer points of damage from each hit your character scores with a piercing or slashing weapon. Unless characters are using a bludgeoning weapon like a club or mace, they'll find that skeletons are hard to hurt.

1. Orc (CR 1/2)

(*Monster Manual* page 203)

And the best low-level monster is . . . the orc! The iconic beast-man savage, the barbaric marauder, bloodthirsty warrior in the service of stronger and darker evils, the orc is simply the classic adversary for a low-level hero.

To be honest, orcs are actually the top pick because they're the perfect representatives of a broad group of creatures known as humanoids. Monsters like goblins, hobgoblins, kobolds, gnolls, and even lizardfolk all provide a very similar sort of encounter — the party fights a handful of savage warriors at a time.

They use armor and weapons just like PCs do and may have champions or leaders who have character classes and use magic like PCs. Some are stronger, some are sneakier, some are halfling-sized and some are human-sized, but essentially it's the same type of encounter regardless of the exact monster involved.

While orcs are often thought of as low-level opponents, you should remember that orcs can have classes and levels too. The run-of-the-mill orc is a 1st-level warrior with poor equipment, but imagine running into an elite orc warband made up of 5th-level barbarians, or an orc battle-priest who's an 8th-level cleric. Now, orcs shouldn't scale up at the same pace at which your heroes gain levels; it isn't fair that your 10th-level heroes find nothing but gangs of 10th-level orcs to fight, when they used to run into gangs of 1st-level orcs. But it is certainly true that a great orc chieftain and his chief bodyguards and advisors may be every bit as tough as a high-level party of adventurers.

Chapter 29

The Ten Best Mid-Level Monsters

Now for the second half of our Top Monsters list, the ten best monsters from Challenge Rating 4 to 9. A creature's Challenge Rating tells you what level of characters a single monster of that type is a suitable challenge for; for example, a CR 2 monster is a good challenge for a party of 2nd-level characters.

These creatures are the most suitable for a mid-level game; usually the party will fight two to three of the lower-CR monsters, or just one of the higher-CR monsters. As before, we've tried to spread out our picks among creatures of different types and different Challenge Ratings. Every monster also includes its Challenge Rating (or CR). If you're a Dungeon Master, you can decide for yourself whether your players are ready to face these sinister creatures.

10. Hydra (CR 6)

(*Monster Manual* page 155)

We got down to number 10 and realized we hadn't chosen a magical beast or monstrous humanoid for the list. So we picked out the hydra (specifically, a seven-headed normal hydra) from among many good contenders for this list. Not only does it carry the banner for the magical beast monster type, it's also a representative of Huge-sized monsters. It's also an example of a monster that rewards a special tactic — using the Sunder combat action to chop off its heads, and having another character ready to seal the stump with fire so that it can't sprout new heads from the wound.

9. Flesh Golem (CR 7)

(*Monster Manual* page 135)

Golems are magical constructs, creatures of nonliving matter given animation through powerful spells and rites. The flesh golem is the most common example of this monster. It's made from bits and pieces of bodies, just like Frankenstein's monster, but the flesh golem is an unthinking machine. As a construct, a golem is immune to many special attacks and effects, including sneak attack damage and critical hits. Better yet, golems specifically enjoy tremendous resistance to many forms of magic. Unless a player character has the right spell, magic just won't affect the flesh golem.

8. Ghost (CR 7)

(*Monster Manual* page 116)

We really went back and forth between the ghost and the vampire, and we decided to go with the ghost. The ghost is the perfect example of an incorporeal monster — a creature that simply doesn't have real substance on the Material Plane, and thus can move through walls, doors, and other obstacles. Dealing with an incorporeal monster requires players to evolve special tactics and employ specific spells and weapons. Ghosts also have the advantage of being infinitely configurable. The Ghost entry in the *Monster Manual* is a *template,* which means it's a package that you add to an existing creature in order to make a ghostly version of it. The sample ghost given in the *Monster Manual* is a 5th-level human fighter.

7. Umber Hulk (CR 7)

(*Monster Manual* page 248)

Here's one of our favorites. The umber hulk is an iconic DUNGEONS & DRAGONS monster — it's a creature invented specifically for the game, something that doesn't really stem from real-world myth or legend. Umber hulks are fun because they are monsters that use a gaze attack. Just like the ghost teaches players to deal with incorporeal monsters, the umber hulk teaches players a set of rules and tactics to overcome a monster that is dangerous to even look at.

6. Beholder (Gauth) (CR 6)

(*Monster Manual* page 25)

Speaking of iconic creatures, here's the beholder! What could be more fantastic than a giant floating eyeball with little eye stalks sticking out, all of which shoot magic rays?

The true beholder is a CR 13 monster, so it's well out of the range of what we would consider a mid-level monster. But there's a lesser version of the beholder called the gauth, which is only CR 6. The gauth's eye rays can put hapless PCs to sleep, damage them, exhaust them, paralyze them, burn them, or dispel their magic. Oh, and if characters look at the big central eye, they're subject to a stunning gaze attack. A gauth is a little fragile for a CR 6 monster, but its ability to inflict a bewildering variety of damage on the party of heroes is unparalleled . . . until they fight a true beholder, that is.

5. Mummy (CR 5)

(*Monster Manual* page 190)

Although creatures such as the ghost or vampire are excellent examples of undead monsters, they're also a little difficult to use in the game because they have a host of special powers. The mummy is an undead monster that's strong, scary, interesting, and also easy for a novice DM to run in game play. Its despair ability can freeze half the party in helpless paralysis as it shambles up to begin pounding on the heroes, and every hit carries the possibility of passing on the dreaded disease of mummy rot.

4. Mind Flayer (CR 8)

(*Monster Manual* page 186)

Another unique creation of the D&D game, the mind flayer is the quintessential evil genius . . . with the ability to stun PCs into helpless paste with its mind blast, then pull out their brains and eat them while the PCs are standing around helplessly watching it happen. If there's a more horrible way to die in the D&D game than that, we frankly don't know what it is. Although a mind flayer is tremendously dangerous on its own, the real threat posed by the monster is its ability to mastermind and command other monsters. A mind flayer is the perfect evil overlord, and it's clever enough to use its minion monsters to wear down a group of heroic adventurers before setting a lethal ambush to finish them off itself.

3. Demon (Vrock) (CR 9)

(*Monster Manual* page 48)

Demons and devils of all sorts are some of the coolest and most powerful monsters in the D&D game. There are four or five that we could have picked to represent the evil-outsider-from-the-infernal-realms niche, but we settled on the vrock as the best example. The vrock is a dangerous melee combatant, but (like many demons or devils) it also possesses several dangerous spell-like abilities and special attacks. Many heroes find that they battle demons, devils, and such things over and over again as they rise to high-level play, and the vrock is a great representative of the type.

2. Troll (CR 5)

(*Monster Manual* page 247)

Although we could have gone with a true giant such as a hill giant or a frost giant for this list, we simply couldn't pass up the troll. A troll is a great mid-level monster that can challenge heroes for a number of levels. Just like the ghost is a great example of an incorporeal monster, the troll is the players' first introduction to a regenerating monster — a creature that's almost impossible to kill outright unless you've got fire handy.

The troll is quite common because it makes a great "meat shield," or dull-witted but physically strong creature that can stand in between the heroes and the evil mastermind. Before the party can get at the evil wizard, mind flayer, or what-have-you, they'll have to cut their way through the troll first. A troll fits well in almost any scenario or monster lair, and it's vile, repulsive, and loathsome. Every player loves to hate trolls, and you know what? The troll deserves it.

1. Young Adult Black Dragon (CR 9)

(*Monster Manual* page 72)

A dragon isn't an exceptionally good low-level monster, but for mid-level and high-level characters, the opportunity to fight a dragon (and pillage its hoard) is the reason you play the game.

A dragon's power varies depending on its color (species) and its age category. The older a dragon gets, the bigger and meaner it gets. A young adult dragon is a handful for almost any party; we chose the black dragon because the young adult black dragon is one of the sample dragons provided in the *Monster Manual,* and a good fit for the top end of mid-level monsters.

A dragon is armed with a number of dangerous and useful abilities — it flies, it's got a great AC and a lot of hit points, it has tremendously good saving throws and spell resistance, it has a deadly breath weapon (acid, in the case of a black dragon), and it can tear you to shreds with its claws and teeth. Old and clever dragons are often potent sorcerers, too.

Chapter 30

The Ten Best Dungeon Master Resources

. . . .

*E*very Dungeon Master can use a little help now and then. Advice, ideas, ready-to-play adventures — every DM should look for these nuggets and horde them like a red dragon hordes treasure.

In this chapter, we examine our Dungeon Mastering libraries and show you which books we go back to over and over when we're actively DMing a DUNGEONS & DRAGONS campaign. Each one makes a great addition to your own library, whether you want to be the Dungeon Master or you just want to better understand the D&D universe.

(You might notice that there are eleven items on this list of ten. We won't tell if you don't. Consider the discussion of D&D miniatures as an added bonus.)

Dungeon Master's Guide

By Monte Cook, Skip Williams, and Jonathan Tweet (published by Wizards of the Coast, Inc.)

One of the three core books that make up the D&D game system (the other two are the *Player's Handbook* and *Monster Manual*), this volume is packed with all the tools and advice you need to become a good Dungeon Master. We constantly refer to this volume while running games, and Chapter 2 ("Using the Rules"), Chapter 3 ("Adventures"), Chapter 4 ("Nonplayer Characters"), and Chapter 7 ("Magic Items") especially get a lot of use. And it's not just for Dungeon Masters; players can find useful details in this book as well, such as the sections on prestige classes and magic items. Make sure you get the 3.5 version of the book, because that's the most current version. You can easily spot the "v.3.5" plate right on the front cover.

Monster Manuals

By various authors (published by Wizards of the Coast, Inc.)

Dungeon Masters are only as good as the challenges they put before the adventurers. And D&D challenges usually include monsters of all shapes and sizes. Make sure, at a minimum, you have the *Monster Manual* available for your game. This volume, one of the three core rulebooks (along with the *Player's Handbook* and *Dungeon Master's Guide*), contains the most iconic D&D monsters, including dragons, beholders, mind flayers, orcs, goblins, gelatinous cubes, and more. When you're ready to expand your repertoire of creatures, think about adding *Monster Manual II*, *Monster Manual III*, and the *Fiend Folio* to your collection. These books don't just provide more monsters; each of them adds something new to the lore of the game.

Player's Handbook

By Jonathan Tweet, Monte Cook, and Skip Williams (published by Wizards of the Coast, Inc.)

One of the three core books that make up the D&D game system (the other two are the *Dungeon Master's Guide* and *Monster Manual*), this volume presents the basic rules of combat and character creation. The DM needs to turn to this book for the rules of the game, and to know what the players are reading when they're away from the gaming table. The lists of skills, feats, and spells usually see a lot of wear and tear by DMs as they build NPCs and adjudicate the rules.

FORGOTTEN REALMS Campaign Setting

By Ed Greenwood, Sean Reynolds, Skip Williams, and Rob Heinsoo (published by Wizards of the Coast, Inc.)

The three core rulebooks (*Player's Handbook*, *Dungeon Master's Guide*, and *Monster Manual*) provide an implied setting for D&D games to take place in. But the setting gets most of its details from the way the rules work and the types of characters and equipment presented. There's no real story or defined location. Story and location come to the forefront, however, in this campaign setting, which presents a traditional medieval high-fantasy world designed specifically for the D&D game system. Whether you want to set your adventures directly in the world of Faerûn, or you want to borrow elements of the world for your own home-brewed campaign, you'll find a wealth of information and ideas in this volume. This is the most comprehensive fantasy world ever built, and it is also used as the backdrop of many novels and computer games. Want to add amazing details to your D&D game? Use this book!

Eberron Campaign Setting

By Keith Baker, Bill Slavicsek, and James Wyatt (published by Wizards of the Coast, Inc.)

The newest of the D&D campaign settings, EBERRON was created specifically to take advantage of the newest edition of the D&D rules. Stressing attitude and tone, this campaign setting highlights action and adventure in medieval fantasy trappings. It's a little different, a little edgy, but it's still D&D. Imagine the movies *Raiders of the Lost Ark*, *The Maltese Falcon*, and *The Lord of the Rings* film trilogy all woven together. That's kind of close to the types of adventures that take place in an EBERRON campaign. Whereas the *FORGOTTEN REALMS Campaign Setting* details the people and places of the world of Faerûn, this book covers the continents and factions struggling in the world of EBERRON. You can set your campaign in this world, or you can borrow elements to add to any D&D campaign. And the book features new races, a new class, new monsters, and new spells, so check it out.

Deities and Demigods

By Rich Redman, Skip Williams, and James Wyatt (published by Wizards of the Coast, Inc.)

Every fantasy world needs a pantheon of gods. Whether the gods fill up the background of the world or strut around on center stage and interact with the populace, no epic fantasy is complete without them. Plus, clerics need them as the source of their divine spells. This volume has all kinds of neat information on using deities in your game, setting up your own pantheons, and allowing player characters to eventually ascend to godhood if they have the right stuff. It's also packed with sample pantheons that are ready to use, including the legendary D&D hierarchy of gods.

Manual of the Planes

By Jeff Grubb, Bruce Cordell, and David Noonan (published by Wizards of the Coast, Inc.)

In the D&D cosmology, most adventures take place on the Material Plane. That's just another way to say the dimension where we keep the world and all the stuff that goes with it, like sun, and moons, and stars. There are other dimensions to explore in the fantasy worlds of D&D, however, a vast array of planes where epic adventures can take place. Many of the most powerful and strange monsters in the game come from these alternate planes, and it's only inevitable that your player characters might want to one day return the favor and visit other planes of existence. This book is all about exploring elsewhere, and the ideas it contains can send your campaign in exciting new directions.

Draconomicon

By Andy Collins, Skip Williams, and James Wyatt (published by Wizards of the Coast, Inc.)

Dragons make up half the name of the game, and this lavish volume presents them in all their fury and glory. In addition to rules, tactics, and the ecology of dragons, you'll find inspiration and adventure ideas on every page of the book. Dragon lairs, draconic adversaries, legendary treasures, and more leap from between the gorgeous covers. And, we admit it — we take this book off the shelf a lot just to look at the wonderful pictures.

Deluxe Dungeon Master's Screen

(Published by Wizards of the Coast, Inc.)

The DM needs something to hide notes and dice behind, and the DM screen was designed just for this purpose. One side faces the players and is covered with great D&D art. The other side features rules summaries and tables that the DM needs to refer to during play, placed conveniently so you don't have to flip through the pages of the books during a tense encounter. We use our DM screens at every game, and so should you.

Adventures

Some DMs pride themselves on always creating their own adventures for their games. We applaud those with the creativity and time to take on this heroic task week after week, but the rest of us need a little help now and then. Wizards of the Coast publishes adventures that you can use as is or modify to fit your own campaign. Grab any adventure that appeals to you, whether it's set in the campaign world you're using or not. You can always make minor adjustments so that it works in whatever world your campaign takes place in.

Some recent adventures to look for include *City of the Spider Queen* (Forgotten Realms), *Shadows of the Last War* (Eberron), and *Return to the Temple of Elemental Evil* (D&D). Another great source for adventure content is *Dungeon Magazine,* published monthly by Paizo Publishing. It contains short adventures and adventure hooks that can be modified for use in any campaign setting.

D&D Miniatures

(Published by Wizards of the Coast, Inc.)

D&D is a game of the imagination, but it works best when you use something to help you visualize combat in three dimensions. Of course, you can use any kind of markers with your battle grid, but when we play, we use prepainted plastic D&D miniatures. Sold in randomly sorted booster packs (though you can find those willing to sell or trade specific figures online), the line features monsters and characters drawn from the D&D game books and novels. Our games are just that much more memorable when we toss a handful of vicious bugbears on the table, or a large troll, or — gasp! — a huge red dragon that towers over the figures that represent the player characters. Miniatures give a sense of scale and help players visualize tactics as combat scenes play out. We love our miniatures, and so do our players.

Chapter 31

The Ten Best Player Resources

*P*layers can get away with just using a *Player's Handbook* and set of dice, but there are a whole lot of cool options waiting in other DUNGEONS & DRAGONS supplements. When we play characters in a D&D game (as opposed to running games as DMs), we often turn to the books listed in this chapter to enhance our characters or to try new options and styles of play.

Glance at the titles listed in this chapter and see if any of the topics appeal to you. If they do, go find the books (check your local game and hobby store if you can't find them in a regular bookstore) and give them a read. They're fun, interesting, and full of things that will get your creative juices pumping. And along the way, you just might find that edge that will make your character better, stronger, and more able to deal with the next challenge your DM throws your way.

Player's Handbook

By Jonathan Tweet, Monte Cook, and Skip Williams (published by Wizards of the Coast, Inc.)

One of the three core books that make up the D&D game system (the other two are the *Dungeon Master's Guide* and *Monster Manual*), this volume presents the basic rules of combat and character creation. It contains everything that players need to create and outfit characters, advance them as they gain levels, and learn the rules of the game. You're going to want to refer to this volume a lot, and perhaps even study it to determine the best way to optimize your character, so make sure you have your own copy.

Race Series Books

By various authors (published by Wizards of the Coast, Inc.)

Every character belongs to a different fantasy race. This series of books explores the intricacies of the core D&D races, and each volume presents a new player character race that you can try out. *Races of Stone* features dwarves, gnomes, and the new goliath race. *Races of the Wild* showcases elves, halflings, and the new raptoran race. *Races of Destiny* explores the lives of humans, half-elves, half-orcs, and the new illumians race. *Races of Eberron* examines the new races presented in the *Eberron Campaign Setting* and shows how they can be used in any D&D game, including shifters, changelings, kalashtar, and warforged. Grab the volumes that focus on the races you like to play, or the races you might want to play in future games.

Deluxe Player Character Sheets

(Published by Wizards of the Coast, Inc.)

These four-page character sheet folios, beautifully printed and set up for the different character classes, are the perfect way to keep track of your character's statistics, abilities, and possessions. No player should pass up the chance to use these premier character sheets.

Hero Series Books

By various authors (published by Wizards of the Coast, Inc.)

Every character class brings something different to the table. This series of books explores the advantages of the core D&D races, presents new class options, and shows how to make your character grow in new and exciting ways. *Complete Warrior* provides martial options that can be used by all classes, though it really speaks to characters with combat-oriented classes, such as the fighter, barbarian, paladin, and ranger. *Complete Arcane* opens up arcane magic to all classes, focusing on new options for arcane spellcasting classes such as the sorcerer and wizard. *Complete Divine* provides divine magic options for all classes, focusing on the primary divine spellcasters, clerics and druids. *Complete Adventurer* explores skill and feat use for all classes while providing new options especially geared toward rogues, bards, and monks.

Expanded Psionics Handbook

By Bruce Cordell (published by Wizards of the Coast, Inc.)

If the D&D game had a fourth core rulebook, this would be it. While it may not be for everyone, the *Expanded Psionics Handbook* adds a new system of special effects to the game — the powers of the mind. Consider this to be a third type of magic, though psionics isn't exactly magic in the sense of the traditional arcane and divine magic described in the core rulebooks. But if you want to play a class or a race with access to a wide variety of mental powers, check out this volume. Psionic classes include the psion and the psychic warrior. The half-giant, githyanki, and thri-kreen are examples of races with psionic tendencies. Psionic powers include *ego whip* (a lashing mental assault that reduces a target's Charisma score) and *mind probe* (which allows a character to explore a target's memories for the answer to a question).

Forgotten Realms Campaign Setting

By Ed Greenwood, Sean Reynolds, Skip Williams, and Rob Heinsoo (published by Wizards of the Coast, Inc.)

The three core rulebooks (*Player's Handbook*, *Dungeon Master's Guide*, and *Monster Manual*) provide an implied setting for D&D games to take place in. But the setting gets most of its details from the way the rules work and the types of characters and equipment presented. There's no real story or defined location. Story and location come to the forefront, however, in this campaign setting, which presents a traditional medieval, high-fantasy world designed specifically for the D&D game system. If your D&D group is using this setting, then this volume gives you insight into the world of Faerûn and all its wonders. There may be parts of this book that your DM asks you not to read, or at least to keep as *player knowledge* instead of *character knowledge* — at least until after the facts become revealed through the course of play. Still, with new feats, spells, and other character options, this volume is indispensable to players using this setting.

Eberron Campaign Setting

By Keith Baker, Bill Slavicsek, and James Wyatt (published by Wizards of the Coast, Inc.)

The newest of the D&D campaign settings, EBERRON was created specifically to take advantage of the newest edition of the D&D rules. Stressing attitude and tone, this campaign setting highlights action and adventure in medieval fantasy trappings. It's a little different, a little edgy, but it's still D&D. Whereas the *Forgotten Realms Campaign Setting* details the people and places of the world of Faerûn, this book covers the continents and factions struggling in the world of EBERRON. Players can gain lots of insight into the world and make use of the various character class, race, spell, and feat options available. As with the *Forgotten Realms Campaign Setting*, there are parts of this book that your DM may ask you to ignore or treat only as player knowledge until that information is revealed during the game.

Arms and Equipment Guide

By Eric Cagle, Jesse Decker, Jeff Quick, and James Wyatt (published by Wizards of the Coast, Inc.)

Your character needs to be prepared for anything and should always have access to the right tool for the job. That's where this collection of armor, weapons, adventuring gear, trade goods, alchemical potions, mounts, and vehicles comes in. With this book and enough gold pieces, your character can get outfitted for any situation.

Weapons of Legacy

By Bruce Cordell, Kolja Raven Liquette, and Travis Stout (published by Wizards of the Coast, Inc.)

This is the ultimate guide to magic items and weapons of heritage, including rules for improving weapons and armor as your character gains levels and experience. Why use a simple *+1 longsword* when you can wield *Excalibur*? This volume tells you how.

Epic Level Handbook

By Andy Collins, Bruce Cordell, and Thomas Reid (published by Wizards of the Coast, Inc.)

Ever wonder what happens after your character reaches 20th level and beyond? This comprehensive volume explores what happens when characters transcend the boundaries of the *Player's Handbook* and enter the realm of epic adventures. If you've ever been interested in playing an extremely high-level character, or if you just want to see what play might be like at those lofty levels, check out this book.

Chapter 32

The Ten Best D&D Novels

As much fun as the DUNGEONS & DRAGONS game is to play, you can't spend all of your time adventuring in the dungeons. That doesn't mean you still can't get your fill of D&D when you're away from the gaming table.

In this chapter, we look at one of the best out-of-game activities you can participate in while still staying in the spirit of D&D — reading D&D-based fantasy novels. Wizards of the Coast publishes a vast array of novels set in the various worlds of D&D, and we introduce you to some of the best out there in this chapter. In addition, we suggest some other fantasy novels that, while not specifically related to D&D, are definitely in the spirit of the game and can inspire players and DMs alike in future game sessions.

Dragonlance Chronicles

By Margaret Weis and Tracy Hickman (published by Wizards of the Coast, Inc.)

This is the trilogy that launched the D&D novels lines, and it holds up today as an epic adventure revolving around a group of adventuring companions not unlike the characters you and your friends play in any D&D game. The epic struggle of the War of the Lance unfolds through *Dragons of Autumn Twilight*, *Dragons of Winter Night*, and *Dragons of Spring Dawning*. Many of the characters and situations introduced in these volumes spin off into new adventures throughout the line of DRAGONLANCE novels.

Dragonlance Legends

By Margaret Weis and Tracy Hickman (published by Wizards of the Coast, Inc.)

This sequel to *Chronicles*, *Legends* explores events in the lives of two popular characters — Raistlin and Caramon. Follow Caramon through time as he struggles to save his brother from a terrible darkness in *Time of the Twins, War of the Twins*, and *Test of the Twins*.

Icewind Dale Trilogy

By R.A. Salvatore (published by Wizards of the Coast, Inc.)

In this thrilling adventure set in the far northern reaches of the FORGOTTEN REALMS setting, you first meet the popular dark elf hero Drizzt Do'urden and his companions. With *The Crystal Shard, Streams of Silver,* and *The Halfling's Gem,* a powerful tale unfolds and sets the stage for the future adventures of the drow ranger and his friends.

R.A. Salvatore's War of the Spider Queen

By various authors (published by Wizards of the Coast, Inc.)

This epic story evolves across five books as civil war and chaos rocks the Underdark. As the most powerful dark elf houses clash in this tale set in the FORGOTTEN REALMS campaign's shadow regions, four heroes seek to save the underworld realm of Menzoberranzan from a terrible, approaching darkness. This series consists of these titles: *Dissolution, Insurrection, Condemnation, Extinction,* and *Annihilation.*

Knights of the Silver Dragon

By various authors (published by Wizards of the Coast, Inc.)

A series of D&D stories written for readers who are ages 8 to 12, it follows the adventures of three children striving to earn their way into the prestigious and honorable Order of the Knights of the Silver Dragon. It's a great way to introduce younger readers to the worlds of D&D. Titles in the series include *Secret of the Spiritkeeper, Riddle in Stone,* and *The Hidden Dragon.*

The City of Towers

By Keith Baker (published by Wizards of the Coast, Inc.)

Set in the world of EBERRON, *The City of Towers* takes place in the magical city of Sharn. Here, four veterans of the Last War are caught up in a plot that involves murder, intrigue, and corruption at the highest levels of power in the city. This novel is a great read and a good introduction to the world of EBERRON.

The Temple of Elemental Evil

By Thomas M. Reid (published by Wizards of the Coast, Inc.)

One of the most popular DUNGEONS & DRAGONS adventures of all time comes alive in this gripping tale of dark magic and ancient evil. As a demon struggles to escape captivity and an evil demigod works to gain control over the foul creature, a band of desperate heroes must enter the cursed temple and find a way to save the world.

The Hunter's Blades Trilogy

By R.A. Salvatore (published by Wizards of the Coast, Inc.)

In the latest adventures of Drizzt Do'urden, hero of the far northern reaches of the FORGOTTEN REALMS world, the dark elf takes a stand to stop the spread of chaos and war across his adopted homeland. Fans of Drizzt will thoroughly enjoy this series, which includes *The Thousand Orcs*, *The Lone Drow*, and *The Two Swords*.

The Year of Rogue Dragons

By Richard Lee Byers (published by Wizards of the Coast, Inc.)

This series of FORGOTTEN REALMS novels explores the ancient secrets of dragons and dragon society. Covering a tale that's integral to the current timeline (the age of Faerûn in which the current edition of the campaign setting takes place), the story deals with events on a draconic scale. Titles in this series include *The Rage* and *The Rite*.

The Savage Caves

By T.H. Lain (published by Wizards of the Coast, Inc.)

The first in a series of D&D action/adventure tales that feature the iconic heroes of the roleplaying game — including Regdar and Lidda! Other titles in this line of novels include *The Living Dead*, *City of Fire*, and *Plague of Ice*.

Novels to inspire

A lot of great fantasy novels have been published. We talk about some of our favorite DUNGEONS & DRAGONS novels in this chapter, and we decided that we should also include a list of past and present non-D&D novels that continue to inspire us and broaden our imaginations. They might not be official D&D novels, but they're certainly in the same spirit, and many of these books inspired our earliest attempts at story and adventure creation. This list is by no means complete or exhaustive. Consider it as a starting point for your own discovery of novels to inspire you and fuel your imagination:

10. *Furies of Calderon* (first in the Codex Alera series) by Jim Butcher

9. *Conan the Barbarian* novels and short stories by Robert E. Howard

8. *The Elric Saga* series by Michael Moorcock

7. *The Adventures of Fafhrd and the Gray Mouser* series by Fritz Leiber

6. *Chronicles of the Deryni* series by Katherine Kurtz

5. *The Riftwar Saga* series by Raymond E. Feist

4. *The Mirror of Her Dreams* by Stephen R. Donaldson

3. *A Song of Fire and Ice* series by George R.R. Martin

2. *The Sword of Shannara* trilogy by Terry Brooks

1. *The Lord of the Rings* trilogy by J.R.R. Tolkein

Glossary

5-foot step: A small adjustment of up to one square in any direction. A 5-foot step doesn't provoke an attack of opportunity, so it's a good way to maneuver around a foe in a fight (or to back away from a foe and give your character room to cast a spell or use a ranged weapon safely).

aberration: A monster type, which includes creatures such as the aboleth, chuul, and umber hulk.

ability: One of the six basic physical and mental attributes of a character or creature: Strength, Dexterity, Constitution, Intelligence, Wisdom, or Charisma. Each ability is given a numerical value (usually between 3 and 18 for a beginning human character). For example, your character might have a Strength score of 15, a Dexterity score of 12, an Intelligence score of 9, and so on. Monsters have ability scores, too, and sometimes they can be way above (or below) character scores. For example, a giant or dragon might have a Strength score as high as 35 or 40!

ability check: A test or check in which you roll 1d20 and then add the ability modifier for the appropriate ability to the resulting roll. For example, breaking down a door is usually a Strength check, and a cleric's turn undead check is a Charisma check.

ability modifier: The bonus or penalty your character gets for having a good or poor ability score. For example, a character with a Strength score of 15 has a modifier of +2 on Strength checks, Strength-based skill checks, melee attack rolls, and melee damage rolls.

action, full-round: Some special actions taken in combat require a whole turn. Examples include making a full attack or charge attack. You may be able to take a 5-foot step in addition to your full-round action.

action, move: Moving up to your character's speed is a move action. You can take one move action and one standard action in your turn, or you can take two move actions. Move actions also cover a number of unrelated activities such as standing up after being knocked prone or drawing a weapon.

action, standard: Most specific things your character can do in a combat situation are standard actions. Examples include casting a spell, using a magic item, or making a melee attack. You can take one standard action and one move action in your turn.

alignment: A basic description of the morality of an intelligent creature, as follows: lawful good (LG), lawful neutral (LN), lawful evil (LE), neutral evil (NE), chaotic evil (CE), chaotic neutral (CN), chaotic good (CG), neutral good (NG), or neutral (N).

animal: A monster type that includes mundane creatures such as lions, tigers, and bears, as well as dire animals, dinosaurs, and giant animals.

arcane spell: A spell cast by a bard, sorcerer, or wizard.

arcane spell failure chance: The chance that a spell fails (that is, the spell is cast to no effect) because the caster was hampered by wearing armor. The heavier the armor, the bigger chance you have of arcane spell failure.

Armor Class (AC): A number representing a creature's ability to avoid being hit in combat. An opponent's attack roll must equal or exceed the target's AC to hit it. Armor Class starts at 10, and is then modified for a creature's size, Dexterity, armor worn, natural armor (tough hide, scales, or thick fur), and magical protections.

attack of opportunity: A single extra melee attack that a combatant may make when an opponent within reach takes an action that provokes an attack of opportunity, such as casting a spell or firing a ranged weapon.

attack roll: A roll to determine whether an attack hits. To make an attack roll, roll 1d20 and add appropriate modifiers for your character's base attack bonus, size modifier (if any), Strength or Dexterity modifier (depending on whether this is a melee or ranged attack), plus any special modifiers that might apply, such as the Weapon Focus feat or a masterwork or magic weapon. If the result equals or beats the target's AC, your character hits.

barbarian (Bbn): A player character class. Barbarians are ferocious warriors who use fury and feral instinct to defeat their foes.

bard (Brd): A player character class. Bards are jacks-of-all-trades who fight well, master many skills, and know some magic. Bards can create magical effects with music and poetry.

base attack bonus (BAB): A basic measure of fighting skill derived from character class and level. For example, a 4th-level fighter has a base attack bonus of +4, but a 4th-level sorcerer only has a base attack bonus of +2.

base save bonus: A basic measure of resistance to various special attacks such as spells or breath weapons, derived from character class and level. For example, a 4th-level fighter has base save bonuses of +4 Fort, +1 Ref, and +1 Will, but a 4th-level sorcerer has base save bonuses of +1 Fort, +1 Ref, and +4 Will.

buff: To use magic to make your character or allies stronger or better. For example, if your character casts *bull's strength* on a fighter buddy, your character is buffing him or her for a fight.

bull rush: A special combat maneuver in which your character tries to shove an opponent out of the way. It's useful for forcing your way through a defended doorway or pushing somebody into a pit.

cast a spell: The shaping of magical or divine energy to create a specific effect by means of words, gestures, or special materials. Only characters of certain classes can cast spells (see *spellcaster*).

caster level (CL): A measure of the power with which a character casts a spell; caster level is the same as the character's level in that spellcasting class. Many spells hit harder or deal more damage when cast by a higher-level character. For example, *fireball* cast by a 5th-level sorcerer (caster level 5) deals 5d6 fire damage, but *fireball* cast by an 8th-level sorcerer (caster level 8) deals 8d6 fire damage.

caster level check: A roll of 1d20 + your character's caster level. If the result equals or exceeds the difficulty class (DC), the check succeeds. Caster level checks are most common performed when a character is fighting a monster that has spell resistance (or SR). If the check is successful, the spell works; otherwise, it fails outright.

casting time: The time required to cast a spell, usually either one standard action or one round. To cast a spell with a casting time of one round, you start on your turn and finish the spell immediately before your next turn.

character: A fictional individual in the game setting, created and controlled by a player or DM. (See *player character (PC)* and *nonplayer character (NPC)*.)

character class: One of the 11 player character types or careers — barbarian, bard, cleric, druid, fighter, monk, paladin, ranger, rogue, sorcerer, or wizard. Class defines a character's talents and basic function in the game.

character level: A character's total level. For a character with more than one class (see *multiclass*), character level is equal to the sum of all class levels.

charge: A special combat maneuver in which a character moves up to double his or her speed and makes a melee attack at the end with a +2 attack bonus. It's good for covering distance to a foe and hitting him or her in the same turn.

check: A method of determining whether your character succeeds or fails when attempting an action. Most checks are either ability checks or skill checks. To make a check, roll 1d20 and add any relevant modifiers. If this result equals or exceeds the Difficulty Class number assigned by the DM, the check succeeds.

class: See *character class.*

class feature: Any special ability, power, or characteristic derived from having levels in a character class.

class level: A character's level in a single class. For multiclass characters, class features generally depend on class level, not character level. (See *multiclass* and *character level.*)

class skill: A skill to which characters of a particular class have easier access than characters of other classes. You can buy class skills at the rate of one rank per skill point, and the maximum rank for a class skill is 3 + character level.

cleric (Clr): A player character class. Clerics are holy crusaders who cast divine spells, wield special power over the undead, and fight well.

command undead: The supernatural ability of evil clerics and some neutral clerics to control undead creatures by channeling negative energy.

concealment: An obscurity that prevents a character from clearly seeing a target. Concealment creates a chance (also known as a miss chance) that an otherwise successful attack misses.

concentrate on a spell: Concentrating to maintain an active spell's effect. Most spells don't require your character to concentrate.

confirm: Table talk for a critical roll made to determine if a critical threat results in a critical hit or normal hit. For example, "I rolled a natural 20, that's a threat. I confirm the crit with a roll of 23." (See *critical hit* and *critical roll.*)

construct: A monster type which includes things that were built and animated through magic, such as flesh golems or shield guardians. Constructs are immune to many attacks and effects.

copper piece (cp): A unit of currency in the game. Copper pieces are worth $\frac{1}{100}$ of a gold piece.

coup de grace: A full-round action that allows your character to attempt a killing blow against a helpless opponent. (*Coup de grace* is French for "stroke of mercy.")

cover: Any barrier between an attacker and defender. Cover grants the defender a bonus to AC.

creature: A living or otherwise active being. The terms "creature," "monster," and "character" are sometimes used interchangeably.

crit: Table talk for a critical hit (or, as a verb, the act of clobbering someone or something with a critical hit). For example, "Did you just crit that orc?"

critical hit: A hit that strikes a vital area. To score a critical hit, you must first score a threat (usually by rolling a natural 20 on an attack roll, but some weapons threaten a crit with a natural roll of 19 or 20, or even an 18, 19, or 20), and then succeed on a critical roll (just like another attack roll). Crits usually deal double damage, but some weapons deal triple or even quadruple damage.

critical roll: A special second attack roll made in the event of a critical threat to determine whether a critical hit has been scored. If the critical roll is a hit against the target creature's AC, then the original attack roll is a critical hit. If the critical roll misses, then the original attack roll is just a normal hit.

cross-class skill: A skill that is not a class skill for a character. Characters may buy cross-class skills at the rate of ½ rank per skill point (or one rank per two skill points). The most ranks you can have in a cross-class skill is one-half of the class skill maximum (3 + character level).

cure spell: Any spell with the word "cure" in its name, such as *cure minor wounds, cure light wounds, cure moderate wounds, cure serious wounds,* or *cure critical wounds. Cure* spells instantly restore hit points lost to damage.

damage: A decrease in hit points, an ability score, or other aspects of a character. The three main categories of damage are lethal damage, nonlethal damage, and ability damage. The exact type of damage is often specified so that you can determine whether the target has any special resistances or immunities that may decrease or negate the damage. For example, if your character casts a *scorching ray* spell dealing 16 points of fire damage at a creature with fire resistance 10, the target only suffers 6 points of damage.

damage reduction (DR): A special defense that allows a creature to ignore a set amount of damage from each hit. DR doesn't protect a creature from energy attacks, spells, spell-like abilities, or supernatural attacks. Many types of damage reduction can be bypassed with the right weapon; for example, a werewolf with DR 10/silver takes 10 points off the damage dealt by any hit, but a silver weapon ignores this defense and deals full damage.

darkvision: The ability to see in total darkness. Many monsters have dark-vision, as do races such as dwarves and half-orcs.

difficulty class (DC): The target number that you must meet or beat with a skill check or saving throw roll to succeed.

dispel: Negate, suppress, or remove one or more existing spells or effects on a creature, item, or area. Dispel usually refers to the *dispel magic* spell.

dispel check: A roll of 1d20 + caster level of the character making the attempt to dispel. The DC is 11 + the level of the spellcaster who initiated the effect being dispelled.

divine spell: A spell cast by a cleric, druid, paladin, or ranger.

domain: A granted power and set of nine divine spells (one each of 1st through 9th level) representing a cleric's area of special interest. A cleric chooses two domains at 1st level and keeps them throughout his or her career.

domain spell: A divine spell belonging to a domain. In addition to the normal daily complement of spells, a cleric can cast one domain spell per day for each spell level his or her caster level allows. Because a cleric has two domains, you can choose level-by-level which domain spell to prepare at each spell level your character can cast.

double weapon: A weapon with two ends, blades, or heads. Double weapons can be used to make an extra attack as if your character was fighting with two weapons.

dragon: A monster type that includes true dragons (such as the black, red, copper, gold, and blue dragons) and dragon-like monsters such as wyverns.

druid (Drd): A player character class. Druids are divine spellcasters who draw their powers from the natural world and gain the ability to take on animal forms as they gain levels.

Dungeon Master (DM): The player who runs the game for the other players. The DM creates the dungeons and lands the PCs explore, decides what sort of monsters or challenges the PCs must overcome, controls the monsters when they battle the adventurers, and referees the game.

elemental: A monster type made up of creatures that embody the elements of air, earth, fire, or water. Elementals can be summoned by *summon monster* spells, and they are immune to many attacks and effects.

energy drain: An attack that saps vital energy, giving your character negative levels. Each negative level gives your character a –1 penalty on attack rolls, saving throws, and checks, and wipes out one spell slot. Negative levels can become permanent level loss.

ethereal: On or from the Ethereal Plane. An ethereal creature is invisible and intangible to creatures on the Material Plane (the "real world" in the D&D game). As such, the creature is capable of moving through solid objects on the Material Plane. Spells such as *ethereal jaunt* allow characters to briefly become ethereal.

experience points (XP): A measure of your character's personal achievement and advancement. Your character earns XP by defeating monsters and overcoming challenges. Characters continue to accumulate experience points throughout their careers, gaining new levels in their character class at certain experience point totals.

fey: A monster type that includes nature spirits or creatures with similar mystic origins, such as the dryad, nymph, or satyr.

fighter (Ftr): A player character class. Fighters have exceptional combat abilities and skills with weapons.

flank: To be directly on the other side of an opponent who is being threatened by another ally. A flanking attacker gains a +2 flanking bonus on attack rolls against the flanked opponent. A rogue can sneak attack a defender that he or she is flanking.

flat-footed: Not yet on guard or ready for trouble. Characters always begin a battle flat-footed, and remain so until they take their first turns in the fight. A flat-footed creature loses its Dexterity bonus to AC (if any) and can't make attacks of opportunity.

Fortitude (Fort) save: A type of saving throw. Fort saves generally apply to things a character resists through sheer physical stamina, such as surviving the effects of a poison.

giant: A monster type made up of big, strong humanoid-shaped creatures, such as ogres, trolls, and true giants.

gish: Table talk for a character who is a multiclass fighter/wizard.

gold piece (gp): The standard unit of currency in the D&D game.

grapple: A special attack or tactic in which a character tries to grab and wrestle an opponent. First, your character has to grab the foe (a touch attack that provokes an attack of opportunity). Then you make a grapple check against your opponent's grapple check. If you equal or beat your opponent's result, your character has him or her grappled.

grapple check: An opposed check that determines your character's ability to struggle in a grapple. A grapple check is equal to 1d20 + base attack bonus + Strength modifier + a special size modifier (–4 if you're playing a Small-sized character, or +4 if your character is Large-sized).

grappling: Engaged in wrestling or some other form of hand-to-hand struggle. When characters are grappling, they're limited to a much smaller choice of actions than normal.

hit: Make a successful attack roll, as in, "My attack's a 27, did I hit?"

Hit Die/Hit Dice (HD): The die or dice rolled to determine how many hit points your character has. For example, a 4th-level fighter has 4d10 Hit Dice, so that character has between 4 and 40 hit points (before adding any Con modifier to each Hit Die). Hit Dice are based on your character's level and class. Hit Dice also serve as a measure of power that determines how vulnerable a character is to certain spells or effects.

hit points (hp): A measure of your character's health. Damage that characters take decreases their current hit points. Lost hit points are restored either by magical healing (by taking a potion of _cure light wounds_, for example), or by natural healing (which requires that the character rest for a certain number of days).

humanoid: A monster type made up of creatures that are very humanlike, such as dwarves, elves, goblins, and orcs.

incorporeal: Having no physical body. Some monsters such as ghosts and shadows are incorporeal. Incorporeal monsters are immune to all nonmagical attack forms.

inflict spell: Any spell with the word "inflict" in its name, such as _inflict light wounds, inflict moderate wounds,_ and so on.

initiative: A system for determining the sequence of actions during a battle. Before the first round of combat, each combatant makes a single initiative check. Each round, everyone acts in order from the highest initiative result to the lowest. Usually, you just use your first initiative roll for the whole fight.

initiative check: A check used to determine your place in the initiative order for a combat. An initiative check is 1d20 + Dexterity modifier + any special modifiers your character may have.

known spell: A spell that an arcane spellcaster has learned and can use. For wizards, knowing a spell means having it in their spellbooks. For sorcerers and bards, knowing a spell means that they selected it to be part of their repertoire.

level: A measure of advancement or power applied to both characters (for example, a 10th-level fighter) and spells (such as a 4th-level spell).

light weapon: A weapon suitable for use in your character's off (or second) hand, such as a dagger.

low-light vision: The ability to see better than a human in conditions of dim illumination. Creatures such as elves and giants have low-light vision.

magical beast: A monster type made up of creatures with magical forms or powers, such as displacer beasts, gorgons, and ropers.

masterwork: Exceptionally well-made weapons or armor. Masterwork weapons give a +1 enhancement bonus on attack rolls. Magical weapons and armor are always masterwork.

Material Plane: The "normal" plane of existence; the "real world" for D&D characters, as opposed to outer planes like the Nine Hells or Pandemonium. (See *plane*.)

melee: Combat at close range, in which combatants are trading jabs, thrusts, slams, or slashes with melee weapons or natural weapons.

melee touch attack: An attack roll made in melee in which characters are just trying to touch foes (usually so that they can deliver a spell of some kind). Because this kind of attack merely requires contact with the target, it ignores bonus to AC granted by armor, a shield, or natural armor.

monk (Mnk): A player character class. Monks are masters of the martial arts and have a number of exotic powers.

monstrous humanoid: A monster type made up of creatures that are only vaguely humanoid in form, such as centaurs, minotaurs, and medusas.

multiclass: A character advancement strategy in which you choose to add levels from a different class than the one your character started off in. For example, if you begin with a 1st-level fighter, when your character reaches 2nd level, your character can become a 2nd-level fighter — or your character can multiclass and become a 1st-level fighter/1st-level rogue, or 1st-level fighter/1st-level sorcerer, or whatever.

natural weapon: Teeth, claws, horns, tails, tentacles, and other such appendages that animals and monsters use as weapons.

nonlethal damage: Some attacks deal nonlethal damage instead of normal damage. When characters accumulate nonlethal damage in excess of their current hit points, they're knocked out. Unarmed attacks (punches, kicks, and so on) and grappling deal nonlethal damage, and characters or creatures can take a –4 penalty on an attack roll with a normal weapon to deal nonlethal damage instead of normal damage.

nonplayer character (NPC): A character controlled by the DM. NPCs can be any of the people your character meets (such as innkeepers, merchants, and the rich noble that asked the party to retrieve a lost or stolen heirloom), as well as the villains or rivals your character encounters (such as evil clerics, sorcerers, rogues, and fighters).

ooze: A monster type made up of mindless, amorphous blobs such as the gray ooze or black pudding.

outsider: A monster type made up of powerful supernatural creatures from other planes of existence, such as demons and devils.

paladin (Pal): A player character class. Paladins are holy warriors who are champions of justice and good.

plane: A different realm or layer of existence, such as the Elemental Plane of Air, the Nine Hells, the Ethereal Plane, or Arborea.

plant: A monster type made up of plant monsters, such as treants or shambling mounds. Plants are immune to many attacks and effects.

platinum piece (pp): A unit of currency equal to 10 gold pieces.

player character (PC): A character controlled by one of the players at the table, as opposed to the DM. Your character is your avatar in the game.

potion: A magic item that's basically a one-shot spell effect that any character can use.

prerequisite: A condition or requirement that must be met before your character can get something. For example, the Cleave feat has Strength 13 and Power Attack as prerequisites — you can't take Cleave until your character has learned the Power Attack feat.

psionics: Special mental powers and attacks that some monsters and characters can use. If your DM isn't using the psionics rules in the game, psionics work the same as spell-like abilities.

race: A character's species or kind. Race determines a character's general size and looks, and it also grants special bonuses and/or negatives to skills and ability scores. For example, if you're playing a 3rd-level elf rogue, your character's race is "elf."

range increment: A measure of how far a missile weapon or thrown weapon can attack without penalty. For example, a weapon with a range increment of 80 feet suffers no attack penalty when used against targets within 80 feet, a –2 penalty from 81–160 feet, a –4 penalty from 161–240 feet, and so on.

ranger (Rgr): A player character class. Rangers are skilled warriors of the wilderness who specialize in defeating certain favored enemies.

reach: The ability to make a melee attack against someone who isn't standing right next to you. Big monsters have natural reach; human-sized characters can get reach by choosing long weapons such as longspears.

Reflex (Ref) save: A type of saving throw related to your character's ability to avoid a threat through agility and quickness.

rogue (Rog): A player character class. Rogues are nimble characters who excel at using skills and making sneak attacks.

round: A single unit of game time, especially in battles. A round represents 6 seconds in the game world (but it might take a lot longer than that to resolve every character and monster action in a single round).

saving throw (save): A roll made to avoid or lessen the effects of a special attack, such as a spell or monster ability. The three types of saving throws are Fortitude, Reflex, and Will.

scroll: A magic item that's basically a one-shot use of a single specific spell. For example, a scroll of *invisibility* lets your character cast the spell *invisibility* one time. Characters can only use scrolls that have spells on their class spell list, and if the spell is too high-level for them to cast normally, they'll have to make a caster level check to pull it off.

silver piece (sp): A unit of currency equal to $\frac{1}{10}$ of a gold piece.

sorcerer (Sor): A player character class. Sorcerers are fragile (they have low hit points) and don't fight well, but they wield powerful arcane spells.

spell: A one-time magical effect. Spells are organized into spell lists keyed to each spellcasting character class and by spell level; higher-level spells are more powerful than lower-level spells.

spellcaster: Any character or creature that has the ability to cast a spell. Bards, clerics, druids, sorcerers, and wizards are primarily spellcasters; paladins and rangers do not begin as spellcasters, but gain the ability to cast spells once they gain a few levels.

spell-like ability: The ability to generate a spell without actually casting it. Powerful supernatural monsters may have a number of spell-like abilities, which work much like spells cast by a character.

spell resistance (SR): A special defensive ability that makes a creature or character hard to affect with spells. In order for an enemy to affect your character with a spell, he or she has to make a caster level check, with your character's SR value as the DC. Some spells work regardless of spell resistance.

spontaneous casting: The ability of a cleric to drop a prepared spell in order to instantly cast a *cure* or *inflict* spell in its place. Druids can use spontaneous casting to drop a spell and instead cast a *summon nature's ally* spell.

stack: Combine multiple bonuses for a cumulative effect. Usually, you only get the best bonus of any given type that applies, but if you gain bonuses of several different types, they'll all work together. For example, a *bless* spell gives a character a +1 morale bonus on attack rolls, but a *prayer* spells gives a character a +1 luck bonus on attack rolls; these two effects stack, so a character has a total of a +2 bonus on attack rolls when under the effect of both spells at once.

take 10: Instead of risking a bad roll on some skill checks, you can simply state that you want to "take 10." This gives you a result as if you'd rolled a 10 on your 1d20 roll, plus whatever modifiers apply. You can only take 10 when your character is not being threatened or distracted; the DM has the final say on whether you can take 10 in any given situation or check.

take 20: If you don't care about time, you can "take 20" on some skills or checks. This gives you a result as if you'd rolled a 20 on your 1d20 roll, plus whatever modifiers apply. You can only take 20 if your character is not faced with any threats or distractions; if the skill he or she is trying to use carries no penalties for failure (such as falling off a cliff he or she is trying to climb); and if he or she has at least two minutes to make the skill attempt (for a skill that normally takes a single action to attempt). The DM has the final say on whether you can take 20 in any given situation or check.

threaten: The area characters or creatures can attack in melee without moving from their current positions. Usually, creatures threaten all squares adjacent to them. If an enemy in a square your character threatens takes an action that provokes an attack of opportunity, your character can get an attack even when it isn't your turn.

turn undead: The supernatural ability of a cleric to drive off or destroy monsters of the undead type.

two-handed weapon: A weapon designed for use in two hands, such as a greatsword. A character can't use a two-handed weapon and at the same time fight with a light weapon in his or her off hand or use a shield.

unarmed strike: An attack made by a character or creature without a weapon. (Most animals and monsters have natural weapons such as claws or teeth, and therefore aren't considered "unarmed"; they don't make attacks of this type.) When your character makes an unarmed attack, he or she provokes an attack of opportunity from his or her foe and deals nonlethal damage on a successful hit. Monks have a special ability to make unarmed strikes without provoking attacks of opportunity and can deal lethal or nonlethal damage as they choose.

undead: A monster type made up of things that used to be alive and that died but won't stay buried. Examples include ghosts, ghouls, vampires, skeletons, and wraiths. Undead are immune to many attacks and effects.

vermin: A monster type made up of giant bugs, such as monstrous spiders or monstrous scorpions.

wand: A type of magic item. A wand lets your character cast one specific spell up to 50 times, depending on how many charges it has in it (new wands always begin with 50 charges). Characters have to have the spell in question on their class's spell list to use a wand (so characters without spell lists generally can't use wands at all).

Will save: A type of saving throw. Will saves test your character's ability to withstand ill effects through mental strength and willpower.

wizard (Wiz): A player character class. Like sorcerers, wizards tend to be physically frail, but they wield powerful arcane spells.

Index

• C •

• *D* •

• G •

EVERY
GOOD
ADVENTURER
NEEDS THE RIGHT
EQUIPMENT

You're going to scale a mountain, take some rope. And when you're off to play D&D®, bring the *Dungeon Master's Guide* **and** *Monster Manual* **along with your trusty** *Player's Handbook* and with all three core rulebooks, you've got everything you need to fine-tune your character, know enemies, and get ready for your turn behind the DM screen. So, stop by your favorite bookstore or shop. And make sure you're packing the gear every player should have.

Want 100% Official Dungeons & Dragons® Content Every Month?

SPECIAL OFFER!
$34.95
FIRST TIME SUBSCRIBERS

IT'S IN THE BAG!

Every month *DRAGON* magazine brings you the best in new challenges and opportunities for your D&D game. From new spells to new magic items to official rules advice and exciting features on the worlds of D&D, *DRAGON* helps you get the most out of your game whether you're a player, a Dungeon Master, or just a fan of all things DUNGEONS & DRAGONS.

DUNGEON magazine rescues time-strapped DMs with three brand new adventures every month, each targeted a different level of play. Full-color maps and illustration reveal treacherous dungeons, fabulous cities, and fanta vistas designed by the best and brightest minds in the industry, and regular columns offer invaluable campai building advice. Get ready. It's time to play.

Check out a free preview of Dragon and Dungeon magazines online at paizo.com/previe